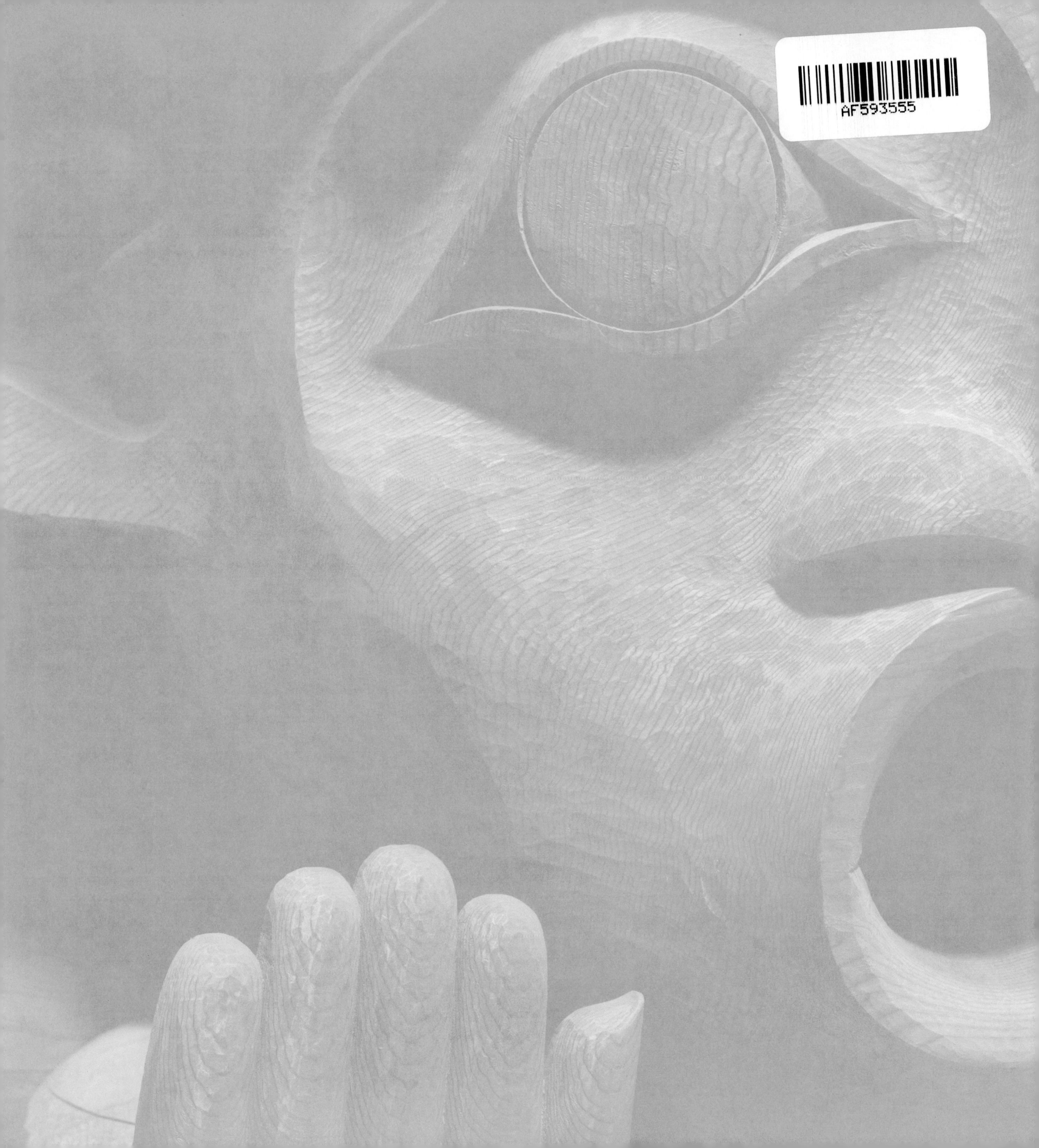

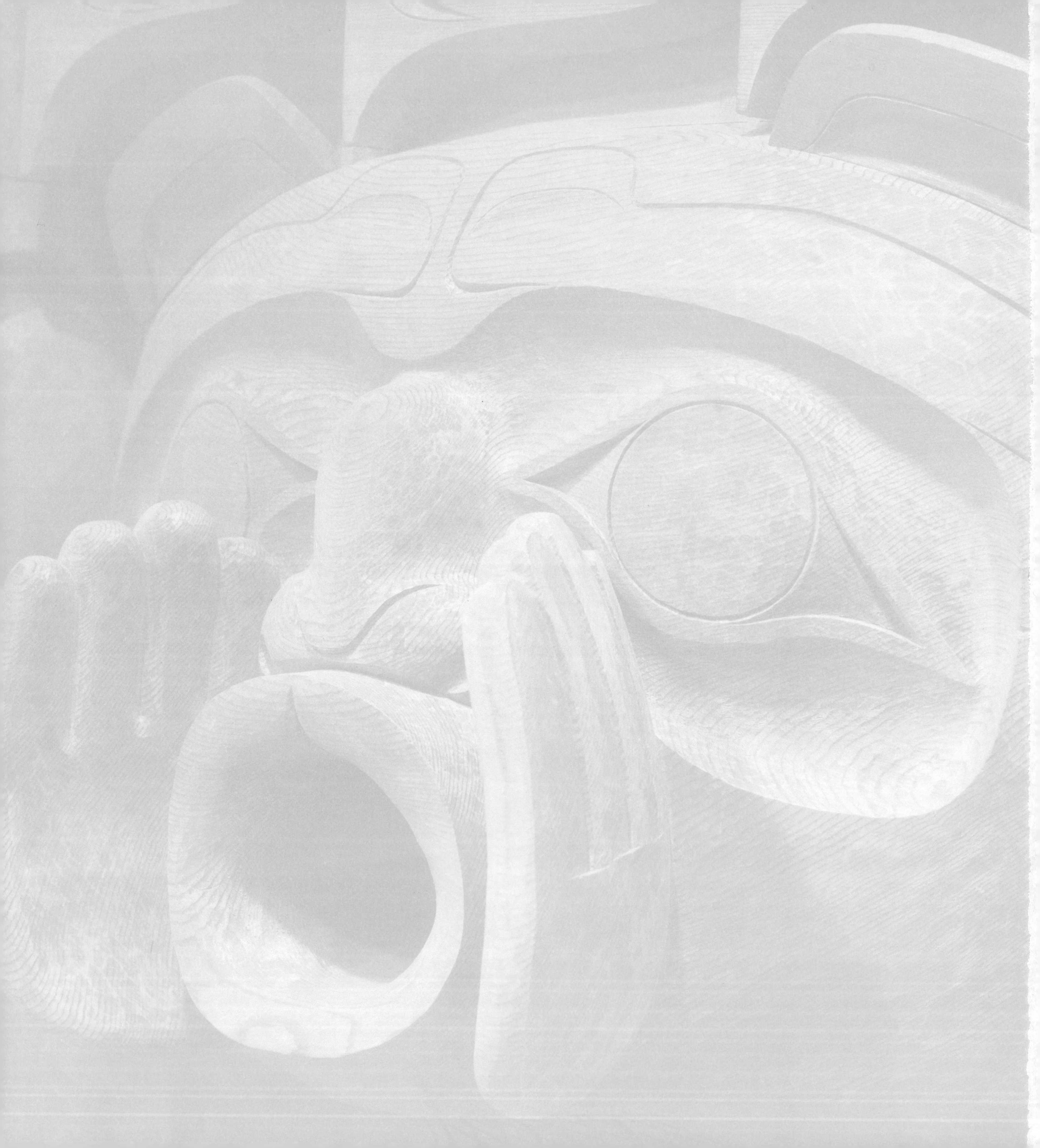

Masterworks *from the* Audain Art Museum

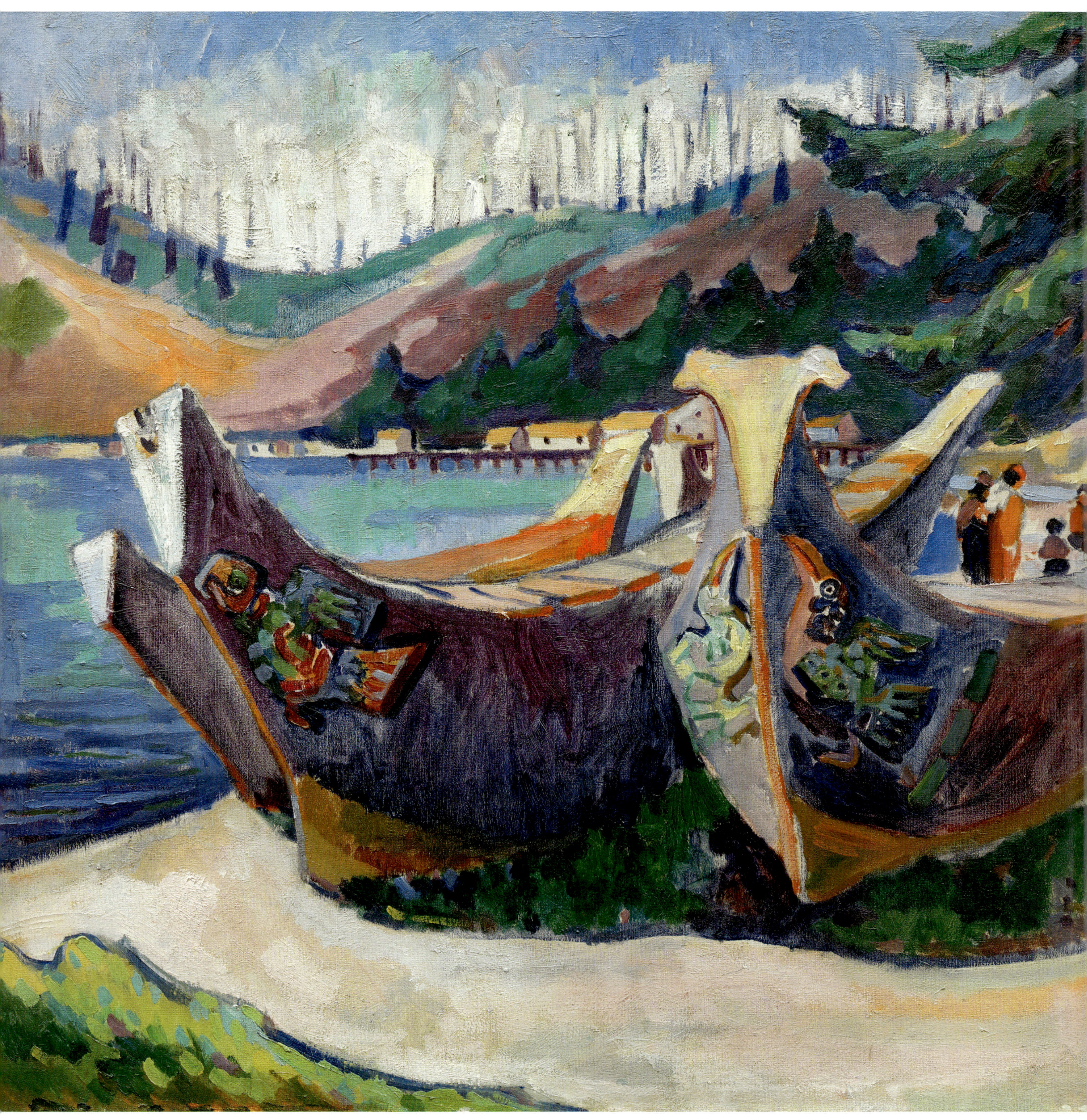

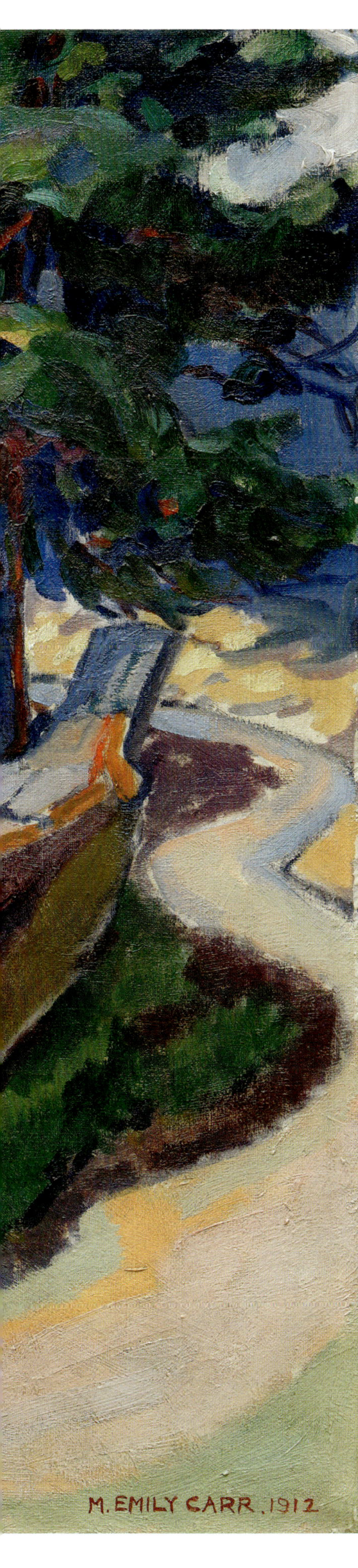

IAN M. THOM

Masterworks *from the* Audain Art Museum

WHISTLER

Figure.1
Vancouver / Berkeley

AUDAIN ART MUSEUM
Whistler, BC, Canada

Contents

Foreword

SUZANNE E. GREENING
Executive Director, Audain Art Museum

From time to time, significant events happen in the art world. These can include a blockbuster exhibition, the death of a famous artist, an artwork that is stolen or repatriated, a record price at an art auction or the opening of an extraordinary art museum.

Early 2016 marks an occasion worth remembering in Whistler, British Columbia. Through the vision and generosity of Michael Audain, a fifth-generation British Columbian, and his wife, Yoshiko (Yoshi) Karasawa, an incredible legacy is being realized in the form of the Audain Art Museum. Not only will the residents of Whistler be able to enjoy the unique cultural and educational opportunities the museum will create for them and for generations to follow, but visitors from around the world will have another important reason to come to our renowned mountain resort.

For more than three decades Michael and Yoshi have been involved with numerous boards of arts institutions, as well as being major philanthropists to educational and cultural organizations throughout Vancouver and across Canada. And since the 1960s, Michael has been an active collector of Canadian and international art, on occasion commissioning local artists.

Having been convinced by others that their extensive art collection should be viewed and appreciated by as many art lovers as possible, Michael and Yoshi began to consider the final resting place for their art. In October 2012, they entered into an agreement with the Resort Municipality of Whistler to build a 2,300 square metre (25,000 square foot) museum—later increasing in size to 5,200 square metres (56,000 square feet)—to house the West Coast portion of the collection. The Vancouver architectural firm Patkau Architects was chosen to design the building.

Among the highlights of this boutique collection is one of the world's most important representations of centuries-old Pacific Northwest Coast masks; over two dozen of the finest works by Emily Carr (lately acknowledged as one of history's most important female artists); and groundbreaking works by the internationally renowned Vancouver photo-conceptualists.

Also featured is the largest collection of British Columbia artist E.J. Hughes's paintings, provided on a long-term loan by Jacques Barbeau and his wife, Margaret Ann Owen; art by some of Canada's most significant postwar modernists, including Jack Shadbolt and Gordon Smith; plus works by internationally collected contemporary artists Jeff Wall, Rodney Graham, Stan Douglas, Geoffrey Farmer, Robert Davidson and Brian Jungen.

Altogether, the permanent collection is a stunning visual journey through British Columbia's art-making history over the last two hundred years. And to ensure that visitors have something new to see on a regular basis, the temporary galleries will host exhibitions of works by important artists from the rest of Canada and around the world.

The Audain Art Museum has been designed as a "Category A" museum, ensuring that it will meet international standards in its environmental and security systems for the care and protection of art. The architects, John and Patricia Patkau, and their entire team of professionals made this complex project a number-one priority for their firm for the three years leading up to the opening, and we are extremely appreciative of their vision and passion to deliver a building that will live in harmony with the surrounding trees and the mountains for a very long time to come.

Construction manager Axiom Builders Inc., headed by Paul Bosa, took on the project and made those plans and drawings come to life in a very short period of time, hiring local trades where possible and following innovative construction processes to ensure that the new building will survive the rigours of a mountainous West Coast climate.

It is important that the museum has long-term financial stability. To this end, an endowment fund has been established with a $25 million target. Donations to the endowment are held in perpetuity by the Audain Art Museum Foundation to generate additional operating funds for the museum. Similar to other not-for-profit cultural institutions, the museum itself is required to raise funds from a variety of sources, including admissions, memberships, facility rentals, retail sales, exhibition sponsorships, and government and foundation grants.

A number of key individuals closely collaborated with Michael and Yoshi in realizing their dream of a home for their priceless art collection. Foremost among them was Whistler resident Jim Moodie, who saw the potential of their vision and opened the way for conversations with the Resort Municipality of Whistler for a suitable site. The council and senior management of the municipality were, fortunately, seeking opportunities to broaden the community's cultural reach and so immediately embraced the magnitude of the benefits and economic impact that a new museum would bring. A spectacular treed site located close to the village centre was selected and, remarkably, just over three years later, the Audain Art Museum will be opening to the public—a testament to the enthusiasm of everyone involved.

Sharing Michael and Yoshi's desire to have the very best of their Northwest Coast art collection available for viewing in the new museum, Ian Thom, Senior Curator–Historical, Vancouver Art Gallery, advised on which works should be included and authored this book. Ian is one of Canada's most respected curators of Canadian art. Since 1979 he has organized temporary and travelling exhibitions and written publications that have had a major impact on the curatorial discourse in the art museum field.

Another eminent curator, Bill McLennan—retired from the Museum of Anthropology at the University of British Columbia—researched and advised on the documentation and provenance of the historical First Nations art and, while interviewing artists, captured stories that were in danger of being lost. The museum is indebted to both Ian and Bill for their connoisseurship and their contribution to our legacy.

From the beginning of this adventure, Michael and Yoshi have had the support and guidance of their board of directors: Sue Adams, Rob Bruno, Neil Chrystal, Councillor John Grills, former councillor Duane Jackson, Eric Martin, John McKercher, Drew Meredith, Jim Moodie and Mayor Nancy Wilhelm-Morden, who have all given freely of their time and expertise to create a firm foundation for the museum.

Michael was fortunately able to invite a number of Polygon Homes Ltd. senior staff to play critical roles in the development and construction of the museum: Goldie Alam, Barbara Binns, Bob Bryant, Celia Dawson and Hugh Ker. We are indebted to them all.

The design and construction of the museum was entirely funded by the Audain Foundation, under the management of Executive Director Chantal Shah, whose board, besides Michael Audain and Yoshiko Karasawa, includes Fenya Audain, Kyra Audain, James Carphin, Robin Elliott and John McKercher.

On behalf of the board of directors of the Audain Art Museum, we would like to thank David and Patsy Heffel and Robert and Jennifer Heffel of Heffel Fine Art Auction House for their financial support in making this book possible.

Construction will soon be finished, the art installed and the museum opened! Speaking on behalf of the staff team, we are passionate about joining Michael, Yoshi and our board of directors on the next stage of this incredible journey in the visual arts.

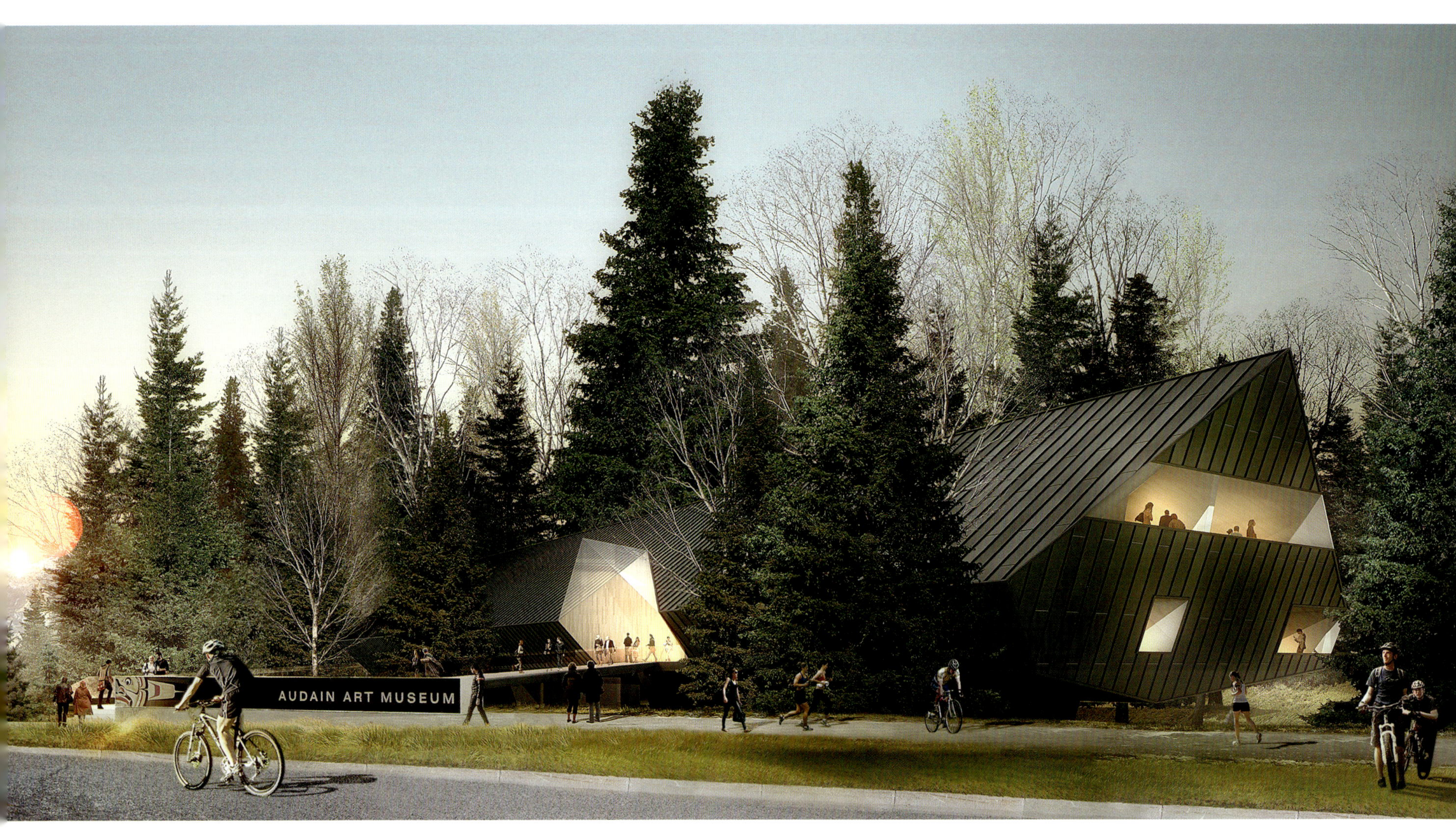
AUDAIN ART MUSEUM

In Conversation with Architects John and Patricia Patkau

JULY 22, 2014

Michael Audain commissioned John and Patricia Patkau, award-winning architects of the Gleneagles Community Centre in West Vancouver, the Millennium Library in Winnipeg and the Goldring Centre for High Performance Sport in Toronto, to design the new Audain Art Museum. I spoke with these two principals of Vancouver's Patkau Architects before the building was completed to discuss the concept and the challenges it presented.

Ian Thom: Art museums are a relatively new area of design for your firm. What problems does an art museum present that you haven't addressed previously in your careers?

John Patkau: Art. Striking the right balance between the presence of architecture and the presence of art is a delicate proposition. How you accomplish a generous, flexible environment for art and simultaneously make architecture with a strong and independent identity is, I think, the greatest challenge.

Patricia Patkau: Another challenge is dealing with gallery space, which for curatorial reasons is without daylight. We needed to think about a completely interior space but also about a counterpoint space—a counterpoint that would connect people to daylight and landscape to provide pause and release within the sequence of gallery spaces.

IT: The site is challenging...

JP: It is. The site appealed to Michael because of the existing forest vegetation, and it appeals to us for the same reason.

PP: Also, it is a site that is separate enough from Whistler Village that it is able to establish its own territory and its own identity.

JP: Some things that might be viewed as challenges actually proved to be opportunities. I am thinking now of the fact that the building is located within a flood plain and so needed to be elevated. The result is a building that will appear to "float" with minimal support within the forest in a way that I think will give it a very strong and unique identity. Deep snow and winter cold also suggest a simple building form.

IT: There is a sense that there is architecture that is quintessentially Whistler (one thinks of ski chalets), and then there is the Audain Art Museum, which is not trying to be Whistler architecture.

JP: Whistler Village is a confection... We wanted a building that has the quality of being direct, inevitable.

PP: The sequence of movement through the site also distinguishes the project. You enter over a bridge, arrive onto a porch and then either enter the museum or continue down to the ground. This public sequence uses specific forms, materials and light in ways that I think people will immediately appreciate. It will ease people out of Whistler and into the museum!

JP: I also think that the experience of the site from within the building is important. The fact that you will be walking along an elevated platform will allow you to experience the landscape differently from when you are on the ground. Perhaps this is similar to the Katsura Imperial Villa in Kyoto, Japan, which is elevated to allow a more aestheticized relationship to the landscape. I think this will be an interesting complement to the exhibitions within the building.

IT: In this building you are using a lot of steel, where often your architecture has been characterized by the use of wood. Was that a challenge for you?

JP: The structure is principally steel because of its bridge-like form, but it is completely concealed to simplify the character of interior spaces, so it really doesn't enter into the architectural experience of the building. The cladding of the building is also steel for very practical reasons. There is an enormous amount of exterior surface by virtue of the building's configuration, so we needed to find a material that was not only durable but cost effective. Standard painted sheet metal was chosen to deal with these challenges. The metal is intended to be a dark, rich, grey tone, like the colour of the shadows in the surrounding forest. People will be surprised at how large the museum is when the structure is complete. The shadow-like colour should make the large volume of the building sit quietly within the site.

PP: The sequence of spaces beginning with the entrance porch, the steps down to the forest floor and the public spaces within the building are lined with wood, which will provide a glowing, inviting liner within the metal carapace.

IT: When you were thinking about this museum, were there other museums that helped inspire the concept for this one?

JP: Even though we haven't designed many art museums, we have been long-time students of them. Whenever we travel, we visit art museums. While we've enjoyed the art, we've also studied the buildings.

One thing we have come to understand from these visits is that there is an architectural opportunity to juxtapose the relatively neutral character of gallery spaces with a more idiosyncratic and assertive realm of non-gallery spaces, providing a textured experience of spaces within.

The Audain Museum has an unusual feature, something we encountered in the Het Valkhof museum in Nijmegen, the Netherlands. After entering, you go fairly directly through the building to a glazed walkway along what would be the back of the building, from which you then enter into the galleries. This is precisely the strategy that we've used here. It allows the museum visitor to enter and move through the galleries in a very controlled way: the lobby first presents the landscape of the interior of the site; from the lobby, a glazed walkway overlooking this landscape runs along the entire "back" edge of the building, from which you enter into the permanent galleries as well as the temporary exhibition spaces. This fundamental organization is key to understanding the plan form of the building.

IT: What was the working process for this project?

JP: This project was representative of how we generally work. We start with a small group, Patricia and myself and the senior person—in this case, David Shone—who will lead the project team through the various stages of design development and construction. We've worked with David for over twenty years and on many projects. Pat and I work together on the initial design. Typically, Pat takes the first initiative to think about the fundamental organization and siting of the building. I'm involved with her at this point, more as a provocateur than anything else. We work trying to get a feeling for how the building will find its place on the site. As the building plan begins to develop, I bring in ideas of building section, form and construction. Pat is fully engaged with this as well, but it is sort of a one-two punch approach. In the end, I believe that the building is completely the result of us together and our larger team.

IT: What is there about this building that marks it as a Patkau building?

PP: Our buildings are all very different from each other. I often think this is one of our problems because there isn't a brand about which people can say, "Oh, I want one of those." Clients have to be brave when they come to us because they don't know what they are going to get. However, there is a consistent scale to our buildings, a scale that tries to keep an intimate relationship between the body and the space. There is also a level of "making," or craft, that is highly recognizable.

JP: There is also a finely tuned response to both urban and natural context.

IT: You have talked about how this building responds to the forest, but Whistler is in the middle of mountains. How does this building respond to mountains?

JP: The site is surrounded by mountains, but it is not characterized by mountains. It is characterized much more strongly by the fact that it is a forested flood plain.

PP: The building acts as a kind of register of the landscape. It is about the different layers of experience as you move up or down within the building, mountains included.

JP: The views from the building to the exterior are very abstract, and they are very singular in their character. This allows the topography and the variation of the landscape to register strongly in your experience.

IT: This is being done on a fairly tight timeline that has necessitated certain decisions in terms of design. Can you elaborate on what some of those decisions have been?

JP: Just to explain how tight the timeline is... Michael's idea of doing a museum project occurred in the summer of 2012. He selected a site in September and selected the architect team in November. After we had initiated the rezoning and approval process with the Resort Municipality of Whistler, Michael decided to significantly increase the size of the building. We then redesigned the project, redid the approvals process with Whistler and still were able to break ground and begin construction in under a year from Michael's first thought of doing the project. The Resort Municipality of Whistler has been extremely helpful in facilitating this process.

PP: We tried to design a simple, linear building and then treat it as an extrusion in which the section changes slightly as you move through it. The proposition was intentionally simple because of the time constraints.

JP: Then, when we had to add area, in order to expand the program, it became more complicated. The addition has added time to the process, but I think that inevitably this time would have been added just because it is a large, ambitious project, with lots of complex technical challenges.

IT: Are there lessons you have learned in this building that you will take to other buildings, or is it a sufficiently unique project that you cannot transfer things to another project?

JP: We learned many things. I think that in some ways this is a very bold building. At the same time, it is a relatively quiet building. This is an interesting combination. It is also an effective formula, especially for building in Canada, where construction budgets are relatively modest.

IT: What do you want the visitor to the museum to go away with in terms of their experience of the building?

PP: I think the Audain Art Museum will have a kind of interiority and a way of gazing out simultaneously, and I hope that these two things will really act together in a powerful way. You can spend hours in some galleries and it

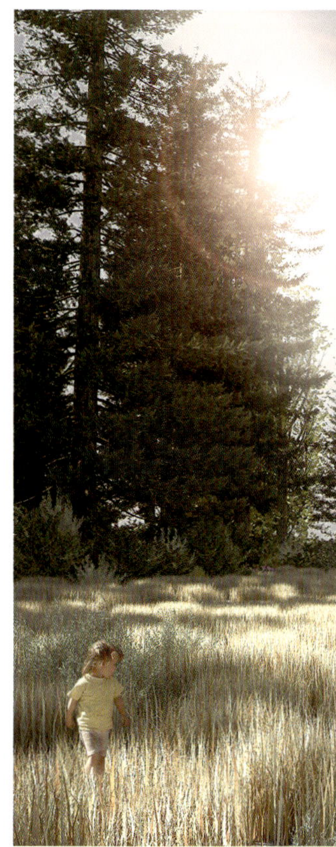

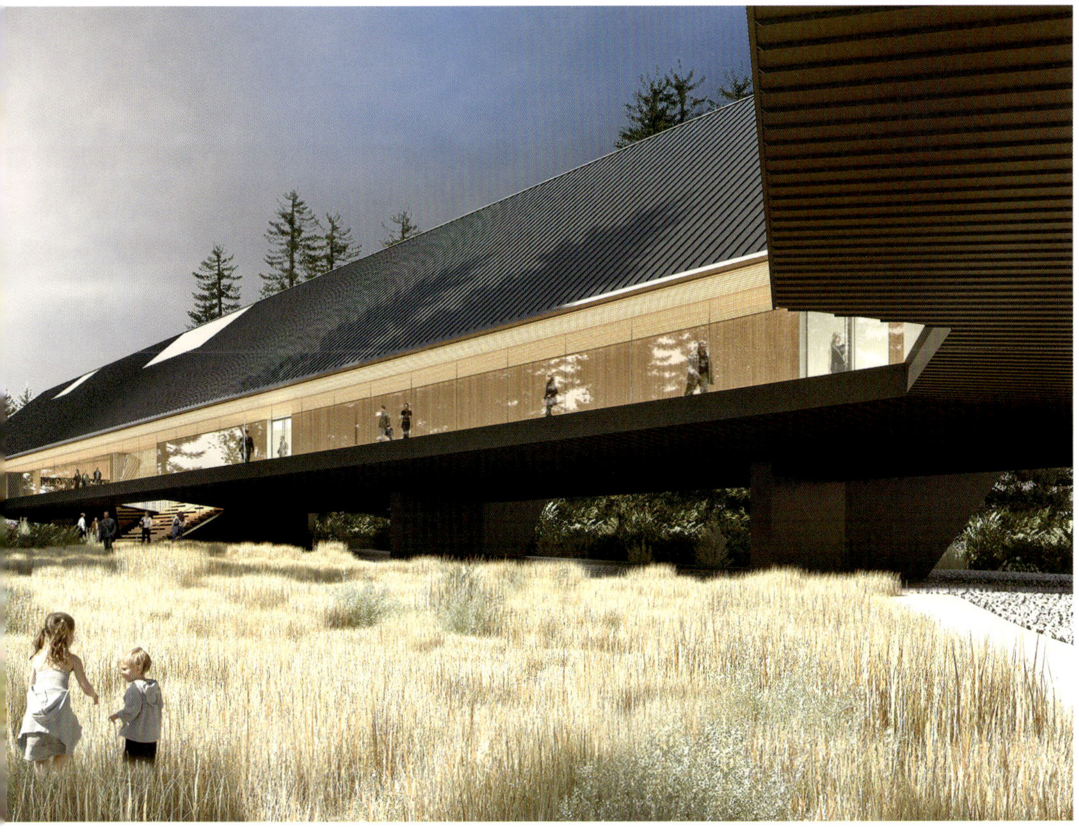

is wonderful, but you come out exhausted, depleted. The fact that you can go back and forth between natural light and landscape and galleries within the Audain Art Museum should allow for a more integrated, reflective and relaxing experience. This museum has a very beautiful location, light and context that will be part of the experience of viewing art, a counterpart to the interiority of gallery space. We hope that people will experience a relaxed intimacy with the art in this situation.

IT: Well, certainly in terms of considering how the art will be installed, one of the things that has been fairly important is to try and give things space to breathe.

JP: My sense is that what the building will be, and what additional potentials it may have, is not fully evident at this point. I have in mind especially, I think, that the complementary quality of the ability to move from the collection to the landscape and back is not well appreciated, and it won't be until the building is complete and the art installed. We are hoping this will be one of the principal successes of the project from an architectural point of view.

PP: We always have that hope. I remember C.Y. Loh, the structural engineer who worked on our house when we first moved to Vancouver, saying after the house was up, "You know, it is better than I thought it was going to be." I've always remembered this comment because I thought . . . that's good.

IT: As an observer who is involved in the project, I am struck by how people keep saying how elegant this building is, its presence within the landscape, the great simplicity of the shape and the very strong lines of the roof, and so on. It is assertive but it is not assertive; it is a very subtle thing to be able to do. The building is itself, but at the same time it is subservient to the purposes of the art.

Introduction

IAN M. THOM

When Michael Audain and Yoshiko Karasawa began to acquire works of art produced in British Columbia, it was never with the intention of tracing the history of art in this province. However, the sheer number of works they've collected now makes this possible, albeit in a less than completely comprehensive way. It is worth examining this collection in some depth because it contains an astonishing breadth of art from the eighteenth century to the present, including exquisite First Nations masks; a wide selection of works by Emily Carr and E.J. Hughes, spanning their entire careers; and stunning examples of modernism, from Lawren Harris and B.C. Binning through Jack Shadbolt, Gordon Smith and Bill Reid to contemporary artists such as Rodney Graham, Jeff Wall, James Hart and Marianne Nicolson.

The first important flowering of artistic activity occurred in British Columbia long before white settlement and contact. In the coastal regions, the First Nations benefited from abundant supplies of food, water and materials to build their homes and carve their poles and masks. This production of artwork accelerated with the arrival of white traders, who introduced metal tools that made carving cedar and native hardwoods substantially easier. The nineteenth century saw a remarkable abundance of First Nations art all along the coast and among the Nisga'a, Gitxsan and others who lived by great northern rivers. It is with works of art from this period that the Audain Art Museum Collection begins.

Collected in the nineteenth century as curios and ethnographic examples rather than as works of art, many First Nations masks travelled far beyond our borders. One of the most remarkable aspects of the Audain Art Museum project has been the repatriation of these exceptional masks to this province. The collection includes superb examples of work by Gitxsan, Haida, Haisla, Heiltsuk, Kwakwa̱ka̱'wakw, Nisga'a, Nuxalk, Salish, Tlingit and Tsimshian artists. Some of these masks are of great rarity (among the few surviving examples), and all are of high quality, great artistry and exceptional beauty, though it has taken the larger Euro Canadian community a long time to recognize this. Although none of the First Nations had words for "art" per se, there was, as these objects vividly reveal, no shortage of creativity, imagination and skill among the carvers and painters of the coast.

It is significant that one of the first British Columbians to recognize the art of the First Nations peoples of this province was herself an artist. Emily Carr, born in Victoria in 1871, has become the best-known British Columbian painter. The Audain Art Museum includes a remarkable representation of her work from most periods of her career. The earliest canvases and watercolours show her adoption of post-Impressionist colour and brushwork in France in 1911 and her initial work in First Nations villages in 1912. Later works showcase her experiments with landscape in the third and fourth decades of the twentieth century, including her return to painting in the late 1920s and her magnificent later totemic works from the early 1930s. Finally, the collection contains several examples of her ecstatic explorations of the coastal forests of Vancouver Island.

Carr was not, of course, the only person to be struck by the visual splendour of the province. Artists such as W.P. Weston and, most importantly, Fred Varley, redefined our understanding of the landscape beginning in the late 1920s. Varley and his students explored the mountainous expanses of the region and produced vivid depictions that remain unmatched in their power and beauty.

Modernism arrived in the province through the curriculum at the Vancouver School of Decorative and Applied Arts (now Emily Carr University of Art + Design) but also through the example of individual artists. Lawren Harris settled in Vancouver in 1940, and his abstract paintings provided direction for many younger painters. The modernism of B.C. Binning was of a different tenor but also provided a new direction for British Columbia painting. As well, Harris, though he was an abstract painter for most of his life in Vancouver, was deeply interested in good painting of all kinds. A keen supporter of Emily Carr in her lifetime and of her legacy after her death, he was also an early champion of the work of E.J. Hughes whose painstaking depictions of the coastal landscape, usually inhabited by humanity, provide a look at the landscape of the region very different from Carr's. Ironically enough, although Hughes's work is now very popular, there was little support for it for much of his painting life. The Audain Art Museum, drawing on its own collection and on a generous long-term loan from The Barbeau Owen Foundation, is able to present, as with Emily Carr, a selection of works that provide a complete view of Hughes's long career.

Painting in Vancouver was extremely active during the 1960s, and one of the most brilliant practitioners of the time was Claude Breeze. His visceral, deeply felt imagery is still remarkably powerful decades after he first made his work. Toni Onley had a more formal, cerebral approach to painting, and his collages from the early 1960s are among his strongest works. (Although the art scene in the 1970s was an active one, the Audain Art Museum does not have any works from the period.)

By the 1980s and 1990s, British Columbia art making saw the remarkable rise of the so-called Vancouver School of photo-based artists. Individuals such as Jeff Wall, Ian Wallace, Christos Dikeakos and Rodney Graham began to produce work that rethought the photographic approach and that was soon noticed both here and around the world. Slightly younger artists such as Ken Lum, Roy Arden and Stan Douglas followed their own paths while building on the examples of the first group. These decades also brought a remarkable resurgence of art making by First Nations people, which resulted from both the increasing market for their work and the slow rebuilding of cultural traditions within communities. Robert Davidson, Reg Davidson, James Hart, Beau Dick and Henry Speck, to name only a few, joined early pioneers such as Bill Reid in producing carvings and bronzes, and their work too was noticed and collected around the world. Major works by all of these artists can be found in the Audain Art Museum. Especially noteworthy is James Hart's monumental *The Dance Screen (The Scream Too)*.

In the 1990s there was also a return to painting among a group of younger artists. The most successful of these were Attila Richard Lukacs and Graham Gillmore.

Our understanding of what is possible in First Nations art is constantly evolving, as seen in the work of Sonny Assu, Marianne Nicolson, Lawrence Paul Yuxweluptun, Brian Jungen, and Shawn and Dean Hunt. These artists, while respecting traditional culture, are very much aware of currents in contemporary art and society. Similarly, the use of photography has shifted and developed in the work of artists such as Rodney Graham, Jeff Wall and Ian Wallace and younger artists such as Stephen Waddell and Tim Lee. Their sense of place and narrative and their relationship to the history of photography is in continual flux.

The Audain Art Museum provides a unique opportunity to consider some of the major artists of the region in a permanent installation that reflects the enormous richness and variety of artistic expression in the province over the last two hundred years. I invite you to learn more about some of the treasures of the collection as you peruse these pages. Enjoy!

Selected Works

Selected Works

Salish Artist

Figure

late 19th/early 20th century

Small-scale woodcarvings of human forms by early Salish artists are extremely uncommon. However, there are a few early larger-scale Salish pieces, including figurative grave boards and old house posts that include figures, and it is from these examples that *Figure* can be connected to the Salish people. In this work, the simplified treatment of the facial features of the two human figures is consistent with early Salish examples. The form of the shoulders of the upper figure also signals that this work is Salish. *Figure* is, however, an exceptional object, perhaps unique in collections of Northwest Coast arts because of its rarity.

What we see is two human figures and two creatures presented in a hierarchical arrangement. The smaller of the two figures is dressed in a garment that still carries traces of red pigment, and is flanked by two animals that climb up the sides. The face of this lower figure is sharply carved with a protruding brow. The brow is connected to his nose, the whole forming a T shape that is the dominant element of the figure's facial features. Completing the face are a pair of inset bead eyes, painted eyebrows and carved lips tinged with red pigment. This figure's body tapers slightly to upraised arms that frame his head, and there are delicate indications of the fingers of his grasping hands. Finally, one notes that he stands on two thin legs that have been broken off above the feet.

This smaller figure is lifting to prominence on his upraised arms a much larger figure with a similar face but with a slightly elongated head and a taller body. The upper figure also appears to be unclothed. His legs are apart, allowing him to be supported by the lower figure and to frame the upper section of the lower figure's head. His arms are oriented downward and held out from his body. His right arm has been broken off just below the wrist, but his left one is complete, and in it he holds a human head by its hair. It is likely that the missing right hand carried a similar trophy, or perhaps the weapon used in the decapitation. The body of this upper figure is fluid in form, with a slightly swelling lower abdomen and broad shoulders, but there are no indications of breasts. We assume, therefore, that this figure is male, despite the absence of genitalia, and that this omission of anatomical detail must have been a conscious decision, since the carver has been careful to delineate the figure's toes and fingers.

The delicacy and precision of the carving, which is particularly noticeable in the details of the small, severed head, are indicative of a hardwood, likely maple, which would have been readily available to a Salish carver. The work, despite its strong frontal form, has clearly been conceived of in the round, because the back has also been finished.

The larger, upper figure is clearly the dominant one, and the display of his victim's head suggests that he is a powerful warrior. Although taking an enemy's head was not uncommon, it was the province of the elite

PROVENANCE: *June Bedford Collection, London; Sotheby's, New York (lot 680, May 18, 2000); Donald Ellis Gallery, New York and Vancouver/ Equinox Gallery, Vancouver; Audain Collection, purchased 2006; Gift of Michael Audain and Yoshiko Karasawa; Audain Art Museum Collection, 2015.003*

▸ Salish Artist
Figure,
late 19th/early 20th century
wood, beads, pigment
70.0 × 15.0 × 11.0 cm
Gift of Michael Audain and Yoshiko Karasawa; Audain Art Museum Collection, 2015.003

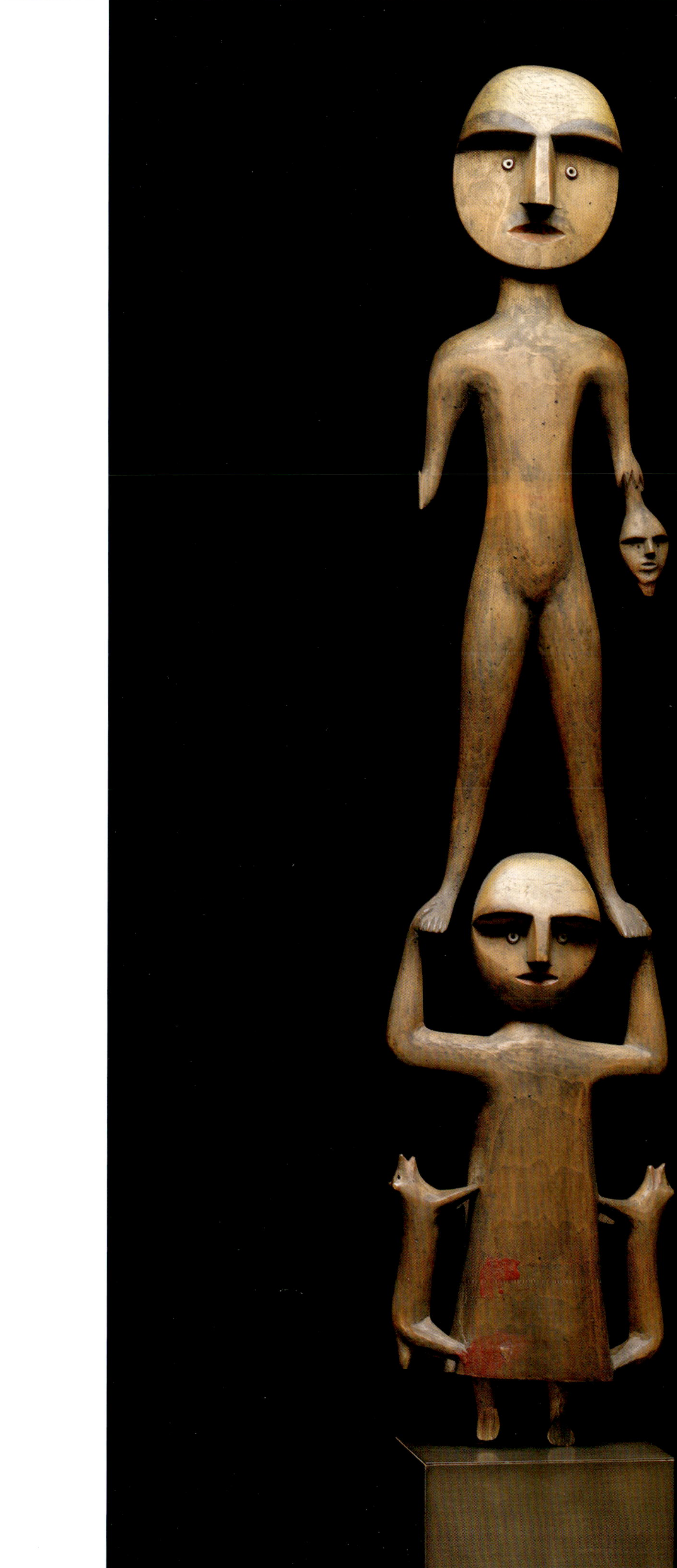

warrior class. The lower figure, who bears this warrior aloft, is most likely a slave. Both his smaller scale and the fact that he is clothed may suggest his lower status. The slave is, literally and figuratively, raising up the dominant warrior in recognition of his battles and victories. The animals at his side are fishers, their faces upturned as they climb towards the warrior above. Quick and decisive hunters, elusive in the wild, fishers are carriers of spirit power.

This object is clearly an assertion of power, but we do not know what it is, how it was used or what it was used for. The fragmentary nature of the carving testifies to its delicacy, and it therefore seems unlikely to have been carved for physical use. Equally, however, it is hard to imagine this sculpture, with the severed head(s), as an early piece of trade art. It is, in short, a mysterious object.

At present, we can appreciate the power and strength of the carving. It also provides an exceptionally rare, if somewhat murky, glimpse into Salish cultural history. The fact that *Figure* is so compelling, even when we know so little about it, reveals the maker as a master carver.[1] ■

Heiltsuk Artist
Articulated Mask (Owl)
c. 1830–50

This bird mask was, as the label it still bears attests, collected at some point in either the late nineteenth or very early twentieth century. The decision to place a label so prominently on the surface of the object is not one a modern collector would have made. While we don't know who collected the mask, it is certain that the early trader who acquired it recognized something of its considerable power. The label reads: "Chinook Indians, Mask worn by Medicine Man." Although this identification is erroneous, the suggestion that this mask has special attributes for healing is probably correct.

As Northwest Coast art scholar Steven C. Brown has suggested, "An articulated mask of this type would probably have been employed in the dramatic recounting of clan and tribal histories, or in the reenactment of encounters with animals and spirit beings, such as were seen in the Tsimshian ceremonial known as Naxnok (the power beyond human). Naxnok mask made visible the spirit power that manifests the physical world as we know it."[1]

This mask displays a remarkable sophistication. As Brown describes it, "This unusual and richly complex bird mask includes an articulated lower mandible and eyes that roll, transforming from bulging orbs to a flatter eye surface... Two small birds are attached to the forehead with pieces of thick hide, allowing them to move slightly with the actions of a skill dancer."[2] This astonishing degree of animation—with the eyes moving, the mouth opening and possibly the small birds above the owl's forehead moving as well—would have been amplified by the metal elements on the rotating eyes, which were likely

PROVENANCE: *Ziff Family Collection, New York; George Terasaki Collection, New York; Donald Ellis Gallery, New York and Vancouver; Audain Collection, purchased 2011*

▸ Heiltsuk Artist
Articulated Mask (Owl),
c. 1830–50
wood, pigment, hide
28.0 × 30.5 × 19.0 cm
Promised Gift, Audain Collection

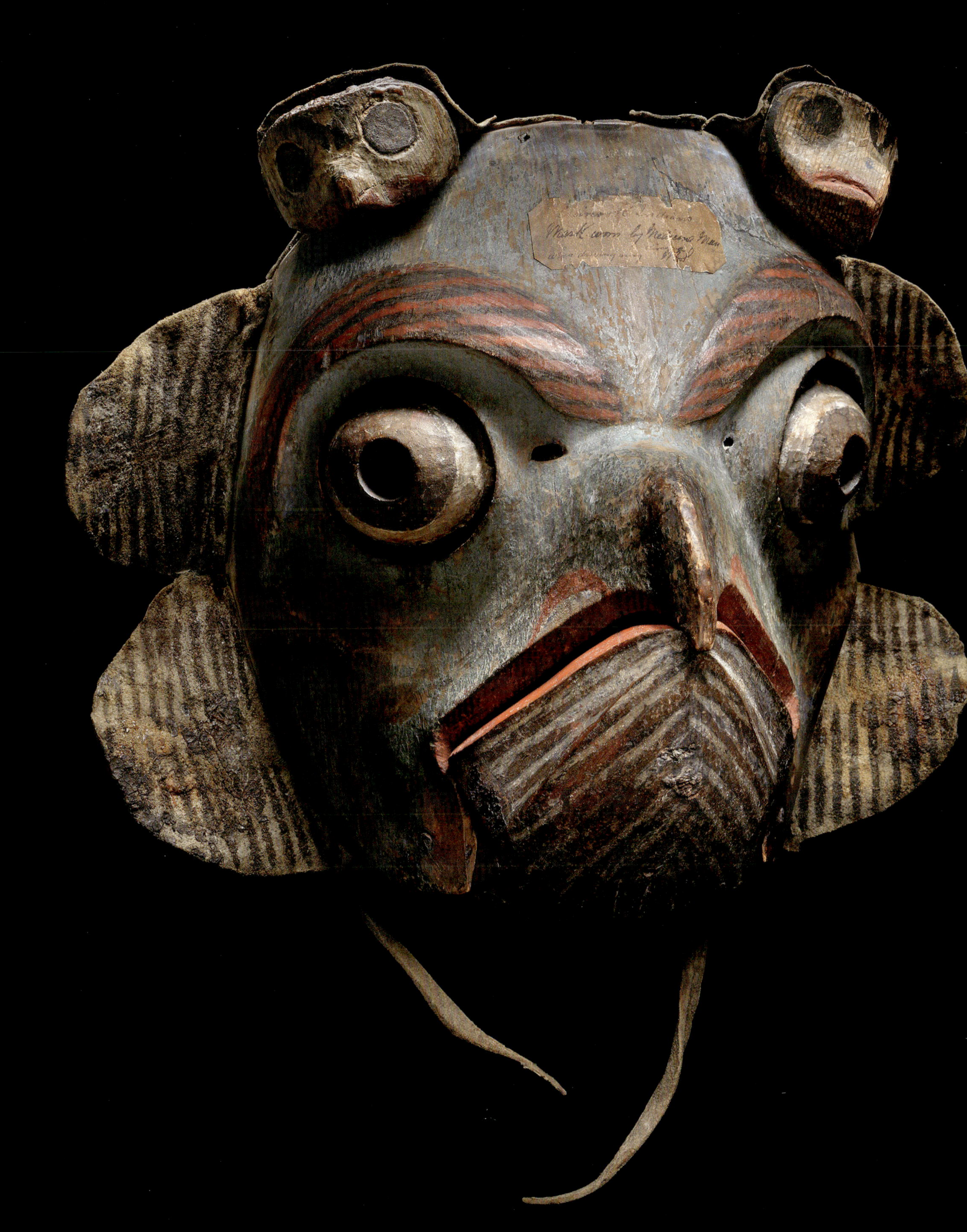
Mask worn by Medicine Man

polished copper. When the mask was danced within a ceremonial context, these would have reflected the firelight. The hide mounts that held the mask on the dancer's head had to be positioned to allow for the operation of both the eyes and the mouth, or as Brown says, "The strings that operate the beak are integrated with those controlling the movement of the eyes."[3] The dancer would presumably also have been making sounds to suggest the cry of the owl. These movements, combined with the sounds, would have made this mask a compelling object to watch being danced.

Although the label mistakenly refers to this mask as being of Chinook origin, the paint, which includes areas of striation, is characteristic of Heiltsuk masks. It includes both mineral pigments that would have been sourced by the Heiltsuk carver or his supplier and red pigment that would have been obtained through trade.[4] The black lines on the raised eyebrows' red paint tone the colour down and make the red of the mouth more vivid. A similar striation is seen in the two half-round shapes on either side of the face, and these lines as a whole tend to amplify the owl's face. The lower portion of the jaw is carved in a chevron pattern that also echoes these patterns.

When the Nisg̲a'a carver Norman Tait (b. 1941) was shown this mask, he suggested that it showed the "'Spirit of the Owl,' the death owl,"[5] and that the smaller heads above represented "the ones that have already gone, nephews, nieces. They are not very significant on the mask, so someone that died at an early age."[6]

Whether it was used in a healing ceremony or in a reenactment of tribal or clan history, or whether it hints of death, what is certain is that this mask has a profound and slightly disquieting resonance. It has all the fierce beauty of an owl. ■

Heiltsuk Artist
Frontlet
c. 1860–80

This extremely beautiful frontlet is a great example of Heiltsuk art and would have been the major part of a magnificent headdress worn by an important chief. Although small in scale, this frontlet is extremely well carved. Only the most essential parts of the eagle are presented here—the face and wings—but these are so vital that we have no need for further anatomical detail. The beak of the eagle protrudes proudly, and the cheeks vividly evoke the bird itself. Equally fine are the small pair of wings that frame a small humanoid face at the bottom of the carving. The presence of the human face emphasizes the unity between man and the natural world and the belief among many First Nations that the creatures of the natural world also have human manifestations. The paint is old, and although somewhat worn, uses the colours that you would expect to see in an old Heiltsuk example.[1]

Frontlets are a mark of high rank and status within the culture. Objects of this much beauty and importance played a significant part in ceremonial life and would have been used in potlatches. It was perhaps in one such ceremony that this frontlet passed out of the hands of the Heiltsuk people and became one of the treasures of the 'Na̲mgis at 'Ya̲lis (Alert Bay). Indeed, this mask was acquired from Yakuglas (Albert Hunt) of that community.[2] This transfer of an object of great importance and luxury from the Heiltsuk to the Kwakwa̲ka̲'wakw reflects the fact that exceptional craftsmanship and beauty were greatly appreciated by First Nations peoples of the coast, no matter the origin of an individual object.

PROVENANCE: *Chief Glakugulus of The Place Where Coppers are Made; Yakuglas (Albert Hunt), Alert Bay; Donald Ellis Gallery, New York and Vancouver; Audain Collection, purchased 2010*

▸ Heiltsuk Artist
Frontlet, c. 1860–80
wood, pigment, abalone
20.8 × 19.2 × 14.7 cm
Promised Gift, Audain Collection

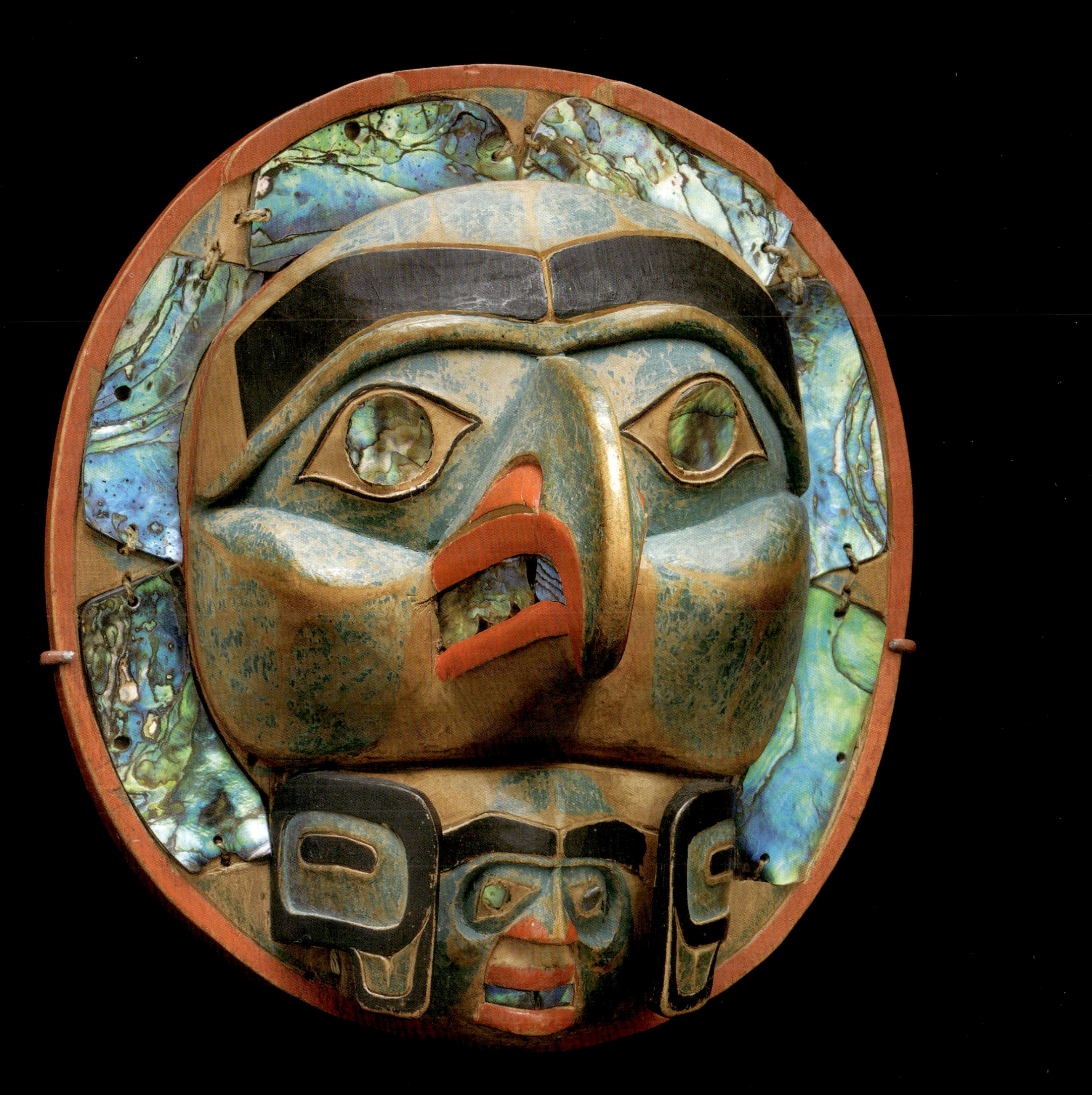

Doubtless, one of the things that was valued about this frontlet, besides the extremely sensitive and subtle carving, was the wonderful use of California abalone. This sparkling blue shell would have been integral to making this frontlet a striking presence in the firelight of a big house ceremony, regardless of where that ceremony was held. This frontlet makes an interesting comparison to two others in the Audain Art Museum Collection: the Kaigani Haida example (page 28) and the magnificent Tlingit headdress (page 52). ■

Haida Artist
Female Portrait Mask
c. 1800

A classic old Haida mask, this work was in the distinguished Menil Collection and was discussed by Bill Reid and Bill Holm in their book *Form and Freedom: A Dialogue on Northwest Coast Art*.[1] It depicts a high-ranking Haida woman; her rank is marked by both the designs on her face (which likely represent tattoos) and the presence of a large labret (or lip plug) in her lower lip. This was a mask intended for use in ceremony, although precisely how it was used remains unknown.

The mask combines elements that are highly realistic, such as the delineation of the nose, lips and teeth, with elements that are highly stylized, such as the eyes, with their incised upper lid, and the ears, which are simple shapes. Although it is called a portrait mask, it is unclear that it depicts a particular individual. Elements such as the shape of the nose and the slightly fleshy area under the jaw are, however, distinctive.

The paint, although faded in some areas, is original. The black, red and blue-green are all characteristic of pigments that came from the Naden River area on Haida Gwaii,[2] and are colours used before the Haida had access to other pigments through trade. The paint is applied both finely and relatively broadly—note, for example, the differences between areas of cross-hatching and the broad swath of the eyebrows. Everywhere, however, there is a careful attention to line, and the linear patterning is masterful. Masks such as this one would have been both carved and painted by the same individual, and although he remains anonymous, he was certainly an artist of genius.

PROVENANCE: *Menil Collection, Houston; private collection, Chicago; James Economos Collection; private collection; Howard Roloff, Victoria; Anthropos, Los Angeles; Douglas Reynolds Gallery, Vancouver; Audain Collection, purchased 2010*

▸ Haida Artist
Female Portrait Mask,
c. 1800
wood, pigment
23.5 × 19.2 × 11.5 cm
Promised Gift, Audain Collection

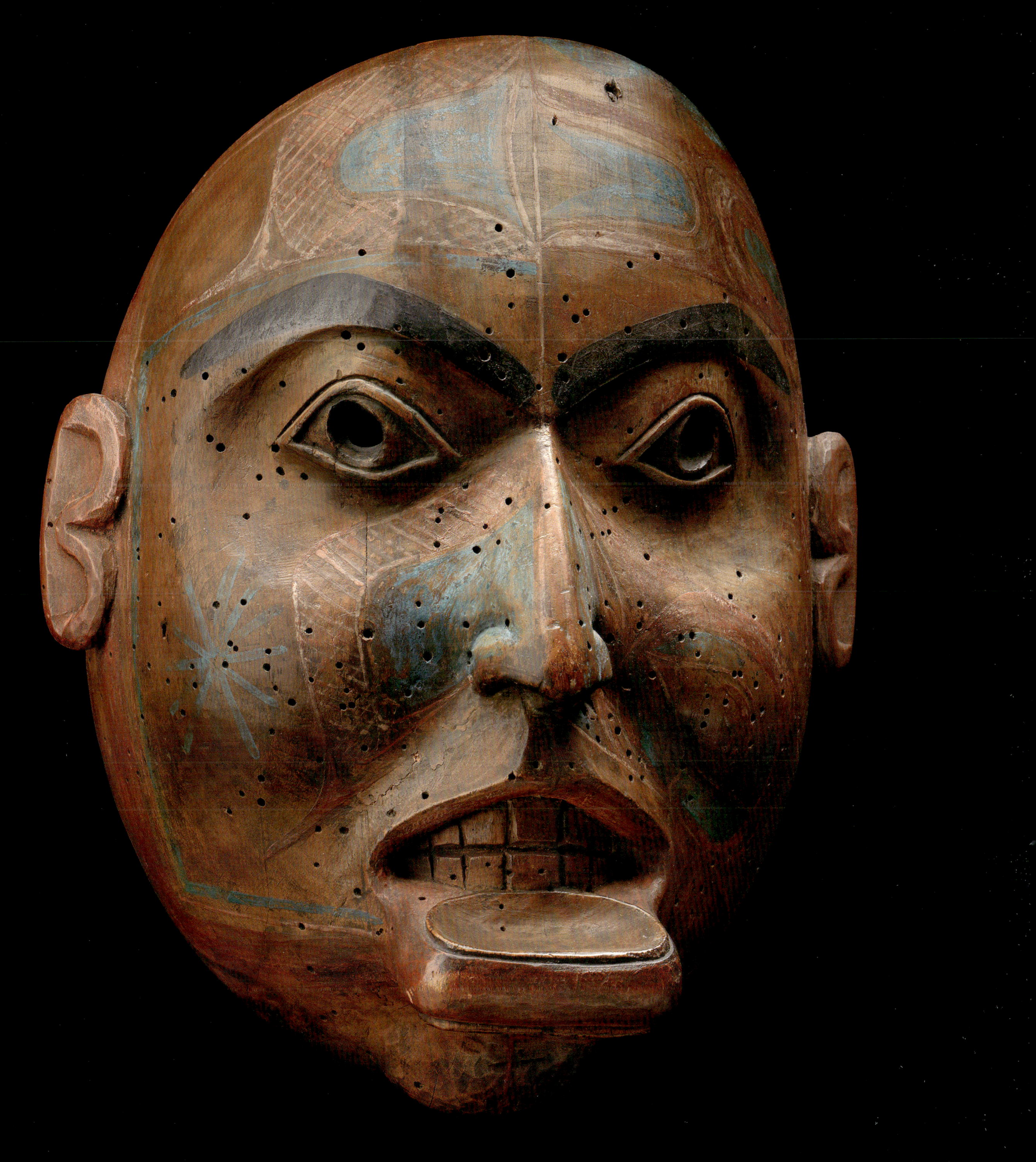

Although the mask has been ravaged by the powderpost beetle, it has lost none of its power and nobility. This woman is someone of consequence, and the level of craftsmanship in the carving reflects her high status. When he saw this mask, the great contemporary carver Robert Davidson (b. 1946) said simply, "That is a very beautiful mask."[3]

To understand why the mask is so beautiful, we need to look at how the painting both matches and contrasts with the carving. The carved face, without the pigment, is remarkably symmetrical. Symmetry generally pleases us in other human faces. The painting, however, is not symmetrical, and this asymmetry leads the eye across the mask's surface, giving the face its vitality. We know that the mask is made of wood, and yet the soft contours of the cheeks and the slightly sagging flesh under the jaw read as flesh, a remarkable and mysterious transformation.

This effect is similar to the transformation that would occur in the dancer who wore and danced the mask. Selected because she could animate the mask brilliantly, the dancer, who may not have been a noblewoman, becomes one, and she embodies the traditions and pride of the Haida people. This noblewoman is human and present and, at the same time, of another spirit world that we can only rarely access. The dancer wearing the mask and the ceremony in which it is used become an important conduit between these two worlds. We cannot help but feel a frisson as we touch this other world.

Similar masks are held in the collections of the Smithsonian Institution, the National Museum of Natural History and the University of Pennsylvania Museum of Archaeology and Anthropology. Scholar Bill McLennan believes all three masks to be by the same artist.[4] ■

Haida Artist
Old Woman with Labret Mask
c. 1840–60

PROVENANCE: *George Terasaki Collection, New York; Donald Ellis Gallery, New York and Vancouver; Audain Collection, purchased 2010*

Unlike *Female Portrait Mask* (page 24), another Haida mask in this collection, which was made for ceremonial use, the carving *Old Woman with Labret Mask* was made for trade. The growing interaction between the Haida and visitors to their islands in the nineteenth century meant there was a market for their carvings.

The fact that this mask has no eye holes shows that it was meant for display rather than for ceremony, and it is one of a number of striking examples of "naturalism"[1] in Haida carving. Perhaps the most notable Haida carver working in this style was Simeon Sdiihaldaa (c. 1799–1889), whose startling masks, which sometimes had eyes that opened and closed, are strongly naturalistic. Although this mask was likely not made by Sdiihaldaa,[2] it certainly demonstrates this naturalistic spirit.

The deeply carved wrinkles in her face convey a sense of her age, and the fact that, as Northwest Coast art scholar Steven C. Brown has noted, they are asymmetrical allows the patterns to "effectively imitate wrinkled skin."[3] These sweeping lines also highlight the eyes, nose and mouth and emphasize the topography of the face. The hair, which appears highly stylized, may originally have been decorated with beading that would have been attached in the holes that run along the top of the mask.

The large labret in her lower lip, the abalone nose ring and the (now missing) abalone earrings, together with the staring eyes, give the mask a bold and exotic look that would have appealed to visitors looking for an unusual memento of their visit to Haida Gwaii. This memorable face would have been a powerful messenger for Haida art and culture, worlds away from where it was carved. ■

▸ Haida Artist
Old Woman with Labret Mask, c. 1840–60
wood, pigment, abalone
25.6 × 22.2 × 12.4 cm
Promised Gift, Audain Collection

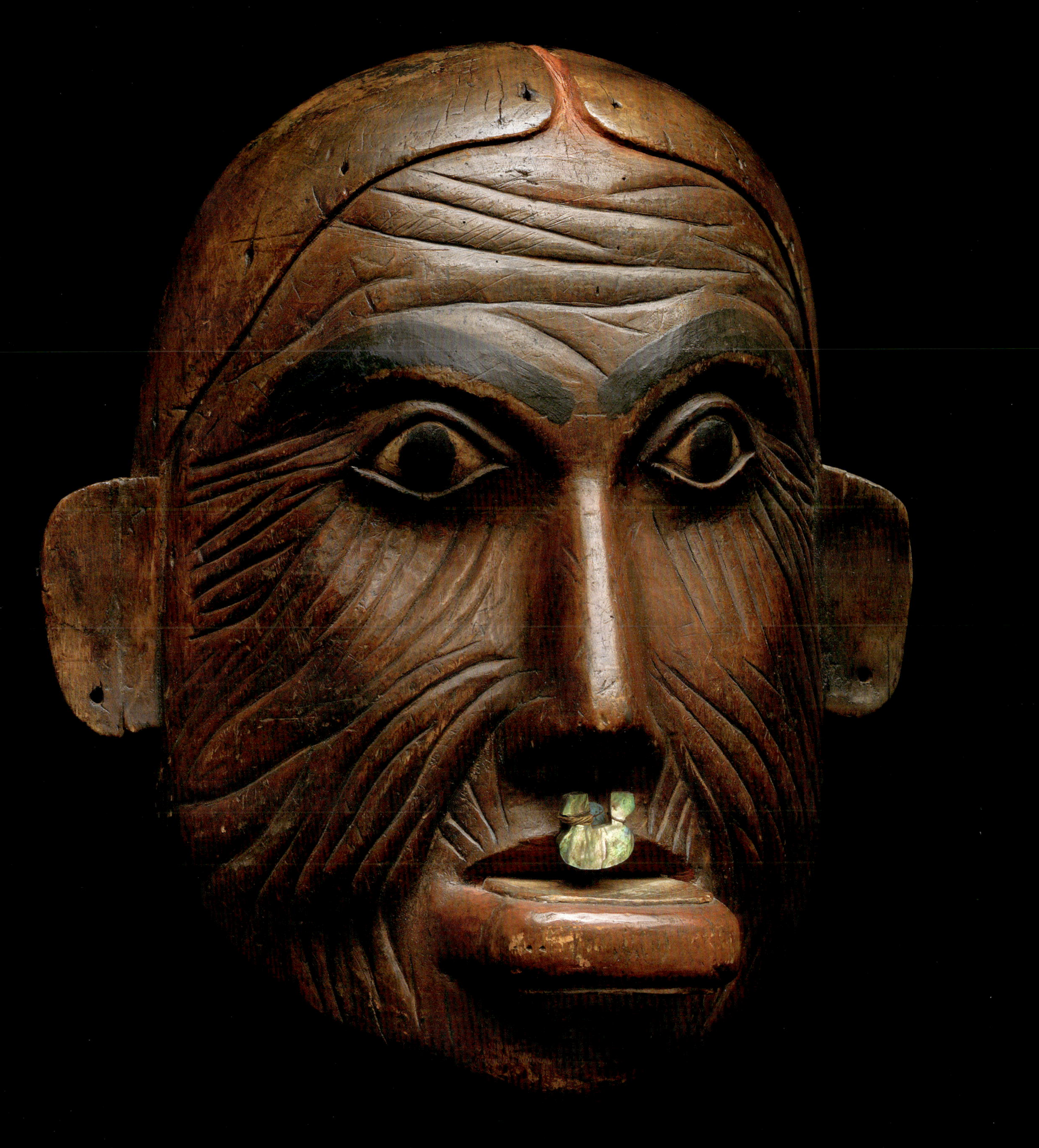

Haida Artist (Kaigani)
Frontlet
c. 1880–90

Although the Haida are synonymous with their island territory, Haida Gwaii, there have also always been Haida people living in southern Alaska, in the area of Hydaburg. In the nineteenth century, there existed a long tradition of family ties between the two regions. Nevertheless, the so-called Kaigani Haida in Alaska also lived in close proximity to the Tlingit, and both Haida and Tlingit influences are visible in their art.

This boldly carved frontlet depicts the figure of Wasco, or Sea Bear, a creature that is a hybrid of a killer whale (or blackfish) and a bear. It is made of a thicker piece of wood, perhaps yellow cedar, and is more roughly carved than one would expect in a true frontlet. On the back, above the lower portion of the frontlet (slightly above the mouth), there is a low shelf-like area that would presumably have rested on the head of the wearer, indicating that this frontlet was likely part of an elaborate headdress and sat on the forehead rather than covering the face.

The headdress would have been decorated on top with walrus whiskers (there are holes to accommodate these along the top edge of the frontlet) and then attached to a support that would have been embellished with ermine skins or other pelts. When this frontlet was worn by the chief who owned it, the area behind the eyes and ears of the Wasco would likely have been filled with eagle down. It is an object that displays the considerable wealth of the individual who commissioned it, being decorated extensively with abalone shell traded from California.[1] Only the wealthiest of chiefs would have been able to afford what would have been an extremely opulent headdress.

This mask has been admired by many carvers, among them Bill Reid (1920–1998), who commented,

> Fantastic frontlet. It doesn't conform to any style of Northwest Coast art, as far as I am concerned, yet when I first saw it years ago, it immediately had a Haida impact. I think that it's one of those funny Haida things that happen now and then. Haida artists worked mostly within a rigid, formal system, but occasionally burst out and did crazy, wild things which out-crazied the other people of the Coast. This has none of the formal organization and classic beauty of the things we associate with the Northwest Coast, yet I find it extremely powerful, potent.[2]

Distinguished carver Dempsey Bob (b. 1948) has observed,

> What is really neat about this is it is a forehead mask carved in the style of a frontlet. That is the frontlet part (front), the lip of the frontlet. It's like a big fin. It could be the Sea Bear; the Haidas call it Wasco. It [ha]s bear ears, and his fin. The back of it is carved in the shape of a frontlet but is actually a dance headdress. There was probably fur on the back and sea lion whiskers on top. When you look at the old stuff and see how creative they really were . . . I wouldn't have thought of this, turning a frontlet into a dance headdress, but that's what they did. This is a really good piece. Look at the depth of the carving."[3]

PROVENANCE: *Adelaide de Menil and Edmund Carpenter, New York; private collection, New York; Sotheby's, New York (lot 111, May 22, 2013); Audain Art Museum Collection, 2013.004*

▸ Haida Artist (Kaigani)
Frontlet, c. 1880–90
wood, pigment, abalone
25.2 × 22.5 × 20.0 cm
Audain Art Museum Collection, 2013.004

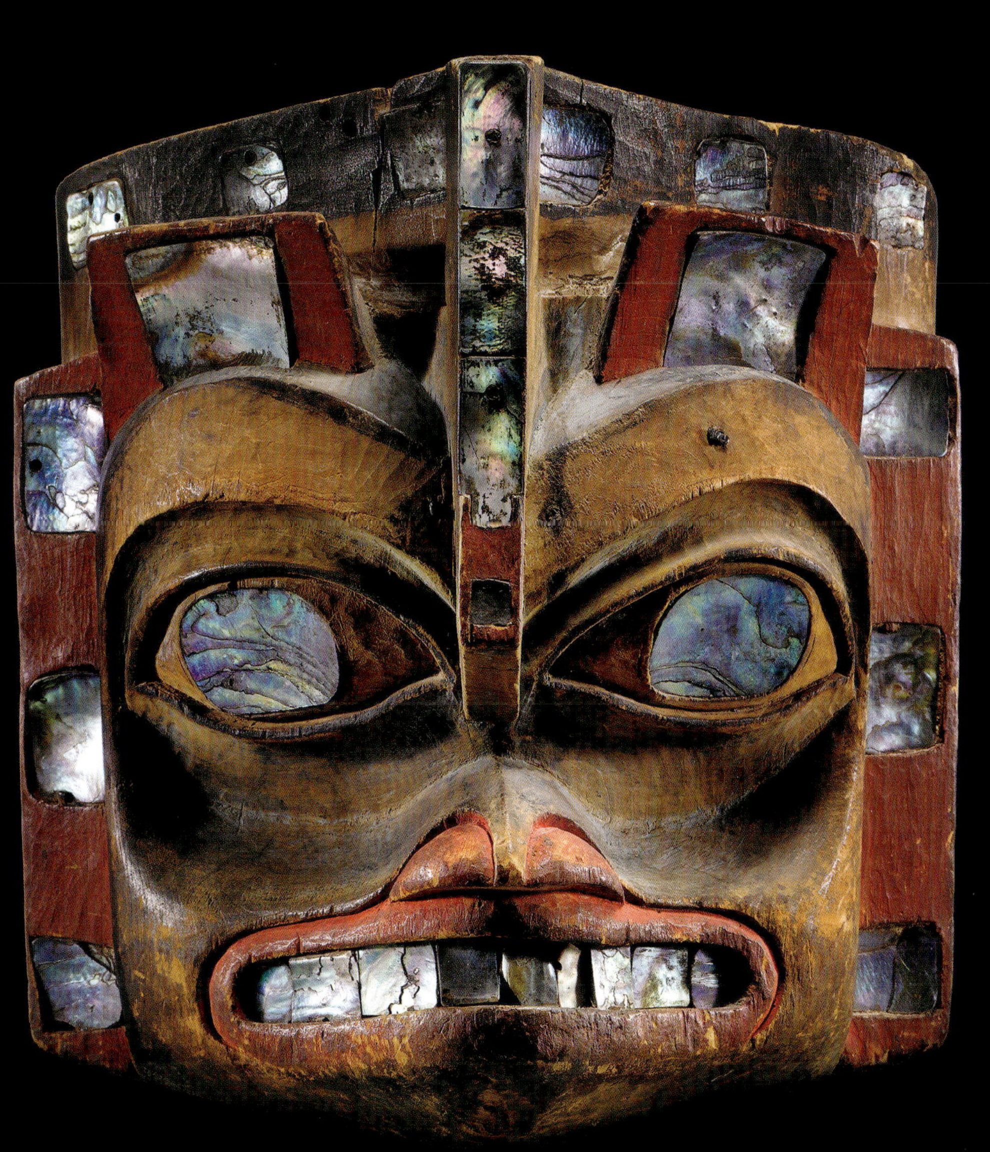

One of the most striking aspects of this frontlet is its lack of a forehead. The face transitions directly from unpainted eyebrows to ears. The upper section of the carving reads not as forehead but as the body of the Wasco, and it supports the dorsal fin that rises above the finely carved nose. It is as if the body of this powerful creature is directly connected to the face without the intervening elements of a head and neck.

The carver Norman Tait (b. 1941) has commented that these "big eyebrows" make the piece look Tlingit. He continues: "Kaigani Haida, that's what I would say. It does have both Tlingit and Haida style. That vertical piece is Tlingit style, maybe the dorsal fin spirit of the whale."[4]

Although this carving has been described by Bob as a dance headdress, and a distinguished chief would have certainly used it ceremonially, it is unlikely that it was danced per se. The wearer of the headdress of which this carving would have been the most important part would have had the right to the Wasco crest and would have been a major figure in any ceremony, but he was likely too august to dance. Certainly, this carving helped to distinguish his rank and importance rather than to disguise or transform his identity.

This carving succinctly demonstrates the importance of the trading relations between First Nations peoples on the west coast of North America. It brings sparkling light in the form of abalone decoration from California. By combining elements of both the finer Haida form (such as the subtle carving of the nose) and the bolder Tlingit form (the eyebrows and dorsal fin), this frontlet amplifies our understanding of Haida visual vocabulary, particularly in the portrait masks in this collection. ■

Kwakwa̱ka̱'wakw Artist
Ancestor Mask
c. 1880

This large and fascinating mask has been in a number of collections, and the exotic nature of the imagery doubtless explains its ongoing appeal. This is not a mask that would likely have been worn by a dancer; rather, it would have been manipulated by a dancer from behind a blanket or screen.

The paint, in traditional colours of red, black and white (now oxidized to brown), is original. Particularly striking, however, are the eyes of the figure, surrounded by the red eyelids and seen against an expanse of black paint. This mask portrays the nuła̱małaga̱mł, one of a group of characters described by George Hunt and Franz Boas in "The Social Organization and Secret Societies of the Kwakiutl Indians"[1] as having distinctive features and behaving in an appalling and fearsome way. Their origin is related in some detail, but the salient points are that the nuła̱małaga̱mł are descended from a hunter who fell in with a group of supernatural figures who lived in a lake and who had "enormous noses and their bodies [were] covered with snot."[2] This experience caused the hunter to lose his senses for a long time. Subsequent nuła̱małaga̱mł were "out of their senses" and had "long noses."[3] Nuła̱małaga̱mł are filthy (which is suggested by the oxidized nature of the mask) and act strangely. "They do not dance, but, when excited, run about like madmen, throwing stones, knocking people down, and crying … They break canoes, houses, kettles, and boxes; in short, acts the madman in every conceivable way. At the close of the dance season they must indemnify the owners for all property destroyed."[4]

PROVENANCE: *Possibly the collection of Professor Aloysius Joyful Copperthwaite, United Kingdom; Graham Osborn-Smith, United Kingdom; The Wax Museum at Brading, Isle of Wight; Robert Ball Collection, United Kingdom; Duke's Collection, United Kingdom; private collection, United Kingdom; Sotheby's, New York (lot 40, May 18, 2011); Audain Collection*

► Kwakwa̱ka̱'wakw Artist
Ancestor Mask, c. 1880
wood, pigment
64.0 × 60.0 × 35 cm
Promised Gift, Audain Collection

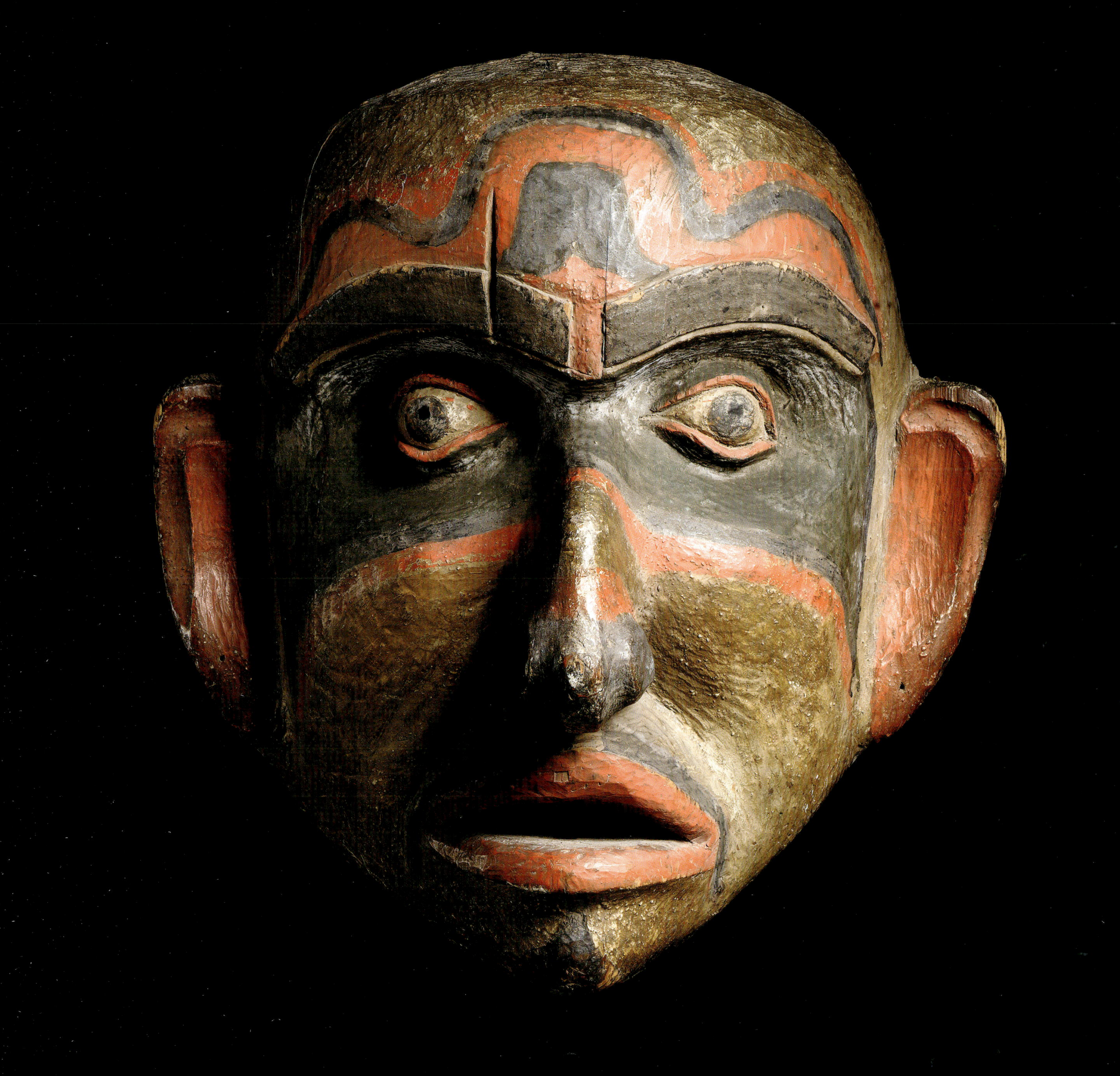

Over time, the behaviour of the nułamałagamł seems to have moderated. The figure has been particularly identified with the Koskimo people, among whom the nułamałagamł is more like a police officer. He appears at the beginning of an event, after first beating on the door, and threatens to discipline anyone who acts inappropriately or in a "disrespectful" manner.[5] Either way, this fearsome-looking figure would have made an impressive presence in a big house as a ceremony was about to begin. ■

Kwakwaka'wakw Artist
Sun Mask
late 19th century

This boldly carved mask comes from the Kwakwaka'wakw Nation, specifically the Koskimo on Vancouver Island, in the area of Quatsino Sound. This is certainly a mask that would have been used in ceremonial events, but the large scale probably means that a dancer did not wear it when it was used.

The main part of the mask is carved from a single block of cedar, and the rays are carved individually and then attached to the larger mask. The presence of three large holes on either side of the face indicates that the mask had either cedar-bark raffia or perhaps an animal pelt attached to further embellish it.

Painted in the traditional Kwakwaka'wakw colours of black, red and white, it has a slightly shiny surface that would have been important for reflecting the firelight when it was being used. The vivid red that covers the lips is carried out into the philtrum, the lower cheek area and the underside of the beak, which gives the black form of the beak additional prominence within the mask face. Red appears elsewhere on the mask, but its use is measured and calculated not to detract from the major punch of red in the lower section of the face. The rays of the sun are outlined in another, somewhat duller, shade of red. The eyes, another cardinal feature of the face, are given prominence by locating them within a large area of black and, though the eye socket is extensively carved, by highlighting only the actual carved eye shape in white. The iris and pupils of the eyes are painted black, and the pupil is a disk of copper that would have been highly polished to reflect the light.

While the rays emanating from around most of the face would suggest that this is a sun mask, in fact this is the face of a thunderbird, as seen in the exaggerated curvature of the beak, which turns in on itself and almost touches the upper lip. The thunderbird is the sovereign of the skies, a mythological being also associated with the sun.

Distinguished Kwakwaka'wakw carver and elder Beau Dick (b. 1955) commented on the origin and use of this mask:

> This mask is Koskimo too, an older style. There are these types of things that could be shown over top of a screen. Go up and down as sun masks and moon masks from behind the screen. Could be carried onto the floor with a blanket, which gets held up and the mask is shown from behind the blanket. It wouldn't necessarily be worn and danced around the fire. It could make an appearance by the doorway then leave. That's another way these masks were displayed. It may or may not be a sun mask. Thunderbird is related to the sun. Some masks had a harness over the head of the dancer.[1]

PROVENANCE: *Erna Gunther, Seattle; Walter Waters, Alaska; private collection, New Jersey; Sotheby's, New York (lot 350, November 15, 1980); private collection, Santa Fe; Sotheby's, Paris (lot 4, June 11, 2008); Audain Collection*

▸ Kwakwaka'wakw Artist
Sun Mask, late 19th century
cedar, pigment, metal
49.2 × 49.2 × 33.0 cm
Promised Gift, Audain Collection

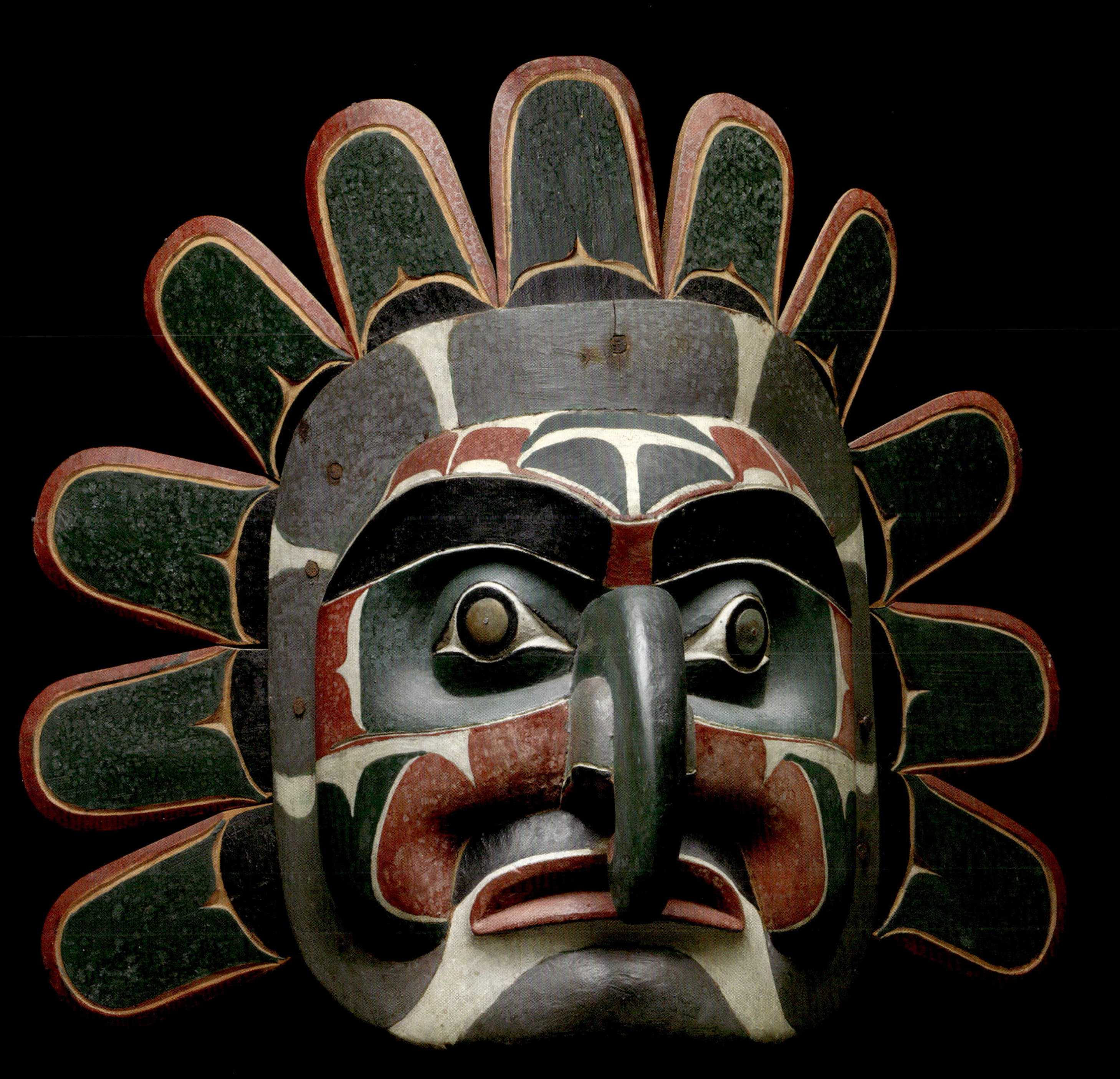

This thunderbird/sun mask is a powerful expression of the traditional Kwakwa̲ka̲'wakw style—both in the carving and painting—and would have been an important part of any ceremony in which it was used. It was once in the collection of anthropologist Erna Gunther, who doubtless recognized the spiritual and cultural force of this compelling mask. ■

Nuxalk Artist
Raven Mask (Bella Coola)
c. 1860–80

Raven was of great importance to the Bella Coola First Nation, and his exploits appear in many stories. He bestowed many benefits on the Bella Coola, or Nuxalk. Among all of Raven's exploits good and bad, one stands out. As anthropologist Thomas McIlwraith noted, "The most spectacular of Raven's exploits was the theft of the sun in order to provide light to the world. For this reason the first raven is referred to as Sanuximatxots, 'The Light Bringer' or Qunqwinim uldida sxen, 'The Unloosener of Light' among other names."[1]

The story of how Raven obtained the sun for the Nuxalk is detailed and deserves retelling in full:

> After they had been living on this earth for some time, *Stältımx̣* married a certain *Sḱqwälut;* they soon had a daughter to whom they gave the name *Nusx̣emtaiän·a*. Much to the parents' joy, she grew into girlhood very rapidly and was soon of marriageable age. Now at this time there was no sun; it was hidden in a container hanging from the roof of *Stältımx̣* house. Raven determined to obtain this for the use of mortals, and decided to become *Nusx̣emtaiän·a*'s child with this aim in view. First he changed himself into a tiny fragment of hemlock needle and placed himself in the cup from which she was drinking. But the girl blew away the fragment of leaf, though she had no idea that it was Raven. Again he tried by changing himself to a piece of eagle down, but again she skimmed it from the surface of the water. The third time Raven became mud. *Nusx̣emtaiän·a* drank this carelessly with the water and was both startled and perturbed to find herself pregnant. Raven had entered her body...
>
> In the course of time *Nusx̣emtaiän·a* gave birth to an infant who was, of course, Raven. Within a few weeks he had grown to a naughty little boy, always demanding new toys, and always crying if he could not get them. One day he saw the sun hanging near the roof and at once he began to cry for the shining thing. He continued until *Stältımx̣* yielded to his grandson's tears and gave it to him to play with. Raven played with it on the floor for a short time, then opened the door and dashed out. As he did so he shattered the container which held light. It became the sun, which has since remained shining. Raven once more assumed his bird form and flew away.[2]

It is this episode in Raven's life that is so important to the Nuxalk and to which this mask refers. How this remarkable rigged mask may have been used is not certain. The carver Latham Mack (b. 1985) speculated that there could have been another mask attached.[3]

PROVENANCE: *Private collection, New York; Donald Ellis Gallery, New York and Vancouver; Audain Collection, purchased 2008*

▸ Nuxalk Artist
Raven Mask (Bella Coola),
c. 1860–80
wood, metal, mirror, cord, pigment
19.5 × 23.3 × 68.8 cm
Promised Gift, Audain Collection

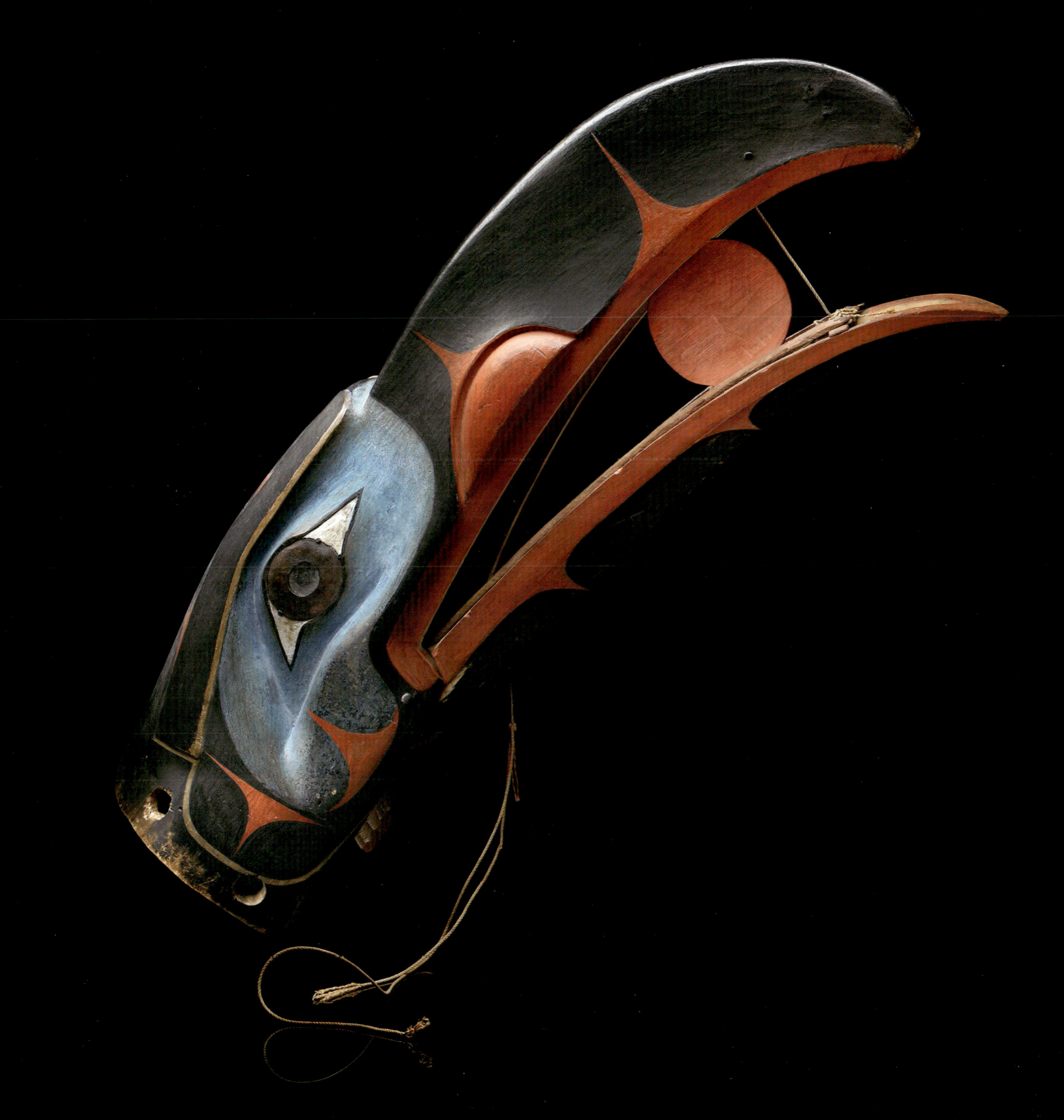

What is certain is that the mask is articulated: when the mouth of the beak is opened, the sun's disk travels along the lower beak towards the tip, and when the mouth is closed, the disk retreats into the bird's gullet.

The paint is original and subtle. Red is used on the edges of the beak and the disk of the sun and as accents on other parts of the head. The eyes are set within an area of deep blue, suggesting the sky. Mack further commented on the qualities of this mask: "It's classic Nuxalk style. They have the cheek coming down off the back. Where the mouth attaches there would be a peg right here, and then they run this line in and it creates the cheek, then it runs back up to the tip of the eye. The eyes are always kind of way down on top of the beak; they almost go straight across at the level of the nose. And everything rolls off the nose up to the front."[4]

The large holes at the end of the beak may have been used to attach this mask to another,[5] or Mack has also suggested, "Usually we will have a piece of wood comes down and ties down and on the side it comes down and we will tie it around our chest and the back one goes down to almost our waist. Then that is what supports the mask. It ties from the bottom on our chest and then there will be a board running down and we tie that on our back. And you dance looking down."[6]

Another possibility is that it held the mask to a cedar-bark ring on the dancer's forehead. Whichever way it was employed, this raven is a remarkably compelling and rare example of early Nuxalk carving and brilliantly encapsulates the complex story of Raven obtaining the sun. One can easily imagine the delight and awe of spectators as they watched the sun travel within the raven's beak. ■

Nuxalk Artist
Earthquake Mask
c. 1880

This striking mask represents the powerful forces of an earthquake. The Nuxalk have various stories about the origins of earthquakes. Anthropologist Thomas McIlwraith and ethnographer Franz Boas document two different ones. McIlwraith records:

> Another supernatural being so far removed from this world that he enters but little the lives of the Bella Coola [Nuxalk], is *Sninia*. He is the male being whom *Ałquntäm* sent down from above in the beginning of time to hold the earth in position, and who has since performed this duty. He lives among the ice of the far north, and has not been seen by mortals for many generations. He holds a rope fastened to the earth; when he is afraid that it has slipped slightly, he takes a new grip and pulls the rope taut, pressing the world against the soles of his feet as he sits with legs extended, as a man would do to hold tight a kicking salmon. It is the tightening of the rope which causes an earthquake. If *Sninia* should lose his grip entirely, the earth would capsize.[1]

Boas reports a slightly different Nuxalk story:

> Our world is called A'neko'oL or QEnk·i'lst, that is "the land below." It is an island swimming in the boundless ocean. In the far east a giant is sitting with legs apart, who is called Alep!alaxtnaiz'. He holds a long stone bar in his outstretched hands. The earth is fastened to this stone bar by means of two stone ropes. Sometimes he gets tired, and moves his hand to take better hold of

PROVENANCE: *George and Rosemary Lois Collection, New York; Donald Ellis Gallery, New York and Vancouver; private collection, Far Hills, New Jersey; Donald Ellis Gallery, New York and Vancouver; Audain Collection, purchased 2009*

▸ Nuxalk Artist
Earthquake Mask, c. 1880
wood, pigment
26.4 × 19.9 × 19.5 cm
Promised Gift, Audain Collection

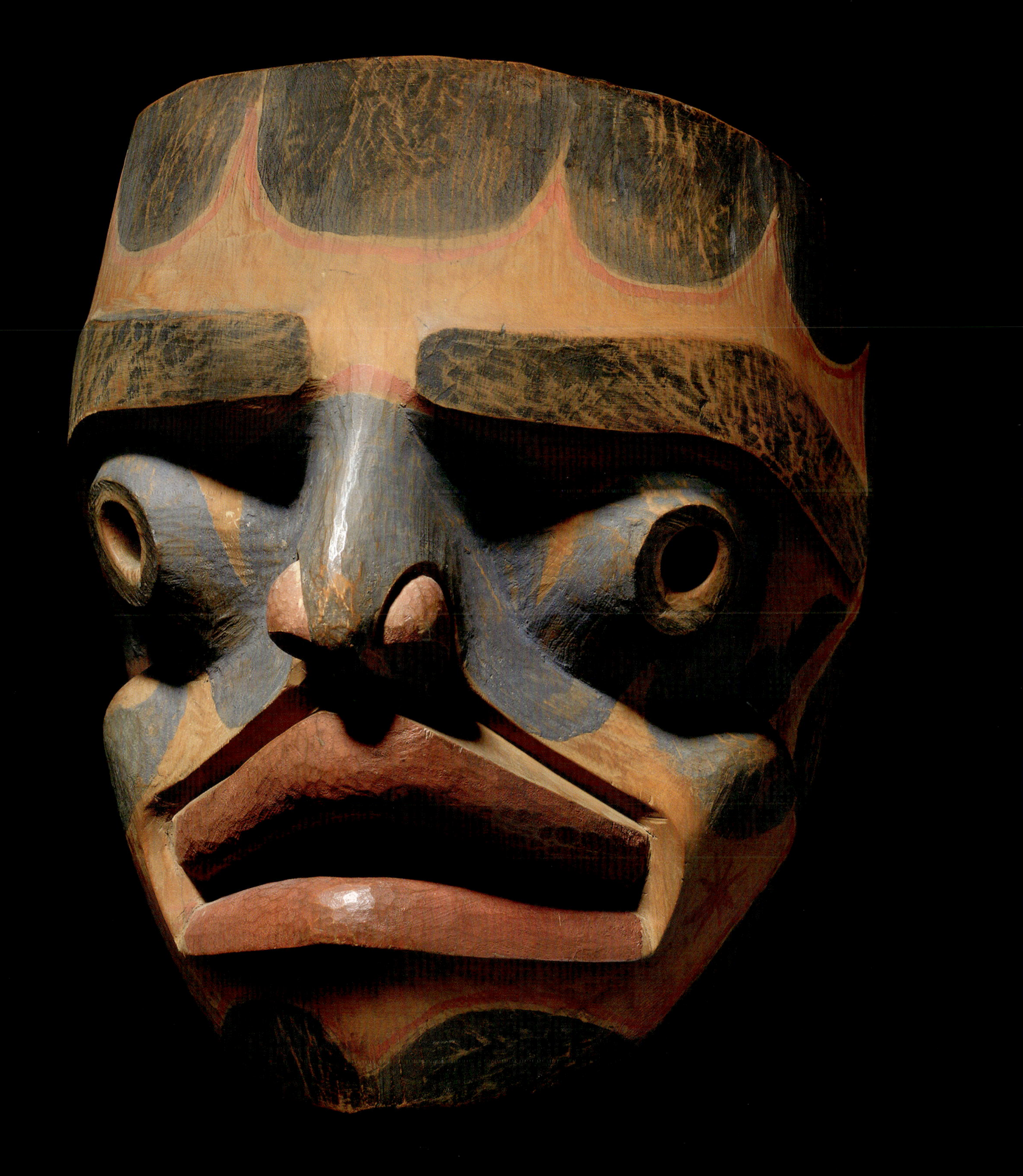

> the stone bar. Then we have an earthquake; and the Bella Coola [Nuxalk] say, "Snenik'pstak·imtols," that is, "He takes hold of our world." When he moves our earth westward, we have epidemics. When he moves it eastward, all sickness disappears.[2]

It appears that the Nuxalk were the only First Nation to have an earthquake mask and dance, and this, of course, may reflect the level of seismic activity in their region. This mask represents an effort to put an identity to a great natural phenomenon, and as McIlwraith reports, it is similar to other dances associated with natural phenomena, such as thunder, the sun and moon:

> The Bella Coola [Nuxalk] believe that an earthquake is caused by the earth slipping very slightly from the grasp of *Sninia*. This being is patron for certain *kukusiut*, and whenever a tremor occurs his protégés call their associates and a dance is held. This may, of course, be at any season, and the ritual during spring or summer is identical with that described for dancers whose patrons are Thunder, the Sun or the Moon. The theme of the song is of the manner in which *Sninia* may also come in the normal manner to his protégés during the ceremonial season, but the ritual is of the usual type and merits no special description.[3]

Immediately after an earthquake, a dance would have been performed using this mask. Not only was it important ceremonially, but Nuxalk carver Latham Mack (b. 1985) considers it "a really interesting mask": "I like how he handles the design on the eye. I actually did this design on a killer whale mask I got a commission for. I wanted to use two U shapes to form that [the eye] because usually the typical one they have a T shape coming down and I had never seen one like this before where it actually meets right here. It's like two U shapes. He carried it over, and I thought I was going to be the first one to do that. I see it's already been done. I like how the lips are really exaggerated. You can see in this a classic Nuxalk piece with the lips defined; the nose is defined."[4]

The mask is deeply carved, with large eye sockets and an incised line above the upper lip that takes the place of the philtrum.

Although carved with greater vigour than finesse, this mask has a considerable force and presence and, like an earthquake, is frightening. The considerable topography of the mask would have made it very effective in the flickering light of a big house fire. ■

Nuu-chah-nulth Artist
Articulated Mask
c. 1840

PROVENANCE: *Seahawk Auctions, Vancouver (lot 193, June 13, 2010); Donald Ellis Gallery, New York and Vancouver; Audain Collection, purchased 2010*

This rare articulated Nuu-chah-nulth mask differs from most others in the Audain Collection. Where we believe that the majority of masks would have been worn and danced by men, this mask was specifically created to be worn and danced by a woman.

The mask is carved from a single piece of wood, likely cedar, with the exception of the nose, which is pinned to the large mask. We see a somewhat forbidding face with a strong, unified brow line and simple ovals for eyes. The painting of two distinct sets of eyebrows moderates the severity of the single carved brow line.[1] The use of a single oval for the eye is unusual, but there are few comparable

▶ Nuu-chah-nulth Artist
Articulated Mask, c. 1840
wood, pigment
33.0 × 16.0 × 7.5 cm
Promised Gift, Audain Collection

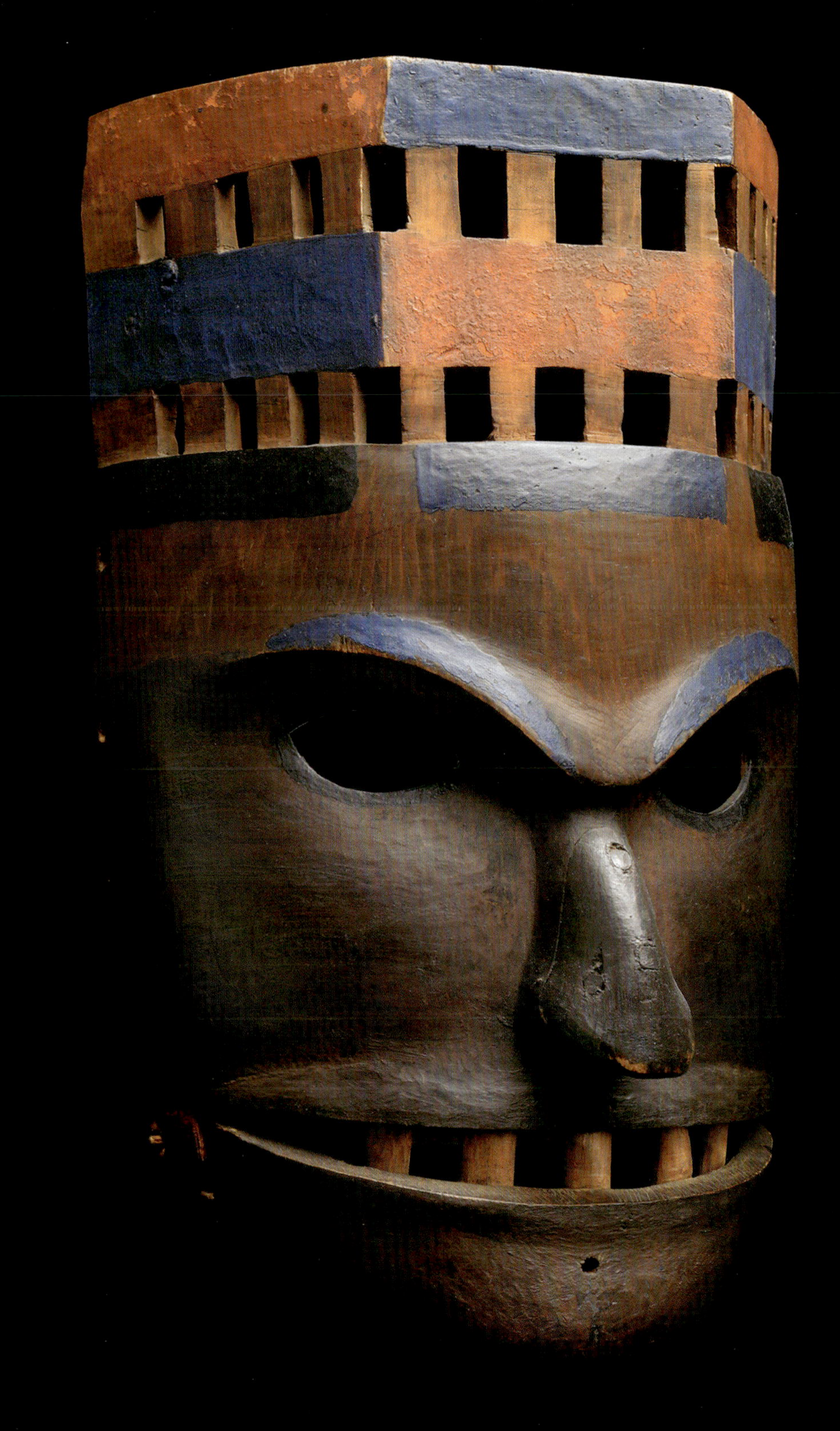

examples extant from this period. The mouth, of which the lower mandible moves, is equipped with three large wooden peg teeth. The whole is painted using red and black pigments in a variety of intensities.

The elongated facial features of the mask strongly suggest that it is a Tla-o-qui-aht (Clayoquot) mask; a mask believed to be by the same artist is held in the Glenbow Museum in Calgary.[2] The mask would have been accompanied by a large fish trap rattle, and the wearer of the mask would have had to animate both. When he was shown an image of this mask, a distinguished carver, who prefers to remain anonymous because he is not of Nuu-chah-nulth ancestry, immediately identified this mask as Tla-o-qui-aht (Clayoquot) from the village of Opitsaht on Meares Island. The artist added, "The woman that wore that mask would use that rattle behind her back. It would be under her blanket. She would go around the house and do her four turns [around the big house]. That's the only time that mask and rattle (fish trap rattle) would be used."

The mention of the fish trap rattle, which is a rattle of a very specific form (a cage with fish),[3] allows us to identify the pierced superstructure above the forehead of this mask, which no other known Nuu-chah-nulth masks share. It is a fish trap, or weir, designed in a U shape to allow water to flow through but to capture the salmon. This element connects the mask directly to the salmon fishery; provides a very specific context in which to imagine this mask in use, in conjunction with the fish trap rattle; and provides a powerful connection between the past and present of the Tla-o-qui-aht First Nation, for whom the salmon fishery is still vital. ■

Gitxsan Artist
Portrait Mask
c. 1880

This rigged mask is likely by the same artist as another *Portrait Mask* in the Audain Collection.[1] The two masks, which were worn in dance ceremonies, are carved and painted in a similar fashion. Both masks are carved from alder, a fine-grained hardwood that allows subtleties in carving and would have been durable enough for repeated use in ceremonies. Each face has prominent cheekbones; a wide, slightly open mouth with red lips; a finely carved nose, painted red at the nostrils; carefully modelled eye sockets; eye holes which form the cornea of the eyes; painted hair that parts in the middle; and peaked eyebrows. Both also show signs of use. Where the larger mask distinguishes itself is in the presence of the headpiece and the rigging: the survival of this delicate painted trade tin headpiece atop the mask is extremely rare. The rigging allows the dancer to open and presumably close the headpiece, a bit like a fan, during a dance.

The nature of the ceremony or dance in which this mask would have been used is uncertain, but the headpiece is likely meant to represent a rainbow. As Northwest Coast scholar and teacher Rocque Berthiaume explains, "The rainbow is a crest in Gitxsan country. It is used as a crest by Fireweed clans. Maybe the headpiece is referencing that. Lots of the older Gitxsan clans incorporate the skies."[2]

Generally, masks, stories and dances were the prerogatives of particular families and could be used only by those families or with their permission. The sky, however, was not a realm that was the prerogative of any

PROVENANCE: *(inset) Equinox Gallery, Vancouver; Audain Collection, purchased 2008*

Douglas Reynolds Gallery, Vancouver; Audain Collection, purchased 2009

▸ *inset*
Gitxsan Artist
Portrait Mask, c. 1880
alder, pigment
24.5 × 19.3 × 16.3 cm
Promised Gift, Audain Collection

▸ Gitxsan Artist
Portrait Mask, c. 1880
alder, pigment, tin
39.4 × 31.5 × 17.0 cm
Promised Gift, Audain Collection

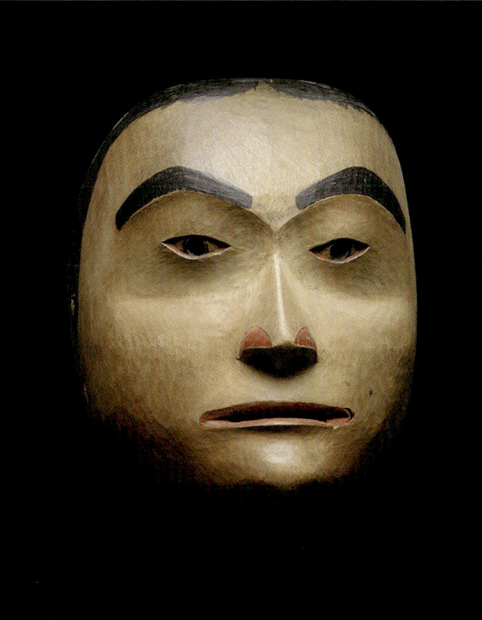

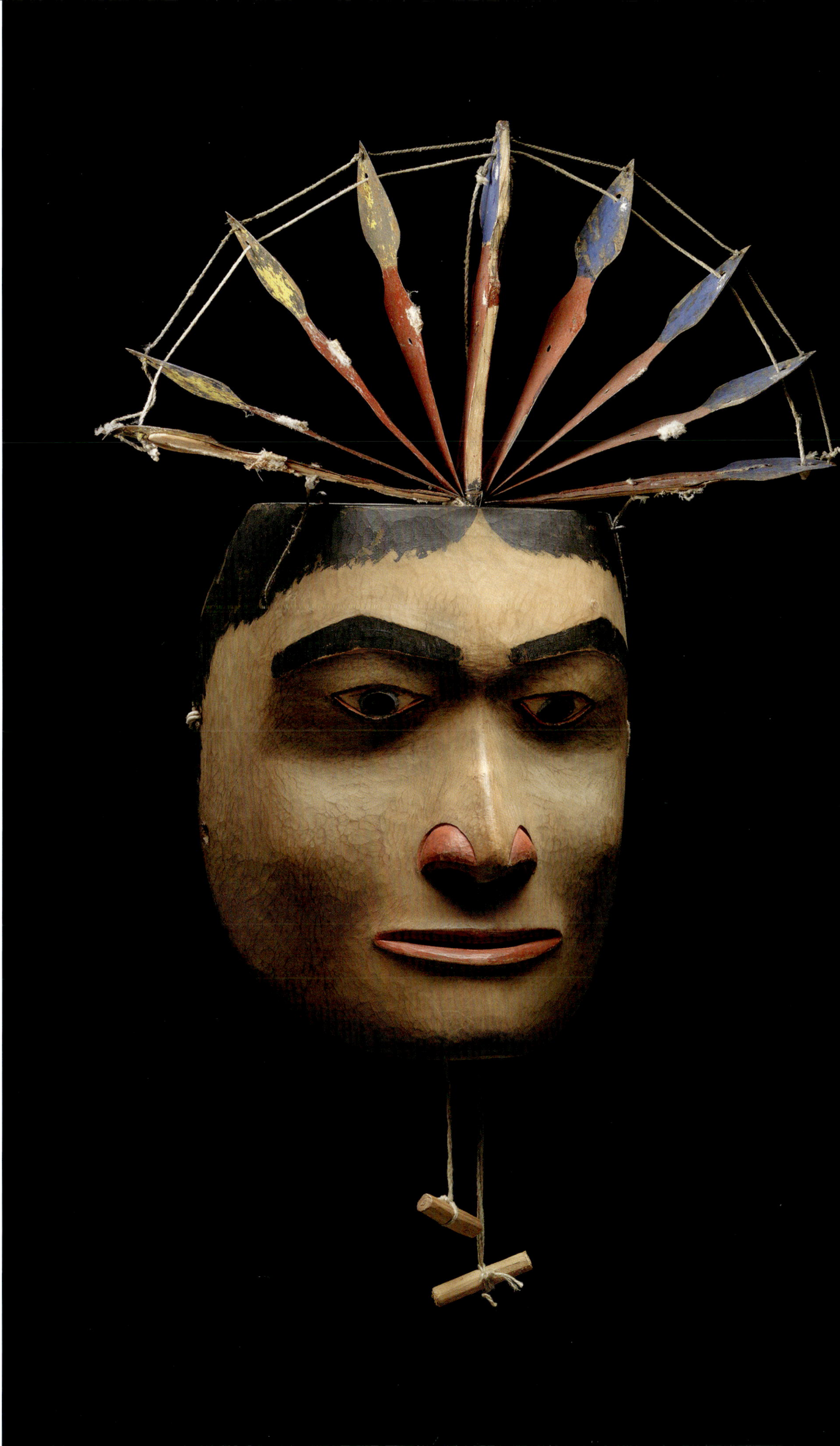

particular family, and therefore the whole clan, rather than an individual, owned the rights to stories about the rainbow.

Assuming the identification of the headpiece as a rainbow is correct, this mask is both human and more than human. The dancer who wore it embodied the sun, which in turn would cause the rainbow to appear. The fact that the rainbow can appear and disappear during the course of the dance, just as a rainbow does in nature, is a particularly interesting aspect. It is easy to imagine that the mask, when used, would evoke the beneficent role of the sun and that the rainbow would suggest the arrival of better weather.

This mask, like its companion in the Audain Collection, has a strong sense of the sublime, of serenity and peace. The face, if not particularly revealing of emotion, is equally devoid of any particular reading, which perhaps supports the idea of a mask for a wider community within the Gitxsan. A haunting image, this mask is the work of an exceptionally accomplished carver. ■

Tsimshian Artist
Portrait Mask
c. 1830–60

This handsome mask, originally collected by the Reverend Thomas Crosby (1840–1914), an English Methodist minister who lived and worked in the Tsmishian village of Lax Kw'alaams (Port Simpson) beginning in 1874,[1] is a fine example of bold Tsimshian carving.

The paint, which is original, is finely applied, and there seems to be a use of black pigment over red in the cheeks and sides of the face. The elegant single line of the upper portion of the eye sockets distinctly and subtly separates the painted eyebrows and encourages the eye to move around the face. When carver and teacher Stan Bevan (b. 1961) viewed images of this mask, he specifically noted this striking element of the design: "I want to point out the design... How he did the eyebrows. It looks like he did a point at the end of the eyebrow, but actually he ran the whole black design through and then ran a red line along the bottom of the eyebrow splitting the black on the face off into an eyebrow."[2]

This mask would have been used within a ceremonial context, but we are uncertain what that context was. Northwest Coast art historian Bill Holm observed, "It's a naturalistic mask... It's a much more stylized representation of a human face: the eye sockets are more designed; the cheeks are outlined in a little carved rim; the lips are more mask-like... It's more of a design than an expression of a real human face."[3] Artist Bill Reid (1920–1998) was interested in the expression of the face too. He noted, "It has a fixed expression, as though depicting a reaction to some immediate situation. When that situation is over, the expression's usefulness and everything else is gone. But that's not to put the mask down in any way. As an object, as an abstract work, it contains many interesting things which make it a beautiful object, obviously the expression of a master carver."[4]

That mastery is seen in the myriad details of this mask—the unusual carved form that surrounds the eyes, moves in towards the nose and then moves out again around the mouth and lips, and that focuses our attention on the most important features of the face; the subtle curvature of the philtrum of the upper lip; the finely detailed nostrils; the division between

PROVENANCE: *Reverend Thomas Crosby, Port Simpson, BC; Museum of the American Indian, Heye Foundation, New York; Adelaide de Menil, New York; George Terasaki, New York; Francesco Pellizzi, New York; Donald Ellis Gallery, New York and Vancouver; private collection, New York; Donald Ellis Gallery, New York and Vancouver; Audain Collection, purchased 2011*

▸ Tsimshian Artist
Portrait Mask, c. 1830–60
wood, pigment
21.0 × 15.2 × 12.5 cm
Promised Gift, Audain Collection

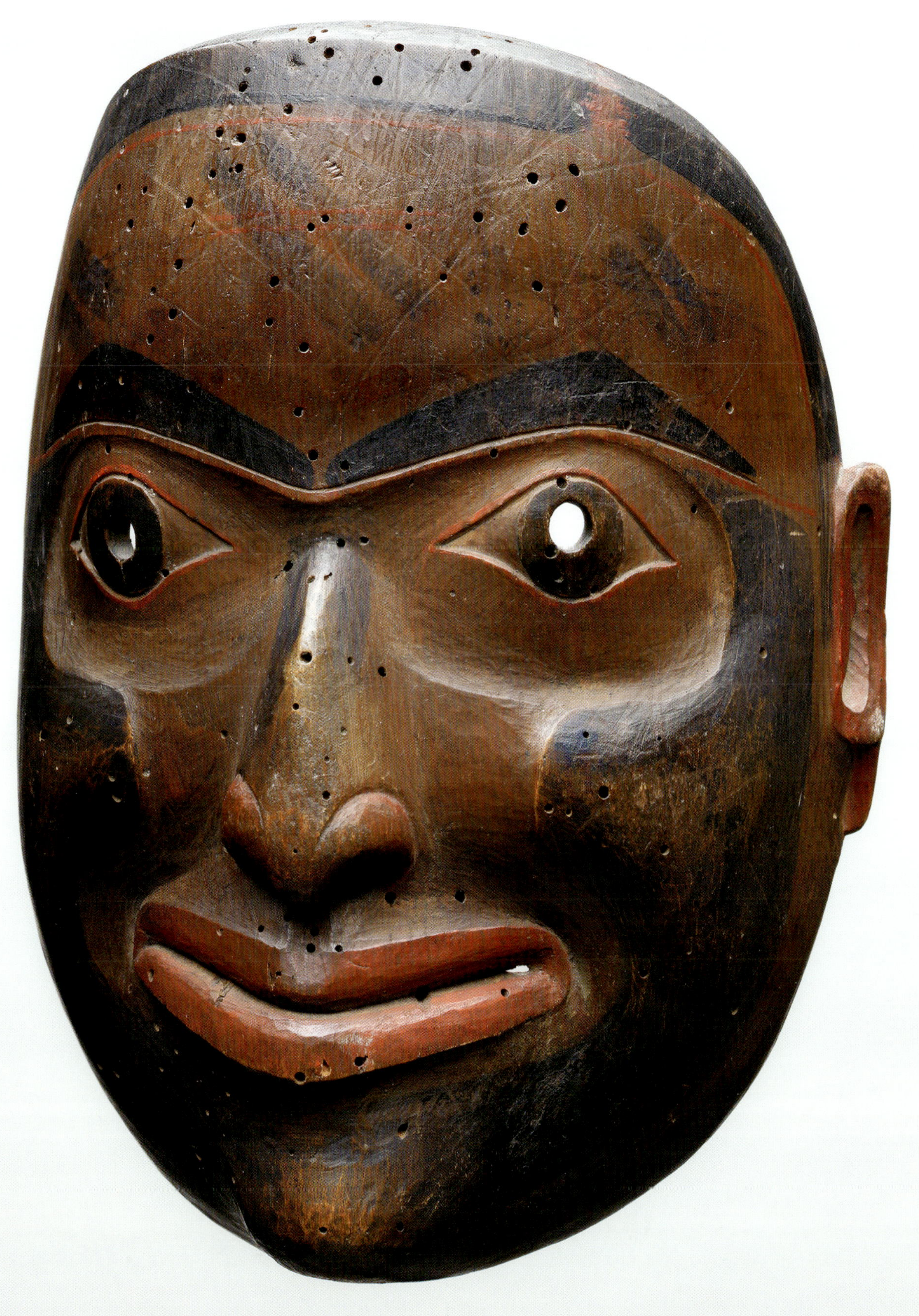

the top of the nose and the brow line; and the way the shape of the mouth and lips counter the shape of the eyebrows—all are marks of refinement and exceptional design. Even without knowing how this mask was used, we can appreciate its power as art. ■

Tsimshian Artist
Chest
c. 1800–50

The Reverend Robert Dundas acquired this splendidly carved box, which might literally be described as a treasure chest, from William Duncan in the village of Metlakatla in the autumn of 1863.[1] It became part of the Dundas Collection of Tsimshian works of art, which the reverend assembled quickly on a single visit to the Christian community. This chest and many other objects remained in the Dundas family until they came to public auction in 2006, 143 years after they were acquired. The works, including this chest, that had been purchased by Canadian collectors and museums from the collection during that sale were then shown in a national tour.[2]

Long recognized as a spectacular example of Tsimshian nineteenth-century carving, this box was the only chest in the Dundas exhibition. Northwest Coast art curator and scholar Alan L. Hoover wrote about its significance:

> Highly decorated rectangular chests often served as containers of a clan's treasures. Masks, ceremonial regalia and woven robes of the noble class were kept in such chests, which were decorated with images designed to protect the contents from adverse spiritual forces. In essence icons for the high-status members of secret societies and ceremonial leaders, these chests held the paraphernalia that made the powers of the chiefs visible and manifest in the world. They were the vessels of social structure and tradition, and kept their important contents from the eyes of the uninitiated.
>
> This particular chest was painted with traditional black and red formline designs, followed by the relief carving of the background and negative (carved-away) areas in the background of the designs. Some of the carved-out areas were then painted with the greenish or blue-green hue that the northern coast artists used so often. The design and carving of this chest are exquisitely executed, offering a grand example of a style that had evolved in this region of the Northwest Coast to a greater extent than anywhere else... In the Tsimshian region, artists pushed the archaic design style toward a new convention of much thinner black and red formlines and much larger carved-out areas that were painted blue-green. The result was an elegant, highly sophisticated style that was inspirational to other artists on the northern Northwest Coast. This chest is a superb example of this design development composed, painted and carved by a master artist.[3]

The greenish or blue-green hue was reserved for the recessed parts of the design because it could be used only with water and therefore was much more vulnerable to wear and chipping when dry. Placing this colour in the lower areas ensured that it was most likely to be preserved.[4]

PROVENANCE: *Reverend Robert Dundas Collection, Scotland; by descent in the family; Sotheby's, New York (lot 34, October 5, 2006); Audain Collection; Gift of Michael Audain and Yoshiko Karasawa; Audain Art Museum Collection, 2015.004*

▸ Tsimshian Artist
Chest, c. 1800–50
yellow cedar, pigment
47.0 × 80.0 × 45.1 cm
Gift of Michael Audain and Yoshiko Karasawa; Audain Art Museum Collection, 2015.004

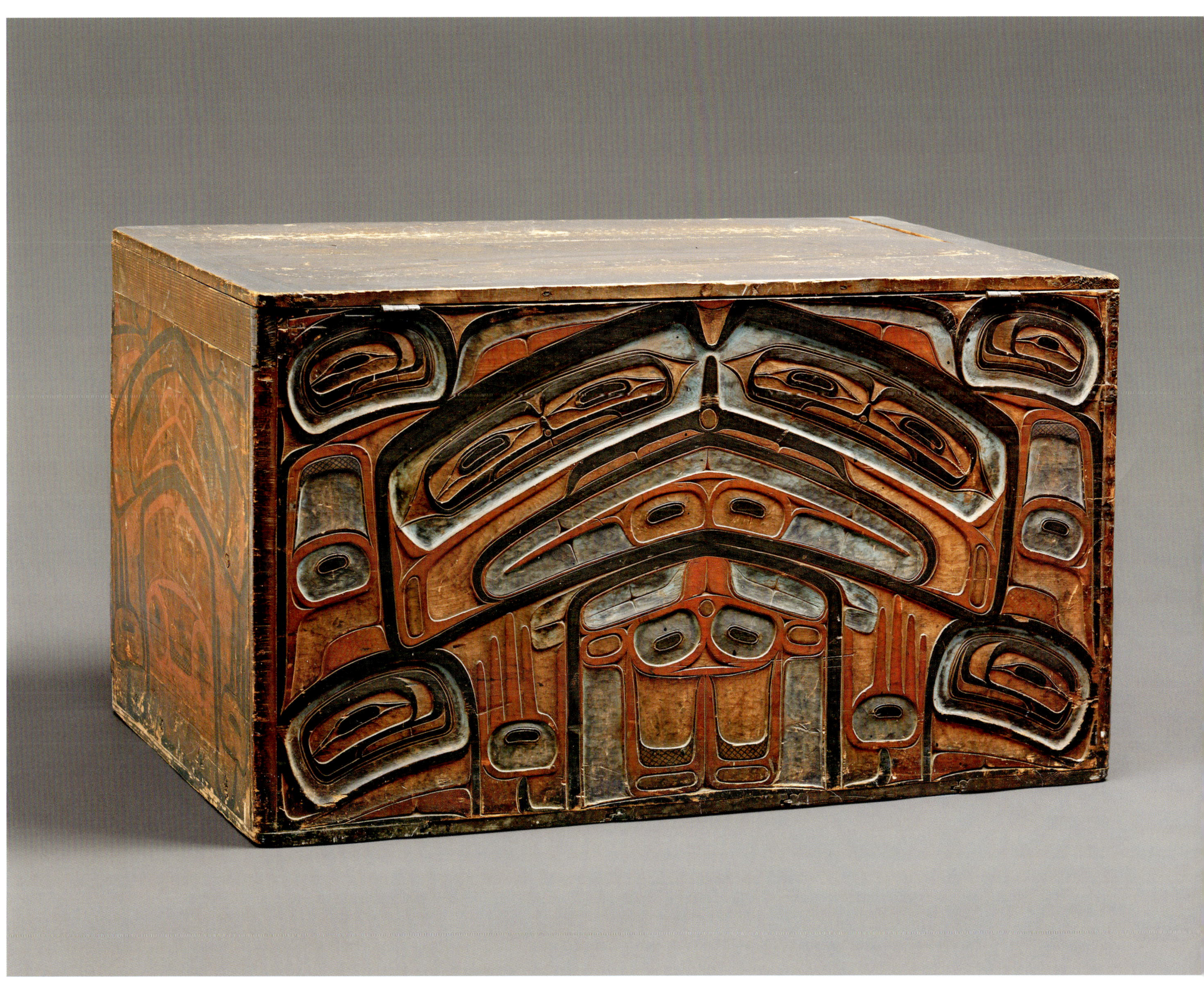

When this box was shown to carver Dempsey Bob (b. 1948), he commented,

> This is Tsimshian. They were some of the best painters, and you look at those old houses. Those paintings are some of the highest achievements of NWC [Northwest Coast] art flat design ever. And this box is part of it… I think this style we are talking about here is a classic style… Some of the best frontlets, rattles and boxes came from the Tsimshian people.
>
> The box is yellow cedar. They would carve yellow cedar because they could get the fine beautiful detail in all the little forms and shapes. That's why it looks so clean… When you look at the really beautiful details of the shapes—like this is a masterpiece, it's a masterpiece.[5]

Interpreting the imagery on boxes such as this one is often difficult. Some of the most significant work in this area was done by Bill McLennan and Karen Duffek. In *The Transforming Image: Painted Arts of the Northwest Coast First Nations,* they write about Tsimshian boxes, "Probably the most commonly represented creature of the box is the shape-changing, whale-eating undersea monster known as Gonakadet, the chief of wealth… Identifiable in Gonakadet's multiple representations may be attributes of killer whales, grizzly bears, humans, beavers, sculpins, and wolves, often portrayed with the suggestion of a hooked nose."[6] They go on to emphasize the idea that the box itself was a carrier of spiritual power, as if the box itself was alive: "In essence, the painted images on boxes and chests were the personification of, and alternative metaphors for, the wealth they contained and the sources from which they derived… The container as a holder of ideas, as well as of material goods and even people, was emphasized throughout the Northwest Coast. It was a box that the trickster/transformer Raven threw open to release light upon the world, establishing the world and its inhabitants in their present form."[7]

This chest was, therefore, far more than a simple container, and the fact that both the bottom and top of the box have been replaced and are not of original design suggests this one has seen much use.[8] The great strength and elegance of the design and its execution, recognized by both Hoover and Bob, more than compensate for these minor faults. It is, quite simply, a statement of genius. ■

Tlingit Artist
Owl Mask
c. 1840–60

This vivid mask is one of the most striking objects in the Audain Collection. In common with some other pieces, the work is articulated—the orange eyelids could once be lifted to reveal the eyes below.[1] As it is, the vivid use of colour calls our attention to the most salient aspects of the owl's eyes and mouth or beak. Originally, human hair probably framed the mask, but it seems to have been replaced at some point by a type of scraggly twine or rope.[2] The mask does retain some of the original strapping to affix it to the user's head, and a remarkable amount of original paint. This includes, in addition to the use of blue-green and orange pigments for the face, eyes, lips and mouth, a pair of boldly painted black eyebrows. The eyebrows are a typical early Tlingit characteristic and can be seen in several masks collected by ethnographer George T. Emmons.[3]

PROVENANCE: *Eugene Chesrow Collection, Chicago; Ziff Family Collection, New York; Sotheby's, Paris (lot 20, June 11, 2008); Donald Ellis Gallery, New York and Vancouver; Audain Collection, purchased 2010*

▸ Tlingit Artist
Owl Mask, c. 1840–60
wood, pigment, hair, hide
25.5 × 23.0 × 16.0 cm
Promised Gift, Audain Collection

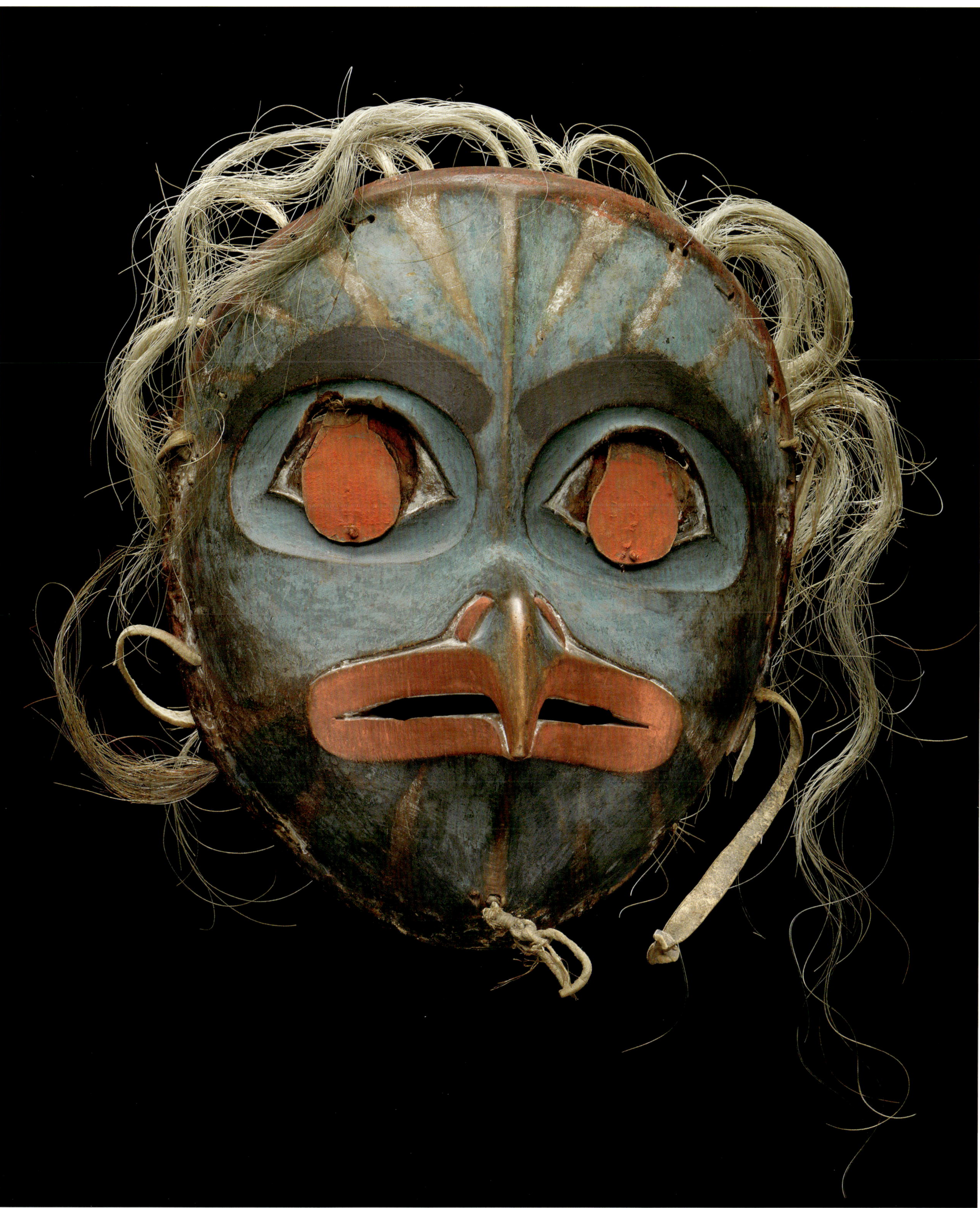

This mask was and is of great spiritual importance. The raised ridges on the forehead, together with the central line and the fine detail of the mouth and beak, are all exceptionally well carved. According to Northwest Coast teacher and scholar Rocque Berthiaume, the movement of the eyes and the unruly hair are "a giveaway that it is a spirit piece ... used by a Tlingit shaman for healing."[4] He adds, "This is a classic example of a mask that they would have worn during a healing ceremony. In the old days the shaman would have had a whole box of these. Different sizes, some would fit in your hand, some you wore. They would have had a number of different pieces. In the old days the shamans made their own pieces. They were healers and also artists. They look a bit roughly made, but they had their own power about them."[5]

Distinguished carver Stan Bevan (b. 1961) has observed that this mask is "a very old piece"[6] and shows clear signs of ceremonial use. Anthropologist Frederica de Laguna reports, "Among the Tlingit, owls were also considered to speak human language—to speak all human languages, in fact. Owls come to tell bad news, usually death or sickness, but also to warn people of impending danger, and people should heed the warnings. Children who cry too much are told they will turn into owls, and there is a story of a girl who mistreated her mother-in-law and, after being shunned thereafter, turned into an owl."[7]

Clearly, the owl performed an important intermediary role between the spirit and human worlds and thus would have been an appropriate mask for a shaman or healer to use. There is, however, something slightly sinister about this orange and blue face, perhaps reflecting the uncertain outcome of any intervention by a shamanic healer. What is undeniable is that this mask has a face that one does not soon forget. ■

Tlingit Artist
Chilkat Blanket (Robe) [Diving Whale Design] c. 1870s

PROVENANCE: *Douglas Reynolds Gallery, Vancouver; Audain Collection, purchased 2007*

Chilkat robes, sometimes called blankets, are one of the most important statements of position and power among First Nations peoples of the Pacific Northwest Coast. The origins of this weaving form, which is associated with the Chilkat Tlingit, are uncertain. Ethnographer George T. Emmons reports,

> According to Tlingit tradition, the art of this type of weaving originated among the Tsimshian ... and was carried to the Chilkat [Tlingit] through marriage or migration from that tribe in early days ... The Chilkats claim, as told to me by Chief Chartrich ... that they owe the knowledge of this blanket to an old woman who, having obtained a blanket from the Tsimshian, took it to pieces and studied out the system of workmanship. The blanket is known to the Tlingit as *nar-kheen* ..., a word said to be of Tsimshian origin.[1]

What is certain is that the finest examples of these remarkable robes are among the highest and most iconic expressions of First Nations material culture to survive. Woven of mountain-goat wool and cedar bark, the Chilkat robe or blanket was the product of months of meticulous work by the weaver, who, traditionally, was always a woman. Before beginning work on the blanket itself, she would have gathered the wool, cleaned it, spun it and dyed it. The designs were usually based on paintings, which were done on cedar boards known as "pattern boards." These boards usually show only half the design, as the design would be reversed to complete the other half of the weaving.[2] The original cataloguing note, probably written by Emmons himself, for a Chilkat robe or blanket in the American Museum of Natural History (artifact E/627) provides a fascinating glimpse into how these magnificent and labour-intensive weavings were made:

> Ceremonial dance blanket (generally known as a Chilkat blanket) "Nar-kheen" [new spelling is Naxine]. The oldest blanket of this type among the Chilkat people and said to have been one of the first ever made. It has been handed down through generations and latterly belonged to "Chartrich," the chief of the Ka-gwan-tan family of the "Chilkat-gwan." The design represents the blackfish. These blankets were greatly prized in the past and were worn on dance and ceremonial occasions over the shoulders as a shawl and tied in the front. They were the work of the women, and in the manufacture no machinery or tools were used. The skin of the Mountain Goat was wet and rolled up in a bundle, hair side in, until the long outer hair and wool was loosened, then it was taken across lap and the fleece was removed by pushing it from the worker with the right hand. When it had been removed, the long hair is picked out and is spun against the hip or leg with the right hand. The strands of wool are rolled up in balls as it is spun. The strands are colored by steeping or boiling in water with colors. The black comes from swamp mud and urine water. The blue from a native stone "Na-hin-ta" and oxide of copper, and the yellow from the long hanging wood moss.
>
> A framework of two upright stakes and a crosspiece is set up, and the warp, consisting of wool enclosing a core of root or bark to give it substance, is secured through loops of spruce root running through holes the length of the crosspiece. The working of the design is done as medallions and the colors are let in where required.
>
> Wooden pattern boards with the design of the whole or half, painted or carved and painted, are placed over the framework and carefully followed. Bags and a curtain of intestine of seal and bear are used to protect and keep clean during working, which took one woman upwards of six months. Certain families only understood the making of these blankets. The designs have become conventional but generally represent some animal or fish or bird, the totem of the owner.[3]

The designs for these works are always highly abstracted, often including, as this blanket does, stylized human faces and references to birds and blackfish or killer whales: the figures on the left and right edges of this robe can likely be read as eagles, and the flukes and fins of a whale form the four corners of the central section. The generalized nature of the design also perhaps reflects the fact that these blankets would have been objects both commissioned by and traded between First Nations along the coast. The crest animals, therefore, would have been those important to all First Nations peoples.

The distinguished Tsimshian weaver Tsymiyaanbiin (Willie White, b. 1960) has said that these robes, which derive their name from the Tsimshian word *haiiet* ("the spirit wrapped around you"), have something of the supernatural in them.[4] Certainly, any great chief who was privileged to wear one of these robes would have felt deeply connected to both the natural and spiritual worlds. These great robes were important heirlooms for the Tlingit people and link the wearer to the ancestral past. ■

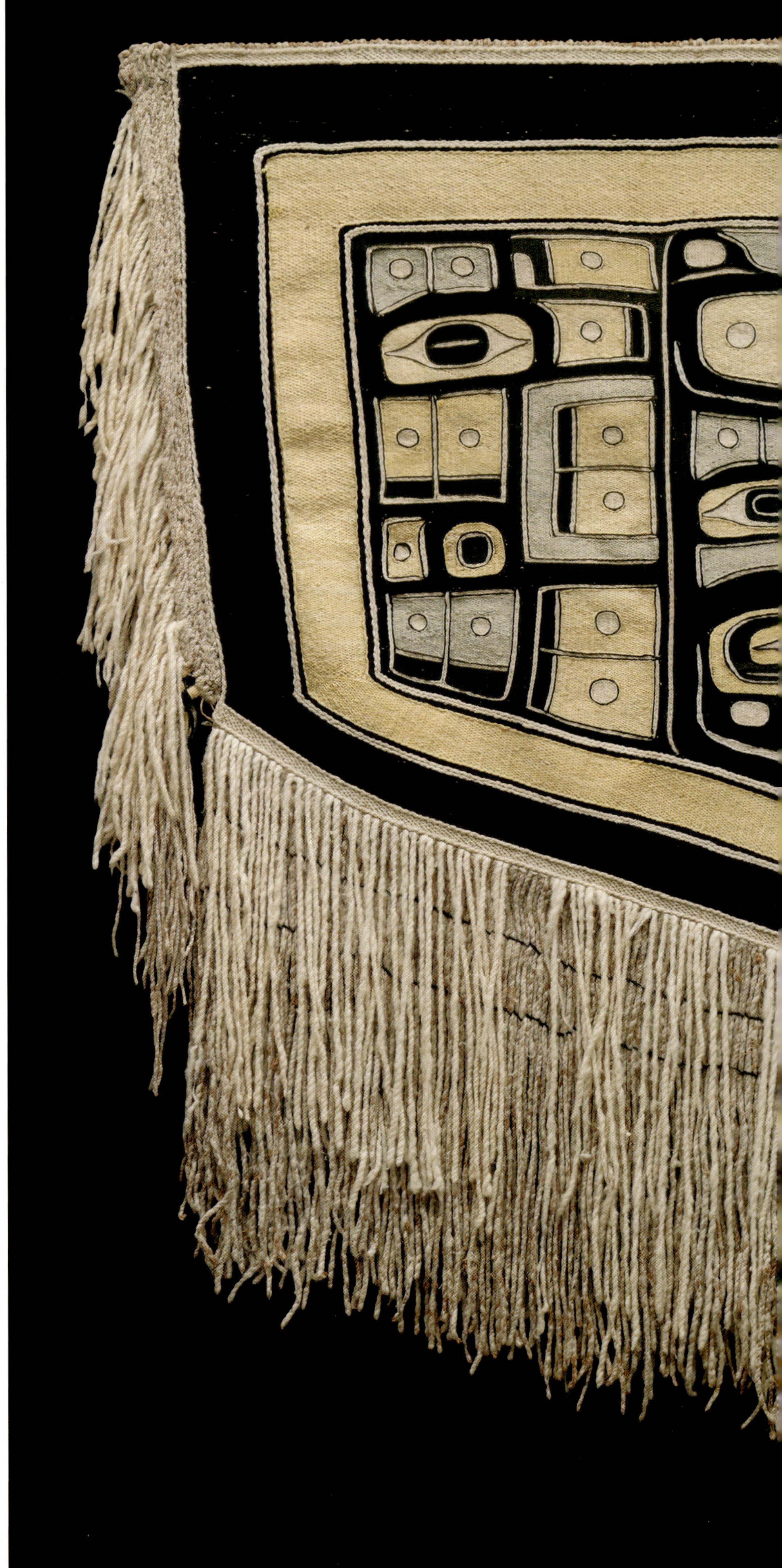

▸ Tlingit Artist
Chilkat Blanket (Robe)
[Diving Whale Design], c. 1870s
mountain-goat wool, cedar bark
127.0 × 189.0 cm
Promised Gift, Audain Collection

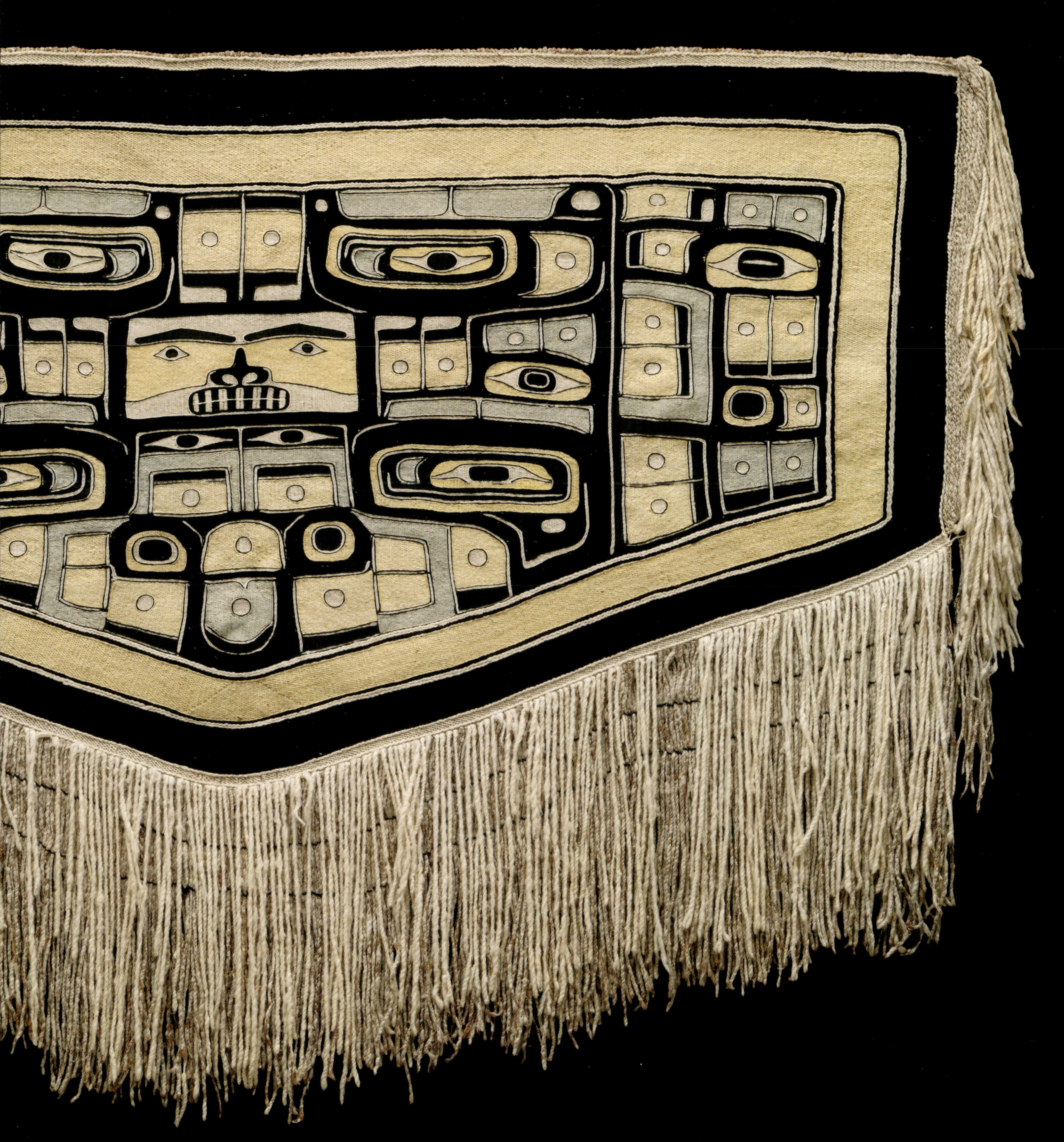

Tlingit Artist
Headdress Frontlet
c. 1840

This impressive headdress was made for an important figure within the Tlingit nation. The wearer of this headdress would have been a significant and wealthy chief. A chief's dance headdress is made up of a number of elements, the most important of which is the carved frontlet that is fastened to a support made of other materials. Often the frontlet has been separated from the rest of the headdress, and to find a headdress as complete as this example is very rare.[1]

The headdress consists of a carved, painted and abalone-inlaid frontlet fastened to a support structure made of baleen strips and covered in cloth. Attached to this support structure are thirteen ermine pelts,[2] and crowning the whole is a thicket of sea lion whiskers. The frontlet figure is that of a beaver hunched on its hindquarters and holding its forearms up. The beaver's tail, which is defined by inlaid abalone, gives visual animation to the central part of the figure.

As Northwest Coast art scholar Steven C. Brown has written, the use of baleen, rather than wood strips, for the support structure, the grooving of the border of the frontlet and the relatively modest usage of abalone support an early dating.[3] Abalone was an important trade item and, as trade and contacts increased between First Nations and Euro-Canadians, it became more readily available later in the century. The abalone here is confined to the beaver itself, with particular emphasis on the eyes, ears and tail. The finely carved details of the beaver are offset by the relative simplicity of the grooved areas. Brown suggests that the earlier style of surface grooving appears to come from an ancient finishing technique once applied to the surfaces of bent-corner boxes, bent-corner bowls and other objects.[4]

"The carver of this frontlet has captured the beaver image in a confident and accomplished style, one that features bold sculptural form with subtle definition and excellent, smooth finish," wrote Brown.[5] Contemporary carver Dempsey Bob (b. 1948) agrees, recently observing,

> Some of the best Northwest Coast carving is in these frontlets. They would commission the best carvers to do these pieces. These pieces are not very thick, but they were so good at sculpture they made it with strong carving. That is what sculpture is: When you look at this face, he brings that face right out. And that's the hard part to do in sculpture. What makes it is the beautiful lines, the socket lines, the eye socket, the mouth; it's all in balance, it's proper. Look at the nice eyebrow; everything is strong and the person that did this—he was a master.[6]

This headdress was designed and constructed to be seen in motion. The chiefly dancer would place eagle down in the top of the headdress, behind the sea lion whiskers, and as the dancer moved, down would float out from the headdress. This, together with the movements of the train of ermine pelts and the robe the dancer was wearing,[7] would have created a splendid spectacle and been seen as an assertion of the wearer's importance and power. ■

PROVENANCE: *Hyde Collection, London, 1934; James Hooper Collection, London; Christie's, London (lot 201, November 9, 1976); Alexander Gallery, New York; Epic Fine Arts/The Masco Collection, Detroit; The Splendid Heritage Collection, John and Marva Warnock, Palo Alto; Donald Ellis Gallery, New York and Vancouver; Audain Art Museum Collection, 2014.017*

▸ Tlingit Artist
Headdress Frontlet, c. 1840
maple, pigment, felt, sea lion whiskers, hide, abalone, baleen, ermine
70.0 × 23.0 × 24.5 cm
Audain Art Museum Collection, 2014.017

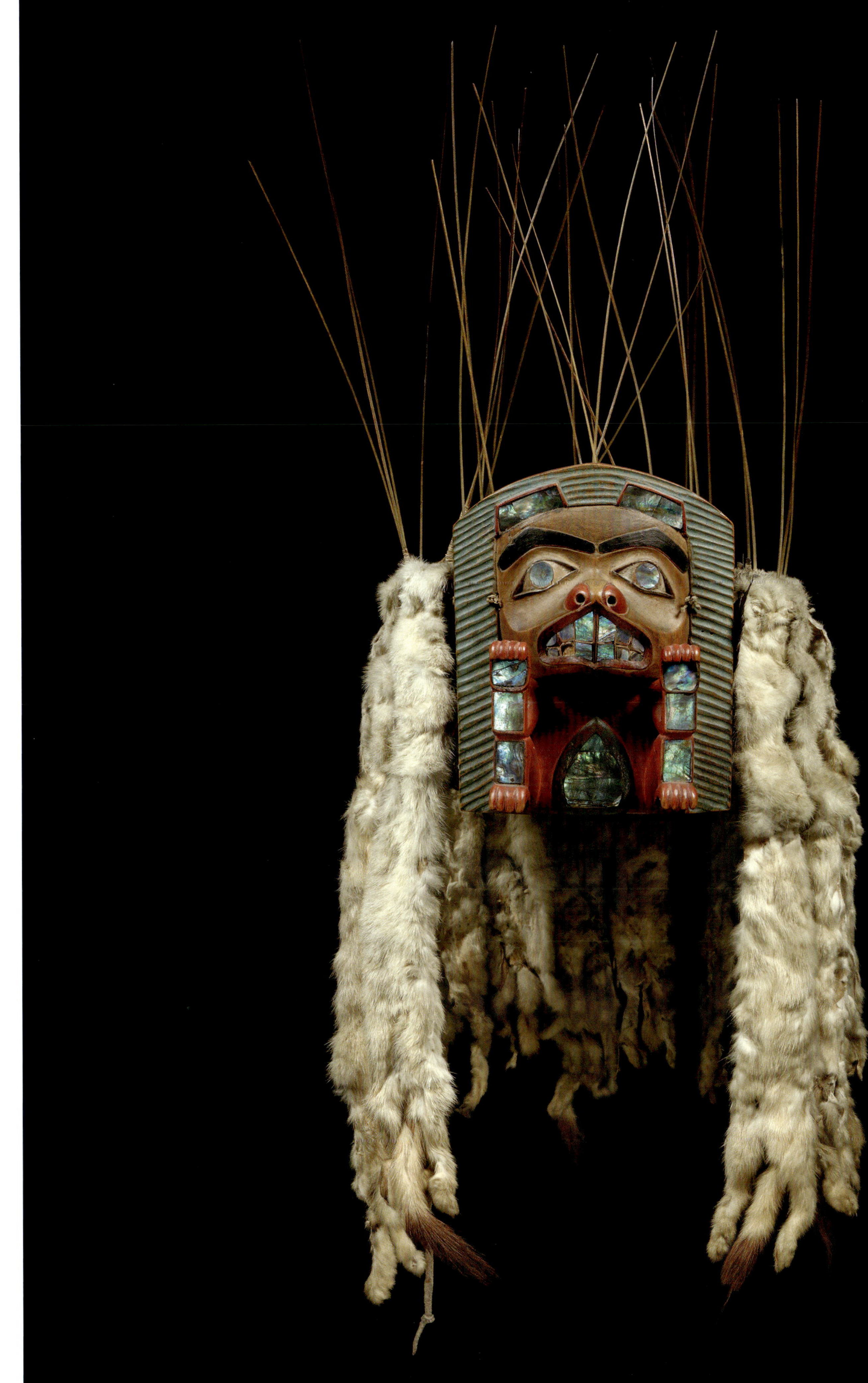

Emily Carr
House with Slanted Roof ~ Brittany
1911

Regarded by many as British Columbia's greatest painter, Emily Carr was born in Victoria in 1871. Like many other Victorian girls, she took painting classes during her childhood, but Carr quickly realized that art would be her métier. Her first formal training began 1890 in San Francisco, at the California School of Design (now the San Francisco Art Institute). Carr returned to British Columbia, in 1893, a competent but not highly skilled artist. A further period of study occurred in England between 1899 and 1904, but Carr was only moderately more accomplished as a painter upon her return to Canada and the period was marred by a lengthy stay in a sanatorium to recover her health. A trip to Alaska in the summer of 1907 exposed Carr to large-scale totemic works by First Nations peoples and changed her choice of subject matter. After two more summers of depicting poles, notably in Alert Bay, Carr decided that she needed further training and that she would go to France, which was then the mecca for many young artists. Carr eventually left Canada in the summer of 1910, arriving in Paris in September. There her approach to painting changed radically.

Emily Carr's brief period of study in France was, in fact, concentrated in the year 1911. After some unsatisfactory classes in Paris and a period of rest in Sweden, she began working with a series of expatriate teachers: the Britons John Duncan Fergusson (1874–1961) and Harry Phelan Gibb (1870–1948) and later the New Zealander Frances Hodgkins (1869–1947). She studied with Gibb in Crécy-en-Brie and, later, in Saint-Efflam in Brittany. With Gibb's guidance, Carr developed a vocabulary of brighter, post-Impressionist colours and a more immediate approach to landscape.

Gibb's students worked outdoors by themselves, occasionally being visited by the master, and then showed the results of their efforts in the evenings. Although Gibb was not an artist of the first rank, he was able to encourage Carr to expand her use of colour and bring a new freshness to her images. While in France, Carr painted villages and scenes from the lives of rural inhabitants. She worked in the landscape and villages and occasionally in the houses of the local people. She was particularly drawn to the architecture of these small French hamlets, and many cottages appear in her paintings from 1911.

House with Slanted Roof ~ Brittany is an unusually large work from this period. It is painted on paperboard, a stiff material that allowed Carr to work directly in front of her subject. While she had worked this way in England, here she does it with a new conviction. *Plein-air* ("outdoor") painting had a long tradition in France, but it had exploded in the nineteenth century—initially with the Barbizon School and most notably with the Impressionists—when paint became available in metal tubes and railway travel allowed people to reach farther afield. Although Carr was receiving Impressionist and post-Impressionist lessons secondhand, as it were, away from the adventurous work of the Fauvists in Paris, she was able to grasp light and colour in a new

PROVENANCE: *Estate of Emily Carr; Dominion Gallery, Montreal; private collection, Ontario; by descent in the family; Heffel Fine Art Auction House, Vancouver (lot 49, November 27, 2003); Audain Collection*

▸ **Emily Carr** (1871–1945)
House with Slanted Roof ~ Brittany**,** 1911
oil on board
85.0 × 70.0 cm
Promised Gift, Audain Collection

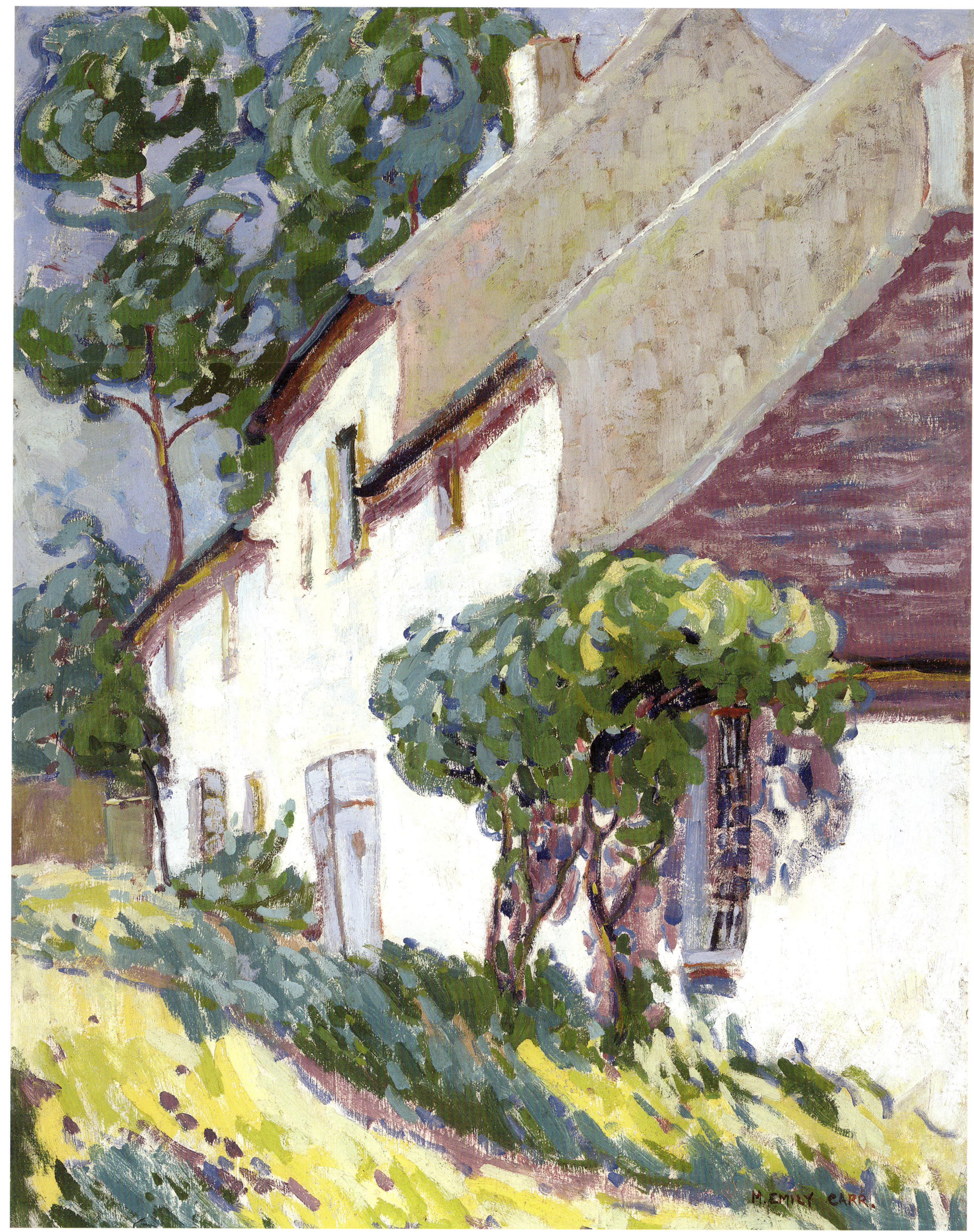
M. EMILY CARR.

way. There is a sense of movement and life in this image, conveyed by her use of colour and by her freer, more expressive handling of the paint. Both the house and nature are flooded with light.

This new confidence would deeply inform Carr's work back in Canada. And when Carr exhibited the results of her studies in France at an exhibition in her Vancouver studio in March and April of 1912, a new chapter was opened in the painting history of the province—modernism had arrived. ■

Emily Carr
War Canoes, Alert Bay
1912

Emily Carr began a long-lasting interest in First Nations subject matter in the 1890s when she first depicted canoes in the local harbour. We don't know when she first saw totem poles, but it was likely during her visit to the Kwakwa̲ka̲'wakw village of 'Ya̲lis (Alert Bay) on Cormorant Island in 1907, on the way to Alaska. The village, which at that time had a number of striking house fronts and poles, was of great interest to her, and she returned to paint in both 1908 and 1909, producing watercolours of the village and at least three watercolours of canoes. Two of these served as the basis for her 1912 canvas *War Canoes, Alert Bay*. The 1908 watercolours, which have the same title as the canvas, closely resemble the larger work.

The major differences between the watercolours and the final canvas are the addition of a group of figures immediately behind the canoes and, more importantly, the intensification of the colour. The canvas reflects her French painting experience, even though this canvas was produced in the studio. As with *House with Slanted Roof ~ Brittany* (page 54), Carr uses colour in an expressive rather than a literally descriptive manner. In this canvas (and in another superb work, *Indian War Canoe [Alert Bay]*, from 1912, which is in the collection of the Montreal Museum of Fine Arts), we see vivid colour—oranges, yellows, purples, blues and greens. The colour contrasts are heightened, and there is electricity in this image that is lacking in the watercolour studies.

What do we see? A group of three beached canoes, two of which have painted decoration—Raven and Thunderbird—on their bows. The sides of the canoes, which we know are made of wood, are purple, and these elegant vessels sit on a patch of green and purple grass or shadow. In the middle ground is a group of loosely painted figures under a great evergreen—which is, naturally, green but also red, blue, yellow and purple. In the background is the village itself, at the foot of a dramatic hillside. Carr has deliberately avoided depicting any of the totems in the village because these would distract from the importance of the canoes.

Carr had collected a couple of model canoes on her trips to First Nations villages, and clearly she had a keen appreciation for the form and beauty of these vessels, which were still fairly common in First Nations villages in the early years of the twentieth century. What is remarkable about Carr's work during this period is her decision to devote her energies to depicting the totems, canoes and villages of the First Nations peoples of British Columbia,

PROVENANCE: *Artist; Martha Douglas Harris, Victoria, 1912; by descent in the family; private collection, Vancouver; Heffel Fine Art Auction House, Vancouver (lot 137, May 10, 2000); Audain Collection*

▸ **Emily Carr** (1871–1945)
War Canoes, Alert Bay, 1912
oil on canvas
84.0 x 101.5 cm
Promised Gift, Audain Collection

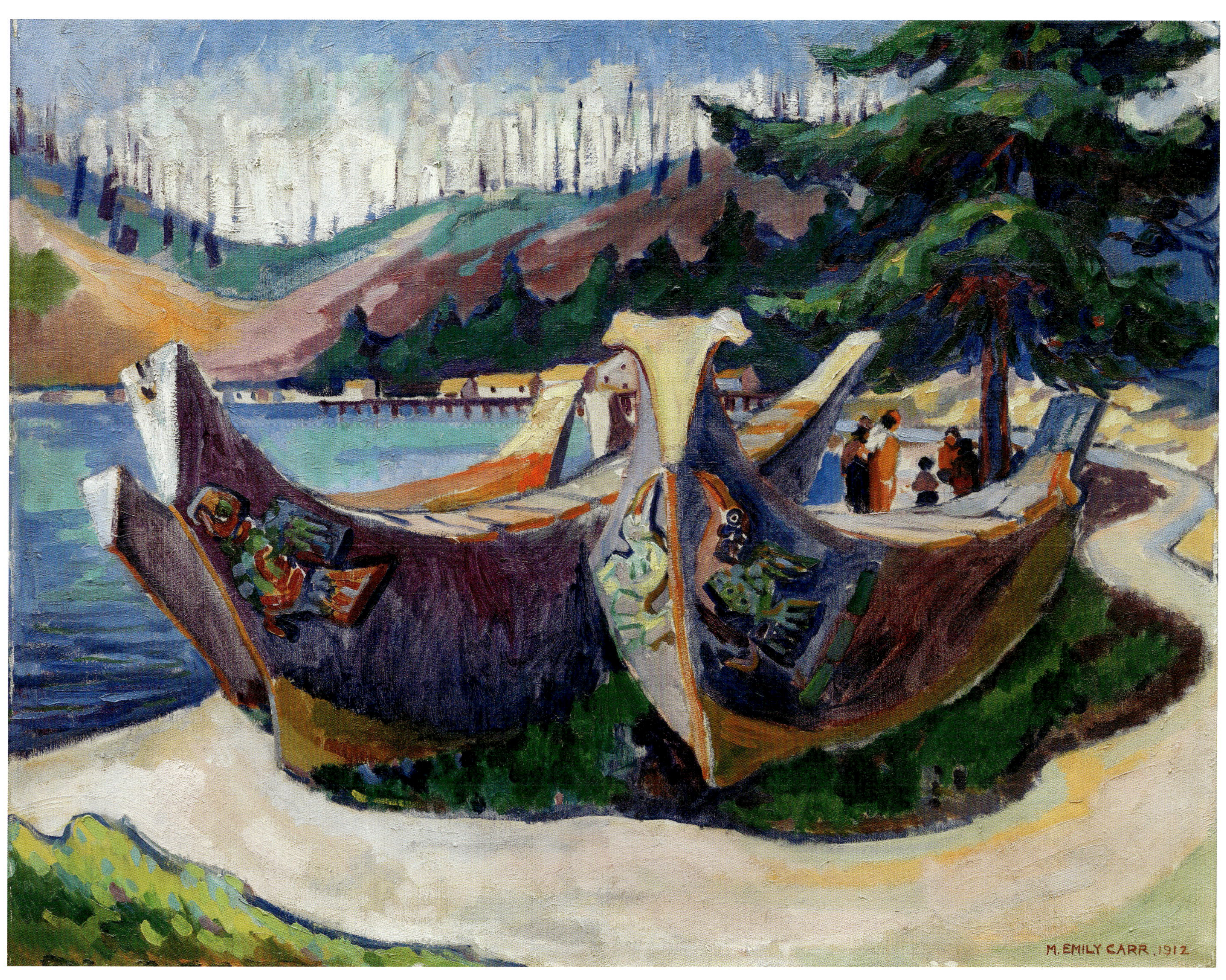
M. EMILY CARR. 1912

which was completely without parallel. These paintings were radical both in how they were painted and in what they depicted.

Carr exhibited over two hundred of her First Nations paintings in Vancouver in the spring of 1913. That exhibition remains without equal as an examination of the visual culture of First Nations people of this province by an artist who was not First Nations. Carr's work, even with what we now know to be many misunderstandings of First Nations culture, was far ahead of its time—so far ahead, in fact, that the exhibition was a failure in Carr's mind because she was not able to sell a large body of these works to the provincial government as a lasting document of the cultural artifacts she feared would soon be gone.

Few people appreciated her "modern" approach to painting, and fewer still her choice of subject matter. *War Canoes, Alert Bay* is one of only a tiny number of works that she sold at the time. Martha Douglas Harris, the first owner of this painting, made a daring purchase when she chose this work for her collection in 1912. The art world would not embrace works like this until fifteen years later, when Carr was a major contributor to the *Exhibition of Canadian West Coast Art: Native and Modern,* which was held in Ottawa in 1927. In that context, where the 1912 canvases were seen with both other Canadian paintings and a large collection of First Nations objects, Carr's work was acknowledged as exceptional and she was welcomed into the larger community of Canadian art. ■

Emily Carr
Memkish
1912

Emily Carr returned from her painting studies in France in the fall of 1911 and exhibited most of the French works in her studio in Vancouver in the spring of 1912. She had begun painting First Nations subjects in the 1890s, in the Victoria area and later in Ucluelet, but first turned to totemic subjects during a 1907 visit to Alaska. Her interest in totems developed further in Alert Bay in 1908 and 1909. And in the summer of 1912 she went north again. Her French training was now brought to bear on First Nations subjects, and Carr began her totemic project in earnest.

The lessons that Carr had learned while working with watercolourist Frances Hodgkins (1869–1947) are clearly evident in this important work. While skilled, Carr's watercolours prior to her studies in France lacked rhythmic power and élan. Hodgkins encouraged Carr to use watercolour more boldly and colour more emphatically, and Carr brought this new directness of approach to her work in the summer of 1912, when she visited a number of Haida, Kwakwa̲ka̲'wakw and Gitxsan villages. The Kwakwa̲ka̲'wakw village of Kalugwis on Turnour Island in Johnstone Strait provided Carr with the opportunity to depict a First Nations house and pole within a landscape setting. For Carr, the most important element of the composition was the pole itself, and she has delineated it carefully. Much of the remainder of the composition—the foliage, the house front and even the sky—has been fairly loosely painted, a legacy of her French training. Yet a couple of vivid touches serve to animate the whole surface of the work: the flashes of red in the

PROVENANCE: *Estate of Emily Carr; Dominion Gallery, Montreal; John Stewart Donald Tory, Toronto; by descent to a private collection, Ontario; Heffel Fine Art Auction House, Vancouver (lot 163, November 25, 2004); Audain Collection; Gift of Michael Audain and Yoshiko Karasawa; Audain Art Museum Collection, 2015.005*

▸ **Emily Carr** (1871–1945)
Memkish, 1912
watercolour on paper
88.0 × 74.0 cm
Gift of Michael Audain and Yoshiko Karasawa; Audain Art Museum Collection, 2015.005

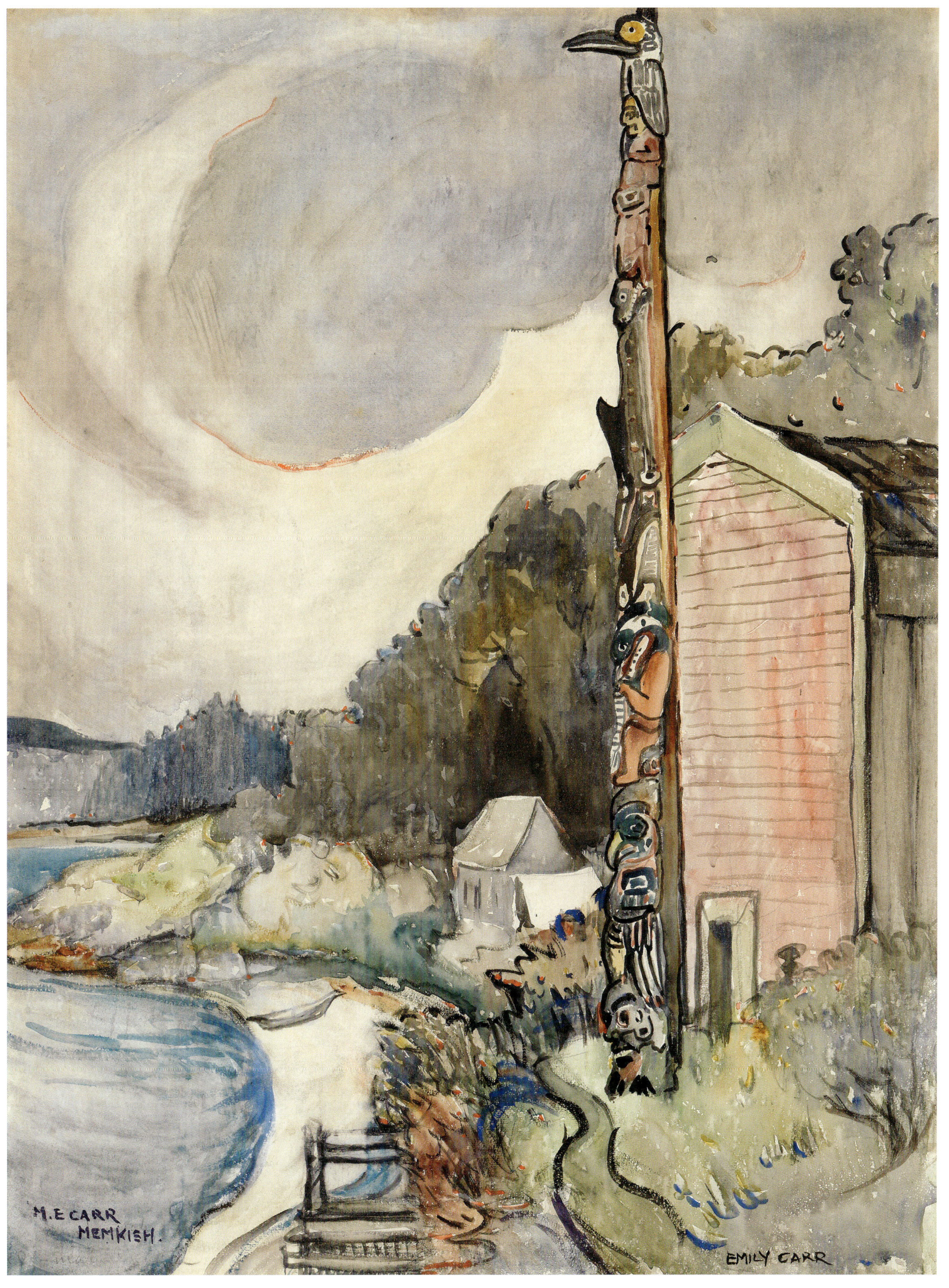
M.E CARR
MEMKISH.
EMILY CARR

sky and the blue within the foreground foliage. These suggest Carr's comfort with stronger, more expressive colour.

The composition is developed with two entry points: the path at the lower right and the beach itself, both of which lead the eye into the composition. Interestingly, Carr has placed the major subject matter, the pole, away from the centre of the pictorial field. This pole had only recently been carved and erected by the great Kwakwaka'wakw carver Charlie James (1870–1938), and its relative newness meant that the paint had not yet been worn away by the sun and rain. A 1913 photograph of the same location by the physician and collector Charles Newcombe shows that Carr took a few liberties with the scene but conveyed the whole fairly accurately. Although this work is a beautiful and satisfying composition, it was not, ironically, a success in the way that Carr had intended.

In Vancouver in the spring of 1913, when she exhibited works done on her northern trip, she delivered a talk entitled "Lecture on Totems," in which she said, "My object in making this collection of totem pole pictures has been to depict these wonderful relics of a passing people in their own original setting: the identical spots where they were carved and placed by the Indians in honour of their chiefs. These poles are fast becoming extinct. Each year sees some of their number fall, rotted with age; others bought and carried off to museums in various parts of the world; others, alas, burned down for firewood."[1] Clearly, for Carr, it was important that these works document a culture that she felt would soon pass away. At the end of the lecture she concluded, "I glory in our wonderful West and I [would] like to leave behind me some of the relics of its first primitive greatness. These things should be to us Canadians what the ancient Britons' relics are to the English. Only a few more years and they will be gone forever into silent nothingness, and I would gather my collection together before they are forever past."[2]

Although the record exists in the works Carr produced, to her chagrin these works were not purchased for the people of the province because they were felt to be not sufficiently accurate in their documentation. In other words, Carr was too much of an artist. Her French training had changed her artistic vision to one that was not compatible with early-twentieth-century ideas of documentation. ■

Emily Carr
Eagle Totem
c. 1930

Emily Carr's participation in the *Exhibition of Canadian West Coast Art: Native and Modern* in Ottawa in 1927 was a turning point in her career. She was embraced by the art community, and on her journey to Ottawa met several members of the Group of Seven: Fred Varley (1881–1969) in Vancouver, and J.E.H. MacDonald (1873–1932), Arthur Lismer (1885–1969), A.Y. Jackson (1882–1974) and, most importantly, Lawren Harris (1885–1970) in Toronto. Encouraged by the praise these artists gave her work, Carr resolved to recommit herself to painting when she returned to British Columbia.

In the summer of 1928, Carr visited First Nations villages on Haida Gwaii and in

PROVENANCE: *Estate of Emily Carr; Dominion Gallery, Montreal; Katherine and Arthur Daly, Montreal; private collection; by descent to a private collection, Vancouver; Heffel Fine Art Auction House, Vancouver (lot 45, November 8, 2001); private collection, USA; Heffel Fine Art Auction House, Vancouver (lot 130, May 17, 2012); Audain Collection*

▶ Emily Carr (1871–1945)
Eagle Totem, c. 1930
oil on canvas
79.5 × 65.0 cm
Promised Gift, Audain Collection

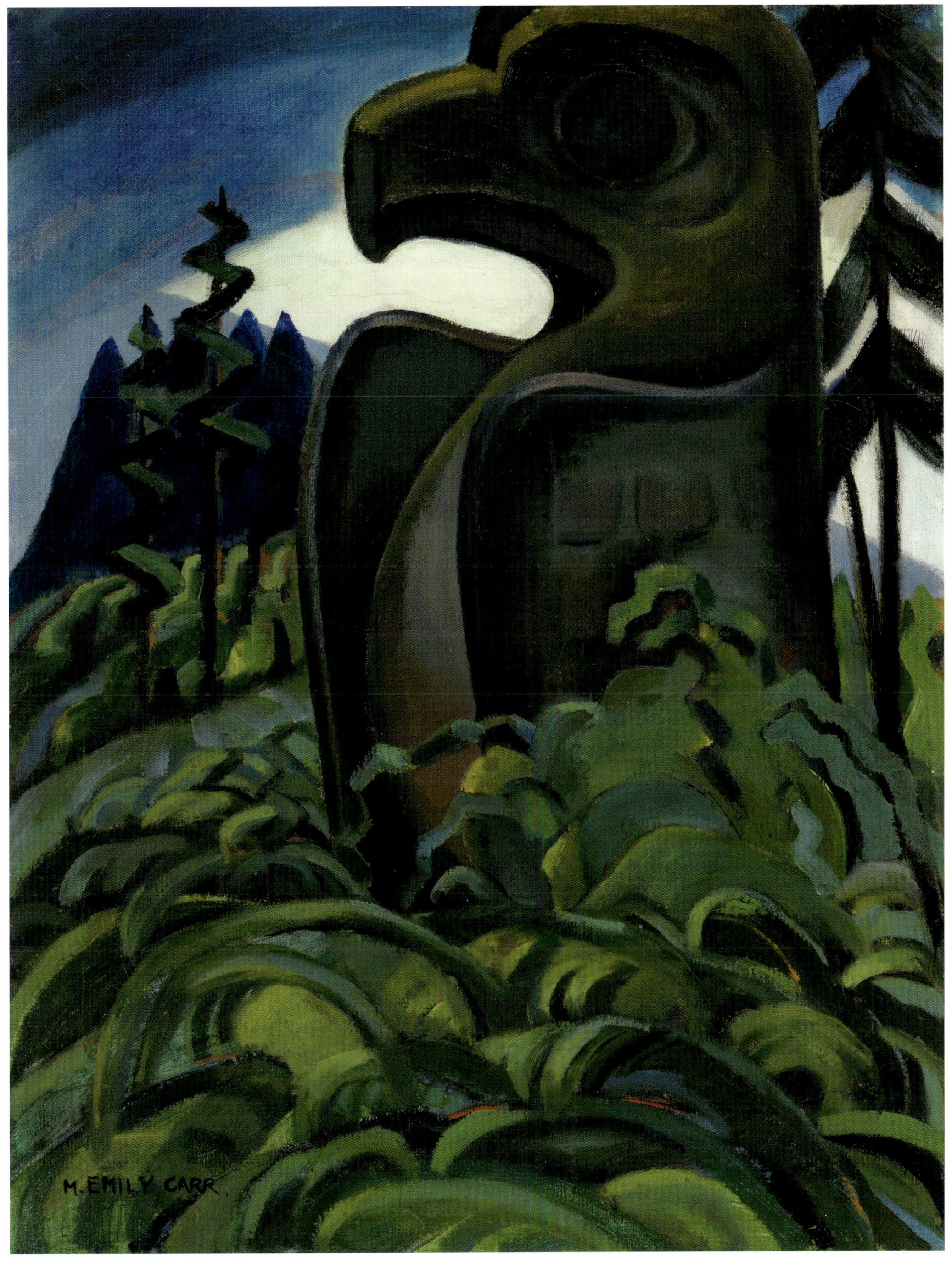
M. EMILY CARR

Kwakwaka'wakw, Nisga'a and Gitxsan territories. In September of that year, she and fellow Victoria modernist Ina D.D. Uhthoff (1889–1971) invited the young American painter Mark Tobey (1890–1976) to Victoria to conduct a master class in painting. The grandeur of Harris's landscapes and Tobey's experiments with Cubist form helped to shape the work she produced in the next few years. She simplified the form of the poles while emphasizing their volume, and she began to give greater attention to their place within the landscape—whether manufactured or natural. Documenting the poles was no longer her primary goal; now she sought a fidelity to the spirit of the pole and the place in which it stood. The deep connection she felt to both the First Nations poles and the natural world can be clearly seen in these later totemic works. These poles, while distinct from the forest, clearly are from the forest and reflect Carr's sense of the connectedness of carved totem and living tree.

Eagle Totem is a powerful example of Carr's mature style. It draws on her study of the totemic figures from journeys in both 1912 and 1928 and shows an increasing attention to the forest landscape. The strong form of the bird is convincing. It has both volume and weight. Solid, immovable, it bridges the vibrating forms of nature in the foreground and the dramatic light of the sky. The close cropping of the image gives the eagle pole both a grand sense of scale and a riveting visual energy. There is a deep conviction in this work that is quite different from and more mature than the confidence of her 1912 paintings.

Carr takes considerable liberties with the natural world. Compare, for example, the trees to the left and right of the totem. These are not trees that could exist in the world, but these shorthand depictions convey what Carr needs them to convey. They read as tangible, if slight, and provide a stark contrast to the weighty presence of the pole. She has expertly balanced the need for a natural setting for the pole with the requirement for realism. The sea of brush that surrounds the pole is just convincing enough to read as flora but never distracts from the main subject—the eagle pole.

The light in the sky, slightly reminiscent of Lawren Harris, is revelatory, allowing Carr to proudly silhouette both the totem and the taller trees. Although the painting is not large in physical scale, it has a very large visual and psychological presence. As a viewer, one can sense and share Carr's wonder at seeing this pole so dramatically set within the landscape. It is an image that stays in the mind and spirit. ■

Emily Carr
The Crazy Stair (The Crooked Staircase)
c. 1928–30

PROVENANCE: *Artist; W.H. and Irene Clarke, Toronto; H.R. MacMillan, Vancouver; donated by H.R. MacMillan to the Vancouver Club; Heffel Fine Art Auction House, Vancouver (lot 130, November 28, 2013); Audain Art Museum Collection, 2013.014*

Emily Carr had accumulated a large body of field sketches (watercolours, drawings and a small group of oils on paperboard panels) from her northern trips in 1908, 1909 and, most importantly, 1912. Many of these depicted First Nations cultures, and several paintings based on these sketches, including *War Canoes, Alert Bay* (page 56), had been well received at the *Exhibition of Canadian West Coast Art: Native and Modern* organized by the ethnologist Marius Barbeau in Ottawa in 1927. That success seems to have prompted Carr to return to this early material before she visited a number of Gitxsan, Nisga'a and Kwakwaka'wakw communities and returned to several sites on Haida Gwaii in 1928.

In her 1908–9 and 1912 trips, Carr had visited Kwakwaka'wakw villages in Knight Inlet—Mimquimlees, Tsatsisnukomi, Karlukwees and Gwayasdums—which provided a wealth of imagery that appears in both finished works and field sketches. These include the watercolours *Communal House (Mimquimlees)*, c. 1908–9, which is held by the Royal British Columbia Museum and Archives, and *Untitled*, c. 1908–9, which is now in a private collection, both of which are closely related to *The Crazy Stair.*[1] *Communal House* depicts the whole of the scene as shown in *The Crazy Stair*, and *Untitled* concentrates on the main welcome figure, which is central to this canvas. Carr was obviously forcefully struck by the power of this figure, for it appears in several works, including a 1912 oil painting titled *Indian Community House*, which is owned by the Hirshhorn Museum and Sculpture Garden, Smithsonian Institution, but its most important appearance is in *The Crazy Stair*. This painting takes its place among major works of the period such as *Big Raven* (Vancouver Art Gallery), *Heina* (National Gallery of Canada) and *Guyasdoms D'Sonoqua* (Art Gallery of Ontario).

The composition consists of a foreshore with a large canoe looming in from the left side; a steep hill with a "crazy stair," which provides the work with the title; and, in the middle ground, a large welcome figure. This figure provides a strong vertical link, slightly to the left of centre, within the image. Carr has heightened the welcome figure and made it considerably more dramatic by lightening the sky behind its head to give it an aureole. The whole image seems to be moving because of the great sweep of foliage in the middle ground from which the welcome figure emerges. Nature and the First Nations figure and house seem to exist in a state of balance, both physical and psychological. The frightening power of the figure is mediated by the embrace and vivacity of the natural world.

A comparison between the watercolours associated with this canvas and the final work reveals that Carr was willing to adjust physical relationships to create a more potent image. She introduces the simple but powerful shape of the canoe, which does not appear in the watercolours. The canoe complements the shape of the welcome figure and provides an opportunity to use colours (red and deep blue) that contrast with the rich greens of the foliage. A comparison between the first watercolour *(Communal House)* and the canvas also shows a shifting of the scale relationships between the house in the background, topped by the large raven, and the welcome figure. In the earlier work, the welcome figure is significantly smaller than the house, and the orientation or direction of the figure has also shifted in the canvas. More importantly, Carr has lowered our viewpoint and elevated the building in the background. This allows the raven on the peak of the house to be silhouetted against a turbulent sky while enhancing the drama of the welcome figure. The image as a whole is a dramatic, if unpeopled, tableau that shows both First Nations totemic figures and the vital forests of British Columbia in a new way.

Carr found a deep spirituality in both First Nations totems and the forest. In works such as *Eagle Totem* (page 60) and *The Crazy Stair,* she manages to combine these two touchstones of her artistic world in a way that is entirely her own. Love these works or hate them, one does not forget the imagery. ■

▸ **Emily Carr** (1871–1945)
The Crazy Stair (The Crooked Staircase), **c. 1928–30**
oil on canvas
110.2 × 65.7 cm
Audain Art Museum Collection, 2013.014

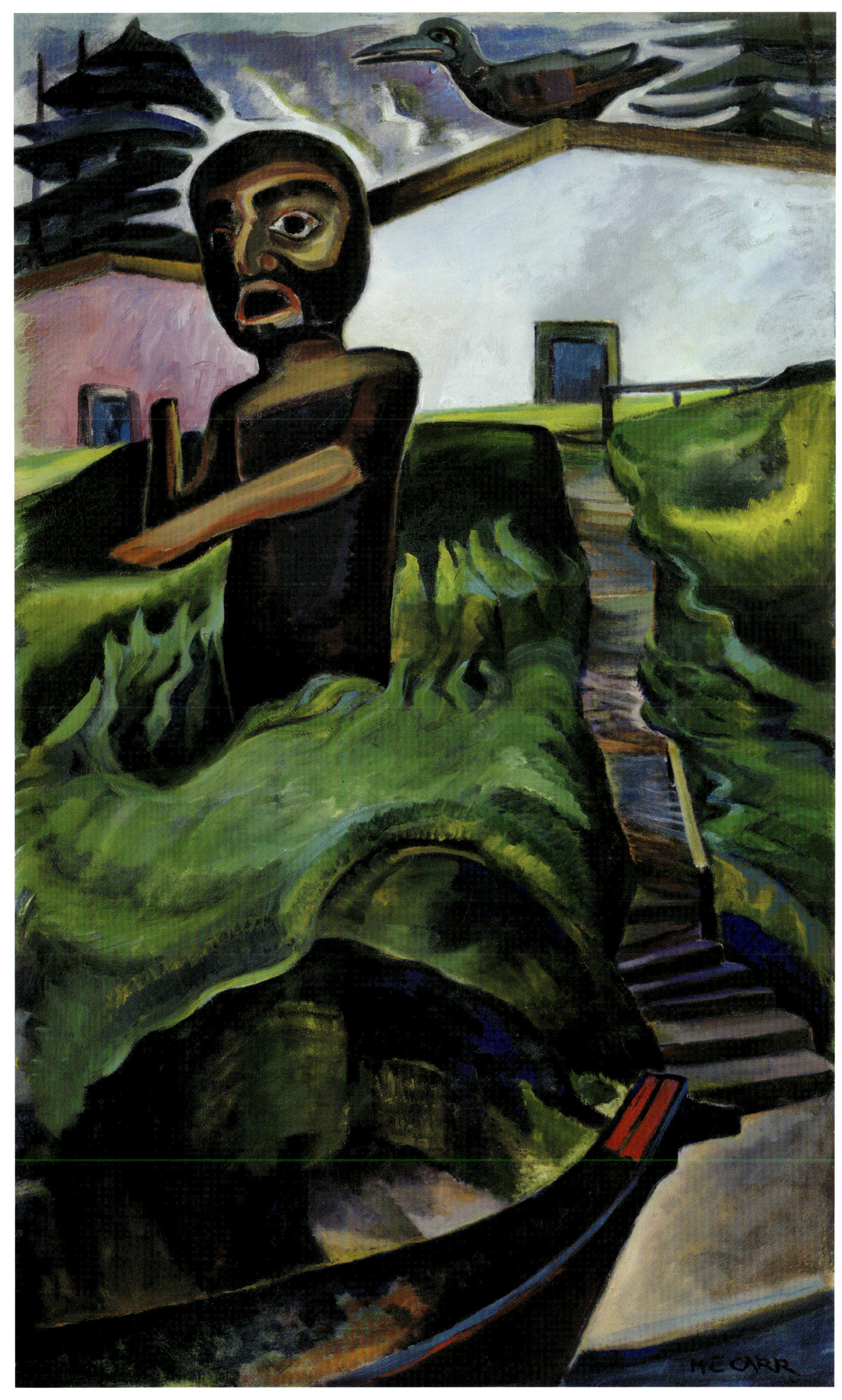
M E CARR

Emily Carr
Quiet
1942

The latter years of Emily Carr's life were marked by a return to the subject matter that had interested her all of her life, the forests of British Columbia. Despite illness and advancing age, Carr produced some of her most radiant oil-on-paper sketches during the last few years of her life. The canvases, in contrast, tend to be summations of ideas that had been present in earlier works. The best of these later works have an almost magisterial quality; carefully considered, they make powerful visual and formal statements. During this period, Carr appeared in group shows as well as a series of solo exhibitions, beginning in Vancouver. There are at least three dated canvases from 1942: *Clearing* (National Gallery of Canada), *Cedar* (Vancouver Art Gallery) and *Quiet*.

Almost certainly the "3 big canvases" Carr refers to in a letter of May 10, 1942, to a friend, fellow artist Nan Lawson Cheney (1897–1985), these works, which are likely her final canvases, are all forest scenes. Two of them, *Cedar* and *Quiet,* examine a deeper forest landscape. As curator and scholar Doris Shadbolt has observed, they are both characterized by an "enclosing wall of green forest close against the picture surface, stretching edge to edge, no sky above, no anchoring earth below, no deep space leading us in."[1] The density of the forest vegetation is clearly seen in the shallow layering of space, and the natural life cycle is made apparent by a young tree on the left, dead stumps on the right and the mature trees in the background.

The trees in this image have a presence that we can almost touch and smell, and the foliage seems to have weight and movement. This is the type of forest that some find oppressive, but Carr introduces areas of light and colour suggesting the life and energy of the forest. The variety of greens—bright first growth, darker mature forest and intermediate colours—is remarkable. The sense of what Carr wanted us to get from this image is suggested by the title: the forest is indeed quiet, but it is neither silent nor still. Shadbolt is certainly correct when she suggests that works such as *Quiet* have a "lyrical tranquility."[2] It is a sense of serenity and deep affection for the landscape that is the accomplishment of this canvas. Produced as a summation rather than a specific portrait of a forest, the composition has a formal elegance and richness that betray how deeply Carr knew and loved her subject. The strength of the painting also shows that Carr, despite her ill health, was still able to depict the British Columbia landscape with a profundity that no one else could match. ■

PROVENANCE: *Artist; Ira Dilworth, Vancouver; Charles Carroll Colby Aikins, Naramata, BC; The Honourable Mr. Justice J.S. Aikins and Anne E. Aikins, Vancouver; by descent to a private collection, Vancouver; Heffel Fine Art Auction House (lot 137, May 27, 2004); Audain Collection; Gift of Michael Audain and Yoshiko Karasawa; Audain Art Museum Collection, 2015.006*

▸ **Emily Carr** (1871–1945)
Quiet, 1942
oil on canvas
130.0 × 86.0 cm
Gift of Michael Audain and Yoshiko Karasawa; Audain Art Museum Collection, 2015.006

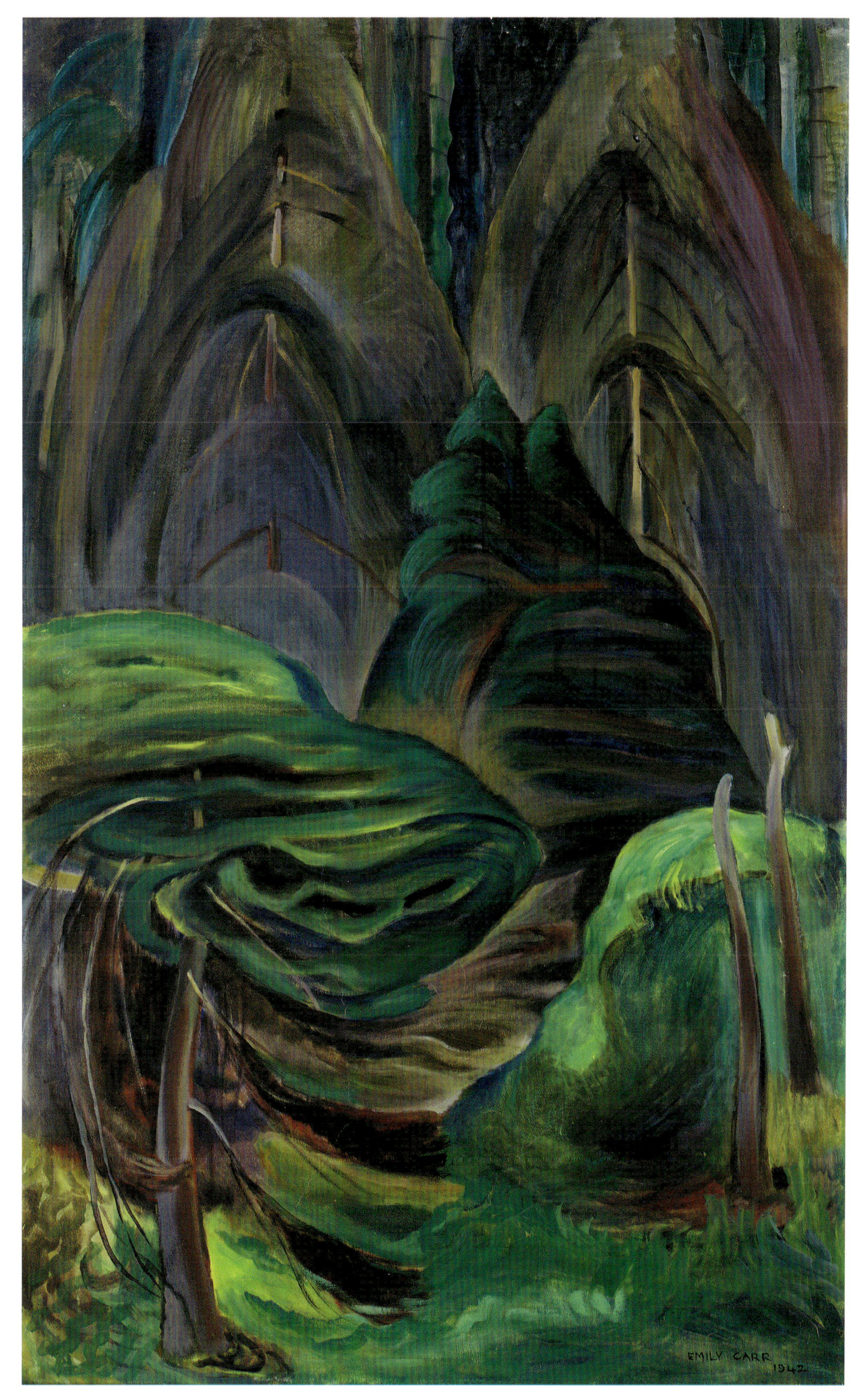
EMILY CARR
1942

Frederick (Fred) Horsman Varley
Dusk—Tantalus Range
c. 1929

Frederick (Fred) Horsman Varley was born in 1881 and trained both in his native Sheffield, England, and in Antwerp, Belgium. After completing his training at Antwerp's Académie Royale des Beaux-Arts in 1902, he returned to England and worked as an illustrator in London. He immigrated to Canada in 1912, settling in Toronto. There he began working at the design firm of Grip Limited, and later at Rous and Mann. These firms were the most important design studios in Toronto, and there Varley met other artists such as Tom Thomson (1877–1917) and J.E.H. MacDonald (1873–1932) and renewed his friendship with Arthur Lismer (1885–1969). By 1914, Varley had joined these artists on sketching trips in Ontario's Algonquin Park. Varley also became involved in art education, working for the Ontario College of Art (now the Ontario College of Art and Design University) in 1916–17. In 1918 he enlisted in the armed forces and served as an Official War Artist, documenting the battle scenes of Canadian troops. After returning to Canada in 1919, Varley joined with six colleagues in early 1920 to form the Group of Seven, and they exhibited their work as a group for the first time in May of that year. He continued to teach, paint and work as an illustrator.

In 1926, Varley accepted a position as an instructor of painting and drawing at the Vancouver School of Decorative and Applied Arts (now Emily Carr University of Art + Design). In British Columbia, Varley was exposed to a completely different landscape than he had known in Ontario, and he responded quickly to his new surroundings. Living in a house on Point Grey Road in Vancouver, Varley regularly saw the magnificent sweep of the mountains rising up from the north shore of Burrard Inlet and the arc of English Bay below. He soon began to explore these mountains. He travelled north of the city to Garibaldi Park and he hiked the North Shore mountains that he saw from Point Grey. He also began to explore these peaks in his work, and his oil-on-panel sketches took on a new vigour and strength that reflected his love of the British Columbia landscape. He wrote to his friend Elizabeth Nutt (1870–1946), who was then teaching in Halifax,

> British Columbia is heaven... It trembles within me and pains me with its wonder as when a child I first awakened to the song of the earth at home. Only the hills are bigger, the torrents are bigger. The sea is here, and the sky is vast; and humans—little bits of mind—would clamber up rocky slopes, creep in and out of mountain passes, fish in the streams, build little hermit cabins in sheltered places, curl up in sleeping bags and sleep under the stars... I often feel that only the Chinese of the 11th and 12th century ever interpreted the spirit of such a country. We have not yet awakened to its nature.[1]

PROVENANCE: *Artist; Milton Blackstone, 1929; by descent to a private collection, Calgary; Heffel Fine Art Auction House, Vancouver (lot 95, May 22, 2008); Audain Collection*

▸ Frederick (Fred) Horsman Varley (1881–1969)
Dusk—Tantalus Range, c. 1929
oil on panel
51.0 × 69.0 cm
Promised Gift, Audain Collection

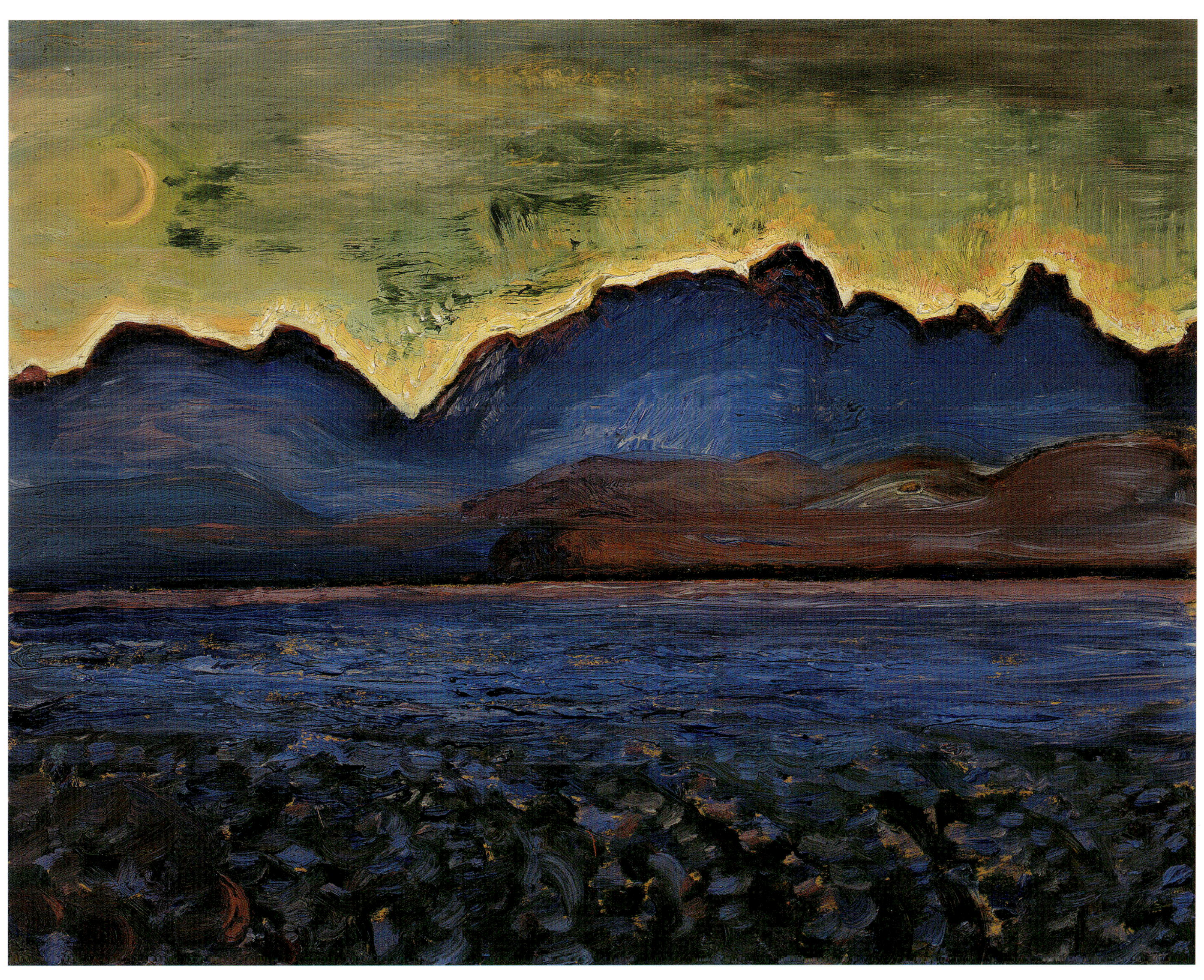

Painter Jock Macdonald (1897–1960), Varley's colleague at the Vancouver School of Decorative and Applied Arts, later characterized this period as follows: "Varley was mainly an outdoor artist during his ten years' residence on the Pacific coast. Almost every week-end he painted in the mountains and in the summers in Garibaldi Park, that unbelievably beautiful virgin country still unknown to tourists, where six-thousand-foot meadows are carpeted with wild flowers, the lakes are pure emerald, the glaciers are fractured with rose-madder, turquoise-blue and indigo crevasses, and the mountains are black, ochre and Egyptian red."[2]

Dusk—Tantalus Range illustrates a subrange of the Coast Mountains that runs northwest from Squamish and that Varley would have encountered on his excursions into the Garibaldi Park area. The resulting sketch is a dramatic depiction of the landscape that uses the brilliant colours Macdonald alludes to and that reflects the sweeping command of space Varley admired in ancient Chinese painting. The eye is not unnecessarily detained by detail in the foreground but is swept back to the brilliant silhouette of the craggy mountain peaks. The contrast between the deep blues and purples of the land and the yellow-orange of the light of the setting sun is intense and powerfully evokes the "song of the earth." The crescent of the moon at the upper left of the composition adds a further element of poetry to the scene.

Although the work is titled *Dusk—Tantalus Range,* which suggests closure and the end of the day, this is, in fact, a landscape of boundless possibilities. Varley has given us enough information to allow our imaginations to visit this scene with him without defining or limiting our reactions to this resplendent vista. ■

Lawren Stewart Harris
Abstraction 119
c. 1945

PROVENANCE: *Artist; LSH Holdings, Vancouver; Stewart Wallace, Vancouver; Kenneth G. Heffel Fine Art, Vancouver; Loch & Mayberry Fine Art, Winnipeg; private collection, Winnipeg; Heffel Fine Art Auction House, Vancouver (lot 46, May 25, 2005); Audain Collection; Gift of Michael Audain and Yoshiko Karasawa; Audain Art Museum Collection, 2015.007*

Lawren Stewart Harris (1885–1970) was born into a well-to-do family in Brantford, Ontario. He spent his childhood in Brantford and Toronto and began his art training in 1904 in Berlin, where he worked with the artists Franz Skarbina (1849–1910) and, later, Adolf Schlabitz (1854–1943), who taught him a rather academic style of painting. He returned to Canada in 1908 and began painting the Canadian landscape and the city of Toronto. In 1909 he joined the Toronto Theosophical Society, and by 1911, through the Arts and Letters Club of Toronto, he had met several other artists who shared his enthusiasm for painting Canada's landscape, including J.E.H. MacDonald (1873–1932). A visit to see the *Exhibition of Contemporary Scandinavian Art* at the Albright Art Gallery (now the Albright-Knox Gallery) in Buffalo, New York, in 1913 had a profound influence on his understanding of what could be accomplished in northern landscape painting and on his use of both light and colour.

With the advent of the First World War, many young artists put their careers on hold. Harris enlisted in the army in 1916 but was discharged in May 1918 following a nervous breakdown that resulted from the death of his brother, Howard, earlier that year. By September, Harris had resumed his art making. With MacDonald and Franz Johnston (1888–1949), he rented a railway boxcar that had been fitted with bunks and a stove, and the three of them embarked on the first of many sketching trips to Algoma, Ontario. And in 1920, Harris, together with MacDonald, Johnston, Fred Varley (1881–1969), A.Y. Jackson (1882–1974), Franklin Carmichael (1890–1945) and Arthur Lismer (1885–1969), formed the Group of Seven.

The landscapes Harris produced in the 1920s have become widely admired and iconic representations of Canada. Throughout the decade, he simplified his composition and reduced his colour palette, reflecting the ideas of Theosophy and his belief that art could have a spiritual function.

When the Group of Seven disbanded upon the death of MacDonald in 1932, Harris felt somewhat distant from his fellow artists. In 1934, he divorced his first wife, Beatrice (Trixie) Phillips (1885–1962), and married Bess Housser (1890–1969), a fellow Theosophist. They left Toronto that year, and in late 1934 Harris began to paint abstractions, working first in Hanover, New Hampshire, and later in Santa Fe, New Mexico, where he became involved with the Transcendental Painting Group and exhibited his work with Raymond Jonson (1891–1982), Emil Bisttram (1895–1976) and others. The Second World War caused Canada to enact currency restrictions, and Harris, unable to transfer funds to support himself and Bess, was forced to return to Canada. In 1940 he settled in Vancouver, where he remained for the rest of his life.

Harris had been painting abstractions almost exclusively for several years by the time he arrived in Vancouver. We know, however, that he remained keenly interested in the outdoors and went hiking and drawing in the Rockies in 1941 with Jock Macdonald (1897–1960). Perhaps the new environment of Vancouver, combined with the two decades of painting the landscape at the beginning of his career, encouraged Harris to reintroduce landscape elements into his work. *Abstraction 119* is one of the strongest examples of his work from the mid-1940s. Geometrical shapes, so important in the ideas of Theosophy, combine with hints of landscape to create a powerful image. As art historian Peter Larisey has written, *Abstraction 119* "gathers together Harris's interest in abstract triangles and other geometric forms, selected natural forms, and tiny, well-contained landscape views similar to his Lake Superior works."[1] Clouds intermingle with geometric shapes (arcs, circles, rectangles and triangles), and there are two framed landscapes in the lower section of the painting: a lake view and perhaps a group of icebergs. There are areas of great depth and others of complete flatness. The paint is at times lightly dappled and at others densely opaque. It is a work that bridges the experiential and the spiritual worlds. Larisey suggests that "Harris probably thought of the work as a fusion of natural and abstract forms that embodied the contribution each can make to spiritual expression."[2]

Although Harris's work was not the earliest abstraction done in British Columbia, it was an important example to younger painters. *Abstraction 119* is an elegant and sophisticated visual dance between abstract and landscape elements. Harris does not allow one to predominate over the other, believing that each is important for allowing viewers to make the journey of the spirit that he felt that art must encourage. As Harris wrote, "In the largely unexplored realm of abstract art, in the realm of new and living ideas for painting, in the reality of a new awareness, we have a creative adventure in harmony with the highest aspiration and search for truth, beauty and expressive evocation and communication in our own day."[3] Harris, in *Abstraction 119,* speaks timelessly and eloquently. It is up to each of us to heed his message. ■

▸ Lawren Stewart Harris
(1885–1970)
Abstraction 119, c. 1945
oil on canvas
171.0 × 141.0 cm
Gift of Michael Audain and Yoshiko Karasawa; Audain Art Museum Collection, 2015.007

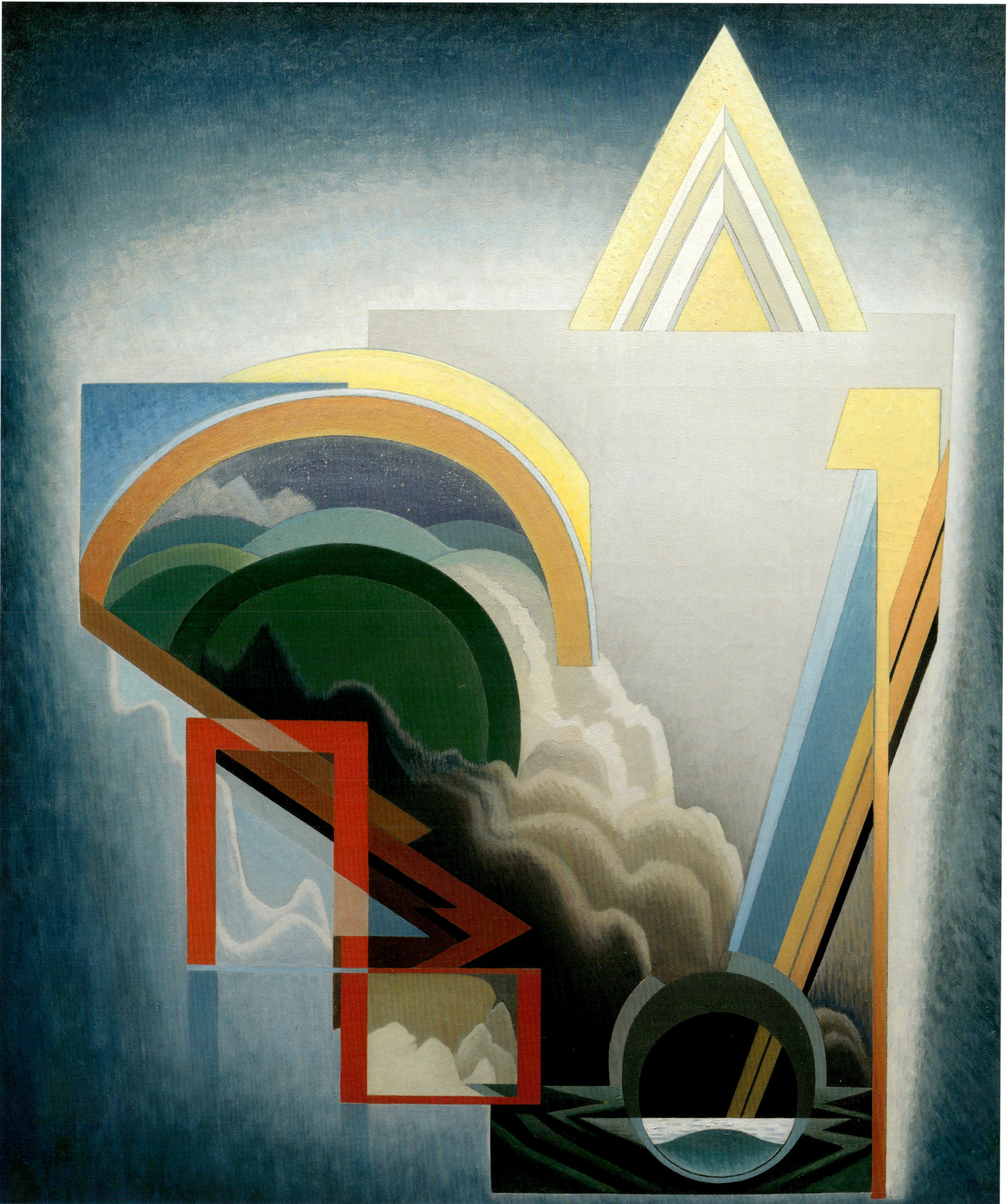

William Percival (W.P.) Weston
Jötunheim
1932

William Percival (W.P.) Weston (1879–1967) was born in London, England, trained initially as a teacher and was, by 1900, working as an educator, a lifelong interest. He was also, however, attracted to the idea of becoming an artist and took night courses at the Putney School of Art and Design. Although he was granted an Art Class Teacher's Certificate in 1904, he continued to take classes in painting until 1908, when he was offered a position as the art teacher at King Edward High School in Vancouver. It was a position that allowed him to combine both his interests, and Weston and his young family arrived in Vancouver in 1909.

Weston soon became part of the small art community in the city, exhibiting his English landscape paintings with the British Columbia Society of Fine Arts only weeks after his arrival in Canada. He later became a founding member of the Canadian Group of Painters, the successor to the Group of Seven as an exhibiting group, and an associate member of the Royal Canadian Academy of Arts, which was formed in 1880 and represented artists and architects from across Canada. As an art teacher and later as the Art Master at the Provincial Normal School, where he trained all of the province's art teachers, Weston's pedagogy formed the basis for all art training of children in British Columbia. His steady employment also left him free to paint as he wished, rather than having to respond to the market in order to sell his works.

Although Weston was a keen hiker and sailor and explored the coast extensively, his initial approach to the landscape was somewhat tentative and steeped in the traditions of English landscape painting. It took him some time to develop what he called "my own language of form and the expression of my own feeling for this coast region, its epic quality, its grandeur, its natural beauty."[1] The paintings are crisply linear and use simple, dramatic form. After a severe bout of phlebitis in 1928 that kept him bedridden for months, he resumed work with a new conviction—images of rocky shorelines, windswept trees and dramatic mountain peaks. Weston summarized his approach to British Columbia's landscape: "The mountains and forests are so gigantic that man seems puny and his slight inroads are comparatively insignificant. If, as I believe, the function of an artist is to express his reactions to the environment, he cannot but record the overwhelming preponderance of nature and omit the human element. Trees two hundred feet high and mountains ranging from five to fifteen thousand feet so outscale man and his works that one hardly notices his presence."[2]

Jötunheim, named for the Norwegian mountain range, is one of a series of dramatic peaks that Weston painted in the Coast Mountains and Fraser Valley in the early 1930s. Although Weston used the names of specific peaks in his titles, he was less concerned with the actualities of topography than with the "grandeur" of nature. Titles such as *Peaks of Silence* (private collection), *High Olympus* (National Gallery of Canada) and *Jötunheim* convey that sense of remote majesty, above the human fray, that interested him.

Weston's choice of subject matter has inevitably led to comparisons with the work of the Group of Seven, Lawren Harris (1885–1970) in particular. Weston's work is, however, quite

PROVENANCE: *Artist; private collection, Vancouver; Heffel Fine Art Auction House, Vancouver (lot 62, November 6, 1997); Audain Collection; Gift of Michael Audain and Yoshiko Karasawa; Audain Art Museum Collection, 2015.008*

▸ William Percival (W.P.) Weston (1879–1967)
Jötunheim, 1932
oil on canvas
108.0 × 117.5 cm
Gift of Michael Audain and Yoshiko Karasawa; Audain Art Museum Collection,2015.008

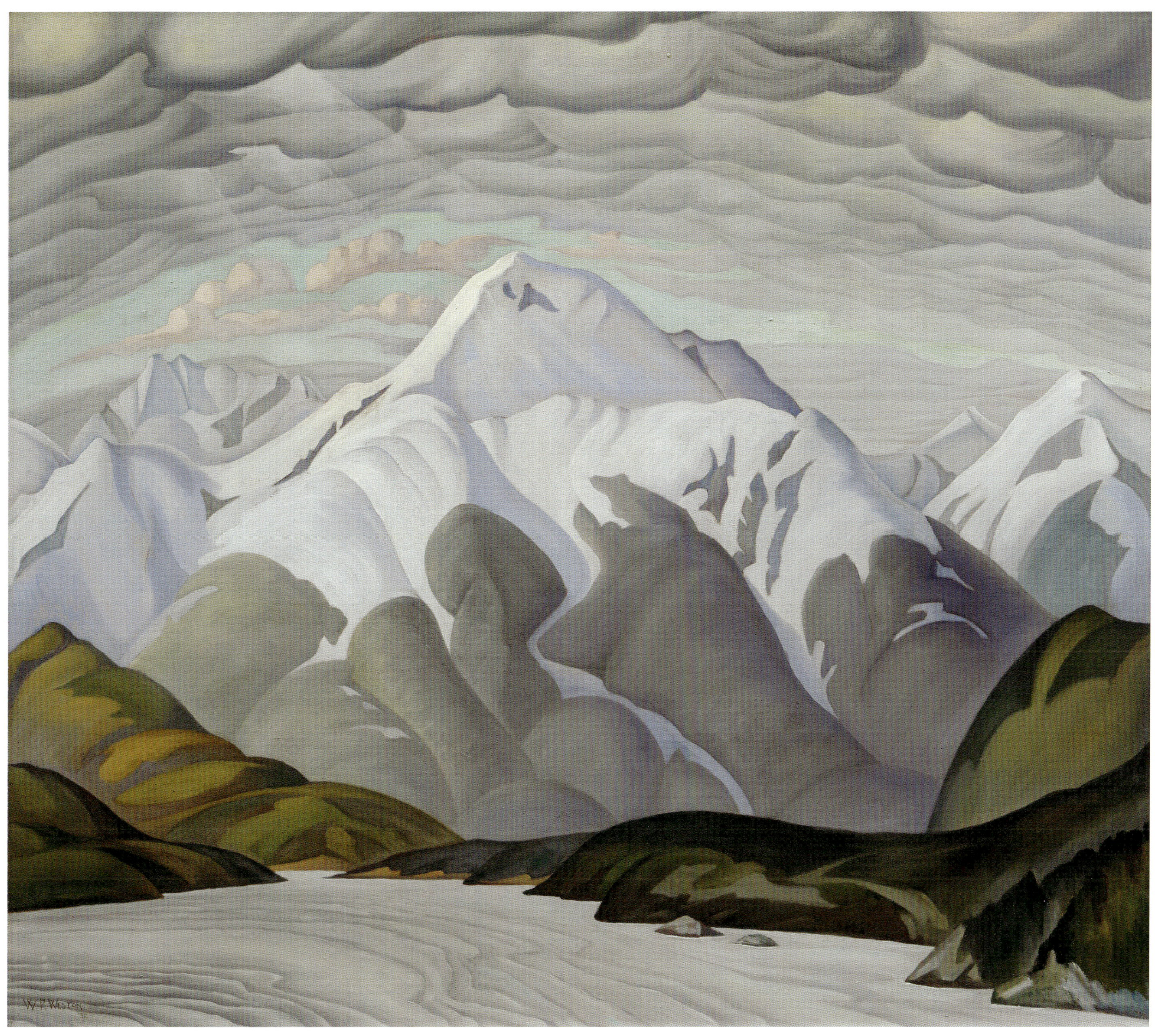

different in character from Harris's depictions of the Rocky Mountains, and Weston always maintained that his work had formed "without knowledge of Harris."[3] There is certainly no mistaking their work. Weston's paintings are warmer, less cerebral and, despite the lack of human presence, more approachable. Weston is interested in the nuances of form, light and colour in a way that has a greater realism than Harris, while never losing a deep sense of awe at the natural world. The handling of paint is also quite distinctly Weston's own.

A close friend of Emily Carr (1871–1945), whom he visited often during the 1930s and occasionally asked for painting advice, Weston had little direct influence on other artists. Once he had found his "own language of form," he was able, in works such as *Jötunheim,* to depict the landscape of British Columbia in a manner that is "heroic, but not brooding."[4] Weston is a singular figure within the art of British Columbia. ■

Edward John (E.J.) Hughes
Taylor Bay, Gabriola Island, BC
1952

Edward John (E.J.) Hughes (1913–2007) is a remarkable figure in the history of British Columbia art. A realist at a time when realism was considered neither modern nor innovative, Hughes chose to depict the landscape of his native province in a way quite unlike anyone else. His fidelity to a vision of a landscape in which people work in harmony with the natural world marks his entire oeuvre.

Hughes was trained at the Vancouver School of Decorative and Applied Arts (now Emily Carr University of Art + Design), where he was a student of Fred Varley (1881–1969), Charles H. Scott (1886–1964) and Jock Macdonald (1897–1960). Following his graduation from art school, Hughes, together with fellow students Paul Goranson (1911–2002) and Orville Fisher (1911–1999), set up a commercial decorating business that specialized in murals, although each man also produced a significant series of prints during the decade. Although the firm received several important commissions (the murals for Nanaimo's Malaspina Hotel, now in the Nanaimo Convention Centre, are the only ones extant), the economic circumstances of the Depression made work as an artist extremely difficult. Hughes worked in the fishing industry during the summers in order to make ends meet.

During the Second World War, Hughes served as an Official War Artist, working in Alaska, Eastern Canada and England. One of the requirements of the war artists was that they be accurate in their depictions of equipment, badges and so on. Hughes's approach to his work involved intensive-looking, elaborate preliminary studies and detailed colour notes done from the motif. His annotation system allowed him to precisely recall colour, both tone and hue, observed in nature, sometimes years later. And this experience later allowed him to develop a highly considered and deliberate approach to image making. After an extremely productive period as a war artist, Hughes was demobilized in 1946 and returned to British Columbia, where he and his wife

PROVENANCE: *Artist; Dominion Gallery, Montreal; Stern Collection, Montreal; Dominion Gallery, Montreal; Jacques Barbeau, Vancouver; The Barbeau Owen Foundation Collection, Vancouver*

▸ Edward John (E.J.) Hughes (1913–2007)
Taylor Bay, Gabriola Island, BC, 1952
oil on canvas
62.6 × 76.2 cm
The Barbeau Owen Foundation Collection

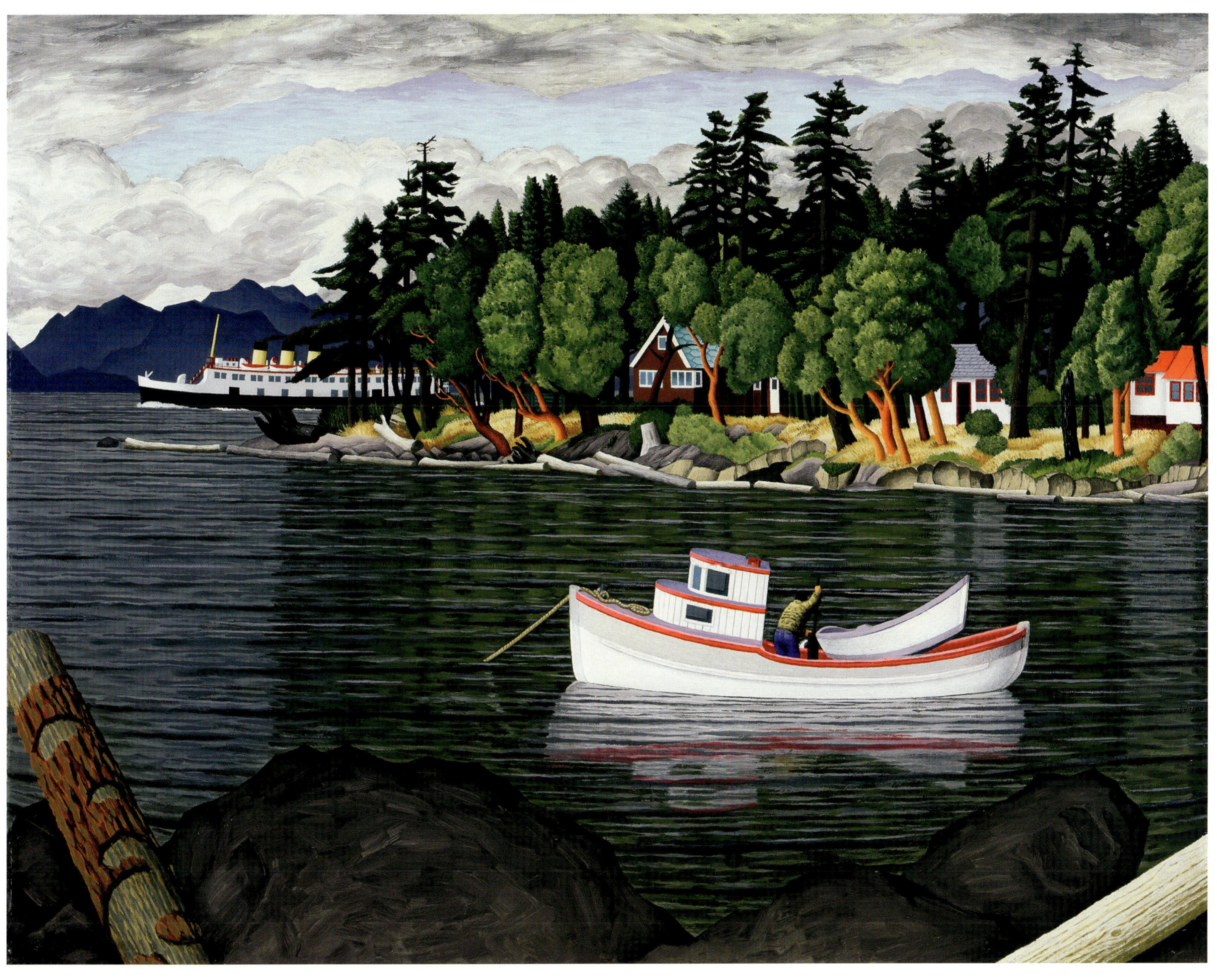

settled in Victoria. The city proved unsatisfactory for his work, and Hughes soon moved north of the city to Shawnigan Lake. He began to produce works that were extremely labour intensive and often required several months, painting twelve hours a day, to complete.

Hughes received some positive notice for his work and made a few important sales to museums. He also enjoyed the active support of Lawren Harris (1885–1970), who in 1947 awarded him the Emily Carr Scholarship, which financed two major sketching trips in the summers of 1947 and 1948. However, life as a painter based in Shawnigan Lake was marginal. An encounter with Montreal art dealer Dr. Max Stern at an exhibition at the University of British Columbia in 1951 was a turning point in Hughes's life. Stern agreed to buy all the works that Hughes had on hand and any new works for the next year. (This arrangement was subsequently extended until the closure of Stern's Dominion Gallery in 2000.)

Taylor Bay, Gabriola Island, BC is one of the earliest new paintings that Hughes sent to the Dominion Gallery. It is based on a drawing done in the summer of 1948, when Hughes had visited a number of locations in the Gulf Islands and lower Vancouver Island and on a subsequent, more elaborate cartoon drawing (also in The Barbeau Owen Foundation Collection) that depicts a quiet but vivid scene. An anchored fishing boat is seen in the middle ground; at the back of the boat, a fisher is preparing to launch a smaller dinghy. The shoreline of Gabriola Island is in the distance, dotted with arbutus trees, conifers and a few cottages. In the far distance is one of the Canadian Pacific coastal steamers that, before the British Columbia Ferry Authority took over the route, linked Vancouver with Victoria and Nanaimo. The whole scene is suffused with a gentle indirect light, which seems to accentuate colour (the red and blue trim of the boat, the orangey-brown trunks of the arbutus). Equally striking is the preternatural calm and the lack of atmospheric perspective. Every aspect of the composition is clearly and precisely described—reflections in the water, foliage on the trees and the textures of the two logs that dramatically enter our field of vision at the lower edge of the composition.

The scene is still, but it is not quiet; movement is implied by the logs, the gently shifting water and the passing steamer (the movement of which is seen in the bow wake and the smoke from the stacks). It is images such as this one that served to create a new image of British Columbia, distinct from the forests of Emily Carr, for all Canadians. ■

Edward John (E.J.) Hughes
Departure from Nanaimo
1964

PROVENANCE: *Dominion Gallery, Montreal; private collection; Granville Fine Art, Vancouver; Audain Collection, purchased 2010*

Edward John (E.J.) Hughes (1913–2007) was born in North Vancouver, but early in his life the Hughes family moved to Nanaimo, on Vancouver Island. He would, therefore, have been very familiar with the Nanaimo harbour and the comings and goings of the Canadian Pacific steamships that linked Vancouver Island to the mainland before the establishment of the British Columbia Ferry Authority in 1958. For Hughes and many other British Columbians, the fleet of coastal steamers—the *Princess* boats—had a romance and a majesty that the newer fleets introduced by the government-owned ferry service lacked. Hughes continued to paint images of these boats, with their elegant lines, triple smoke stacks and serried rank of lifeboats, long after they had ceased to service the West Coast. SS *Princess Victoria,* for example, was launched in 1902 and decommissioned in 1952.

It is likely that *Departure from Nanaimo,* which depicts the *Princess Victoria* about to leave Nanaimo's harbour for a trip back to Vancouver, is based on observations that Hughes made on his major sketching trips in the Gulf Islands and lower Vancouver Island in the summers of 1947 and 1948. By 1964 when Hughes painted this work, this coastal steamer service was no longer running, and Hughes was depicting a nostalgic world rather than the present. The vessel in the right foreground is another Canadian Pacific ferry, perhaps SS *Princess Joan.*

Hughes has been conscious of painting the scene in a way that suggests authenticity. For example, although boats such as the *Princess Victoria* carried passengers, freight and vehicles, they were not double-ended ships, which meant that the boats had to be backed away from the pier and turned before beginning their journey. This explains the extensive bow wake as well as the smaller stern wake of the ship in this image. Hughes, who was always a master of water surfaces, has paid particular attention to the anatomy of the waves, and they read very convincingly. So too has he paid considerable attention to the geography of Nanaimo harbour. In the background are the cliffs of Gabriola Island and the tip of Jack Point to the right, and, closer to the ferry, Protection Island, complete with a few houses and a small lighthouse. Protection Island, the site of a mine, had, however, been abandoned since 1938, so Hughes uses some artistic licence in this painting.

Hughes was always conscious of providing human interest in his work. In this composition, a small boat and boatman animate the left foreground, and the *Princess Victoria* itself has several people aboard on both the fore and upper decks. These figures allow viewers to imaginatively place themselves within the pictorial space. The complex layering of the composition allows the eye to be led from foreground to middle and distance, but the main action of the work, the turning of the *Princess Victoria,* is strategically isolated between two densely painted areas—the fore- and backgrounds.

The focus that Hughes brings to this composition is remarkable and persuasive, even if it is not entirely realistic. Compare, for example, the scale of the boatman in the foreground with the size of the passengers aboard the *Princess Victoria*. These are not consistent with the distance between them. Similarly, Hughes subtly adjusts his viewpoint within the composition to allow the scene to be viewed as clearly as possible. Whereas the whole image is seen from an aerial perspective, the boatman seems to be depicted from a higher vantage point than the docked steamer. These revisions to reality, however, demonstrate Hughes's skills as an artist. He convinces us of the reality of the scene, and we are there with him.

This work, like many of Hughes's best paintings, gives us a timeless view of the past. It vividly evokes the majesty of the *Princess Victoria,* the vitality of the Nanaimo waterfront and Hughes's delight at our place within the natural world. ■

► Edward John
(E.J.) Hughes (1913–2007)
Departure from Nanaimo,
1964
oil on canvas
120.0 × 143.0 cm
Promised Gift, Audain Collection

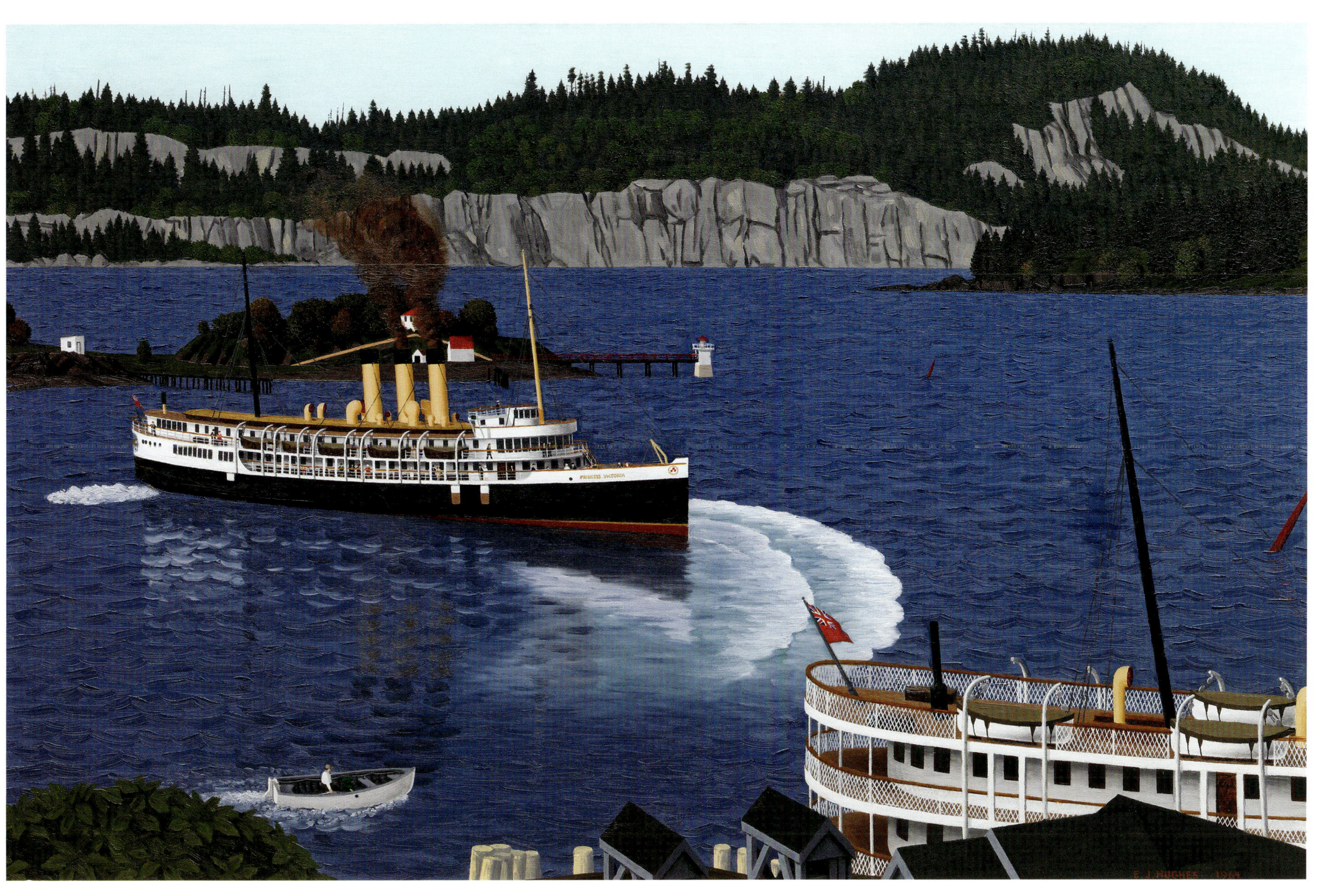

Bertram Charles (B.C.) Binning

Triptych of Nautical Symbols

1955–56

Bertram Charles (B.C.) Binning was born in Red Deer, Alberta, in 1909 but came to British Columbia as a child and lived and worked in Vancouver for most of his life, until his death in 1976. He trained at the Vancouver School of Decorative and Applied Arts (now Emily Carr University of Art + Design) and, beginning in 1932, became an important teacher there. In the late 1930s, Binning felt the need for further training and travelled to England, where he studied at the Ozenfant Academy with sculptor Henry Moore (1898–1986) and painter Bernard Meninsky (1891–1950). Although the approaching Second World War curtailed his studies abroad, he was able to absorb a great deal about modernist painting while in London, and saw Picasso's *Guernica* when it was exhibited to raise funds for the Republican side of the Spanish Civil War.

Upon his return to Canada, Binning resumed teaching and began to exhibit drawings and watercolours extensively. These elegant and often amusing drawings were characterized by a superb command of line and an intimate knowledge of the coastal life of British Columbia, and Binning soon gained a national reputation as an artist. Always a keen modernist, Binning was also active as an architect, designing his own iconic house in West Vancouver in 1940. He seems to have done more drawing than painting in the early 1940s, but in 1947 he took a leave from his duties at the school and returned to

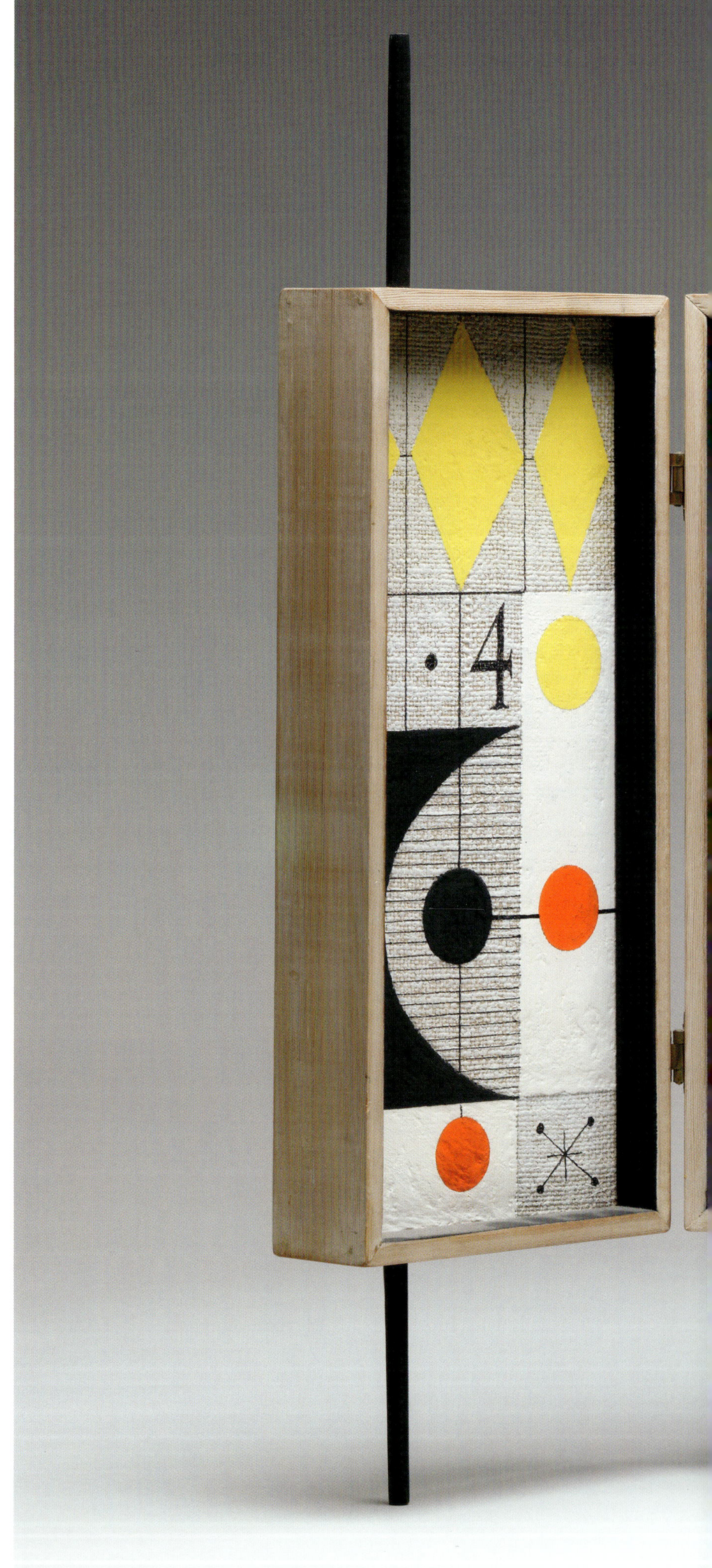

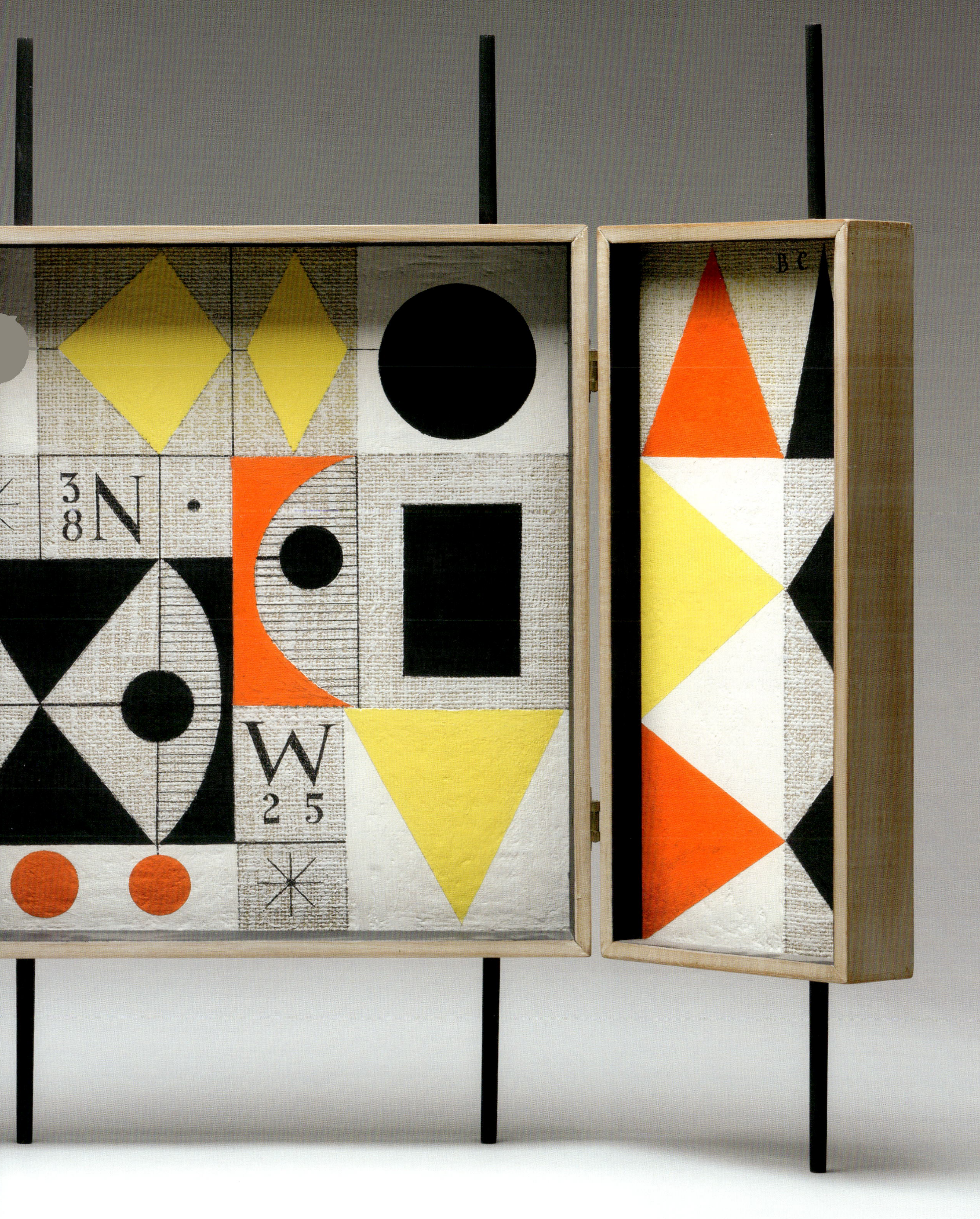

3 8 N
W 25
B C

painting. He was determined to find a modernist style that could be his own voice. The paintings from 1948, which combine both realism and abstraction, were universally lauded. Soon these works entered major public collections, including the National Gallery of Canada, the Vancouver Art Gallery and the Art Gallery of Toronto (now the Art Gallery of Ontario).

A year later, Binning joined the faculty of the School of Architecture at the University of British Columbia and, in 1952, became the founding director of the Faculty of Fine Arts (now the Department of Art History, Visual Art and Theory). Among Binning's responsibilities at the university was to teach art history, which fit well with his deep interest in the art of the past. Although he produced a number of major public murals during this decade, he also experimented with mosaic. This led him to visit Italy, and there he saw many altarpieces whose form—a central image and two side panels—he modernized in a small number of triptychs that are unique in Canadian painting.

Triptych with Nautical Symbols is a superb example of these works. It combines the form of the altarpiece with Binning's vivid sense of colour and design, his love of texture and his great affection for the sea and sailing. The rough burlap painting surface is treated with gesso to accentuate the texture and/or to provide a solid base for the oil paint. Throughout the composition, delicate lines and the unpainted texture of the burlap balance large areas of flat colour. The horizontality of the triptych form is counterbalanced by slender pegs that protrude above and below the frames and recall masts. The painting's title is slightly misleading, because though the diamond, circle and triangular shapes recall nautical flags, they do not replicate them. Moreover, the inclusion of what seems to be a boat registration number (Z901), several other numbers, and letters representing the directions east, north and west is more allusive than literal.

More important is the sense of visual rhythm that animates the whole work. The simple palette of colours, each of which is repeated in every panel, reads electrically. Compounding this feeling is the fact that the work can be viewed both closed (only the outside surfaces of the two side panels are visible) and open (the inside surfaces of the side panels and the central image are visible). The elegant but taut pattern of the closed triptych becomes more airy and more vivid when the triptych is opened. Carefully considered, exquisitely crafted and minutely executed, *Triptych with Nautical Symbols* has, nevertheless, a carefree élan and sense of fun, which every viewer can respond to. ■

PROVENANCE: *Artist; Private collection, Saanichton; Heffel Fine Art Auction House, (lot 8, November 6, 1997); Audain Collection; Gift of Michael Audain and Yoshiko Karasawa; Audain Art Museum Collection, 2015.009*

▶ Bertram Charles (B.C.) Binning (1909–1976)
Triptych of Nautical Symbols, 1955–56
oil, gesso on burlap mounted on board
58.4 × 60.0 × 22.0 cm
Gift of Michael Audain and Yoshiko Karasawa; Audain Art Museum Collection, 2015.009

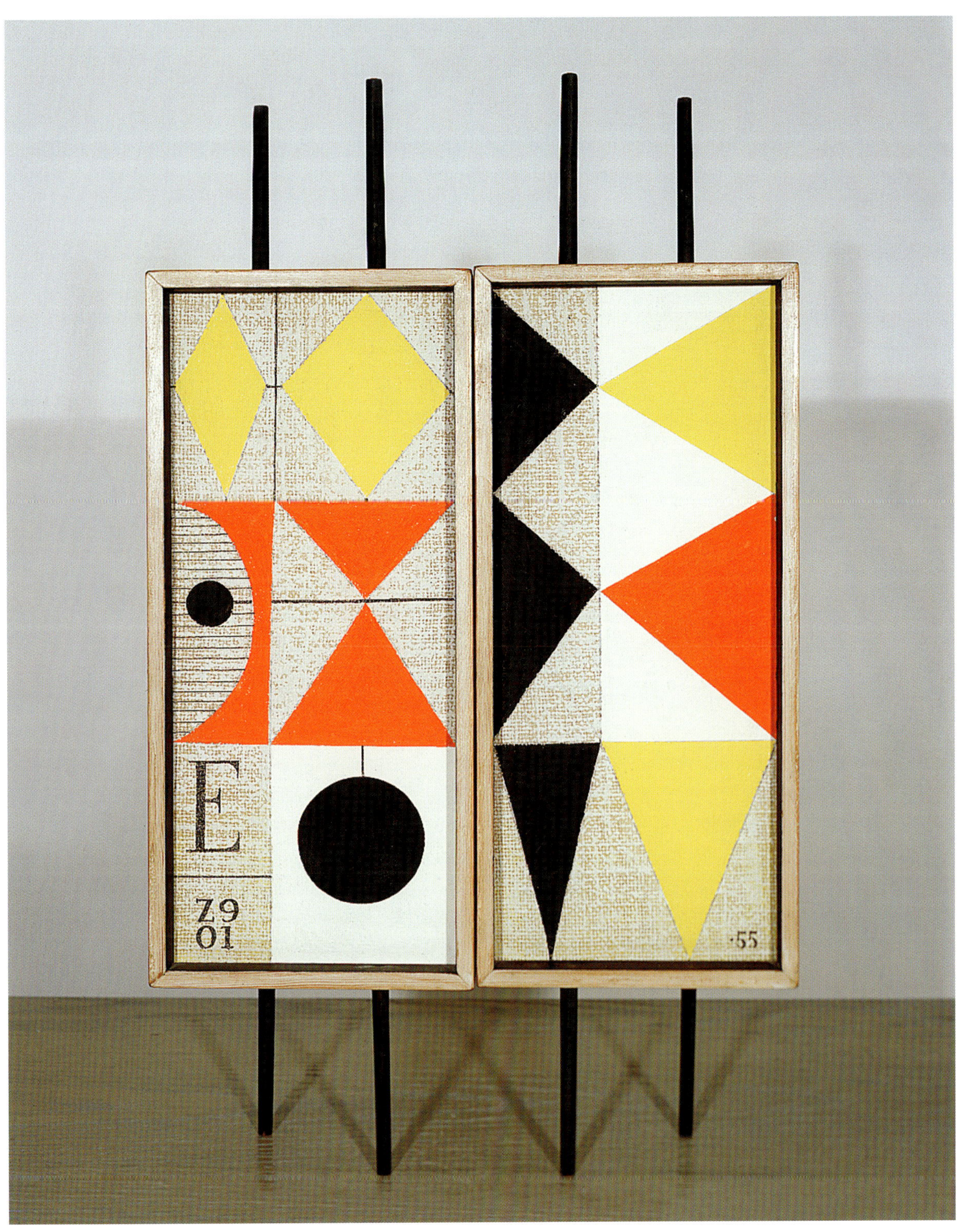
E
·55

Claude Herbert Breeze
Transmission Difficulties: The Dignitaries
1968

Claude Herbert Breeze was born in Nelson, British Columbia, in 1938 but was raised in Saskatoon. His art training began with a period of study with the Saskatchewan realist Ernest Lindner (1897–1988) in 1954–55, and he was subsequently taught by Art McKay (1926–2000) and Kenneth Lochhead (1926–2006) at the Regina College School of Art, University of Saskatchewan, from which he graduated in 1958. He spent a further year (1959) at the Vancouver School of Art (now Emily Carr University of Art + Design) and then worked as a medical illustrator at the University of British Columbia. At that time, he began to exhibit his paintings in Vancouver. In the 1970s, he moved to Ontario, where he taught first at the University of Western Ontario and then, in 1976, at York University, where he is now an emeritus professor. He became a member of the Royal Canadian Academy of Arts in 1974 and is represented in collections throughout Canada.

Drawing his images from the media, Breeze created a series of paintings whose searing commentary on social, sexual, racial and equality issues are among the most memorable examples of painting in 1960s Vancouver. They are also antithetical to the prevailing interest in abstraction that was current in Vancouver at the time. Taking his cues from both the powerful work of German Expressionism and Pop Art, Breeze produced images that were vividly coloured but also socially and politically vital. He recently commented, however, that "my biggest mature art influence had/has been *Persian Miniatures*, after I saw an exhibition of the works in Vancouver at the VAG [Vancouver Art Gallery]. It seemed to me a perfect balance of my visual aesthetics that could be translated into modern terms."[1] The miniatures were tightly controlled, dense narrative paintings, something that, as Breeze notes, could deal with contemporary subjects.

In 1967, Breeze began to produce works based on the form of the television screen, including a series of paintings entitled *The Home Viewer* and a second series, *Control Centre*, as well as a group of collages and charcoal drawings. Common to all these works are the strong edges that define the TV screen's shape and that can both contain images and draw the eye in. It is a form that is easily recognizable by today's viewers.[2] Of course, during the period when Breeze was producing these works, colour television was in its infancy in Canada, broadcasts having only begun in July 1966. His paintings were, therefore, referencing the increasingly ubiquitous medium of television but also adding another element to the experience—brilliant and expressive colour.

Transmission Difficulties: The Dignitaries was one of two paintings made on the same day. Whereas *Transmission Difficulties: The Operation* (National Gallery of Canada) depicts an apparently screaming patient whose lower extremities seem to have exploded on the operating table lying in a room alone, *Transmission Difficulties: The Dignitaries* depicts two members of the judiciary and a cleric (perhaps

PROVENANCE: *Artist; Bau-Xi Gallery, Vancouver; Audain Collection, purchased 1991; Gift of Michael Audain and Yoshiko Karasawa; Audain Art Museum Collection, 2015.010*

▸ Claude Herbert Breeze (b. 1938)
Transmission Difficulties: The Dignitaries, 1968
acrylic on canvas
115.0 × 185.5 cm
Gift of Michael Audain and Yoshiko Karasawa; Audain Art Museum Collection, 2015.010

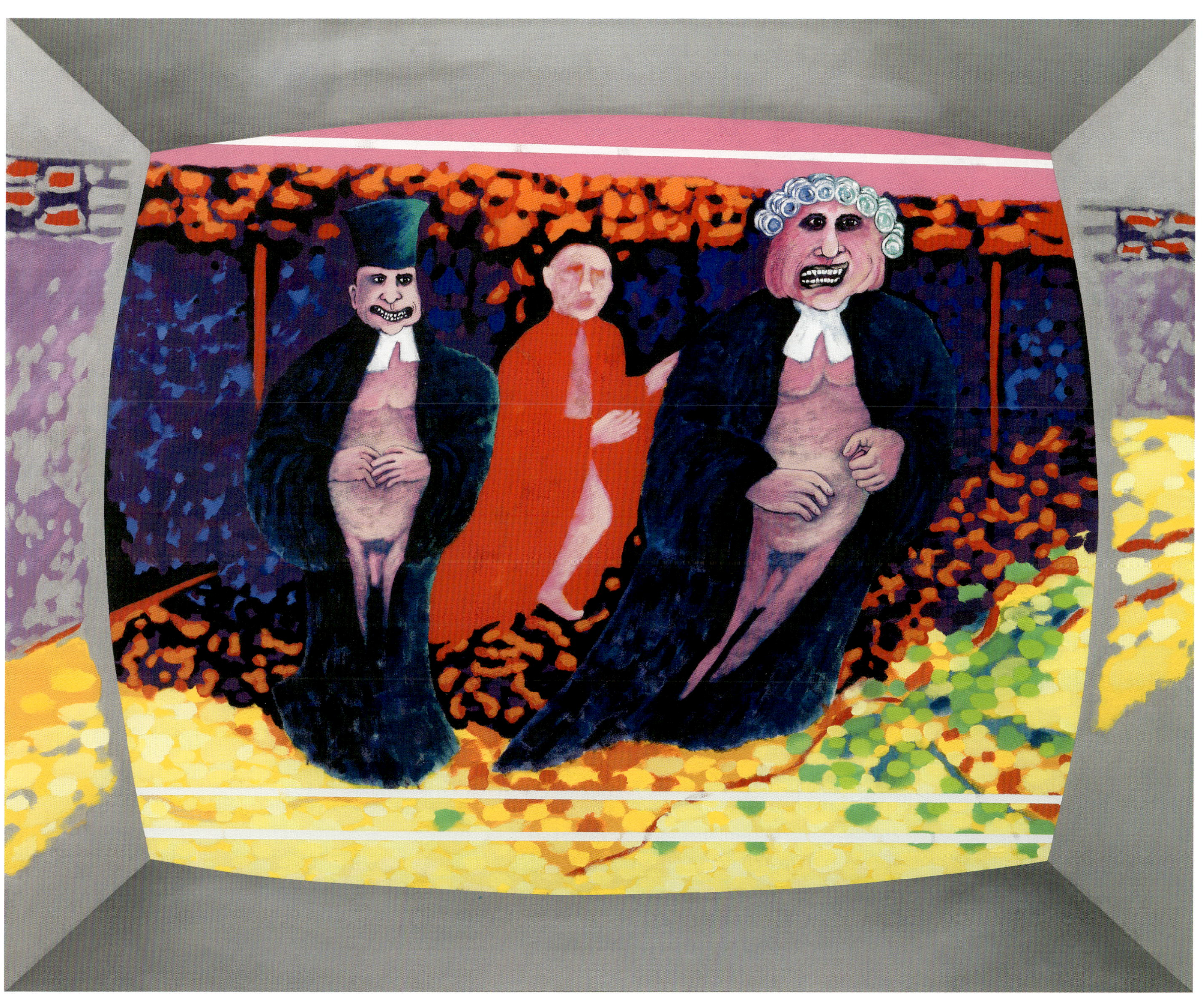

a Catholic cardinal) in a very unflattering light. They are, in the case of the two lawyers or judges, literally exposed, with their bloated bodies and genitals visible. The cardinal, while not exposed, is clearly naked under his vestments. All of the figures seem to rise up from the visual noise of the background, almost as wraiths wrapped in the robes of their offices. The faces of the two legal men appear to be in rictus, suggesting menace rather than humanity. As Breeze commented, "The painting's subject, images and interpretation seem obvious as to my intent of creating a visually social/political statement on religion, law, justice, etc. while using rather traditional painting aesthetics."[3]

Though Breeze may have used "rather traditional painting aesthetics," works such as *Transmission Difficulties: The Dignitaries* were viewed as controversial at the time they were produced. Far from respecting these bastions of society, Breeze has exposed them as leering and corrupt in both body and mind. The headline of one review trumpeted, "Claude Breeze's shockers strip the skin off the Sick Sixties."[4] This painting was also included in a solo exhibition of his work organized by curator Doris Shadbolt for the Vancouver Art Gallery in 1971. Although it was not Breeze's first solo exhibition, *Claude Breeze: 10 Years* was a major milestone in Breeze's career and included a national tour. When asked by a reviewer about his role as a painter at that time, Breeze replied, "I am a painter, an observer within the system—not without. My function is to observe, analyze and criticize. Above all I must make people aware of human and social depravity."[5]

This is surely one of the messages of this work, but its tremendous power as a visual image should not detract from the enormous skills as a painter that Breeze displays in his use of colour and composition. Today, almost fifty years after it was painted, *Transmission Difficulties: The Dignitaries* has lost none of its ability to shock, and Breeze's critique of the elites of religious and legal office remains pointed. The painting offers another view of the Swinging Sixties and the days of free love. It also reminds us that things have not changed much and that we must remain socially and politically aware. ■

Norman Antony (Toni) Onley
Juno
1962

Born in 1928 in Douglas on the Isle of Man, Norman Antony (Toni) Onley immigrated to Canada with his family when he was twenty. Between 1942 and 1946 he had trained at the Douglas School of Art (now the Isle of Man College of Further & Higher Education), specializing in watercolour, and following his arrival in Canada he studied further with Carl Schaefer (1903–1995) at the Doon School of Fine Arts in Ontario. After the sudden death of his first wife, Mary, Onley moved to British Columbia with his two daughters in 1955, joining his parents, who had retired to Pentiction. Two years later he won a scholarship to the Instituto Allende, an art school in San Miguel de Allende, Mexico. Onley spent three years in Mexico, and during that time began to explore abstraction under the tutelage of the painter James Pinto (1907–1987). He began to use collage extensively and sent some of these works back to Vancouver

PROVENANCE: *Artist; Audain Collection, purchased 2002; Gift of Michael Audain and Yoshiko Karasawa; Audain Art Museum Collection, 2015.011*

▸ **Norman Antony (Toni) Onley** (1938–2004)
Juno, 1962
oil, collage on canvas
130.0 × 115.0 cm
Gift of Michael Audain and Yoshiko Karasawa; Audain Art Museum Collection,2015.011

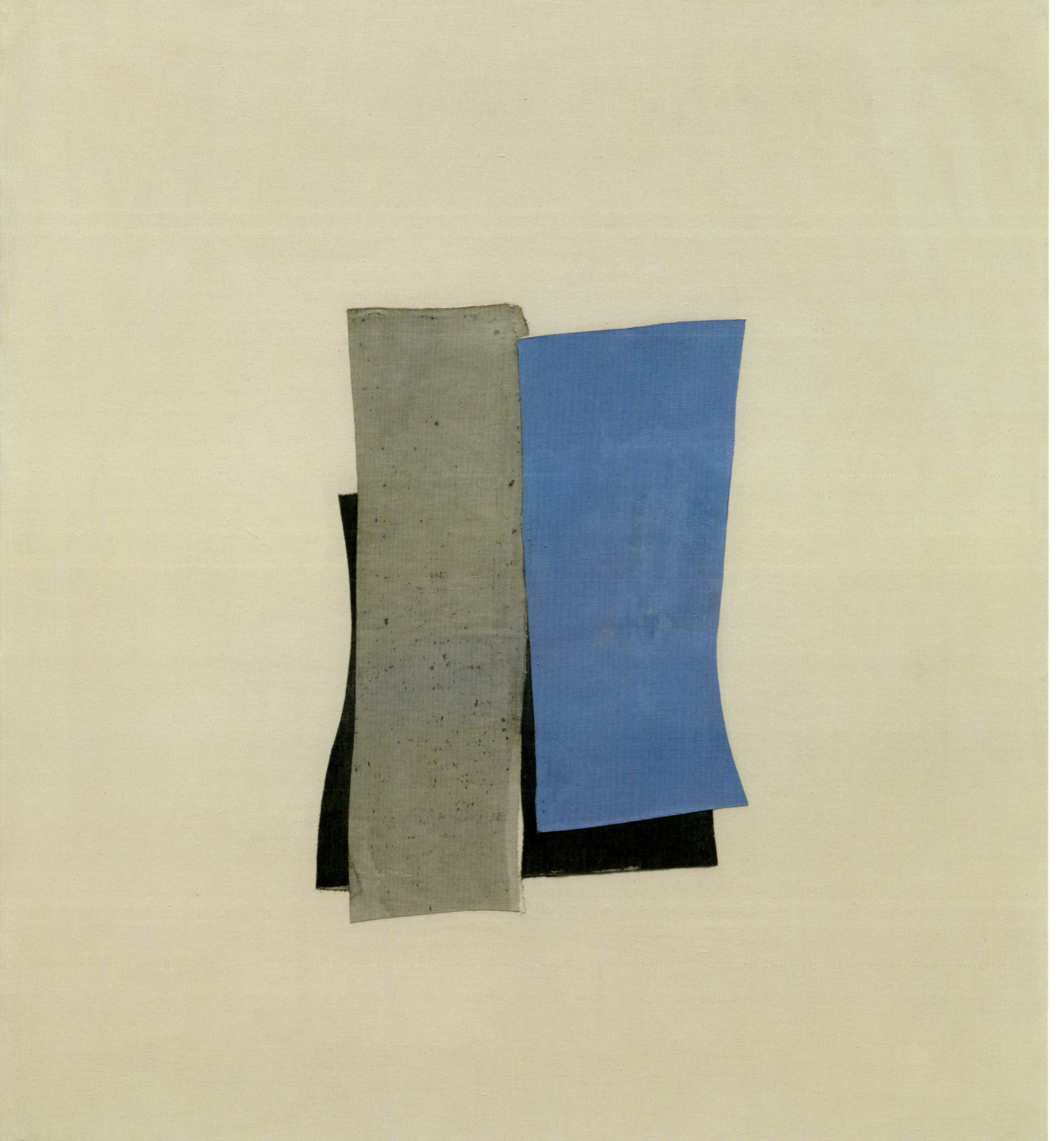

for exhibitions, including his first solo exhibition at the Vancouver Art Gallery in 1958.

Upon his return to British Columbia in 1960, Onley settled in Vancouver. He had produced a number of collages in Mexico, some quite colourful, but these were for the most part paper-on-board works. Oil-on-canvas collages became his main preoccupation in Vancouver, and he first came to larger public attention for a series of highly reduced abstractions, notably forty largely black and white works, the *Polar* series, which he began in 1961. These refined and tightly controlled works were widely admired and resulted in a major commission, a mural for the Queen Elizabeth Theatre in 1961. In 1964, Onley also spent a year in England where he expanded his printmaking activity.

Juno is a brilliant example of one of his minimal but elegant abstractions. Onto an unprimed canvas, Onley has glued three small, irregularly cut canvas shapes in grey, black and a faded blue. By subtly shifting these shapes, causing them to overlap, Onley has, without the use of line or shadow, managed to introduce an enormous sense of depth and volume into the composition. The black shape is on top of the bare expanse of the canvas, and the grey and blue shapes are on top of the black but also impinge upon the raw canvas. The blue shape is the foremost, as it surmounts the canvas itself and both the black and grey shapes, creating depth. Although the work is almost square, the irregular collaged shapes are slightly more vertical, thus introducing a subtle upward motion to the work. The painting is an important example of the abstraction that dominated 1960s painting in the province.

The composition has a quiet strength, which is perhaps why Onley titled the work *Juno,* after the Roman goddess, daughter of Saturn and sister and wife to Jupiter. She was a goddess of both power and subtlety, attributes that are reflected in this composition. Onley's collage work reflects his sure compositional sense and his belief that much can be said with minimal means. For many, works such as *Juno* represent the apogee of Onley's career as an artist. However, the works were not easily saleable, and Onley, with a family to support, sought a new vocabulary that might make his work more appealing to a wider audience. He found it in 1965, when he began to produce small landscape paintings of dramatically simplified natural forms, in watercolours, prints and acrylics. He did not, however, abandon collage, and some of his finest late works are small paper collages that recall his experiences in Mexico. A lifelong pilot, Onley died when his amphibious plane crashed into the Fraser River in 2004. ■

William Ronald (Bill) Reid
Killer Whale
1984

PROVENANCE: *Artist; Buschlen Mowatt Gallery, Vancouver; private collection, Yukon Territory; by descent to a private collection, Yukon Territory; Heffel Fine Art Auction House (lot 172, November 15, 2005); Audain Collection; Gift of Michael Audain and Yoshiko Karasawa; Audain Art Museum Collection, 2015.012*

William Ronald (Bill) Reid was a pivotal figure in the history of First Nations art in British Columbia. Born in 1920 in Victoria, Reid had a father of Scottish-German descent and a Haida mother, though as a child Reid had little, if any, exposure to Haida traditional art. As an adult, Reid worked in radio, eventually becoming an announcer for CBC Radio, and while in Toronto in the late 1940s, took a jewellery course at the Ryerson Institute of Technology (now Ryerson University). His two years of study, accomplished during the day while he worked at night for the Canadian Broadcasting Corporation (CBC), gave him a strong technical knowledge of European traditions of jewellery making. When he returned to British Columbia with the CBC in the 1950s, Reid began to study and explore his Haida heritage. The curator and writer Doris Shadbolt has described this process as Reid "becoming Haida."[1]

Reid began by copying examples of Haida art that he found in museums and books. In 1957 he travelled to Victoria to work with master carver Mungo Martin (1879–1962) on a totem pole; it was the first time that Reid had worked on a large scale, and this experience seems to have been a turning point in his career. The following year he left the CBC to devote himself full-time to art, a decision no doubt assisted by a major commission he received in 1958 from the University of British Columbia (UBC)[2] to carve a series of Haida poles and house fronts for the new student residences of Totem Park. Reid worked on this monumental group, together with Kwakwaka'wakw master carver Douglas Cranmer (1927–2006), from 1958 to early 1963. (This assemblage of sculptures is now located behind the Museum of Anthropology at UBC.)

Reid continued his work as a jeweller and sculptor after completing the Haida village for UBC and, in 1967, began a series of gold boxes with three-dimensional figures surmounting their lids. These boxes, which looked back to the example of the work of Haida master carver Charles Edenshaw (1839–1920) in argillite, are among Reid's most accomplished works. During this period, Reid began to make a name for himself in international art circles and lived in both London and Montreal before returning to Vancouver in 1972. The following year, Reid was diagnosed with Parkinson's disease, a progressive, degenerative disease that affects the nerve cells in the part of the brain that controls body movements. Initially, this did not greatly affect Reid's work, but gradually he became less able to perform fine movements and he began to use assistants on large-scale projects. He continued to work in Vancouver until his death in 1998.

Reid's remarkable and important *Killer Whale*, completed in 1984, is the first monumental sculpture created in bronze by a British Columbia First Nations artist.[3] Commissioned for the Vancouver Aquarium, it is a familiar sight to thousands of visitors to the city. The composition did not, however, begin as a bronze. A three-dimensional killer whale first made its appearance in Reid's work on a gold box in 1971. However, this bronze began as a small, finely detailed and exquisitely carved boxwood carving (now in the collection of the Bill Reid Gallery of Northwest Coast Art), which depicts an orca or killer whale leaping above the waves. This carving became the starting point for a series of models and enlargements that culminated in *Killer Whale*. Reid was assisted in this process by the Vancouver sculptor George Norris (1928–2013) and by younger Haida artists such as James Hart (b. 1952) and Don Yeomans (b. 1958).

Although *Killer Whale* exists in a variety of smaller-scale formats, the most memorable is this 1.3 metre version. In this striking image, Reid combines the use of the three-dimensional sculptural form with the language of Northwest Coast First Nations art—the ovoids and U forms. This combination of naturalistic form and Haida design elements is characteristic of Reid's work and is one of his most significant contributions to sculpture.

The killer whale is, of course, a major predator and has been an important sea creature for the Haida for millennia. Here, Reid's dynamic depiction brings this monarch of the seas vividly to life: its fierce teeth and the enormous dorsal fin clearly demonstrate its power, but the ovoids and other forms define this whale as Haida. It is a startling, memorable and profoundly moving image of the relationship between the Haida and the natural world. ■

▸ William Ronald (Bill) Reid
(1920–1998)
Killer Whale, 1984
bronze
180.0 × 50.0 × 64.0 cm
Gift of Michael Audain and Yoshiko Karasawa; Audain Art Museum Collection, 2015.012

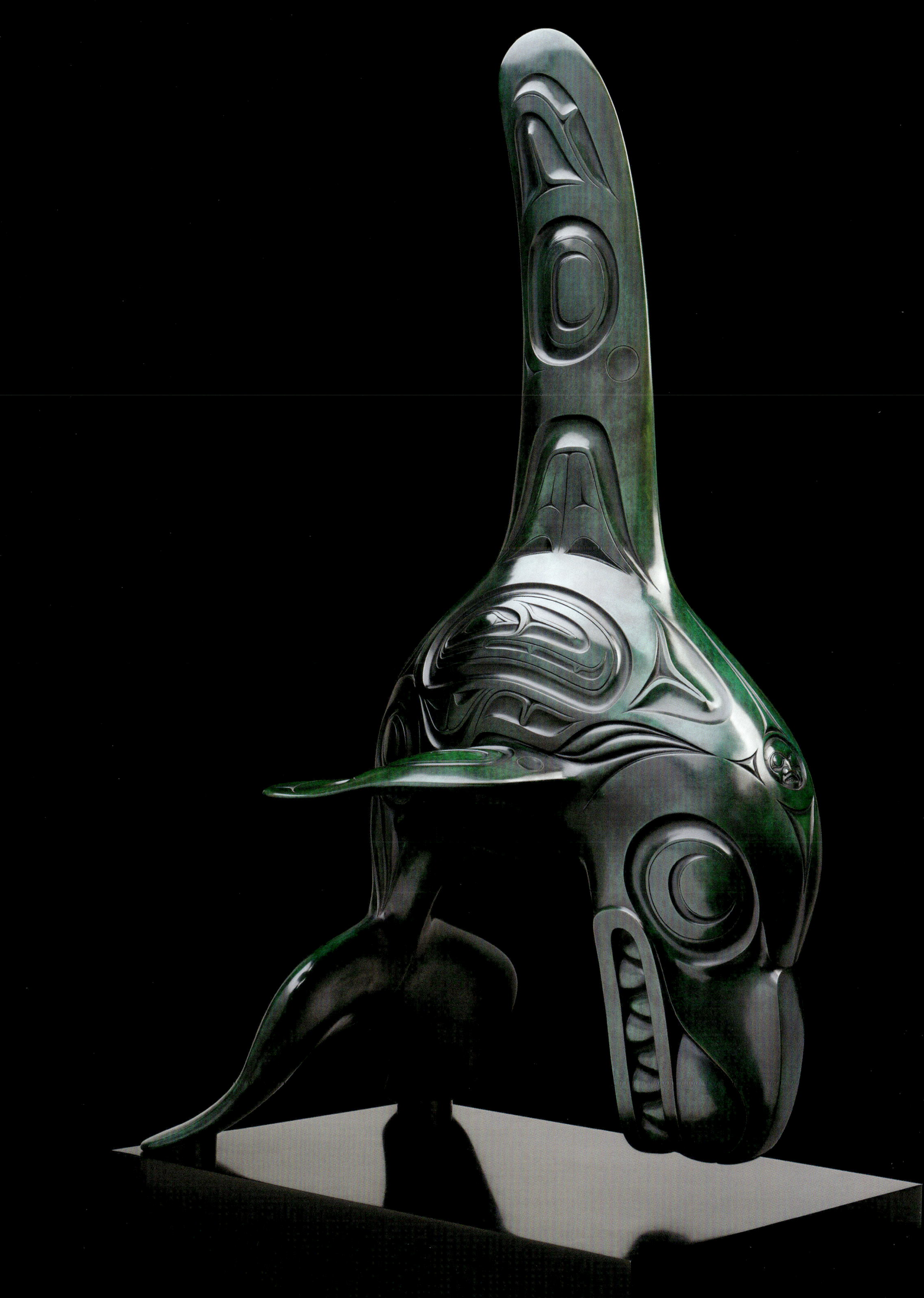

Jack Leonard Shadbolt
Butterfly Transformation Theme 1981
1981

Jack Leonard Shadbolt was born in Shoeburyness, England, in 1909 and came to Canada with his family in 1912. After a brief period in Nelson, British Columbia, the family settled in Victoria and Shadbolt grew up there. His informal artistic training began in 1925 when he met artist and academic Max Maynard (1903–1982) and went on sketching trips with him, but Shadbolt's main course of study was education and he went on to have a long teaching career in public schools in Duncan and Vancouver. In 1928, while attending the Provincial Normal School in Victoria, he had his first formal art classes with W.P. Weston (1879–1967). When Shadbolt moved to Vancouver in 1931, he took classes at the Vancouver School of Decorative and Applied Arts (now Emily Carr University of Art + Design), and in 1932 he began exhibiting his work. He also studied with painter Othon Friesz (1879–1949) and sculptor and painter André Lhote (1885–1962) in Paris in 1938. Upon his return to Vancouver from Paris, Shadbolt took up a teaching position at his alma mater, which had recently been renamed the Vancouver School of Art. He would remain there until he retired in 1966, except for a few years during the Second World War when he enlisted and was sent abroad. Shadbolt worked in Vancouver until his death in 1998.

The Second World War was a critical period in Shadbolt's life because his travels exposed him to much contemporary art, to the dramatic bombing of London and, through his work cataloguing photographs of Nazi concentration camps, to the horrors of genocide. Following the Second World War, Shadbolt sought to create a style that would encompass the range of his experience and the connection he felt with the environment. In the course of digging the foundations for a house in Burnaby that he was having built for himself and his wife, Doris, whom he had married in 1945, he became fascinated with the insects and grubs he encountered there and the idea of life cycles within nature. It would be another twenty years, however, before he began to explore in his work the theme of butterflies, a subject he would return to again and again.

Although Shadbolt had given up his position as Head of Painting and retired from teaching in 1966, he was a man of prodigious energy. He made thousands of works of art throughout his career, wrote several books and was a keen advocate for the value of the arts. He continued to hold solo exhibitions (there were more than one hundred during his career) and receive major commissions across Canada. He and Doris established a foundation for the visual arts and created the VIVA Awards to recognize mid-career artists, and he was recognized with several honorary degrees and an Order of Canada. In the 1970s, when he and Doris travelled extensively, working serially became a significant part of his practice. *Butterfly Transformation Theme 1981*, which reads from left to right, is a superb example of one of his series works and a

PROVENANCE: *Artist; Bau-Xi Gallery, Vancouver and Toronto; Laing and Kathleen Brown, North Vancouver, purchased 1984; Audain Collection, purchased 2006; Gift of Michael Audain and Yoshiko Karasawa; Audain Art Museum Collection, 2015.013*

dazzling display of Shadbolt's skills as a painter and colourist.

This massive work, more than seven metres in width, was the centrepiece of an exhibition of Shadbolt's butterfly works held at the Art Gallery of Greater Victoria in 1988. That show also featured his most monumental and important exploration of the subject, a tapestry entitled *The Choice* (1984–85, Vancouver Art Gallery) which art historian Scott Watson has described as a "grand opus."[1] In a statement for the exhibition, Shadbolt wrote,

> I saw the butterfly as a powerful symbol of the natural and spiritual will to survive through change and transformation—a symbol all the more potent in contrast with the fragile and ephemeral beauty of its subject. I created my own abstract paraphrase where, by raw and intense design, by alteration of scale and by supercharged psychological transcription I could pitch the implications of human overtone to the extreme. And the butterfly's dangerous flight over gulfs of space and migratory distance, subject to instinctive compulsion, offered me the possibility of a heroic metaphor.[2]

Shadbolt's own words also perhaps best describe the cumulative effect of *Butterfly Transformation Theme 1981*: "The forms emerge from a seemingly mechanized origin of hard, emblematic boldness, move through a muffled dark passage where deep red flashes emerge off the wings, thence to a bold, heraldic white and yellow stasis, then through chittering of black and yellow dazzle, through a passage of muffled mauves again into a dark . . . rhapsody out into the light once more and into the bacchanale."[3] It does indeed have a sense of the heroic, the struggle of the fragile butterfly not only to endure but also to thrive. It also suggests that order may emerge out of chaos. And it is, finally, a profoundly optimistic work that, for Shadbolt, has larger implications that we can all bring to the vagaries of our own lives. ■

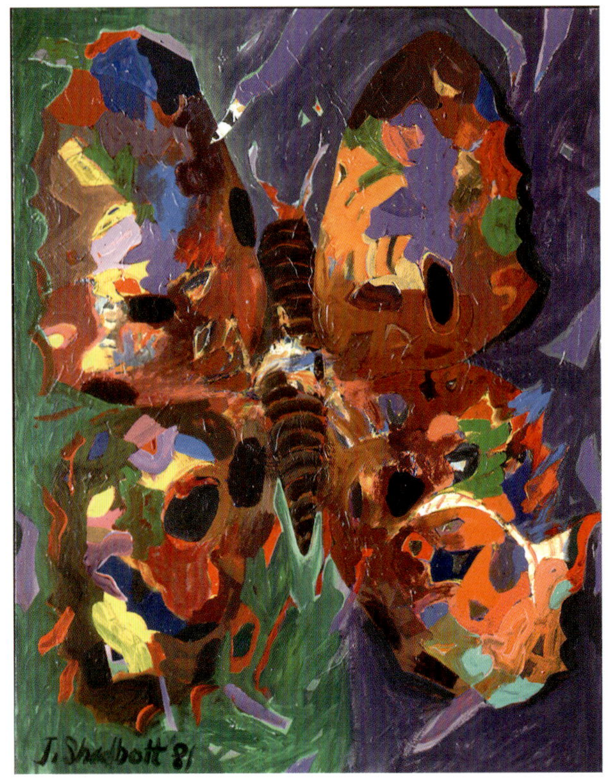

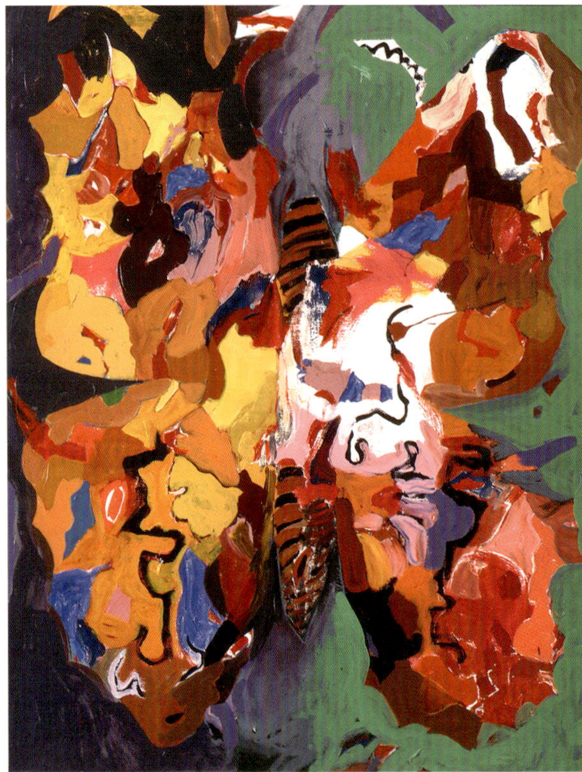

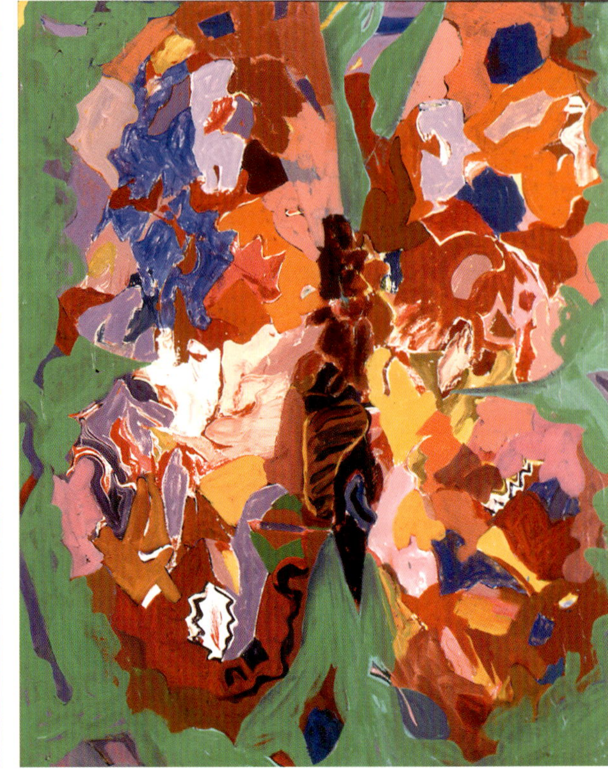

▶ Jack Leonard Shadbolt
(1909–1998)
Butterfly Transformation Theme 1981, 1981
acrylic on canvas
six panels, each 162.5 × 121.9 cm
Gift of Michael Audain and Yoshiko Karasawa; Audain Art Museum Collection, 2015.013

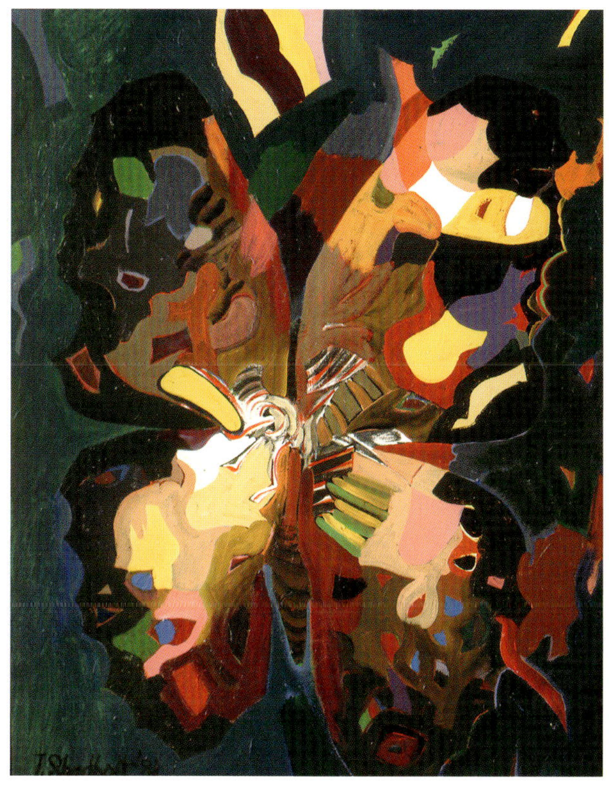

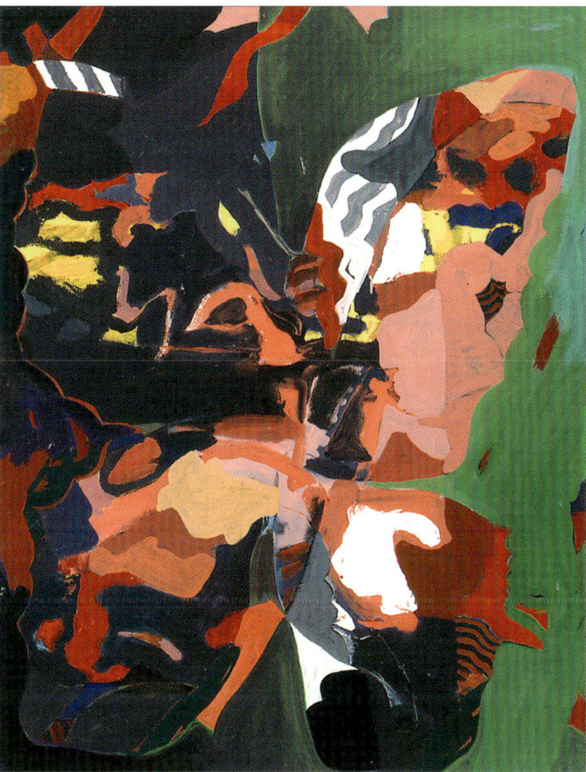

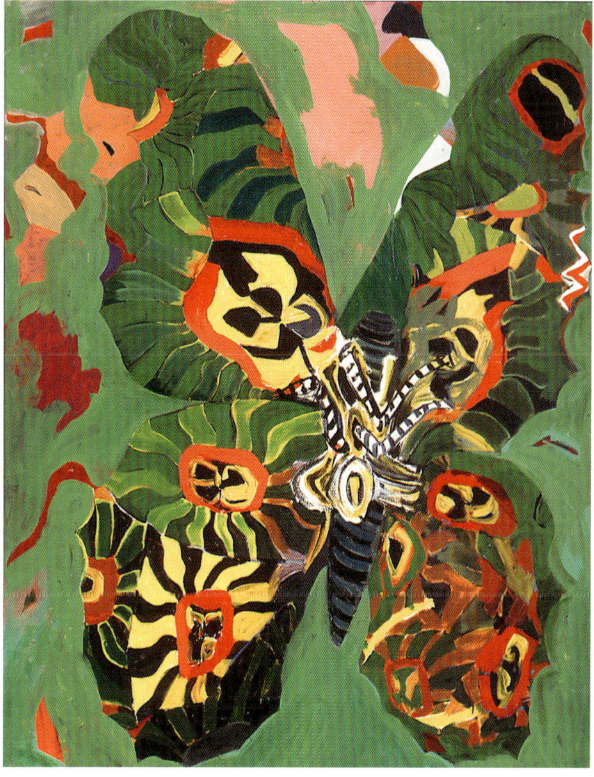

Gordon Appelbe Smith
Winterscape
1991

Gordon Appelbe Smith's exhibition career has spanned more than seventy years and has been marked by enormous changes in both his life and his work. Born in East Brighton (Hove), Sussex, in 1919, Smith immigrated to Canada with his mother and brother in 1933. The family settled in Winnipeg. Smith's father had been an amateur watercolourist and had given his two sons some lessons, but it was only in 1937 that Smith began his formal art training, as a student at the Winnipeg School of Art (now the School of Art, University of Manitoba). At that time he also worked part-time at the design firm Brigdens of Winnipeg and taught children's art classes at the Winnipeg Art Gallery. This early exposure to teaching was significant because it would mark a direction for his future.

The advent of the Second World War saw Smith join the Royal Winnipeg Rifles, and he later transferred to the Princess Patricia's Canadian Light Infantry, with which he served overseas. On a brief holiday in the summer of 1940, he visited Vancouver for the first time and met Marion Fleming (1918–2009), who became his wife in 1941 before his deployment to Europe. This meant that Vancouver became his new home.

Severely wounded in Sicily in 1943, Smith recuperated in Tunisia and later England, returning to Vancouver in 1944. While undergoing continued therapy for his injuries, Smith completed his high school education, had his first solo exhibition at the Vancouver Art Gallery and, in 1945, enrolled in the Vancouver School of Art (now Emily Carr University of Art + Design). He worked with Jack Shadbolt (1909–1998), Charles H. Scott (1886–1964) and others, graduating in 1946. He began teaching at the Vancouver School of Art the same year. In 1951, he took further training at the California School of Fine Arts (now the San Francisco Art Institute), working with painters Elmer Bischoff (1916–1991) and James Budd Dixon (1900–1967). Smith had, since the mid-1940s, worked during the summers at the Provincial Normal School (a facility that trained schoolteachers) in Vancouver, and in 1956 he joined the Faculty of Education, where he taught with distinction until his retirement in 1982.

Smith's artistic career has been widely varied. He has done important commissions, and he's worked both representationally and abstractly. There have, however, been a few constants in his work. The first is a deep commitment to the act of painting itself—a relish for the character and reality of paint, whether oil or acrylic, and how it interacts, feels and looks on a painted surface. The second is an intense observation of the world, whether the wonders of the natural landscape or the minutiae of human endeavour. The third, and perhaps most important, is an interest in challenging himself and confronting new problems. This means he has been willing to abandon the direction his art has taken if he feels that it is no longer working. In short, Smith has never rested on his laurels, considerable though they may be.[1]

Winterscape is perhaps the most successful of a series of dramatic paintings from the early

PROVENANCE: *Bau-Xi Gallery, Vancouver; Audain Collection, purchased 1993; Gift of Michael Audain and Yoshiko Karasawa; Audain Art Museum Collection, 2015.014*

► Gordon Appelbe Smith (b. 1919)
Winterscape, 1991
acrylic on canvas
173.0 × 257.5 cm
Gift of Michael Audain and Yoshiko Karasawa; Audain Art Museum Collection, 2015.014

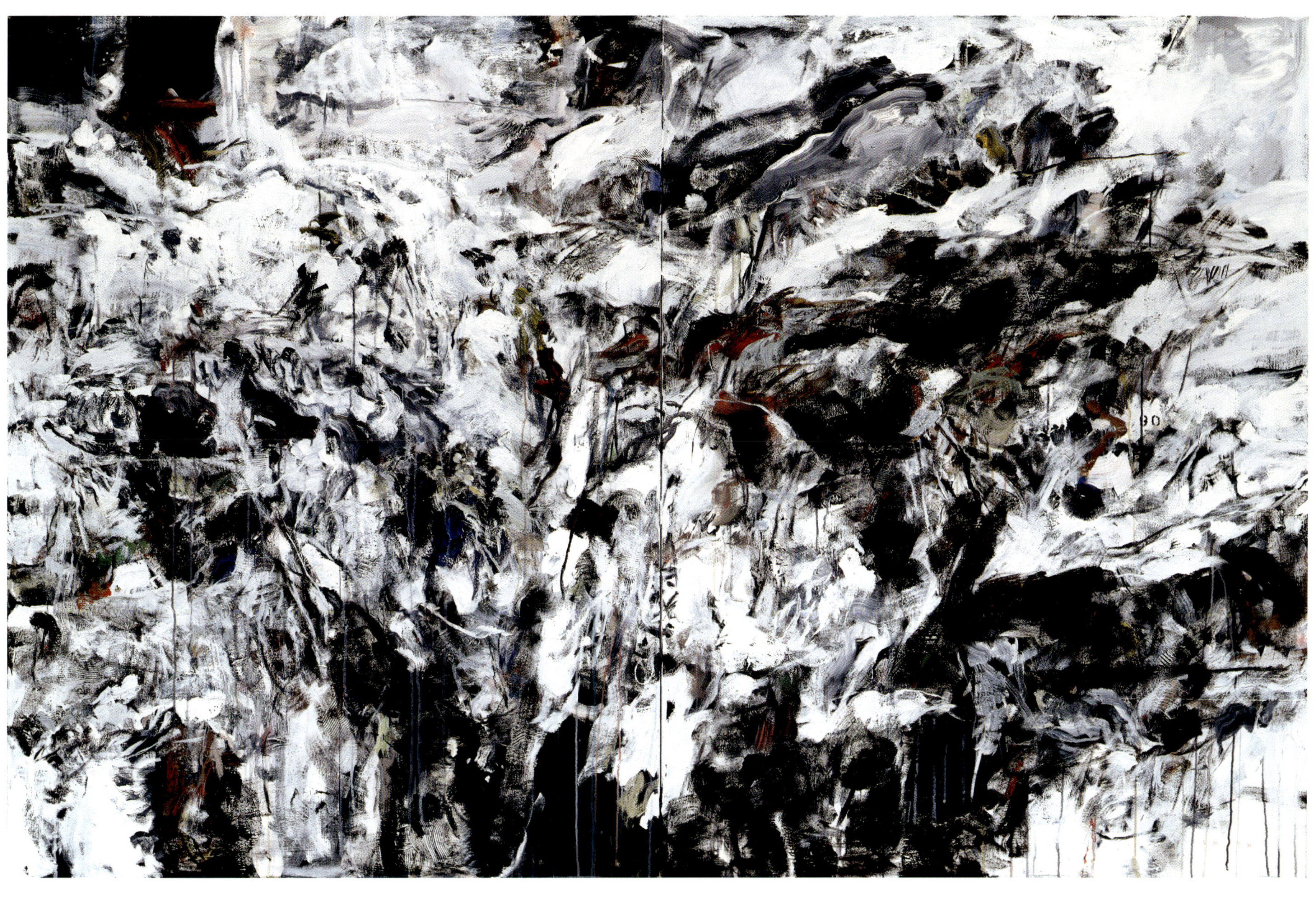

1990s that explore the boundaries between representation and abstraction, between order and chaos. The work itself is a powerful contest of black and white, and though it is based on close observation of the natural world, it borders on complete abstraction. One reads it both as a close viewing of the complexity of the natural world and as an exciting and vivid display of paint handling. The work is full of drips, slashes and bright spots of colour. A pattern of black lines throughout the image resolves into twigs, and the title reminds us that we are looking at a representation of a landscape covered in snow. Smith does not want us to forget the fact of the paint itself, however, and both the scale of the painting and the absence of easy reference points for us to orient ourselves (sky or foreground) make exploring the painting a visual and emotional adventure. We feel the excitement of Smith's attack as a painter and the chill of this wintery scene. It is an image of the natural world but one that approaches the abstract, and it is this series of tensions that give *Winterscape* its power. Just as we think we understand and know the work, some other aspect of it emerges, challenging us as viewers, just as the image challenged Smith as an artist. ■

Takao Tanabe
Strait of Georgia 1/90: Raza Pass
1990

Takao Tanabe was born in the small settlement of Seal Cove, British Columbia, in 1926. This community, now a part of Prince Rupert, was strongly associated with the life of the coast. His father worked as a fisher and his mother worked in a cannery. The community was also home to a number of lumber mills. When Tanabe was eleven, the family moved to Vancouver. Tanabe continued his schooling there until 1942, when, like other Canadians of Japanese ancestry, he and his family were interned in a camp. The camp, which had no facilities other than those the internees themselves could build, meant that Tanabe's education came to an end. In 1944, he moved to Winnipeg, joining his older siblings, who had been employed in farm labour during the Second World War.

Following the war, Tanabe was at loose ends and, in 1946, enrolled in the Winnipeg School of Art (now the School of Art, University of Manitoba). The following year, when Joseph Plaskett (1918–2014) replaced Lionel LeMoine (L.L.) FitzGerald (1890–1956) as the main painting teacher at the school, Tanabe was introduced to ideas about painting that opened the world of art to him. After graduating in 1949, Tanabe spent much of the 1950s studying in New York—where he worked with artists Hans Hofmann (1889–1966) and Reuben Tam (1916–1991)—and in Europe and Japan. He also spent several years in the 1960s living in New York and in the 1970s working at the Banff Centre, but British Columbia

PROVENANCE: *Equinox Gallery, Vancouver; Audain Collection, purchased 1994; Gift of Michael Audain and Yoshiko Karasawa; Audain Art Museum Collection, 2015.015*

► Takao Tanabe (b. 1926)
Strait of Georgia 1/90: Raza Pass, 1990
acrylic on canvas
142.7 × 186.0 cm
Gift of Michael Audain and Yoshiko Karasawa; Audain Art Museum Collection,2015.015

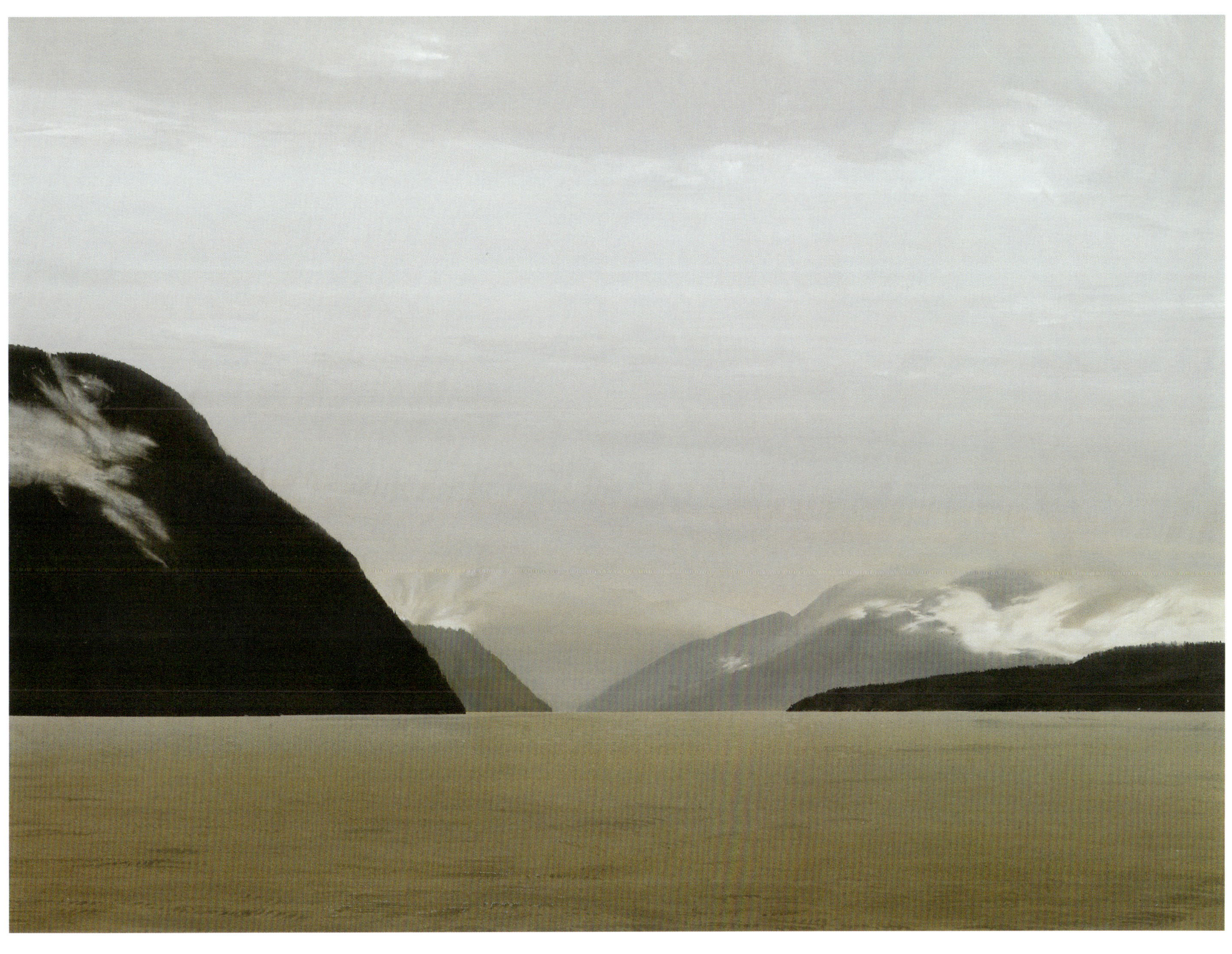

remained his home, and he returned to the province permanently when he retired from the Banff Centre in 1981.

Tanabe has had a long career as a designer and painter. Although much of his early work is abstraction, he shifted towards landscape-based work in the early 1970s when he accepted the position in Banff. Throughout that decade he produced a series of remarkable images of the prairie landscape, images that owe a great deal to the ideals of *sumi* painting, which he had studied in Japan. Using expansive washes of acrylic paint, Tanabe produced images that depict the landscape in its essential elements—land and sky. Devoid of human presence, these works inhabit the realm between abstraction and representation and depict the prairie in an absolutely telling and individual manner.

Since the topography of the coast did not allow for the almost minimal representation of the landscape that had marked his work of the prairies, Tanabe's challenge when he returned to British Columbia was to find both subjects that interested him and a new approach to painting. He continued to be interested in landscapes without people and, usually, without evidence of manufactured things; however, the quality of light and colour and the atmosphere of the coast were quite different from the prairie. Beginning in the early 1980s, Tanabe began to produce an extraordinary series of paintings that have redefined how the coastal landscape is seen.

Strait of Georgia 1/90: Raza Pass is a magnificent example of Tanabe's highly personal vision of this landscape. A sweeping view across the Strait of Georgia, it is a deceptively simple work that slowly reveals its depth and beauty. Composed in a symphony of subtle colours—greys, browns, blues, black and white—the image is both remarkably specific and evanescent. The composition works brilliantly to lead the eye inexorably into the distance, an effect accomplished by subtly lightening the colour of the surface of the ocean as the eye moves into the distance. The overlapping shapes of islands also move from dark to light, marking a visual and psychological journey. There is infinite variety in the delicate colour shifts, and the work is atmospheric in the best way possible: timeless and majestic while vividly evoking the damp grey light of the coast. Tanabe has achieved that most elusive of goals for an artist: he has convinced the viewer of the truth, the absolute rightness of his vision. No one who has seen a Tanabe painting of British Columbia's coastal waters can look at the landscape the same way again. ■

Sonny Assu
1884–1951
2009

PROVENANCE: *Artist; Equinox Gallery, Vancouver; Audain Collection, purchased 2009*

Sonny Assu was born in Richmond, British Columbia, in 1975 and is of mixed Caucasian and Kwakwa̱ka̱'wakw ancestry. He has spent his life in urban settings and has only come to a full appreciation of his aboriginal ancestry in adulthood. His early interest in art was largely centred on comic books, and it was during the course of his studies at both Kwantlen College (now Kwantlen Polytechnic University) and Emily Carr Institute of Art and Design (ECIAD, now Emily Carr University of Art + Design) that he developed a sense of both aboriginal art and fine art. A critical aspect of Assu's art making has been his determination to place himself within a modernist context while maintaining a significant relationship to First Nations traditions and art. As he once wrote, "I've taken he notion of tradition and combined it with modern imagery to form a new discourse."[1]

Unlike many other First Nations artists, Assu did not develop his art through an apprenticeship with an older artist. He learned instead through the traditions of Western art schools and their pedagogy, though at ECIAD he did work extensively with the Aboriginal Program manager, Brenda Crabtree, who taught him to make traditional drums and weave cedar bark. Another instructor, Michael de Courcy (b. 1944), taught him about Pop Art and Andy Warhol.[2] Assu, while very much cognizant of his ancestry as a Kwakwa̱ka̱'wakw man, uses tradition and traditional forms where they can inform and enhance his work within a contemporary context. As he has noted, "I'm a contemporary artist. My art is rooted in tradition but not traditional."[3] For example, he will use formline design, which he taught himself through extensive practice and studying books such as Bill Holm's *Northwest Coast Indian Art* and Hilary Stewart's *Looking at Indian Art of the Northwest Coast,* where he feels it is appropriate for the aesthetic aims of his artistic practice.

Perhaps nowhere is Assu's complex relationship to his Ligwilda'x̱w (We Wai Kai) Kwakwa̱ka̱'wakw heritage and the world of popular culture more evident than in *1884–1951,* one of his most celebrated and accomplished works. It is a striking and subtle installation piece that combines a profound respect for the history of the troubled relationship between First Peoples and the Government of Canada with a sardonic examination of the ubiquity of the "to-go" coffee cup. The magic of the work is that it does this in a remarkably elegant and beautiful way, with a great sensitivity to both the formal properties of composition and materials.

What we see before us are sixty-seven spun copper cups, with lids discarded on an old Hudson's Bay blanket. The cups are exactly the same size as a Starbucks "grande" cup, which has become a ubiquitous feature of urban culture around the world. The Hudson's Bay blanket immediately conjures up the history of trade and exploitation of First Nations peoples by this and other firms. The use of copper is important, for this metal was of singular

▸ *overleaf*
Sonny Assu (b. 1975)
1884–1951, 2009
spun copper cups with lids (67), Hudson's Bay blanket
dimensions variable
Promised Gift, Audain Collection

significance on the Northwest Coast. The only metal to which the First Nations seem to have had access prior to contact with European traders and settlers, copper was used as an expression of wealth within these cultures. A shield-like copper would have been displayed by a chief at a potlatch, while household goods, artworks and other items were distributed to potlatch guests as a demonstration of the wealth of his family and nation. Occasionally, in an act of either "boasting or shaming," the copper would be "broken and distributed amongst chiefs"[4] at the potlatch. So Assu has set up a complex relationship between waste, as seen in the discarded cups, and wealth, which is referenced in the use of copper.

The title of the work, *1884–1951*, and the number of cups are also of considerable significance. In 1884, the Government of Canada enacted the Indian Act, which continues to govern the lives of most First Nations people in Canada and that established residential schools and banned the performance of the potlatch and other traditional ceremonies. The government's aim with the act was to assimilate First Nations into the dominant Euro-Canadian culture. This prohibition remained in effect for sixty-seven years, until 1951. As Assu has recently written, this strategy bore "very little fruit for the colonial government and drove the Potlatch culture underground for 67 years."[5] In a reflection on the work's complexity and richness, Assu has stated, "The discarded piling of the cups references our movement towards becoming a disposable society; the Canadian government's act of cultural genocide and its systematic discarding of the First People; and the poetic, utopian nature of wealth distribution of the Potlatch practicing peoples."[6] ■

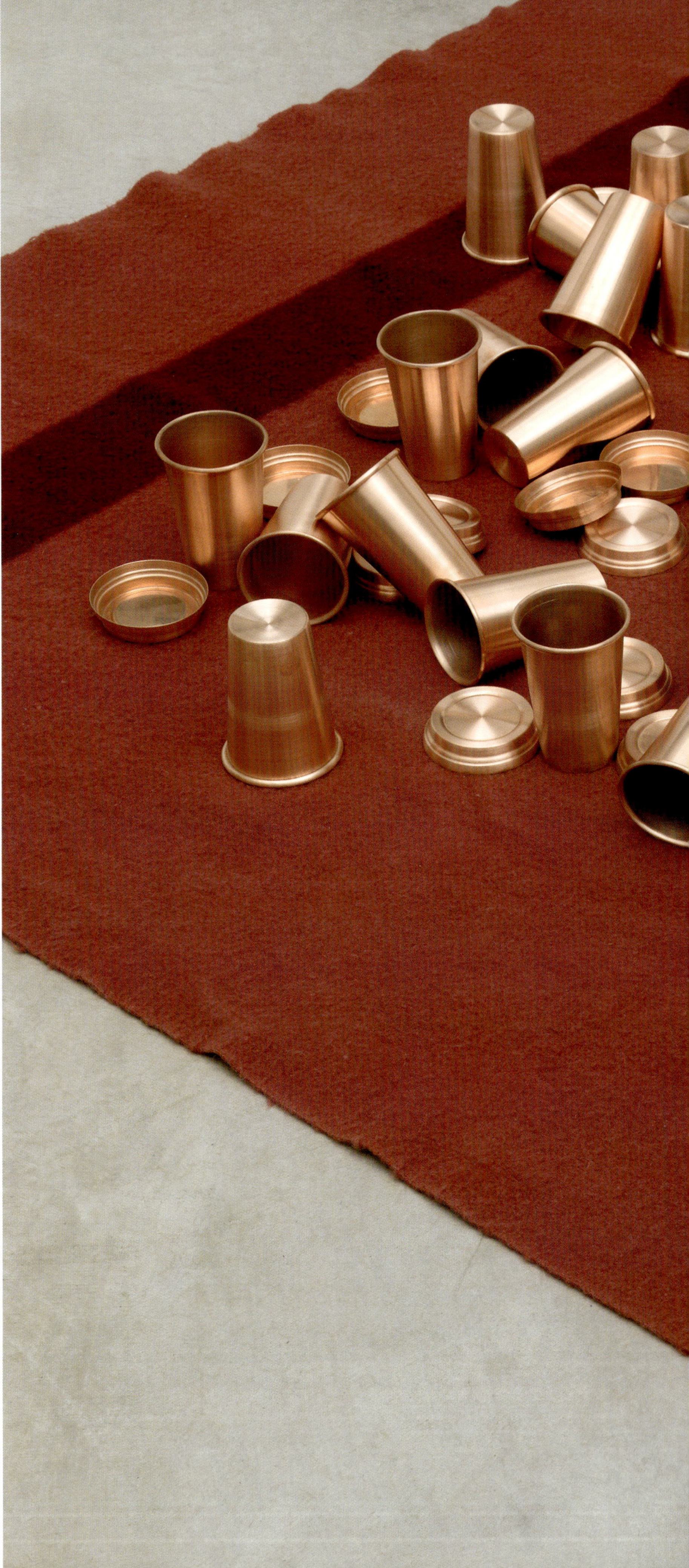

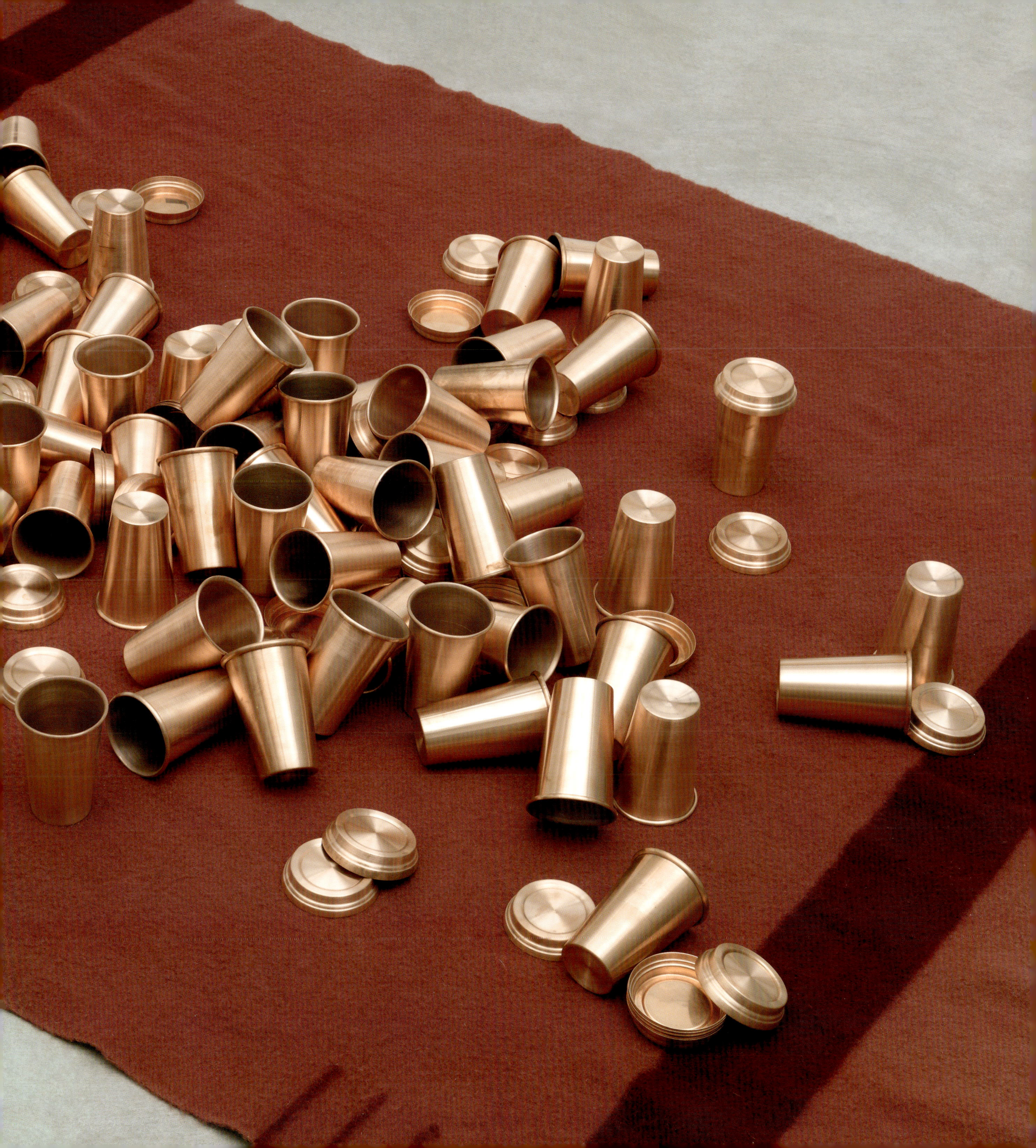

Dempsey Bob
Northern Eagles Transformation Mask
2011

Your vision, how you see, what you try, what you do, that is what is important.—Dempsey Bob[1]

An artist of Tahltan and Tlingit ancestry, Dempsey Bob was born in Telegraph Creek, British Columbia, in 1948. He spent part of his childhood in Port Edward, near Prince Rupert, and while he recalls doing a great deal of drawing as a child he had no familiarity with traditional art forms and did not imagine that art lay in his future. A turning point came in 1969 when he joined a friend in a class being taught by the Haida carver Freda Diesing (1925–2002). Bob says of this period of his life, "So I just sort of fell into it really and I met the right people at the right time, like meeting Freda because there were no teachers at that time. She was our only school, the only person that was willing to help us."

Bob responded quickly to Diesing's encouragement and advice. Although there were few resources readily available, Diesing encouraged her students to look at older First Nations carvings. Bob says, "She showed us what the really great old pieces were and how they were made. It saves a lot of time because when you are searching for stuff, you don't really know what you are looking for. You can learn, but it takes time. She saved us a lot of time by showing us what to look for, where to look for symbols and what to do. That was really good."

Diesing, keenly aware of the importance of teaching, encouraged Bob to teach in Alaska and to investigate his Tlingit ancestry. In 1972, seeking further training, Bob enrolled at the Gitanmaax School of Northwest Coast Indian Art in 'Ksan near Hazelton, where he worked with master carvers Earl Muldoe (Delgamuukw, b. 1936), Walter Harris (1931–2009) and Ken Mowatt (b. 1944). By 1974 he had settled in Prince Rupert and begun his career as an artist. Bob knew that he had to develop his own approach to art making. He also realized that he needed to travel extensively to study older Tlingit works and that understanding them might provide the basis for his own style. Dempsey Bob's eagerness to learn and explore, "to go [his] own way," has characterized all of his work and his career as a teacher. As he once put it, "I think that if you stop learning you are finished." Remembering the importance of a good teacher in his own development, Bob was one of the founders of the Freda Diesing School of Northwest Coast Art in Terrace and continues to act as an advisor to the school.

Bob has been widely recognized for his remarkable skills as a carver, his profound understanding of materials and his rich imagination. *Northern Eagles Transformation Mask* is a wonderful example of Bob's ability to reimagine a traditional form, in this case the transformation mask. He describes the traditional Tlingit migration story that it references: "A group of Eagle people[2] were forced to leave their homes and resettle elsewhere and therefore required to transform themselves." The way he has chosen to depict transformation is highly innovative. Whereas a traditional transformation mask moves and changes to reflect

PROVENANCE: *Artist; Audain Collection, purchased 2011*

▸ Dempsey Bob (b. 1948)
Northern Eagles Transformation Mask, 2011
yellow cedar, acrylic
58.4 × 40.6 × 15.2 cm
Promised Gift, Audain Collection

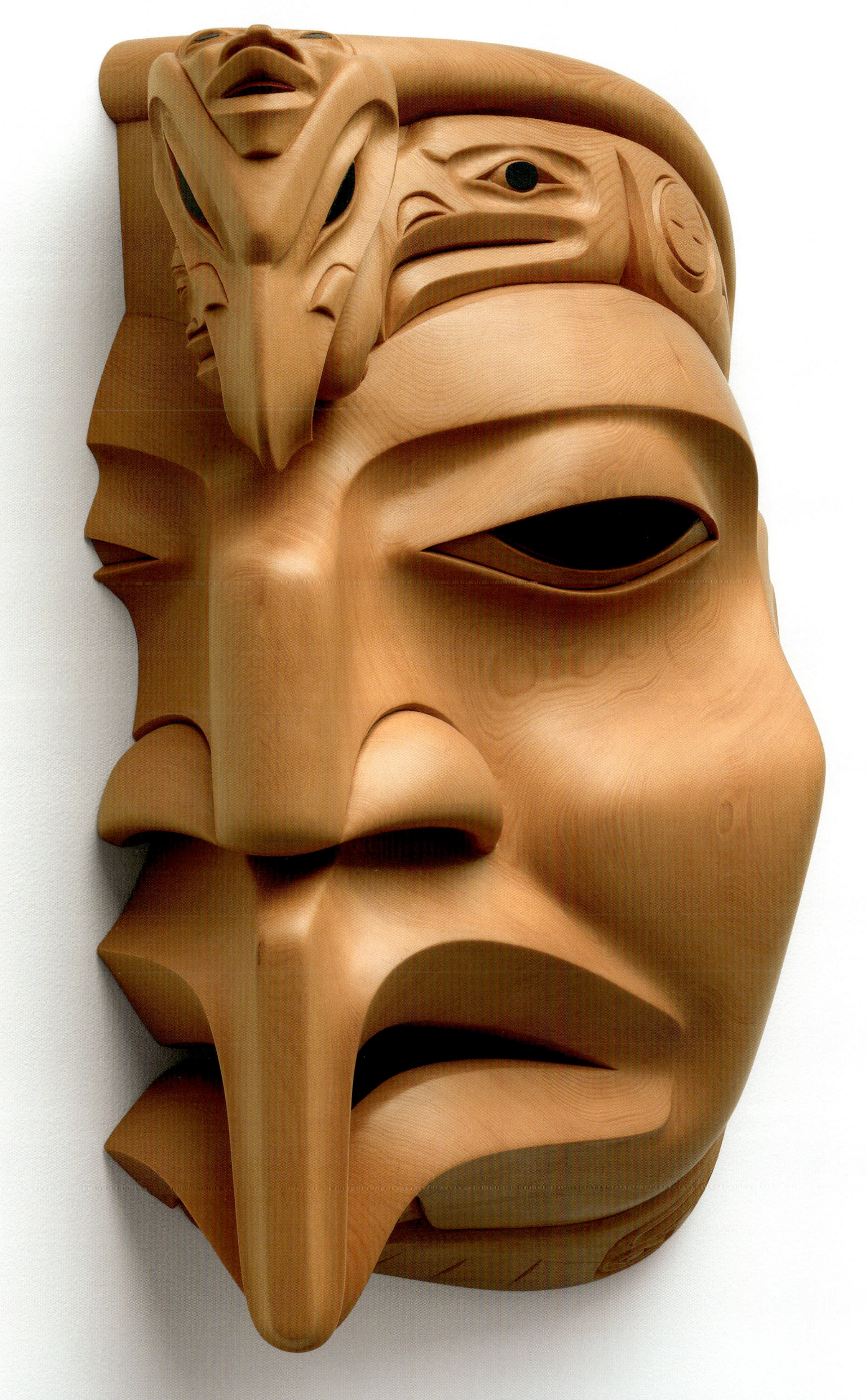

the transformation—an eagle, for example, would open to reveal a human face underneath—this mask catches the beginning of the transformation in a single, asymmetrical block of wood. It is a man "turning into an eagle; his mouth is turning into a beak." Bob further describes the complex imagery of the sculpture, which unfolds almost cinematically:

> I did the little faces underneath, under his chin, to represent the Eagle People. And there's a human on the lip of the mask and then you can see at the top he has got a headdress, and the headdress and carvings on the forehead is the way we show our clan symbols and that's an eagle on there. Then there is Eagle transforming and coming out of its mouth, and a little human on its head, on the eagle's head, the main centre part. And on the sides I did almost like a background. It could be of a crescent moon or something, but I did an eagle in there too. I sculpted it right out, with a lip around it. This is sort of like its eagle headdress to show all eagles. Like there's an eagle in the main figure, an eagle coming out of its mouth and an eagle on the sides. Then what I did different on the other side. On the other side of the main centre eagle there's a human. I changed his face on this side, but you have to look at this side to see it. Then I did a little face on the top, which is Eagle's.

Bob envisions the transforming figure as "emerging from the wall," an idea he thought about during an earlier collaboration with Maori carvers, when he was given too small a block of wood to create a warrior. "So what I did was I got the idea to split it from the corner... I use the corner as my centre line. Technically it shouldn't work, but I make it work in the piece and I make it merge right into the wall." The fluidity of Bob's carving enhances the natural beauty of the wood, and this fluidity is also expressed temporally as this man/eagle figure transforms before our eyes. Accented by only the slightest touches of paint, the work reflects Bob's belief that "if you have really strong sculpture you don't need a lot of paint."

Northern Eagles Transformation Mask reflects Bob's relationship to tradition, spirituality and his own very contemporary vision. He has described his evolution as an artist as trying to "get back to really simple strong forms." In this haunting image, he has masterfully reached his goal, but the real magic of this piece is the complexity of the stories and traditions it so tellingly evokes. ■

Robert Charles Davidson
Dogfish
1999

PROVENANCE: *Artist; private collection, USA; Douglas Reynolds Gallery, Vancouver; Audain Art Museum Collection, 2013.009*

Born in Hydaburg, Alaska, in 1946, Haida artist Robert Charles Davidson grew up in the village of Masset and began carving under the guidance of his father, Claude Davidson (1924–1991). Equally important for Davidson as a young man was his interaction with his grandmother Florence Davidson (1896–1993), who told him many old stories and taught him much about the old ways. At the time, Davidson felt that much of this teaching was not very relevant to him, but as he has matured as both an artist and a man, the importance of these talks with his grandmother has increased.

Davidson's early carving success led him to work with Bill Reid (1920–1998) for several months beginning in 1966. Concurrently (1967–68), he attended the Vancouver School of Art (now the Emily Carr University of Art + Design), where he developed the drawing skills that remain at the heart of his work today. The time spent with Reid allowed Davidson to develop quickly as an artist, and in 1968 Reid recommended him for a teaching job at the Gitanmaax School of Northwest Coast Indian Art at 'Ksan. It was the beginning of Davidson's long career mentoring younger artists.

Davidson's own artistic career has been wide ranging, and he has excelled in several important areas—sculpture, printmaking, jewellery making and painting. He has also become an important Haida singer, and his dance group, the Rainbow Creek Dancers, is one of the most distinguished on the West Coast. Prior to 1969, when Davidson carved and raised a pole in the village of Masset, he had felt that his large-scale carving and the ceremony surrounding the pole raising were separate events. That occasion, however, demonstrated to him that ceremony and art are part of a continuum of Haida culture and history.

Davidson has a long-term fascination with the shark, or dogfish, and *Dogfish* is his largest version of this subject to date. Almost two metres in height, over a metre in width and almost sixty centimetres in depth, the sculpture has a monumental presence and enormous visual power. The dogfish was one of Davidson's father's crests, but Robert Davidson also notes that the great Haida artist Charles Edenshaw (1839–1920) also often depicted the dogfish.[1] Davidson first explored the dogfish's complex form in two prints from 1969 and in three-dimensional form in a rattle from 1971. In the 1970s, Davidson completed a series of six dogfish masks. The exercise was to rough out the mask in a single day and then individually complete each mask differently.[2] He attributes his interest in the dogfish to the challenges of its form but he has also said, "It is just a face that I am fascinated by; it has so many subtleties, so many parts to it."[3]

Although it is sometimes erroneously referred to as a mask, Dogfish is a wall sculpture. It was never conceived of as a mask or an object that might be used in dance or ceremony, unlike the large-scale Shark Mask

(1986), which is danced by the Rainbow Creek Dancers. Davidson has employed many media—bronze, aluminum and many types of wood—but the heart of his sculptural work has always been red cedar, which is found in abundance on Haida Gwaii. Red cedar is also amenable to carving, and the tall trees are the perfect material for the totems that Davidson has carved throughout his career. Indeed, Dogfish is carved from a cedar offcut that Davidson kept from a large commission he received in 1986 in which he created a series of poles for the Donald M. Kendall Sculpture Gardens at the PepsiCo world headquarters in Purchase, New York.

To carve *Dogfish,* Davidson began by working on the mouth, and then moved to the forehead, eyes and nostrils. His sensitivity to both the wood itself and the sculptural form is seen in the remarkable variety of carved surfaces: there are areas that are flat, curved, convex and concave, solid and pierced. A particularly interesting and subtle touch is the use of negative space to depict the dogfish's lower teeth.[4] One of the central tenets of Davidson's sculpture has always been a profound sensitivity to proportion. This is seen here in the powerful, upward curves of the gills, which are balanced by the downward shape of the mouth and lips. The thin carved lines of the gills and forehead decoration are further balanced by the thickness of the red and black lines of the lips, nostrils and eyebrows. The elegant variation of the width of the lines used to carve and delineate the eyes gives them considerable animation and power. And the use of these traditional colours—black and red—on a very untraditional object is an example of how Davidson is both traditional and exploratory in his work.

Although it reads powerfully when seen straight on, *Dogfish* is very much a relief sculpture and Davidson has been fully cognizant of the fall of light on the carving. Areas of shadow and highlight help give the carving depth and substance viewed both at a distance and up close. The interplay of the forms of the face and the planes of the carving are both elegantly simple and enormously visually powerful. This is a serious and impressive image, and the dogfish is clearly a creature to the reckoned with. ■

▸ Robert Charles Davidson
(b. 1946)
Dogfish, 1999
red cedar, acrylic
181.0 × 110.0 × 58.0 cm
Audain Art Museum Collection, 2013.009

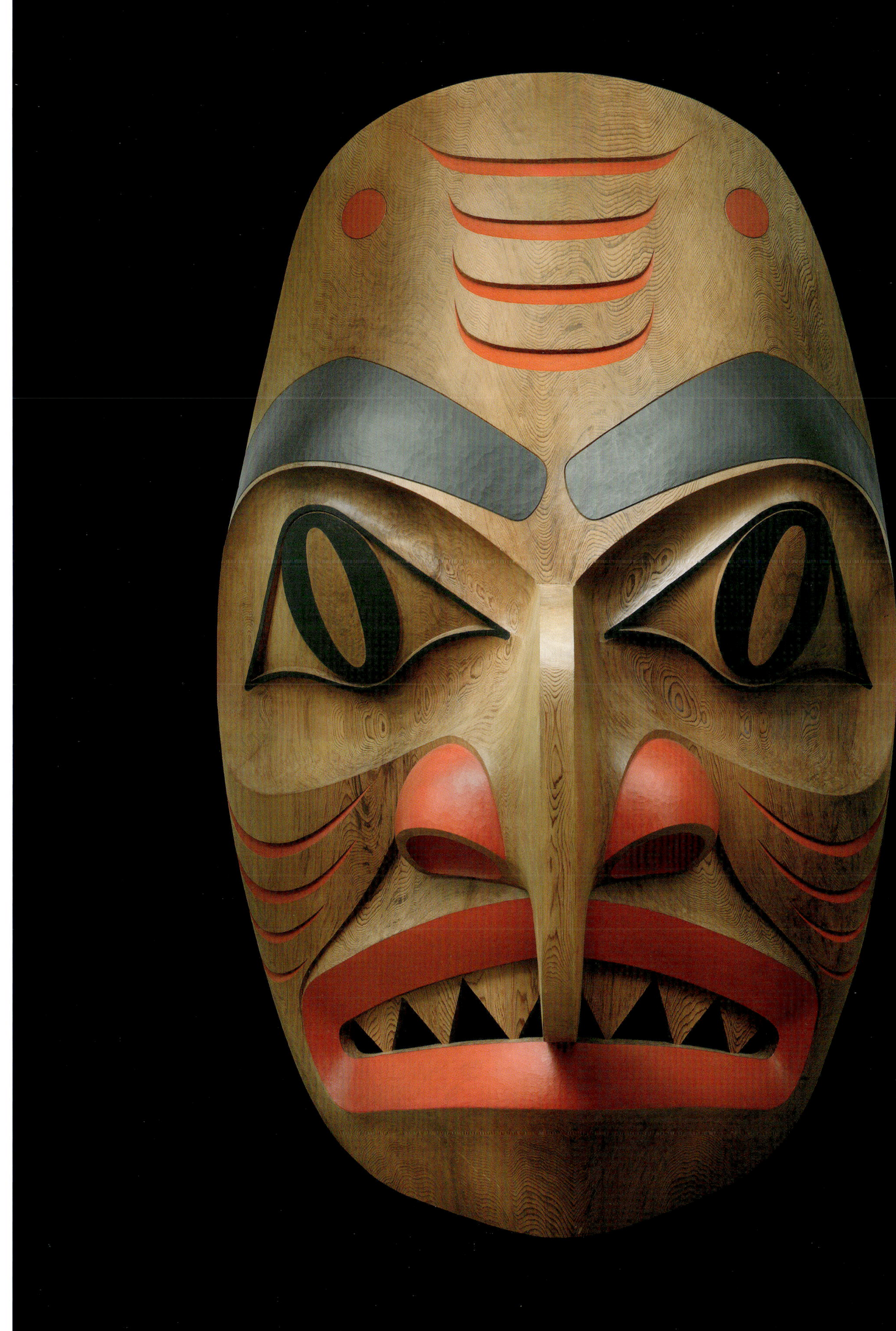

Robert Charles Davidson
Relaxed Symmetry
2003

All contemporary First Nations artists today face the challenge of working in ways that relate to both the traditions of their culture and the realities of modern life. Throughout his career, Robert Charles Davidson (b. 1946) has explored the idea of what Haida art is and can be. This process, which he has several times referred to as "expanding the circle,"[1] has led him to notable innovations in a number of areas of his work. While he was not the first to make screenprints, Davidson is the most distinguished practitioner among First Nations artists working in this medium and one of the most important printmakers in Canada. His use of varied colour and different forms has enlarged our understanding of the possibilities of Haida art. Similarly, his sculptural works have expanded beyond traditional woods (red and yellow cedar, alder, maple) to include epoxy powder–coated aluminum and bronze, and his methods (including boat-building techniques, in his sculpture *Nung Stung Supernatural Eye*, 2006) have helped to move Haida art in new, non-traditional directions. And his approach to painting first on paper and then on canvas has enlarged both his own practice and that of many other First Nations artists who have followed his intrepid lead.

While Davidson will never abandon his Haida roots as an artist, he is constantly pushing himself to make his practice "exciting and challenging at the same time."[2] Davidson wants to retain this sense of excitement both for himself as the maker of the work and for the viewer, and nowhere is that more evident than in his embrace of abstraction. While it can easily be argued that Haida traditional art is highly abstracted (the question of whether a creature is a hawk or an eagle is often posed when looking at a traditional object), Davidson has taken this process to a new level. He recently suggested that he wanted to make a Haida work of art using only two lines and colour. This extreme simplification is only possible because Davidson is so skilled.

Relaxed Symmetry is a wonderful example of his striving to challenge the pre-existing limits of his practice and to expand the possibilities of his art. The work is an exercise in both design and form and a consummate example of his superb skills as a carver. While there may be suggestions of the natural world for some, Davidson sees the work as purely abstract. When asked about the title of this work, Davidson explained: "It came because I was getting kind of tired of symmetry but even so it is fairly symmetrical. If you did a rubbing of one and flipped it over, it is not bang on and so that was really my statement."[3]

Interestingly enough, Davidson first developed this composition in drawings on paper, a method that he continues to use for most of his sculpture. This paper maquette would, ironically, have allowed Davidson to make the work completely symmetrical, but he deliberately chose not to do so. Employing wood from a single milled red cedar board, he completed one panel and then the other. Each panel is divided in half vertically, and within each half is an exquisitely refined carved element that stands in relief. It is both simple and exceptionally exacting. Davidson recently described his

PROVENANCE: *Artist; Douglas Reynolds Gallery, Vancouver; Audain Collection, purchased 2007; Gift of Michael Audain and Yoshiko Karasawa; Audain Art Museum Collection, 2015.016*

▸ Robert Charles Davidson (b. 1946)
Relaxed Symmetry, 2003
red cedar, acrylic
diptych, each
116.8 × 58.0 × 4.7 cm
Gift of Michael Audain and Yoshiko Karasawa; Audain Art Museum Collection, 2015.016

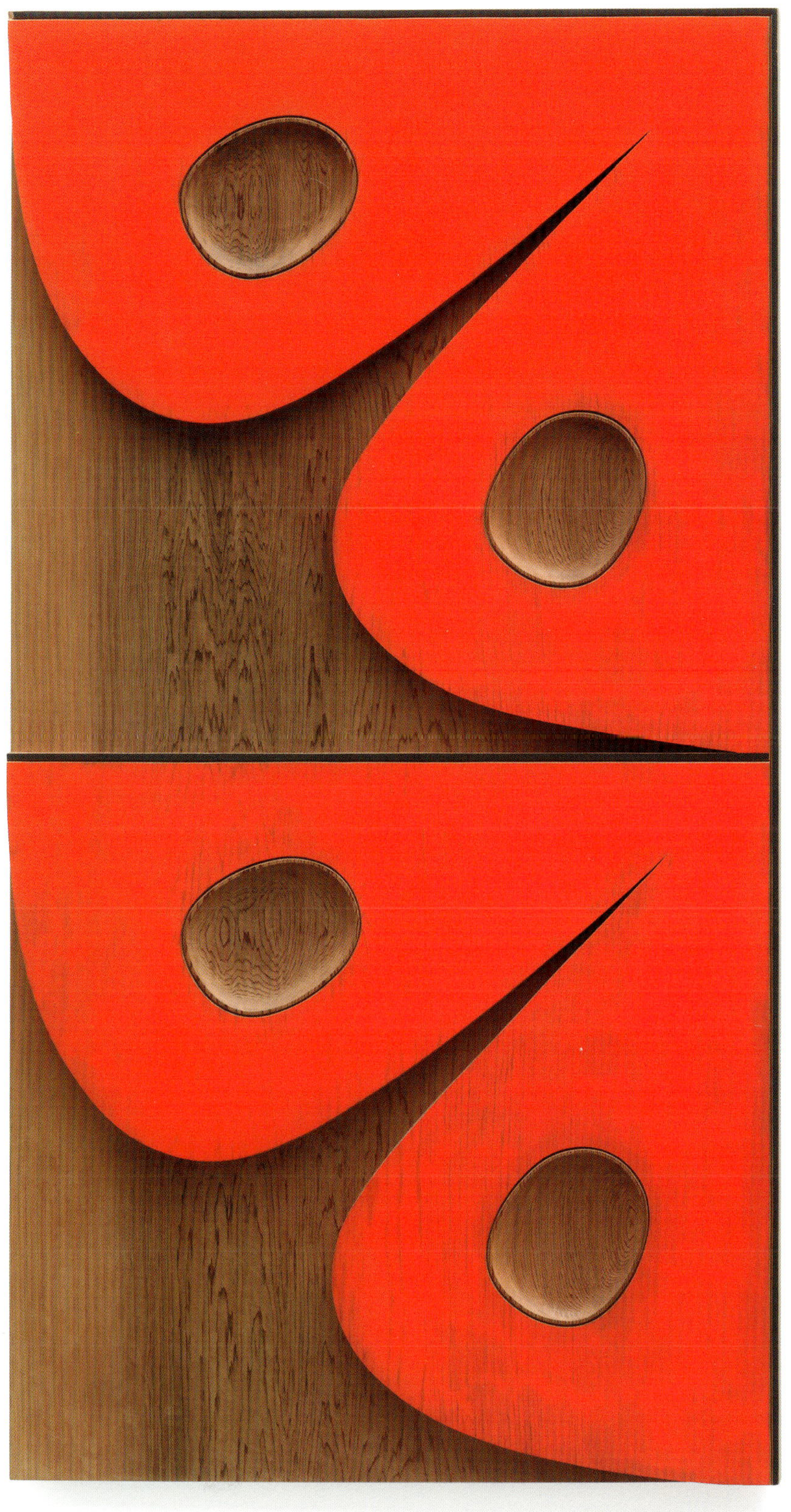
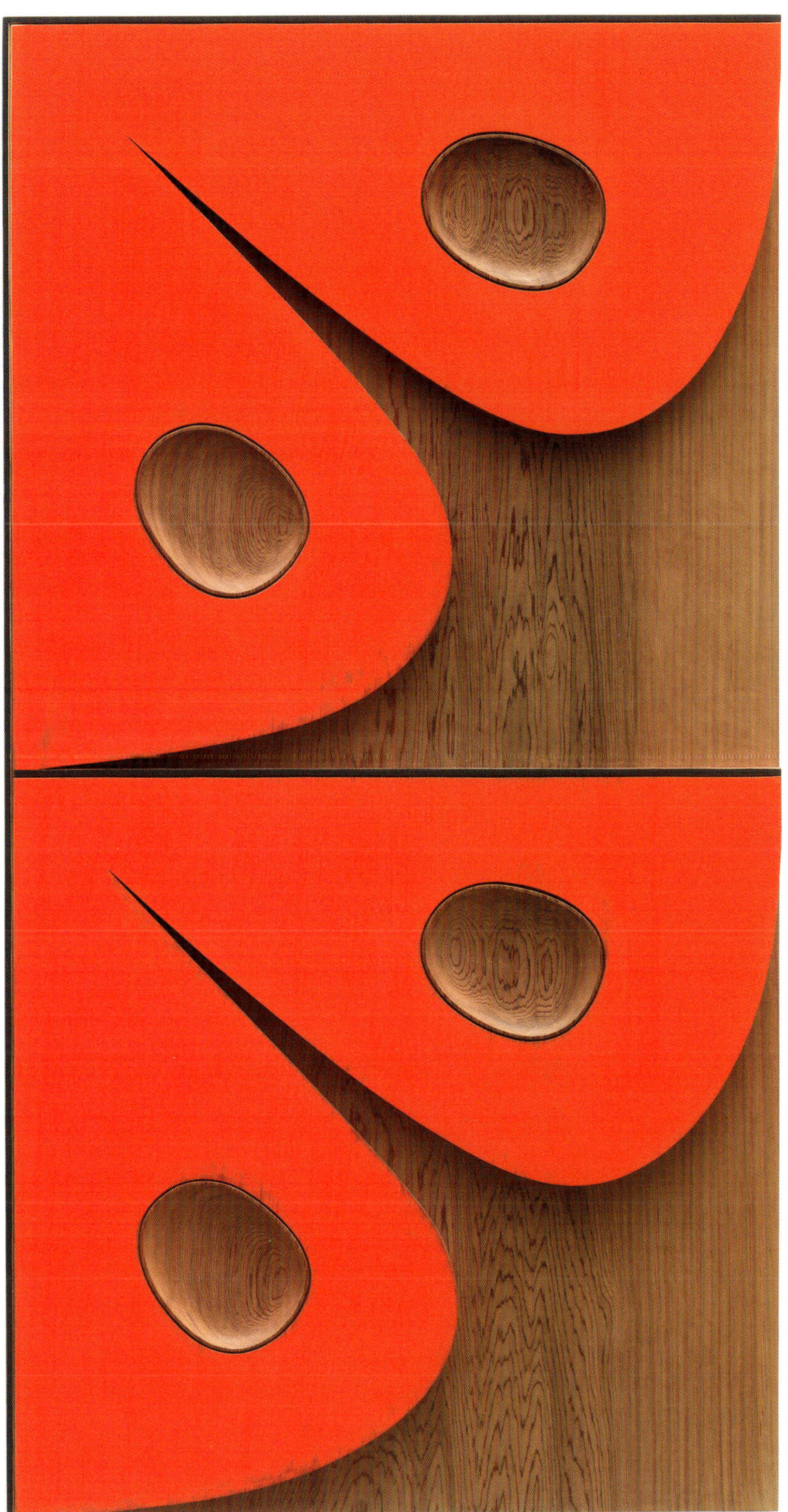

sculptural process: "I like to use the peeling the orange comparison. The object is already in the wood, so all the artist does is peel away that peeling. But we all have different ways of peeling the orange. Sometimes you go too far or else you don't go far enough and that is where intuition comes in."[4]

Here the process of peeling the orange is highly refined, and the success of the work rests on delicate tensions between curved and straight lines, expansion and compression of space, the raw texture of the cedar and the flat surface of the painted areas. A single carved line defines each of the shapes in this work, both delineating the shape and animating the composition as the eye runs along it. The shapes may be opening up and they may be closing. Similarly, depending on the orientation of the two panels around the central axis, which Davidson is happy to have changed,[5] the composition as a whole either expands outward or closes inward. The subtle use of line occurs not only in the carving but also in the use of paint. A single black line divides the panels, and this straight line is balanced by two black egg-shaped lines within the lobes of the larger carved shapes. Inside these egg-shaped lines, Davidson has carved out a concave area. The sides of these shapes have been carved in a gentle curve, providing a contrast to the verticality he's used to carve the sides of the larger shapes. Davidson has suggested that the black lines provided him with a guide for his carving, but they serve a larger compositional function by giving greater definition to the carved areas. Although this work displays a greater sense of freedom and is "more spontaneous, less analytical"[6] than some of his early work such as *Dogfish* (page 109), Davidson is the first to admit that only an artist with "ten thousand plus hours of study" can "get to this level."[7]

Relaxed Symmetry is an image that has both élan and power. It appears effortless but is, in fact, testimony to Davidson's enormous level of commitment to his art. He comments, "Even though it is only one line, that one line will take two or three days for me to do it right."[8] The magic of the work is that it reveals no sense of the work that has gone into making it but an enormous sense of visual delight and ease. It is relaxed. ■

James Hart
The Dance Screen (The Scream Too)
2010–13

PROVENANCE: *Commissioned for Audain Collection, 2008; Gift of Michael Audain and Yoshiko Karasawa; Audain Art Museum Collection, 2013.015*

I tell younger people all the answers are in the old pieces.—James Hart[1]

Born in 1952 in the Delkatla community of Masset, Haida Gwaii, James Hart had a white father and a Haida mother. Perhaps because of his mixed ancestry, he was not sent to residential schools and spent much of his childhood with his grandparents, who were fishers. Following his schooling, Hart spent some time in the fishing industry. It was not until 1978, when he was hired to assist Robert Davidson (b. 1946) in creating the Edenshaw memorial house in Masset (regrettably now destroyed), that Hart turned his attention to art.

The experience of working with Davidson and other artists in Masset laid the foundation for another important period of training, with Bill Reid (1920–1998) in Vancouver. Beginning in 1980, Hart participated in a number of major projects, most notably the great *Raven and the First Men* (Museum of Anthropology, University of British Columbia). By this point in his career, Reid was suffering from Parkinson's disease, and Hart and others became his carving hands. While he worked with Reid during the day, Hart would complete his own pieces in the evening. Inspired by the ideas current in Reid's studio, Hart began to undertake some major experiments of his own, and in 1982 he was the first First Nations artist in British Columbia to complete a bronze sculpture of a pole. The success of this work encouraged a number of other First Nations artists, including Reid himself.

After working for Reid for four years, Hart began to pursue his own projects exclusively. While he has continued to expand his artistic practice, Hart has also devoted considerable time to learning Haida traditional ways—the language, ceremony and cultural values. He has spent extensive time with Haida elders and has carved and erected a major pole in Old Massett village in honour of his family. At this event in 1999, Hart inherited the traditional title Chief 7idansuu, which had previously been carried by master carver Charles Edenshaw (c. 1839–1920), his ancestor.

A spirit of experimentation, closely tied to a deep study of the older Haida pieces, has always characterized Hart's work and nowhere is that more evident than in his most important work to date, *The Dance Screen (The Scream Too)*. A monumental, elaborately carved screen that was three years in the making, it is without precedent in Northwest Coast art. Although there are many examples of dance screens, none extant have the complexity, power and ambition of Hart's recent work. Although the vocabulary of the screen is strongly tied to Haida tradition—a great mother bear, killer whales, frogs, bear cubs (in human form), eagle, raven, beaver, salmon and salmon people—no one would mistake this for an old work. The fact that it is conceived of as a free-standing work has necessitated a major support

James Hart (b. 1952)
The Dance Screen (The Scream Too), 2010–13
red cedar, yew wood, abalone, mica, acrylic
332.0 × 479.0 × 35.7 cm
Gift of Michael Audain and Yoshiko Karasawa; Audain Art Museum Collection, 2013.015

overleaf
The Dance Screen (The Scream Too), 2010–13
details

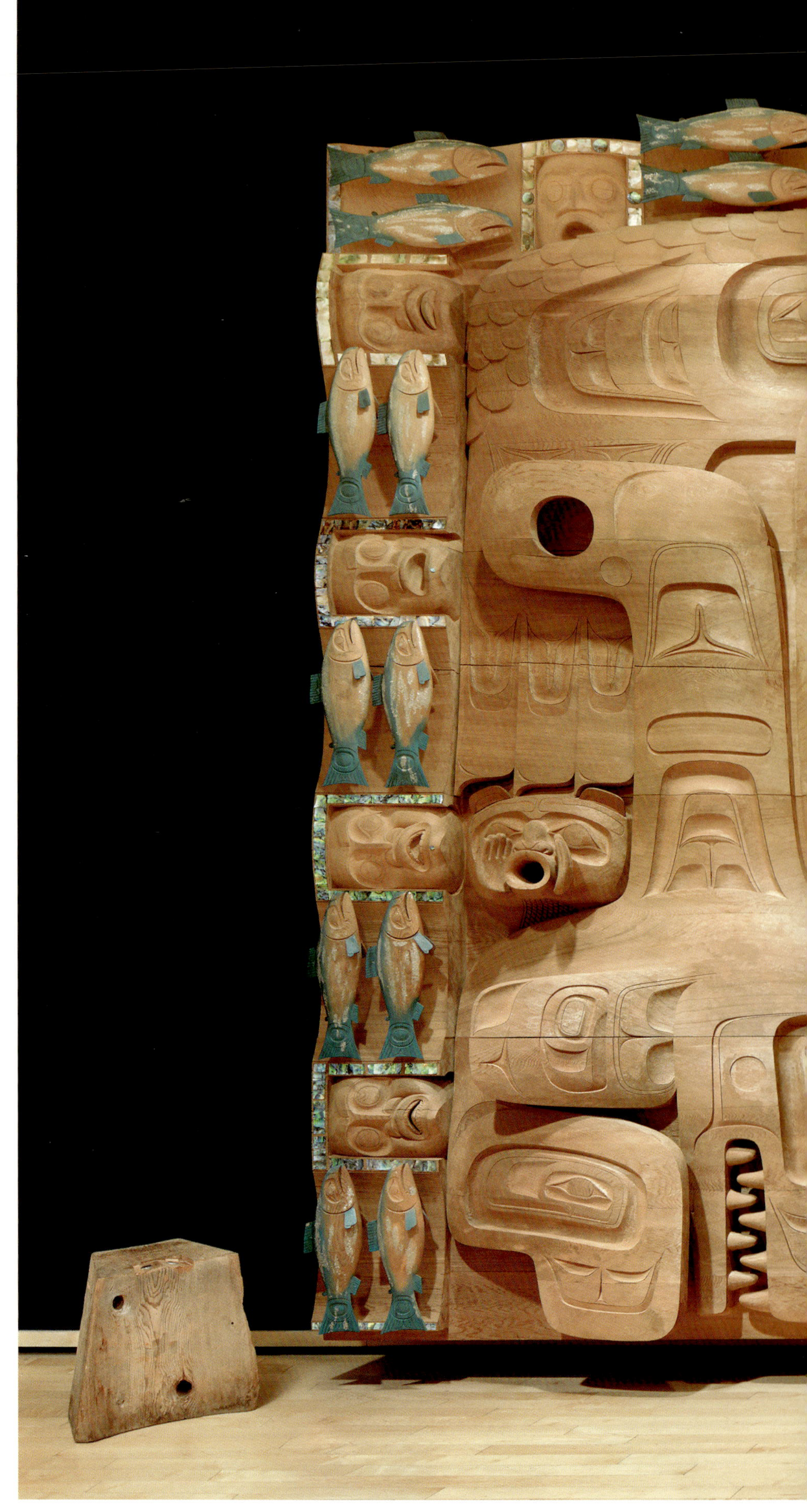

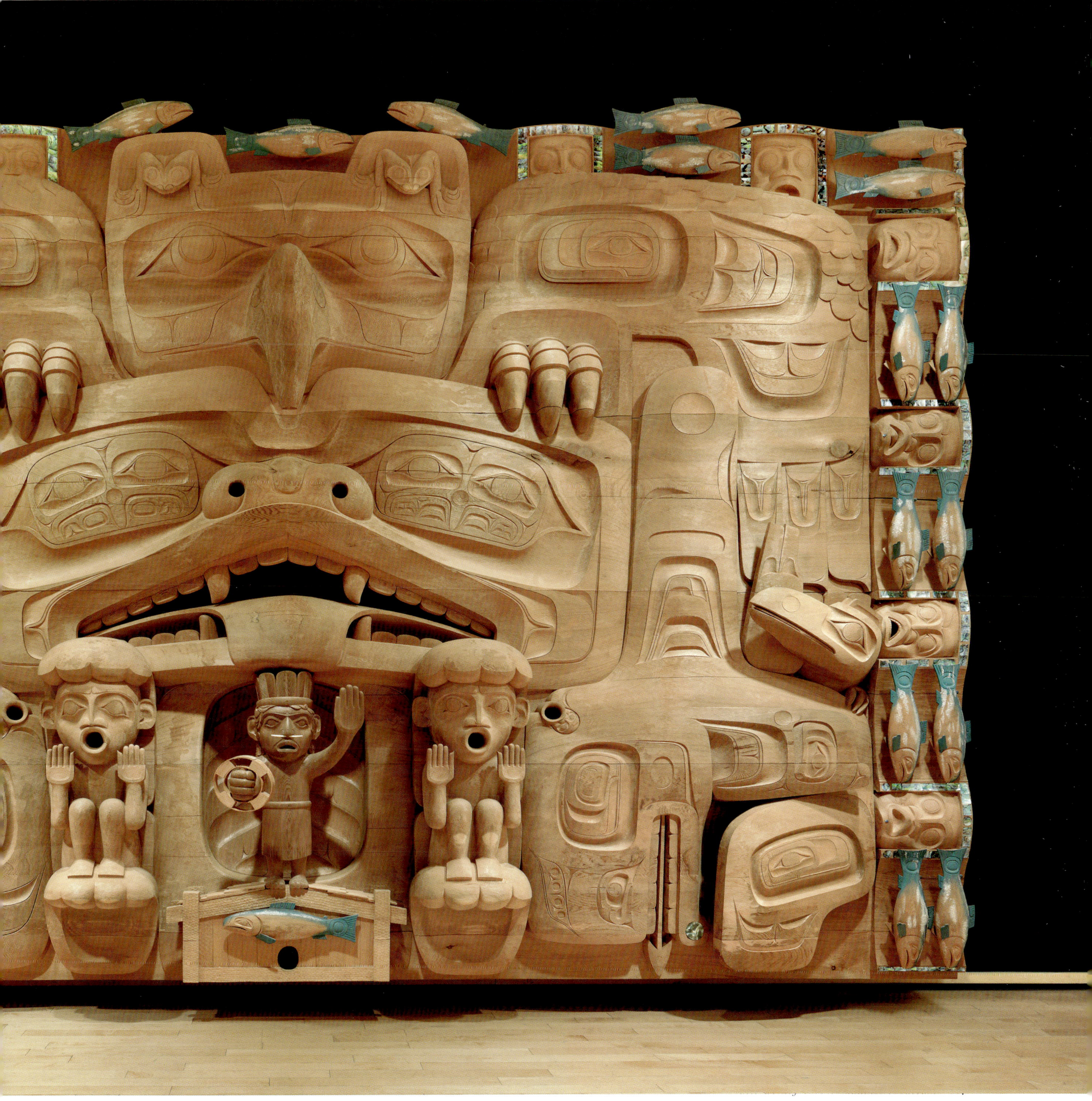

structure that, while hidden, securely places this dance screen in the present day.

Initially commissioned in 2008, *The Dance Screen* began with extensive drawing (a method that both Davidson and Reid emphasized to Hart during his training), and its evolution has been lengthy and complex. Much traditional Northwest Coast design is symmetrical and, at first glance, so is *The Dance Screen*. Closer study reveals, however, that the work, while balanced, is distinctly different on each side of the centre line. To the left as we face the screen is the male realm, represented by the male killer whale, with his massive dorsal fin and large teeth; tucked behind this figure is a beaver crying out. To the right is the female side, shown by a female killer whale, with her smaller dorsal fin and speared tongue, and tucked behind her is the figure of the mischievous raven. In the centre of the sculpture is a massive bear mother figure standing guard over two bear/human cubs that rest on her paws. The bear mother is surmounted by a huge figure of an eagle with frogs emerging from its ears. Around the border of the work is a school of salmon alternating with salmon people. At the base of the entire work is a shaman figure, holding an elaborate rattle and standing atop a model house. Finally, not to be overlooked, behind the shaman figure is a carved door. The shaman figure can be removed and this door opened to allow passage between the world we inhabit and the spirit world animated by the creatures we see on the screen.

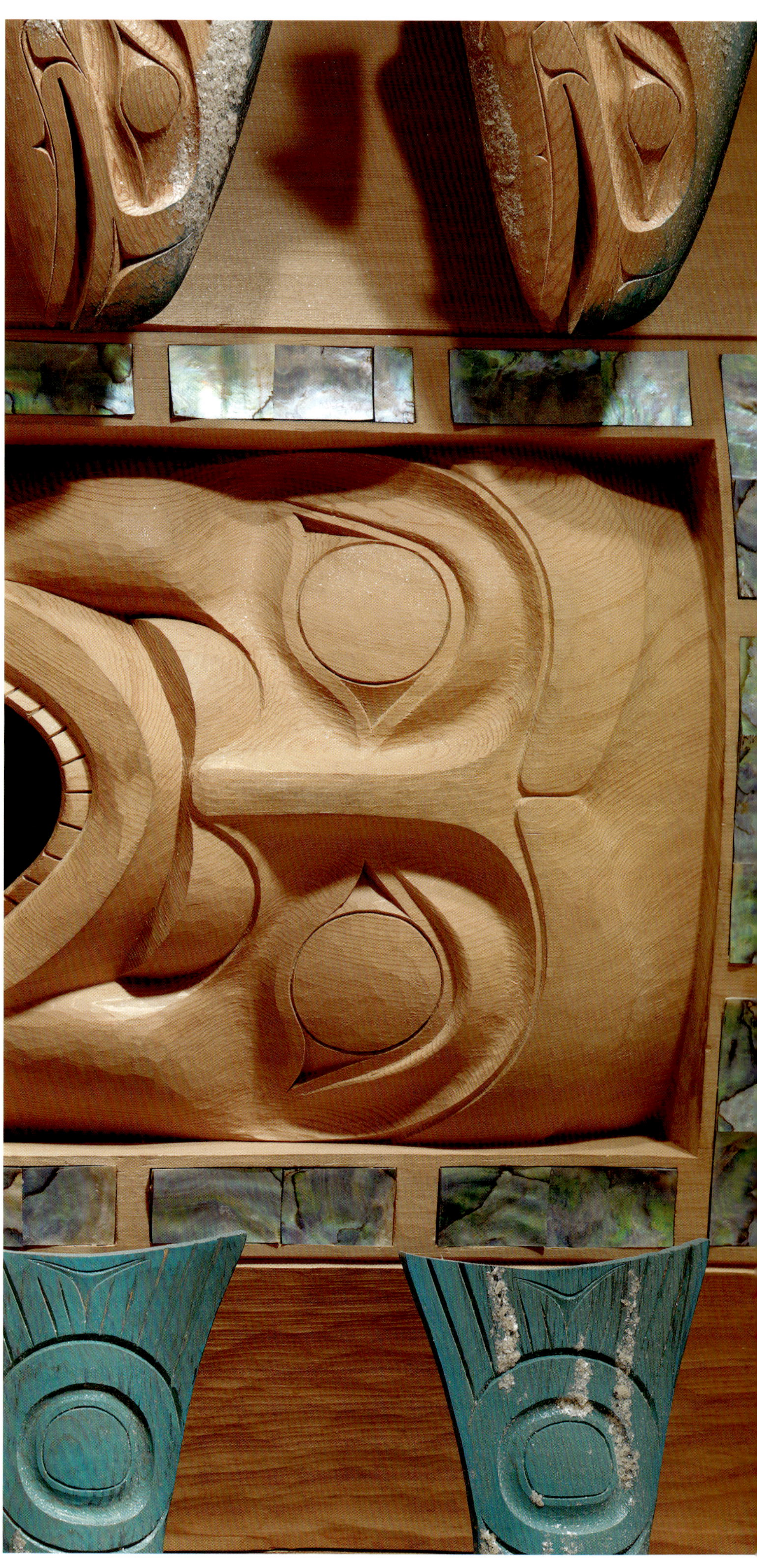

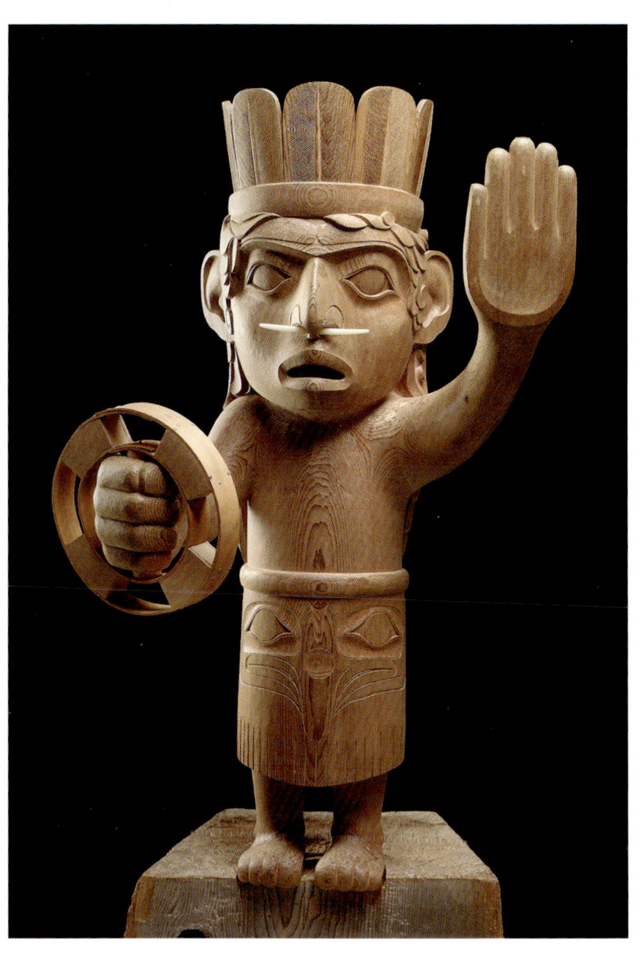
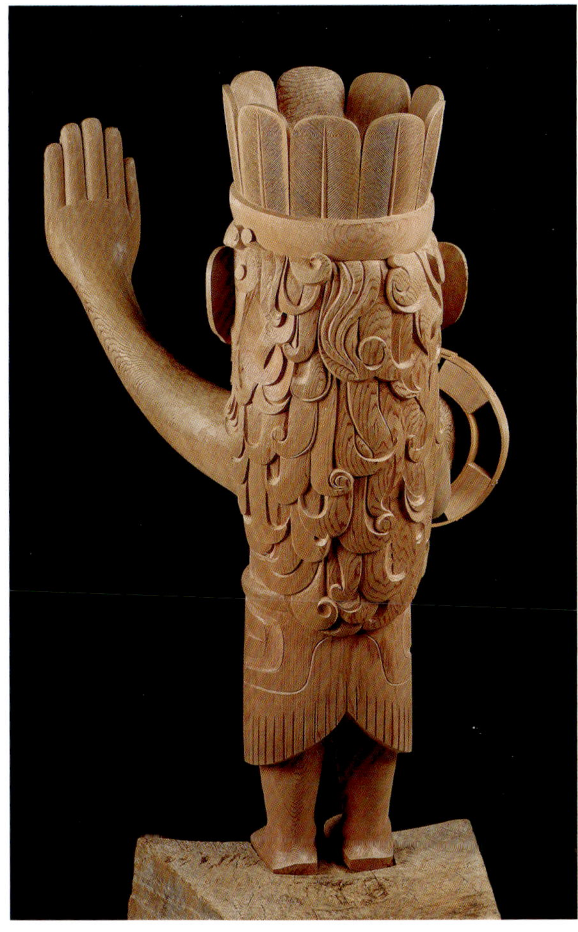
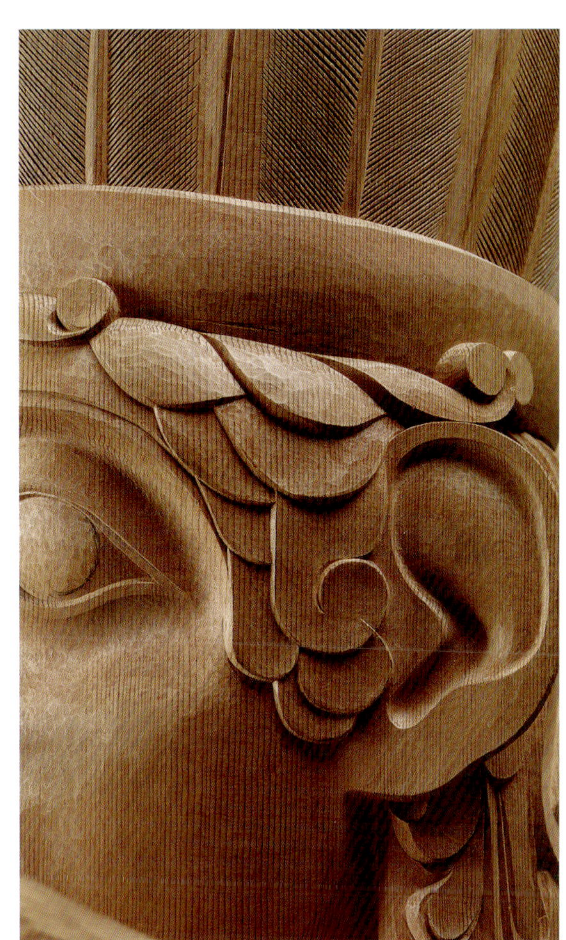
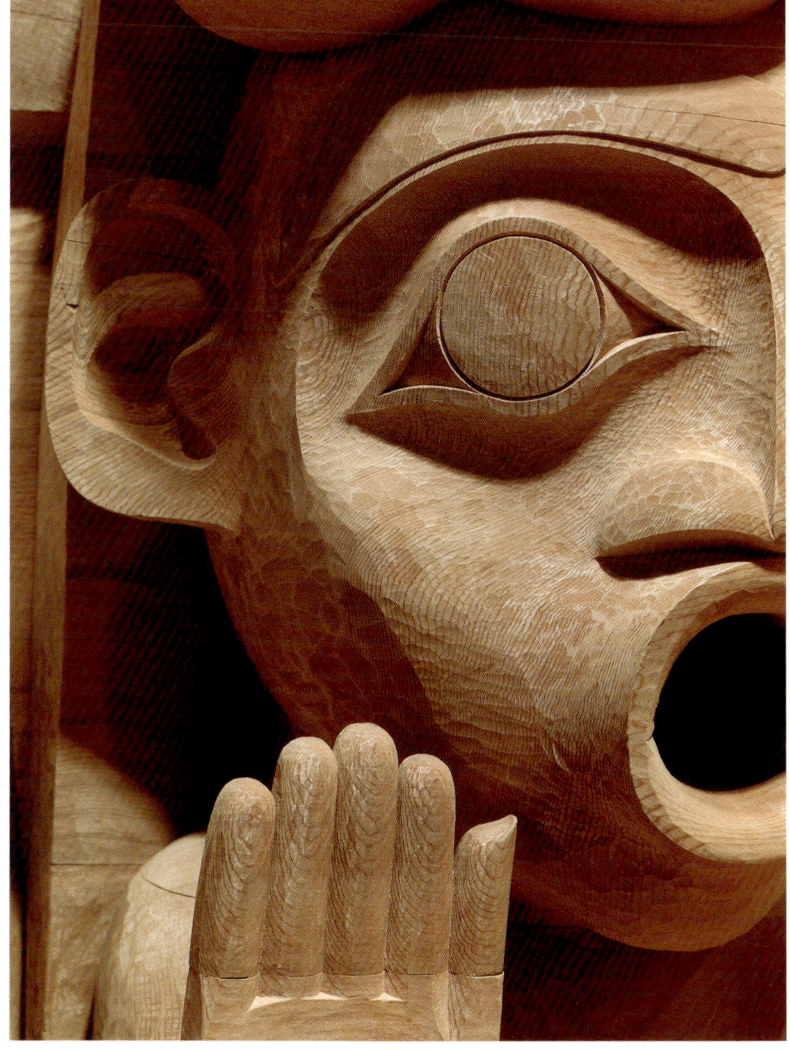
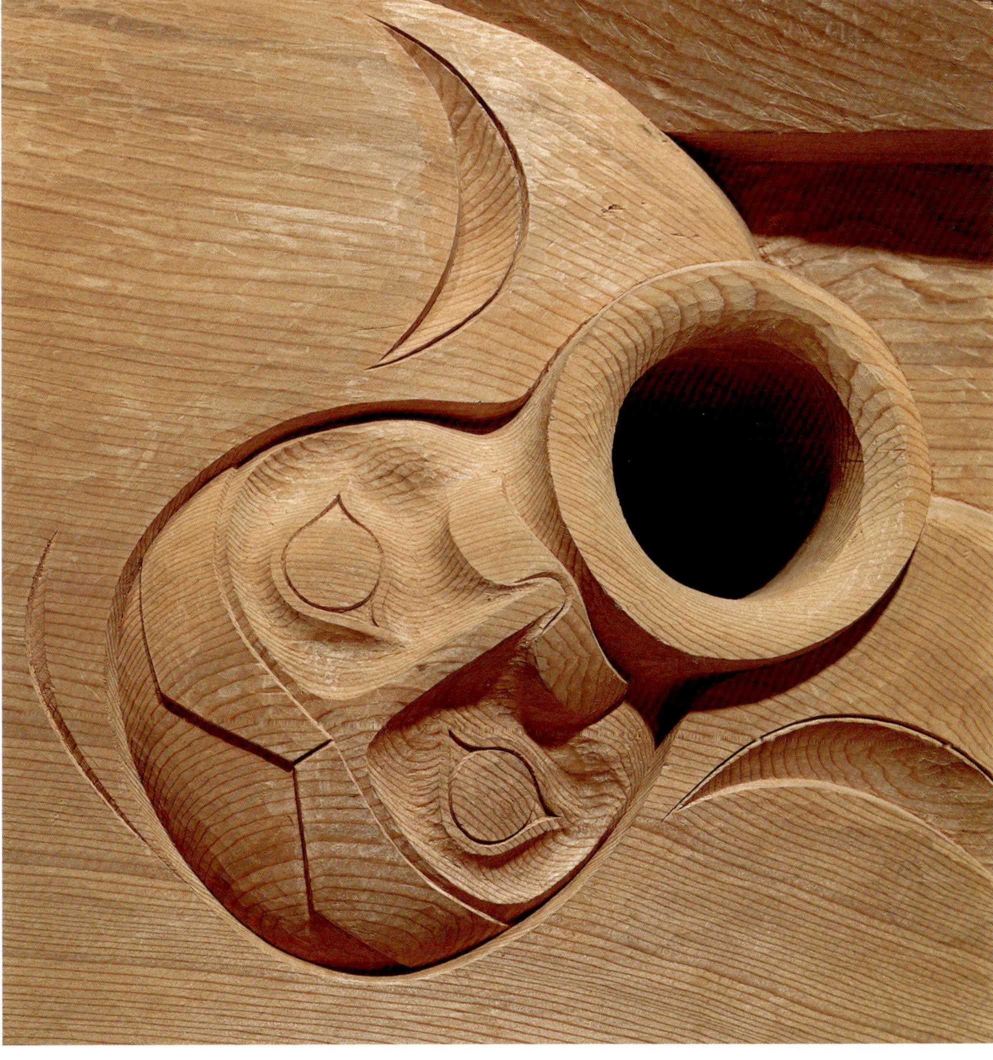

The Dance Screen (The Scream Too) recalls Hart's early work as a fisher rather than as a carver, and it is a wake-up call to all of us to protect the salmon. Every creature in this ecosystem that Hart depicts is dependent, directly or indirectly, on the health of salmon stocks. In Haida history, all creatures have both a human and an animal existence. The small house at the base of the screen is the salmon house, and when the salmon return to that house, they shed their salmon skins and assume human form. Knowing that the Haida depend on the continuation of this ancient life cycle throughout their entire lives is central to our understanding of this work. The screen, when danced, would allow dancers to move from behind it (the spirit realm) to in front of it (our world). In this way, Hart emphasizes the connection of this work to the traditions of the Haida.

Like a great totem, a work of this scale and importance is not accomplished by a single artist. The design is clearly Hart's, but like others before him, he needed other hands to complete the work. Hart had several assistants on the project—his son Carl Hart, John Brent Bennett, Leon Ridley and Brandon Brown. Hart, working with these younger artists, has continued the traditions of Haida learning (by watching a master and by doing) in which he participated himself. The immensity of this endeavour is clear when one realizes that it took several years just to assemble the wood. Hart decided to use fire-killed red cedar from Haida Gwaii. The trees had died in a forest fire nearly a century ago, but the trees themselves remained standing and the wood had slowly been drying since then. Hart selected seven massive pieces of timber to make up the whole work, and he needed to be able to match the individual pieces of wood precisely in order to realize his design.

The finished dance screen is unique because of two major factors: the enormous depth of carving and the fact that it is free-standing rather than incorporated into the rear of a big house. Its title, *The Dance Screen (The Scream Too),* alludes to the famous image by Edvard Munch (1863–1944), and is therefore both a statement about Haida traditional life and culture and a work that speaks to the issues of the present. Hart wants us to be very much aware of our responsibility to shepherd the natural world rather than ruthlessly exploit it. ■

Beau Dick
Dzunukwa Mask
2007

PROVENANCE: *Artist; Douglas Reynolds Gallery, Vancouver; Audain Collection, purchased 2007; Gift of Michael Audain and Yoshiko Karasawa; Audain Art Museum Collection, 2015.017*

Kwakwaka'wakw artist Beau Dick is perhaps the most important figure currently working in 'Yalis (Alert Bay) on Cormorant Island. Born in the village in 1955, he trained with his grandfather, his father and his uncle Henry Hunt (1923–1985). This training began when Dick was fourteen and worked for his grandfather, "hollowing out his masks, painting, sanding for him."[1] This experience gave Dick a great sensitivity to cedar. His skills were further enhanced when he spent a period in Victoria working with Hunt, who taught him "how to sharpen the knives, use the adze, you know, his techniques." Dick later worked with many other artists, including Tony Hunt (b. 1942), Bill Reid (1920–1998), Robert Davidson (b. 1946) and Doug Cranmer (1927–2006). He was part of a team of carvers working under the direction of Cranmer that recreated the 'Namgis Big House in 'Yalis. This wide variety of carving experience gave him a remarkable facility with and a great feeling for the potential of a piece of wood. He notes, "I pick up a piece of wood and I find that the destiny of it is there."

Dick credits another uncle, Jimmy Dawson, with enriching his knowledge of Kwakwaka'wakw tradition and history: "I learned a great deal from him. Knowledge that is passed on, family history, mythological history, protocols, meanings, origins behind things." Dick's appreciation for Kwakwaka'wakw heritage has caused him to become involved in ceremony and the Hamatsa society (a secret ceremonial society) of his nation and it has both imbued his work with the long traditions of Kwakwaka'wakw culture and embedded it within them. Of his art's potential enduring legacy, Dick has commented, "I would hope that future generations will simply look at what I have done and forget who I was, but see it as part of the culture."

Dzunukwa (Tsonokwa or Zunoqua) is a figure that would have been very familiar to all Kwakwaka'wakw, particularly the people of 'Yalis. She is considered a distant ancestress of the 'Namgis people, through her son Tsilwalagame. While respected as a bringer of wealth, she is best known as the Wild Woman of the Woods. Kwakwaka'wakw children were told that if they misbehaved, Dzunukwa (who as a full figure is often seen with a basket on her back) would come and gather them up in her basket and devour them in the woods. Her main sustenance came from eating miscreant children. Her fearsome aspect was accentuated by the call she made—*Hu*—which was sometimes said to be the sound of wind in the forests. Dzunukwa is used in Kwakwaka'wakw dances, and she often appears to mark the end of a feast or potlatch, perhaps to encourage rowdy youngsters to obey their elders and go to bed.

Beau Dick has carved Dzunukwa many times, as a small mask that would be worn in a dance and in larger versions such as this mask.

Although this mask has never been used in a ceremony, if it were to be, it would be carried in front of a dancer rather than worn. Instantly recognizable as Dzunukwa, the figure is large and fierce-looking. There is little or nothing of the feminine and no gentleness in the face of this Wild Woman of the Woods. The use of black over red paint gives her skin an unworldly look, which is enhanced by the bedraggled hair, moustache and goatee. Even her eyebrows are prodigiously hairy. Dick has put particular emphasis on her large lips and open mouth—perhaps howling, perhaps ready to devour a child. The remarkable finesse of Dick's carving, the subtle flow of the folds of the nose and convincing roundness of the lips, as well as the hurt appearance of the squinting eyes, all allow Dick's Dzunukwa to occupy a frightening netherworld—not quite human, but not alien enough to be inconceivable as a different being. Her large size compounds the sense of awe and dread that we feel when confronted by this image, and we can easily imagine how disturbing this figure would be if it were danced in the flickering light of a big-house fire.

This Dzunukwa is firmly rooted in the traditions of the Kwakwa̱ka̱'wakw people, but by choosing to carve the mask so large, Dick has also securely placed this as a contemporary work. It serves as a bridge between Kwakwa̱ka̱'wakw tradition and the modern non–First Nations world, a role which Dick himself also performs with rare distinction. As he has commented, "I express with my hands our people's identity with my artwork, whether it is in a gallery or is used in ceremony. And that is my job, to express our identity, not only in ceremony or its true context but [also] in this modern day. Then these pieces are out there doing their job." ■

► Beau Dick (b. 1955)
Dzunukwa Mask, 2007
red cedar, horsehair, acrylic
133.0 × 65,0 × 40.0 cm
Gift of Michael Audain and Yoshiko Karasawa; Audain Art Museum Collection,2015.017

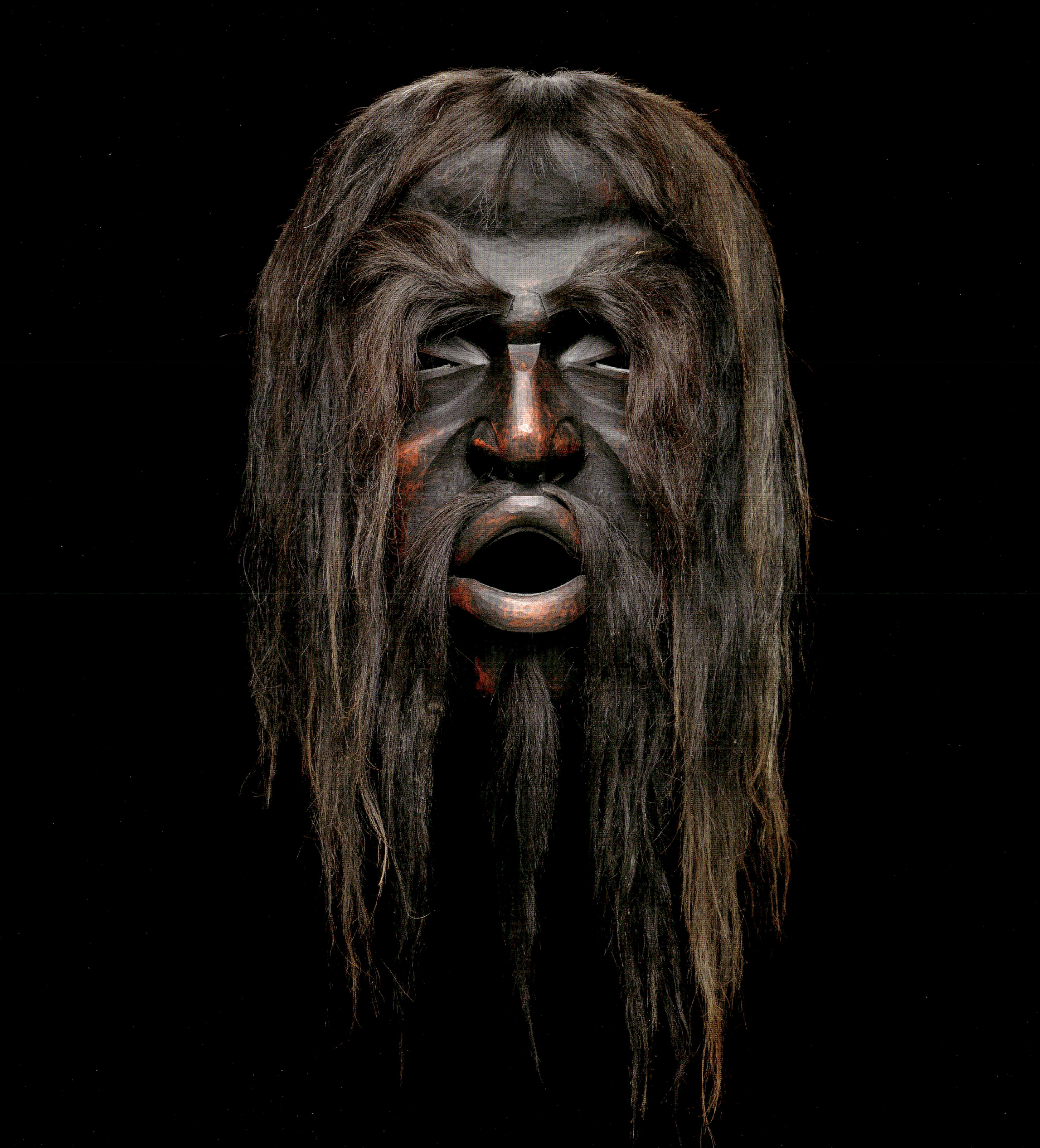

Philip Gray

Porcupine Hunter Mask

2010

Born in Vancouver in 1983, Philip Gray is an artist of mixed Cree and Tsimshian ancestry. Despite the fact that some of his family members are carvers, he grew up in the city and had little exposure to his traditional cultures until he joined a dance group through the aboriginal Synala Housing Co-op, where he lived as a teenager. Ceremonial dance was, therefore, his first exposure to Tsimshian culture, and it remains an important part of his life.

At school he was constantly drawing, though these were generally copies of figures from books and comics. In 1998 Gray was among several young people who assisted the Coast Salish artist Gerry Sheena (b. 1964) in carving a pole during the summer, and it was this exposure to carving that made Gray realize that art was his vocation. He began a process of self-education and a more formal apprenticeship with Sheena.

While working with Sheena, Gray feels he learned the fundamentals of design, basic cutting and using a straight edge and other tools. More critical, however, was his extensive reading and his study. Books such as Bill McLennan and Karen Duffek's *The Transforming Image: Painted Arts of Northwest Coast First Nations* gave Gray an appreciation of form and style, and of the finesse and subtlety of Tsimshian design. When he was unable to find a Tsimshian art teacher, Gray took a three-day design workshop with Haida artist Robert Davidson (b. 1946), who helped him to enhance both his carving and design skills. Although his training had been with Salish and Haida carvers, Gray was interested in moving his own style towards Tsimshian design, which he describes as a "lot more human looking, [with] subtle detail."[1] By 2002, Gray felt confident enough of his skills as a carver to begin selling his work to dealers in Vancouver.

Story, ceremony and dance are important for Gray, and he makes a distinction between masks made for ceremonial use and those made for the market. He has commented that there is "a lot more soul for the works for ceremony with an actual story, but I will use general versions of the old stories for commercial pieces."[2] His experience as a dancer also determines that his masks, even if not for ceremony, could be worn and danced.

Porcupine Hunter Mask is a masterful display of the skills of this young carver. It shows his response to the form and quality of his materials, the grain of the wood being enhanced by both his carving and the paint. The subtle detail of Tsimshian design can be seen in the painting of the eyebrows and the mouse design on the cheek of this mask. Gray has retold the narrative of this striking image:

> The mask is a Tsimshian story about a porcupine hunter that was very successful in this task. It got to the point where the chief of the porcupines was fed up with how many of his people he was trapping. He sent out some warriors to capture the hunter and they brought him to his big house. There he sat the man at one end of the house near the fire. The Chief's people started to drum and sing as he danced around the fire. As he came up to the

PROVENANCE: *Artist; Douglas Reynolds Gallery, Vancouver; Audain Collection, purchased 2010*

► **Philip Gray** (b. 1983)
***Porcupine Hunter Mask*, 2010**
red cedar, acrylic, porcupine quills
60.9 × 38.1 × 25.4 cm
Promised Gift, Audain Collection

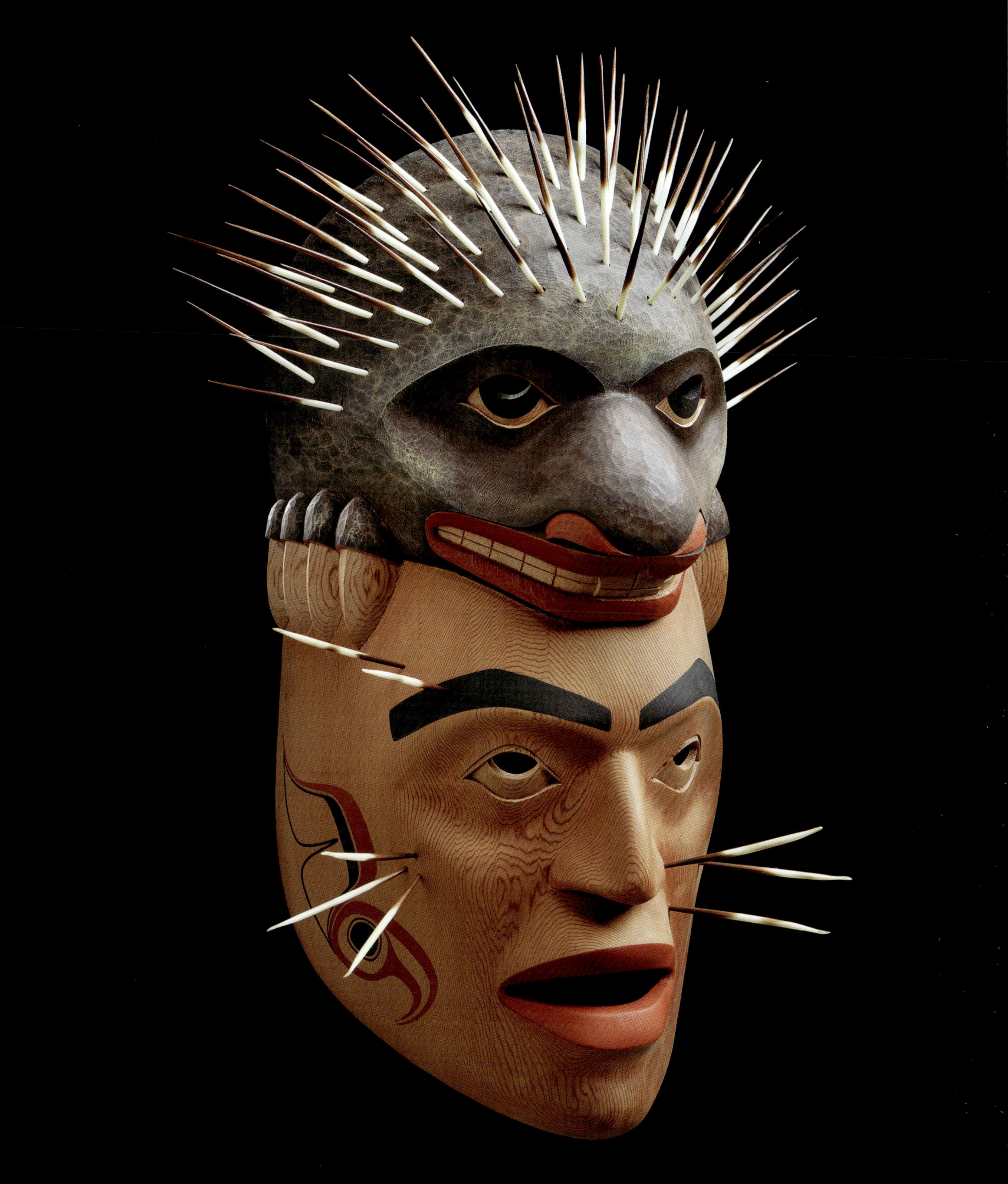

hunter, he would stand in front of him and ask: "What is my name?" He had no idea what his name was and couldn't respond, so the chief struck him in the face with his quill-covered tail. The large porcupine chief would dance around the fire, again and again, with each turn asking him the same question. The man would guess incorrectly and would be struck once again by the giant animal. The hunter was near death, with a bloodied and swollen face. While the chief took one last turn around the fire, Mouse Woman approached the man. She whispered to him the name of the chief. So when he was asked for the last time, he answered correctly. The porcupines rubbed medicine on his face to heal his wounds and take away the swelling. They warned him of his overhunting and sent him on his way.[3]

The mask is a remarkable encapsulation of the complex emotions and actions that drive the story, which strongly appealed to Gray. Both protagonists—porcupine and hunter—are vivid and memorable. One can easily see within their expressions their determination to prevail, and this conviction is something that is not soon forgotten. ■

Brian Jungen
Variant I
2002

PROVENANCE: *Artist; Catriona Jeffries Gallery, Vancouver; Audain Collection, purchased 2002; Gift of Michael Audain and Yoshiko Karasawa; Audain Art Museum Collection, 2015.018*

Brian Jungen's work first attracted international acclaim with the series entitled *Prototypes for a New Understanding*. Created between 1998 and 2005, the series grew to a total of twenty-three works that involved the brilliant reworking of a luxury athletic shoe, specifically the Nike Air Jordan. Jungen took apart this apparently unsympathetic source material and reassembled the shoes to create striking sculptural works that are reminiscent of First Nations masks from the British Columbia coast. With their white, red and black colour, the shoes evoked, for Jungen, the traditional colours (specifically red and black) found in First Nations masks.

Jungen was born to a Dane-zaa mother and a Swiss father in Fort St. John, British Columbia, in 1970. He completed his education in Vancouver, graduating from the Emily Carr College of Art (now Emily Carr University of Art + Design) in 1992. His exhibition career began five years later, in 1997, with both a solo exhibition in Calgary and a group exhibition in Vancouver. Since that time Jungen has exhibited extensively around the world, creating works that combine ideas of contemporary art and aboriginal culture.

Appropriating seemingly unsuitable consumer materials as a source for his artwork has characterized much of Jungen's career to date. Moreover, he is not afraid to challenge convention, as he describes: "I went to a sports store and purchased a number of pairs of Air Jordan sneakers and began to dissect them, which in itself was interesting in that it was almost a sacrilegious act: cutting up and 'destroying' these iconic, collectible (and expensive)

► Brian Jungen (b. 1970)
Variant I, 2002
Nike athletic footwear
132.1 × 108.0 × 21.0 cm
Gift of Michael Audain and Yoshiko Karasawa; Audain Art Museum Collection, 2015.018

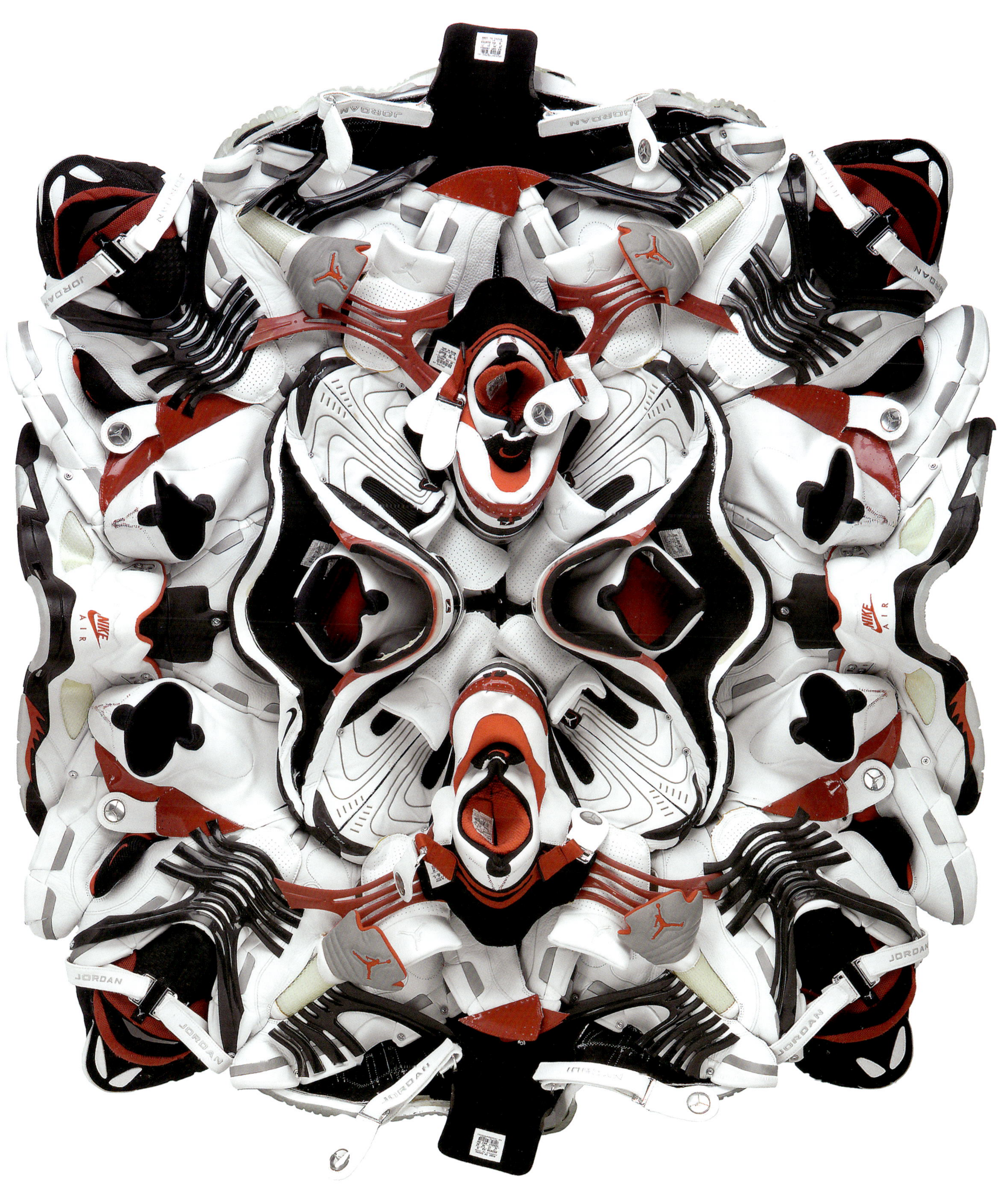
JORDAN
NIKE
AIR

shoes."[1] What marks Jungen as an artist, however, is that while he does destroy the sneakers, it is so that he can create something else. Far from being sacrilegious, Jungen's actions might be described as sacred and creative in the best way, turning something highly prized yet literally pedestrian into a work of art that is transcendent.

Variant I is not part of the *Prototype* series, though it uses the same source material. It was Jungen's first use of the Nike Air Jordans in a work that does not echo First Nations masks, and it was done in the middle of the series. The *Prototypes* were limited to twenty-three works because Michael Jordan's number, when he played basketball for the Chicago Bulls, was 23. *Variant I* thus allowed Jungen to explore the use of the Air Jordans in a way that was unrelated to First Nations masks.[2] (It is important to note, however, that Jungen never saw the *Prototypes* as masks because they were never used in ceremony. They were always seen as art objects that alluded to rather than copied older First Nations material.) *Variant I* may be seen as a bridge between the earlier, more contained *Prototypes* and the later, more expansive ones.

Here Jungen addresses the history of modernist painting rather than the traditions of First Nations mask making. (Interestingly, First Nations masks allow the wearer to transform themselves into the creature or entity represented in the mask, and Jungen's work here might be said to accomplish a parallel transformation.) The pattern that Jungen has created seems to suggest that there is an explosive outward movement from a central point. The swirling lines created by the colours and shapes of the shoes and by their stitching suggest a sense of boundless energy (akin to the swirling forms of Abstract Expressionist art), and yet Jungen has contained this energy by making the form of the work roughly square. He has given the work axes by emphasizing the tabs of the sneaker's tongues at the top and bottom of the composition and by emphasizing the sole elements at the right and left edges. With this work, Jungen brilliantly explicates the challenging place that people of mixed ancestry often occupy within the world: neither of one culture and place nor of another. While Jungen has clearly spent a great deal of time thinking about his own First Nations ancestry and cultural ways, he cannot divorce himself from the outside world and his interest in modern art. *Variant I* sits between these two worlds and requires us to consider both of them when we view the work. It is a hybrid, and as such tells us much about our world and how each of us must adapt to survive and succeed. ■

Marianne Nicolson
Tunic for a Noblewoman: In Memory of 'Wadzidalaga
2009

Kwakwaka'wakw artist and scholar Marianne Nicolson was born in Comox, British Columbia, in 1969. She grew up in Victoria and Vancouver but spent summers in the ancestral territory of her family in Kingcome Inlet on British Columbia's central coast. Nicolson, who always wanted to be an artist despite the fact that it was not the cultural norm for women within Kwakwaka'wakw culture, has long been interested in her culture's stories and ceremony. She has completed doctoral studies in

PROVENANCE: *Artist; Audain Collection, purchased 2009*

► *overleaf*
Marianne Nicolson (b. 1969)
Tunic for a Noblewoman: In Memory of 'Wadzidalaga, 2009
acrylic, brass, copper, silver, coins, abalone shell on wood
diptych, each 129.5 × 124.4 × 7.7 cm
Promised Gift, Audain Collection

Kwak̓wala (the language of her people), the first person ever to do so, and her artistic practice is strongly rooted in the language and traditions of the Kwakwa̱ka̱'wakw and her own family.

Nicolson studied art at Emily Carr Institute of Art and Design (now Emily Carr University of Art + Design), and in addition to her regular program of studies she worked extensively with Kwakwa̱ka̱'wakw carver Wayne Alfred (b. 1958), who taught her the traditional forms and carving. As a painter, her work has been marked by both a desire to locate herself and her family within the Kwakwa̱ka̱'wakw culture but also within the larger world. As she has commented, "The work is also biographical, an attempt to explore who I am and what is my place in the world. First step, who are your parents? And I have tried to go back further. Politics occupies a large sense of my identity and my desire to keeping the culture strong."[1] This means that the work has a profoundly personal meaning as well as a larger political purpose: "My desire for making artworks wants to understand the human experience. I do have an agenda. I do feel that we are, as a people, struggling to preserve our cultural traditions. As I grew up, I felt that I wanted this tradition to continue, even if the manifestation changed."[2]

Tunic for a Noblewoman: In Memory of 'Wadzidalaga̱ was first exhibited in *Continuum* at the Bill Reid Gallery of Northwest Coast Art in 2009. That exhibition presented work by a number of First Nations artists that explored "the complexity of the terms of exchange between the historical past and the contemporary presence of cultural and artistic practice."[3] This is, of course, exactly where Nicolson places the work she makes for the non-Kwakwa̱ka̱'wakw community. While acutely aware of the traditions and forms of Western painting, her imagery is informed by Kwakwa̱ka̱'wakw culture and history. This duality of purpose is manifest in all of Nicolson's work and is certainly true of *Tunic for a Noblewoman*.

The two panels present a considerable visual spectacle. Rich in texture and form but subtle in their use of colour and design, they are given greater depth by their reference to the life of Nicolson's grandmother, 'Wadzidalaga̱ (Emily Mary Scow). The tunic form references traditional garments worn by Kwakwa̱ka̱'wakw people. It also recalls the life of 'Wadzidalaga̱, whose birth in 1913 is marked in the pattern of pennies and in the sixteen quarters inlaid as eyes on the eight coppers that recall the birth of each of her sixteen children before she died at the age of forty-three, in 1956. They also reference the Kwakwa̱ka̱'wakw practice of giving away coins to mark the birth of a child. There are larger references to Kwakwa̱ka̱'wakw values in the *sisiutl* (double-headed serpent) that adorns the tunic. For Nicolson, the *sisiutl* "represents the traditional balance between the value of men and women amongst the Kwakwa̱ka̱'wakw."[4] Finally, Nicolson has painted the decoration of the tunic as if it were made of dentalium shells, which have a specifically feminine reference because these shells were, in addition to being a currency among First Nations of the coast, used in puberty rites for girls.[5]

While one can appreciate this striking work as a powerful formal visual statement, the painting is immeasurably enriched by understanding its larger context for Nicolson and the Kwakwa̱ka̱'wakw. *Tunic for a Noblewoman* is very much of the present, but it has complexity and sophistication and, through its strong connection to the past, it also has great depth. ■

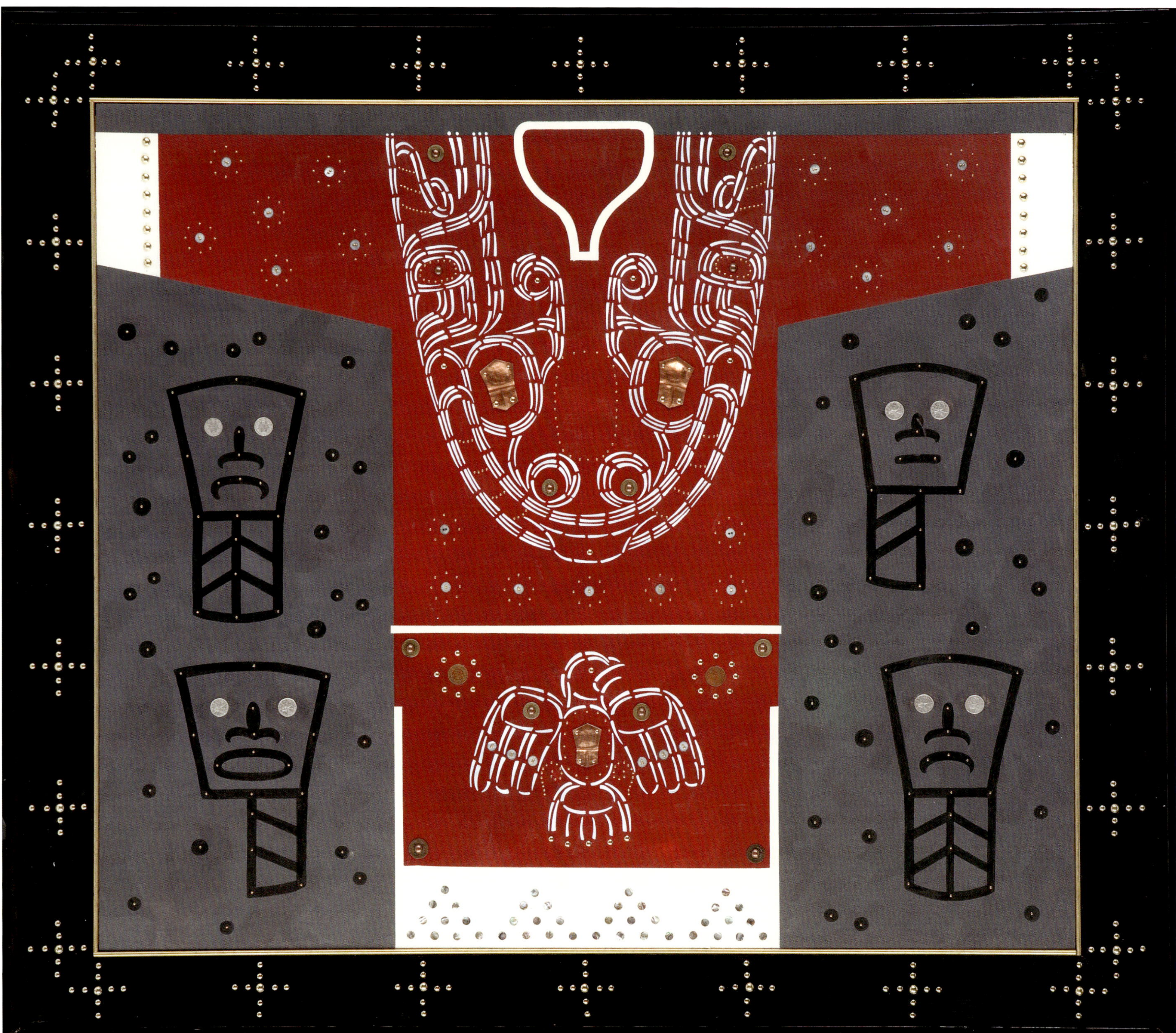

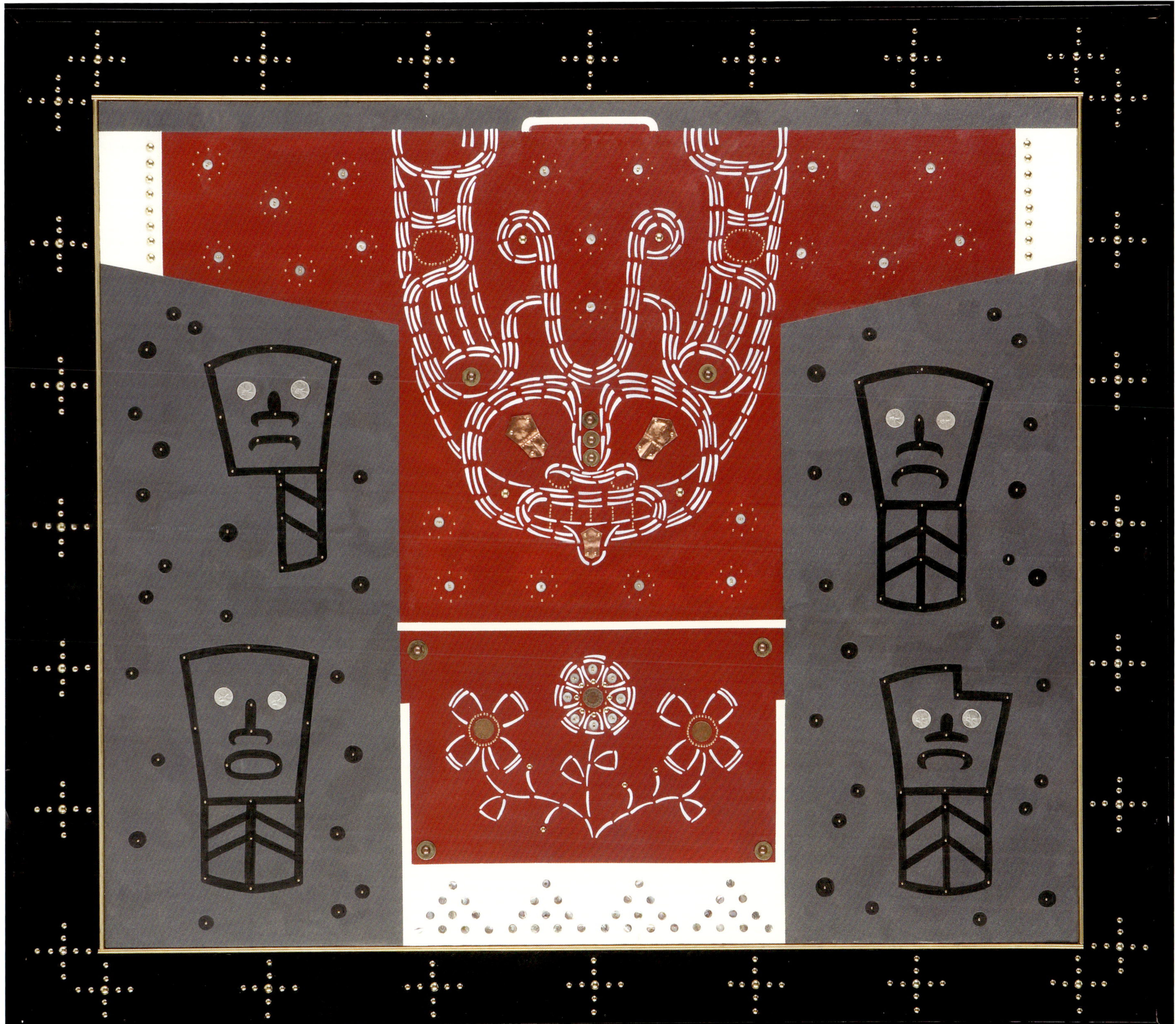

Jay Simeon
Sea Wolf and Killer Whale Mask
2008

Born to a Haida father and a Paigan mother in 1976 in Fort Macleod, Alberta, Jay Simeon moved to Vancouver after early childhood, following the divorce of his parents. He first saw Haida work in books shown to him by his father, and Simeon's aunt, Sharon Hitchcock (b. 1952), an experienced argillite carver, provided him with his first training. Working with her, he spent a great deal of time drawing, and drawing remains a critical part of his process today. He reinforced this solid knowledge of Haida design elements during a design course that he took with Robert Davidson (b. 1946) in 2000–1. Simeon has applied this knowledge to a variety of media—gold, silver, argillite and wood—and he has excelled in all of them. It is, however, as a woodcarver that he is most keen to establish his reputation because "all the great ones did wood."[1]

Simeon wants to position his work in the larger traditions of Haida art and, at the same time, to be seen as a contemporary artist. "Older pieces are really important to me. I look at older pieces all the time," he says, but explains that he is interested not in copying older masks but in drawing inspiration from them. At the same time, he is also influenced by the world around him today. Constantly refining his skills and the use of the ovoid, U form and formlines allow him to move his work towards "the intangible essence of the art."

Simeon conceives his work completely before he begins carving. This is through a process of either drawing or visualizing the final piece. Although he has only been carving wood since 1997, when he studied with artist Gary Leon (b. 1968), he has quickly emerged as one of the most gifted carvers of his generation. *Sea Wolf and Killer Whale Mask* is a splendid example of his vision as an artist and his mastery of carving. Of this mask—or perhaps more correctly, headdress—Simeon has said, "Sea wolf, in the story he would catch the killer whales and then put them in front of his house; in argillite sculptures, he always has three. He has his breakfast for the morning, orcas. Teeth are inlaid holly wood, paua shell, copper on eyes. Don't think that a dance exists for him. I am going to take it to the point where it could be danced and be brought to life. It is something that will be worn on top of the head and see through the cedar bark." That Simeon has created a mask or headdress capable of being used in ceremony speaks of his conscious connection to older traditions of ceremony, even though he has, because of the circumstances of his own life, had little direct experience of ceremony. His interest in illustrating an older legend of the sea wolf, or wasco, despite the fact that he doesn't know of a dance directly connected to this figure suggests that Simeon is, like fellow Haida Robert Davidson and James Hart (b. 1952), interested in expanding the traditional language.

Simeon's powerful and fearsome sea wolf shows enormous sensitivity to his materials. It has a precision in carving that compares to the exacting requirements of argillite. Yet as

PROVENANCE: *Artist; Spirit Wrestler Gallery, Vancouver; Audain Collection, purchased 2008*

▶ Jay Simeon (b. 1976)
Sea Wolf and Killer Whale Mask, 2008
alder, holly, horsehair, cedar bark, paua shell, copper, acrylic
58.4 × 35.6 × 25.3 cm
Promised Gift, Audain Collection

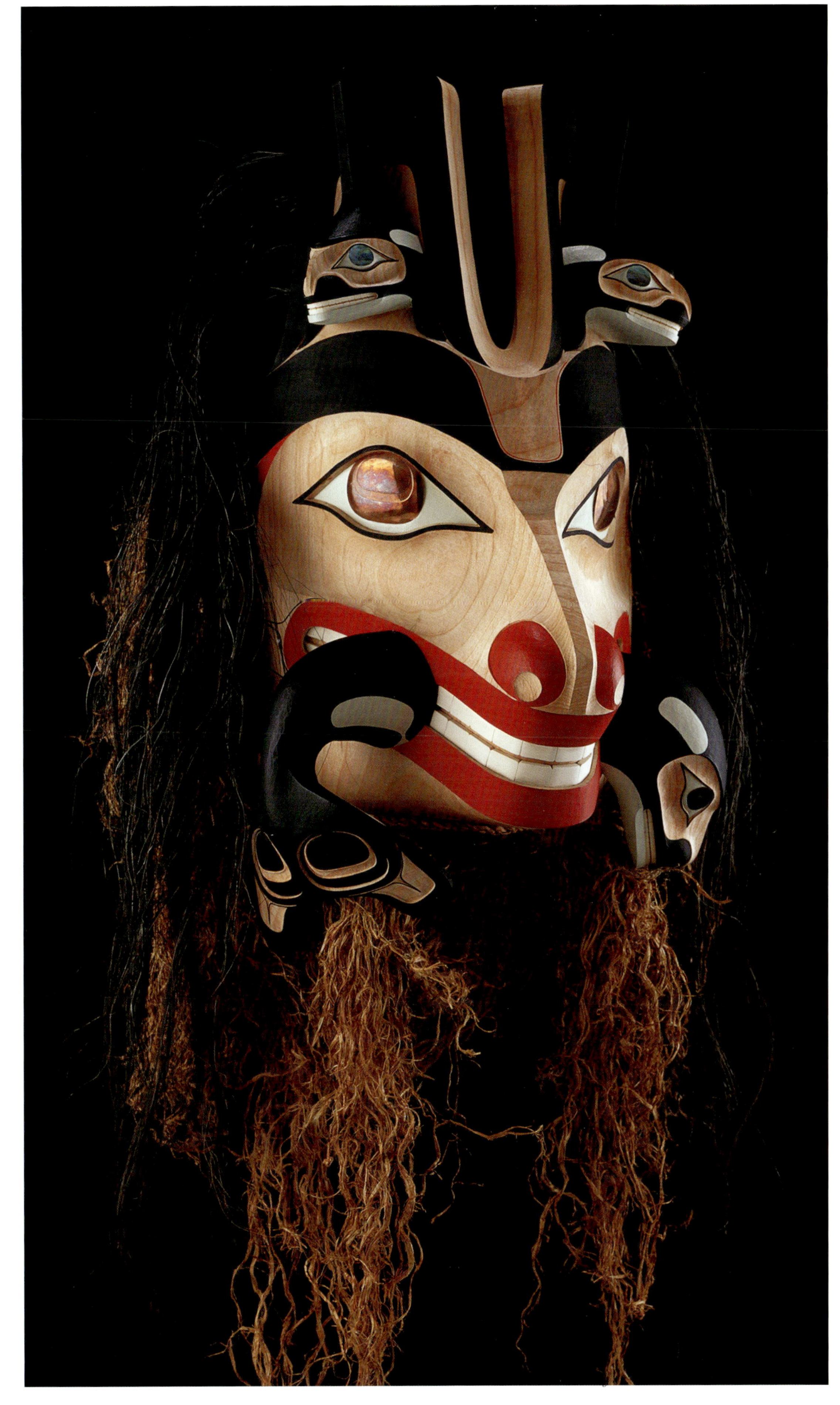

he notes, "It is alder. It was a huge block. You carve alder right away and it is like butter if you carve it quickly. It forces you to move quickly." He has also sensitively used additional materials—holly wood, paua shell, cedar bark, horsehair, acrylic paint and copper—to enrich the wood. The warm colour of the alder contrasts with the vivid red of the sea wolf's lips and nostrils. Simeon's attention to formal composition is seen in the two upper killer whales, which echo the form of the whale being devoured by the sea wolf and, more subtly, the curve of the nostrils. Even if there is no dance for this figure, one can easily imagine how effective this sea wolf could be if danced.

Simeon is interested is broadening what Haida art means, including using European techniques in his jewellery and expanding the image of what is Haida. This sea wolf allows Simeon to forcefully express his convictions: "I'd like people to get a sense that we're still here, not even as Haida artists but Haida people, and that we are moving forward with it." *Sea Wolf* is very much still here and, while respecting the past, is part of an art that is moving forward. ■

Henry Speck Jr.
Hok Hok Headdress
2004

Kwakwa̱ka̱'wakw master carver Henry Speck Jr., son of the important artist Chief Henry Speck (1908–1971), was born in Alert Bay in 1937. Like many First Nations people of his generation, he was forced to attend school within the residential system. In Speck's case, he was perhaps somewhat more fortunate than most in that the school he attended was the St. Michael's Indian Residential School in Alert Bay itself. Nevertheless, Speck was not permitted by the school to participate in traditional Kwakwa̱ka̱'wakw ceremony and, despite his father's artistic career, did not pursue this vocation as a young man. Instead, he worked in the fishing and logging industries for several years.

Life in remote coastal logging camps is one of periods of intense work, punctuated by periods of intense boredom. The men in the camp often have little with which to entertain themselves, and as Speck says, "I decided that I would do a little bit of carving, then my boss talked me into it."[1] In 1972 Speck, needing a home base between logging jobs, moved with his wife to Hegams (Hopetown Village) on the south shore of Watson Island, dividing his time between carving and logging. He did not become a full-time carver until 1984, when he was in his late forties.

Hegams had no electricity in 1972; therefore, any carving that Speck did was done by hand. He had had no training as an artist, except for a brief period in 1963 when he assisted his father in completing a mural for the big house in Alert Bay. Brief though that training was, Speck gained a strong sense of design. Following his father's advice "never to copy anybody," he began to slowly develop his own artistic approach. "I study a lot of artists' carvings but I never copied," he comments, adding that he paid particular attention to the work of the Hunt family: "I admire their wisdom and knowledge, and I always did."

Initially, Speck carved entirely for the tourist market and produced only a limited number of masks. It is difficult to imagine

PROVENANCE: *Artist; Spirit Wrestler Gallery, Vancouver; Audain Collection, purchased 2005; Gift of Michael Audain and Yoshiko Karasawa; Audain Art Museum Collection, 2015.019*

▸ **Henry Speck Jr.** (b. 1937)
Hok Hok Headdress, 2004
red cedar, cedar bark, marine enamel
88.0 × 188.0 × 30.5 cm
Gift of Michael Audain and Yoshiko Karasawa; Audain Art Museum Collection, 2015.019

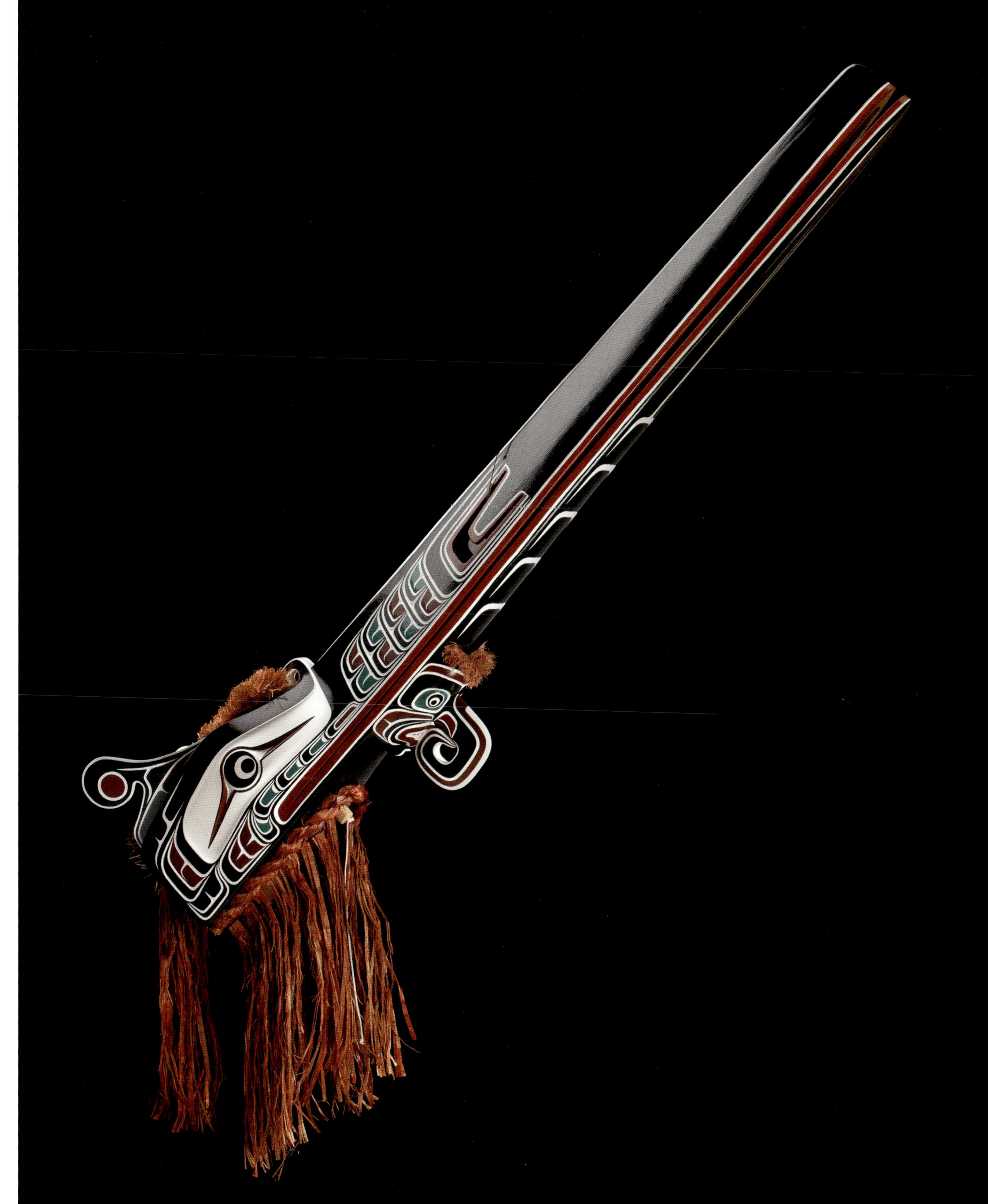

now when Kwakwaka'wakw communities conduct so many important ceremonies, but during Speck's youth and even when his father worked on Alert Bay's big house in the 1960s, there were virtually no masks available for ceremonial purposes. These complex masks had been forbidden for years, and few carvers had the skills to make them. Through his keen observational skills and a great deal of practice, Speck slowly emerged as a major carver of Kwakwaka'wakw ceremonial masks. He is particularly renowned as a carver of three supernatural bird headdresses: Galukw'amhl (The Crooked Beak of Heaven), the Raven Hamatsa or Cannibal, and the Hok Hok. All of these creatures, when then are used traditionally, appear in the Tseyka (Red Cedar Bark Ceremony), worn by initiates of the Hamatsa or cannibal spirit, Baxwbakwalanukwsiwe'. By donning these headdresses, the human dancers become the embodiment of a cannibal spirit.

Speck's masks, such at this Hok Hok headdress, are all intended for use in ceremony even if they have not, in fact, been danced. The dancer would wear the headdress atop his head and, unable to see clearly when wearing it, would have an attendant during the ceremony. The enormous beak, which characterizes this cannibal bird, is rigged to allow the dancer to open and close it, making a loud and terrifying noise. The intended ceremonial use also dictates the use of shiny marine enamel paint rather than acrylic paint. The marine enamel in the traditional colours of black, white and red would glisten in the firelight of a big-house ceremony.

Speck's skills as a carver allow him to produce masks directly, without preliminary drawings, and they are prized for their precise detail and light weight, which is an important attribute for a mask that is danced. Speck has carved the Hok Hok mask several times and has a strong vision of the form in his mind: "I visualize it right away. I see it right away. I look at wood and do measurements and all that and I go from there." The carving is, however, complex, and Speck prefers to do his work alone.

It is perhaps ironic that Speck, who had so little exposure to ceremony when he was growing up, should have emerged as such an important carver of Kwakwaka'wakw ceremonial masks. While his masks would function brilliantly within a ceremonial context, they are so highly prized by collectors that few ever do. Nevertheless, Speck's work on masks such as this Hok Hok are an important link to the Kwakwaka'wakw traditions of the past and are works of art deeply imbued with a sense of the richness and power of that culture. Speck says, "When I used to talk to the elders, they used to tell me that you are going to be doing this when I'm gone, and it has now come true." Now an elder himself, Speck continues to tell the old stories and pass them on to younger generations, both Kwakwaka'wakw and non–First Nations. ■

Don Yeomans
Creator
1985/2008

PROVENANCE: *Artist; private collection; Artist; Douglas Reynolds Gallery, Vancouver; Audain Art Museum Collection, 2013.006*

One of the major challenges for artists of First Nations ancestry is to locate themselves and their art practice within the contemporary world. Don Yeomans is an artist of Haida and Métis ancestry who has been able to distinguish himself through the power of his ideas and the excellence of his carving. Born in Prince Rupert, British Columbia, in 1958, Yeomans took his first art training with Freda Diesing (1925–2002), who was teaching classes in Prince Rupert. Although he excelled in these studies, he did not believe that he was destined to work as an artist. He felt there was a stasis within First Nations traditional arts that was unappealing.

Despite these reservations, and though he had little thought of pursuing a career within First Nations art circles, Yeomans enrolled in a fine arts program in Vancouver, where he tried his hand at a variety of media. At Langara College he learned "a language that made perfect sense, and it sort of gave me an instant application to what I was doing with Native art, to break things down to the units of universal understanding. Is it balanced? How is the rhythm of the piece? Does it flow? Is it harmonious in colour? All principles that nobody in the Haida art world told me about or in the Native teaching realm really delves into and yet it is pertinent to all types of design, all types of art."[1] Upon finishing his schooling, Yeomans realized that there were possibilities for him within Haida art that would combine tradition and the realities of the world he found himself in.

In 1978, Yeomans joined Robert Davidson (b. 1946) and many others in Masset, Haida Gwaii, to work on the Charles Edenshaw Memorial Longhouse. The experience was useful in that it taught him the importance of planning within his work. As he has commented, "The most critical thing for me was layout, how to do it precisely, how to measure it, how to check your lines and your cuts, true the log, technical things that were very useful." At the same time, Yeomans was interested in maintaining a sense of spontaneity within his work, and an intensive period of study and work with Gerry Marks (b. 1949) and Phil Janze (b. 1950) beginning in 1979 allowed him to enhance this facet of his work. In the early 1980s, Yeomans accepted a position teaching First Nations art with the Victoria school board, which meant that he had to immerse himself in the art of not only the Haida but also other coastal First Nations in the province. In order to teach his students, he needed to have a sense of what their cultural style was.

By 1986 Yeomans had left teaching. He then began a period of work with Bill Reid (1920–1998) in Vancouver. A highly accomplished carver in his own right by this time, Yeomans worked with Reid because he wanted to be able to question the older artist about his philosophy and approach to art and art making. He benefited greatly from the experience and realized that all of his teachers—First Nations and non–First Nations—shared a trait: they "sought outside the culture to enrich their art." While respecting the traditions of the past, artists such as Diesing, Davidson and Reid were not afraid to develop new forms and expand our understanding, and they had all clearly distinguished themselves. This spirit has informed all of Yeomans' work. He has used the language of formline to express himself, even if it is at times uncomfortable and difficult.

Nowhere is this approach more apparent than in *Creator,* a complex work that Yeomans has visited twice in his career. The work, first completed in 1985, reflected the anger and disappointment Yeomans felt regarding the role of Christianity in First Nations communities. The raven, traditionally the trickster in First Nations culture, is cruelly crucified on a Christian cross. In the first version of this work, the cross was made of stainless steel and evoked many associations—modernity, white culture and, of course, the Crucifixion itself. The raven, carved from glowing yellow cedar, was starkly contrasted with the slick, shiny surface of the steel. The work also reflected Yeoman's belief "that the Natives gave up their culture, gave up their ideology for technology." Several years later, Yeomans was able to buy back the work from the collector who owned it, and he decided to reconfigure it.

In the 1990s, as part of his continuing exploration of new sources for his art beyond the confines of Haida culture, Yeomans had become increasingly interested in Celtic patterns. In the years since he'd first created this work, Yeomans had "realized that Christianity had a lot to offer. I mean this is in retrospect. I did that piece twenty-five years ago but I've seen things in my life since then, like my father becoming a Christian and how that transformed him as a human being and made him a better person. I felt the need to go back and respect the religion, make the cross more ornate, give it as much focus as the bird."

Without forgetting the enormous damage that Christianity brought to First Nations communities, Yeomans now feels that the story has greater complexity and that there is good as well as bad. The *Creator,* now on a Celtic cross, has a somewhat more gentle impact but maintains a distinct, contemporary edge. It forcefully reflects Yeomans' belief that "culture has to expand. If I am to be represented by an idea, that is the idea that I want to put out there, that culture is inclusive; it is not trapped in one period in history that was your glory days." ■

▸ Don Yeomans (b. 1958)
Creator, 1985/2008
yellow cedar
76.2 × 60.9 × 17.8 cm
Audain Art Museum Collection, 2013.006

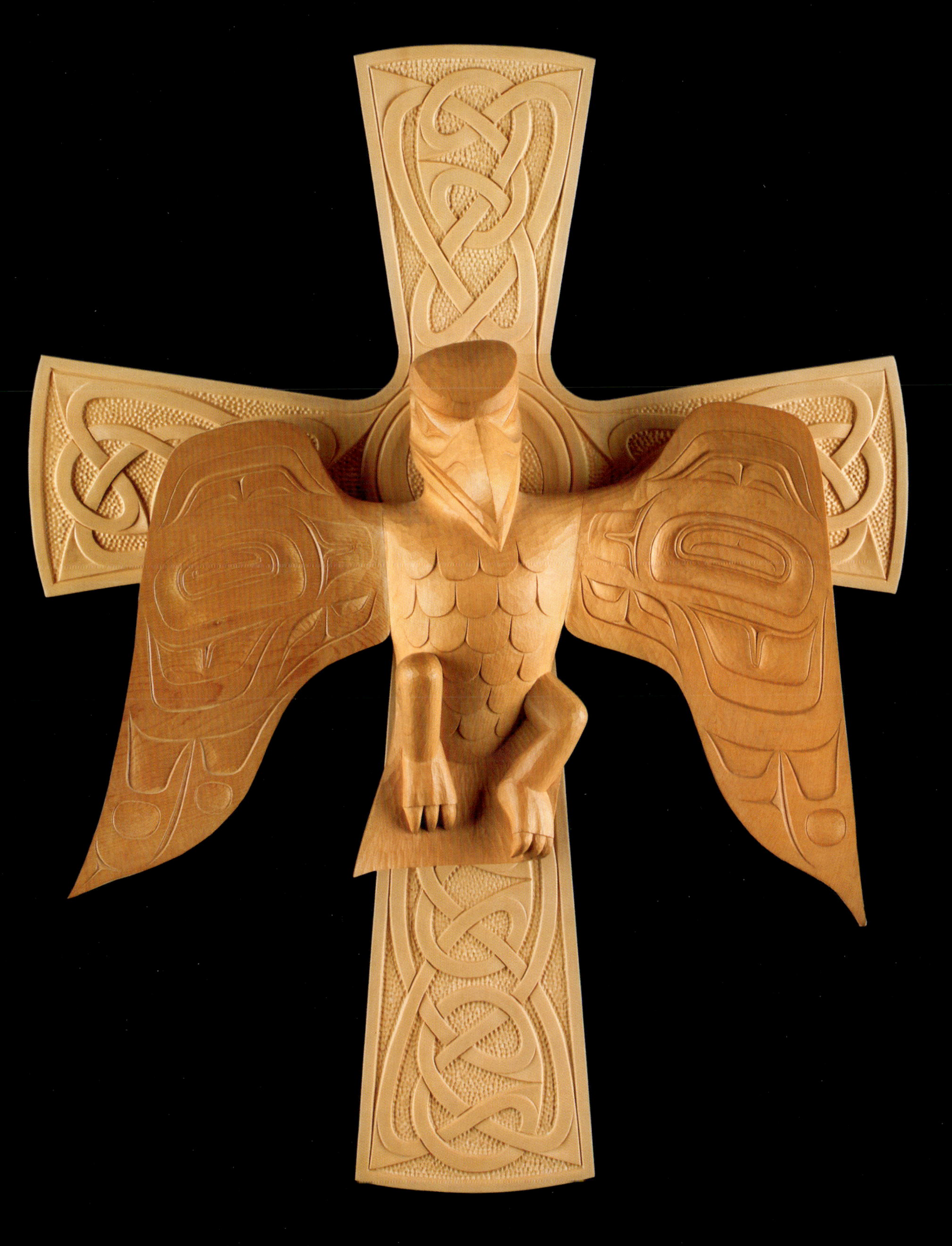

Lawrence Paul Yuxweluptun

Clearcut to the Last Old Growth Tree

2013

All art is political to a greater or lesser degree, but few artists have made their political views as central to their practice as the Coast Salish/Okanagan artist Lawrence Paul Yuxweluptun. Born in Kamloops in 1957, Yuxweluptun was deeply immersed in the political and cultural struggles of First Nations people through the activity of his father, Ben Paul, who was an official of the Union of British Columbia Indian Chiefs and fought long and hard for fishing and other ancestral rights. Although Yuxweluptun himself did not choose to become an activist in the usual sense, his work gives voice to strongly held views about the environment, the place and treatment of First Nations people within Canadian society and their continuing struggles to achieve full equality within the country. This is a struggle that Yuxweluptun feels is a long way from finished.

As a child, Yuxweluptun spent time in the residential school system, even though his family lived off-reserve. In later years he attended school in Richmond, British Columbia, where he experienced what he describes as "blatant racism."[1] Deeply interested in art as a child—as he says, "to me it was just a natural form of thinking"—Yuxweluptun realized that he wanted to give voice to his concerns and felt that traditional forms of art making were not equal to the task. "How do you carve the experience of a reservation or a residential school?" he asks. Following high school, after a period of time that he describes as "hanging out with Indians," Yuxweluptun enrolled at the Emily Carr College of Art and Design (ECCAD, now Emily Carr University of Art + Design) in 1978. A quick study, Yuxweluptun worked in a variety of media but gravitated strongly to painting. However, this was painting that was more strongly influenced by a variety of European traditions than by First Nations forms. Yuxweluptun cites his influences as "the world, my television, certain people: Geronimo, Sitting Bull, Chief Seattle, Gandhi, Churchill, Rembrandt, Vermeer, Degas, Cézanne, Picasso, Vincent, Bugs Bunny, Yeats, Michelangelo, Bob Marley." While fiercely proud of his heritage, he felt that "someone had to change the order of things. The gauntlet had to be thrown down to challenge the whole notion of what art is. Not Indian art, not good Indian craft—Indian art."

With his great range of influences, Yuxweluptun felt the freedom to ignore rules of tradition, form and subject matter. By the time of his graduation from ECCAD in 1983, he had already developed a distinct and uncompromising voice. In his words, "I was one of the first Native artists to pry an anthropologist off my leg." His work developed in two ways. The first, which he calls "ovoidism," employs the traditional ovoid form in highly abstract and original ways. Of the ovoids he says, "They are an extension of an existential conceptual symbolic of duality of colour and thought. They are

PROVENANCE: *Artist; Audain Collection, purchased 2013*

▸ Lawrence Paul Yuxweluptun (b. 1957)
Clearcut to the Last Old Growth Tree, 2013
acrylic on canvas
268.0 × 175.2 cm
Promised Gift, Audain Collection

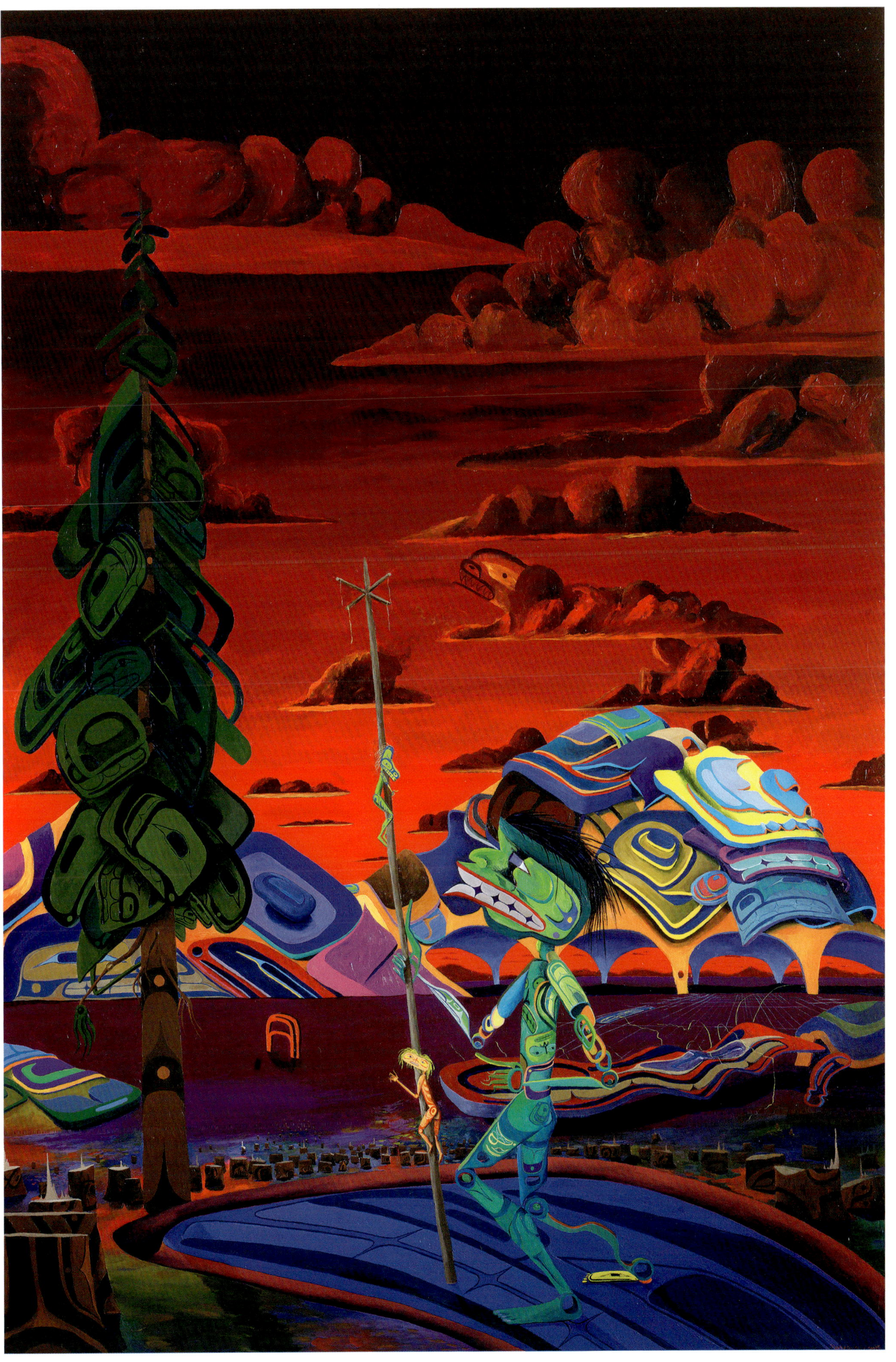

an expression of the time that I live in. So that it is free thinking, to think and express what I am thinking, the feelings of death, the feelings of residential schools, anything is possible. They are a very expressionistic symbol." Of the second, which is more strongly narrative, he says, "My mind is about surreal symbolism. I'm a symbolist realist. From my cultural background, I transformed symbols."

Yuxwelptun's subject matter is the "hard things [that] have to be said, need to be said"—the depredation of the environment, the ongoing insults of the Indian Act, aspects of "Post-Colonial Distress Syndrome that all of the residential school children suffered." He describes an early realization that has shaped the course of his own life and his art:

> Key moment in my life: sitting down at the back of a hall, any Indian hall, I don't even remember where it was. Maybe it was Williams Lake. It was a summer day and there was a meeting, when I was about seven or eight, and there were all these Indians and one white man. I realized that they are talking to themselves. That guy was paid to sit there; he was not going to do anything. The Indian Act was designed to oppress our people and I knew then that I had to speak for myself. I wanted no part of the reservation and what stays on the reservation.

More recently his work has commented that the land base on which First Nations people have lived since their earliest days is being continuously eroded by the exploitation of natural resources and urban development. In his words, "All the salmon is gone: I cannot even feed my grandmother now, I cannot make an offering to the Great Spirit."

Clearcut to the Last Old Growth Tree offers us a sense of the power of Yuxweluptun's visual language and political engagement. It is an electric image of a decimated landscape, with only a single tree remaining. A shaman stands before the tree, unable to do anything. The background hills are covered with ovoids and suggest that even in this devastated state the landscape is inhabited by traditional beliefs and culture. It is, however, a deeply pessimistic view of how we have treated the world and, as such, a highly politicized statement about the need to preserve rather than exploit the environment. It is a call for more robust action by the whole of humanity to prevent the destruction of the natural world. Despite its strident tone, the painting is astonishingly colourful and vivid. Indeed, Yuxweluptun notes, "The artist has never had so much of a colour theory to work with. There is a lot more colour to be dealt with. It creates a different colour theory."

Yuxweluptun has a strong sense of the history of both the First Nations people and their treatment within this country and the history of art. His wide-ranging visual interests come together in works such as this one, works that are powerfully contemporary. As he notes, "I'm always watching the now, my presence is in the now." Politically and aesthetically engaged and challenging, Yuweluptun's work is among the most memorable painting being done today. His paintings give voice to his experience and that of other First Nations people who regularly have a "bad colonial day." The work is often edgy, provocative and never dull, and while Yuxweluptun is under no illusions about the ability of his work to change larger social ills, he wants his voice to be distinct and clear. As he says, "I try to make an ugly painting that is beautiful, and I try to make a beautiful painting that has something ugly to say." He succeeds, and we are all the better for it. Clearly, he has taken part of the formal language of Northwest Coast First Nations art to an entirely new place, and painting has allowed him to speak clearly and freely. As he comments, "Nothing is out of bounds to me. I am not confined to a traditional three-dimension format. My hands are not tied. Artists should challenge everything." ■

Stan Douglas
MacLeod's Books, Vancouver
2006

Born in Vancouver in 1960, Stan Douglas grew up in the city and attended Emily Carr College (now Emily Carr University of Art + Design), from which he graduated in 1982. He had already had a solo exhibition the previous year and has since gone on to have major solo exhibitions around the world. He has also received numerous major awards for his work in video and photography, including the International Center of Photography Infinity Award in 2012 and the Scotiabank Photography Award in 2013. The subject of several monographs, Douglas's work is dense and complex, multilayered in its examination of both history and the present. He has recreated realms that relate to actual historical events and made work that imagines possible events. A deep level of research characterizes all of his work, and the resulting images are both startling and astonishingly beautiful.

MacLeod's Books, Vancouver is one of a series of seven photographs of Vancouver and the interior of British Columbia that Douglas took in 2006 when working on his video installation *Klatsassin,* which was first exhibited at the Vienna Secession that year. Although the photographs were taken while Douglas worked on *Klatsassin,* he regards them as a separate body of work and has shown them separately. They trace what Douglas describes as "an increasing abstraction of the landscape as you go from one to the other."[1]

Beginning in the gold-rush town of Barkerville, Douglas documented "different types of landscape as we go from the West Coast rain forest to the more desert area of central BC and finally we get to the last two pictures of Vancouver. There is one of the Maritime Worker's Hall,[2] and we see a view of Vancouver Harbour which, if you know the harbour well, makes no sense because we are seeing things which are tens of miles apart from each other in the same image, so it is almost like Cubist landscape, where inside is outside. And following with this abstraction or condensation of landscape in the form of MacLeod's Books."

Although it is set in the well-known Vancouver bookstore and is quite different from the remaining landscape images in the series, *MacLeod's Books, Vancouver* is, for Douglas, a landscape photograph: "In two ways it is a landscape photograph. In one case there is the midden that the proprietor of that bookstore, Don Stewart, had made. He has got a desk in the middle. It is like a midden where he knows where everything is but to anyone else it looks like a complete jumble. So there is a stratification of information over time that accumulates there. Plus, I imagine each book being a compressed version of the history of BC or a history of BC landscape."

The photograph is a documentary image. Taking the photograph early one morning before the store opened, Douglas "shot it as

PROVENANCE: *Artist; David Zwirner Gallery, New York; Audain Collection, purchased 2006; Gift of Michael Audain and Yoshiko Karasawa; Audain Art Museum Collection, 2015.020*

[he] found it." The fact of a space heavily layered with accumulated history and meaning is, however, very important for Douglas. He notes,

> In a place like MacLeod's Books we are looking at the accumulation over time of somebody's decisions about what that place should be—what goes where, why it goes there, how it is going to be organized, how it is negotiated by the body. So it is seeing the relation of somebody living in that space. In a way we are inside his brain. I mean, it is an interesting place to be, and I wanted people to visit it through this photograph—which we can do in a photograph of that scale and that kind of detail, that we can't do necessarily in life because it holds things in a fixed position, in a position in time, so you can actually scrutinize it in a way that you would never do in reality or in film.

In order for the image to be immersive in the way Douglas wanted, he needed to make a large-scale picture so that "you feel yourself in the image and most importantly it has got enough detail that you can actually read the titles of the books."

This is an image that is remarkably compelling. As Douglas notes, it looks like "a jumble," yet we sense that there is an order to the apparent chaos. If we take the time to look at this densely packed, visually rich image, the stories that we as viewers may take away are, quite simply, limitless. ■

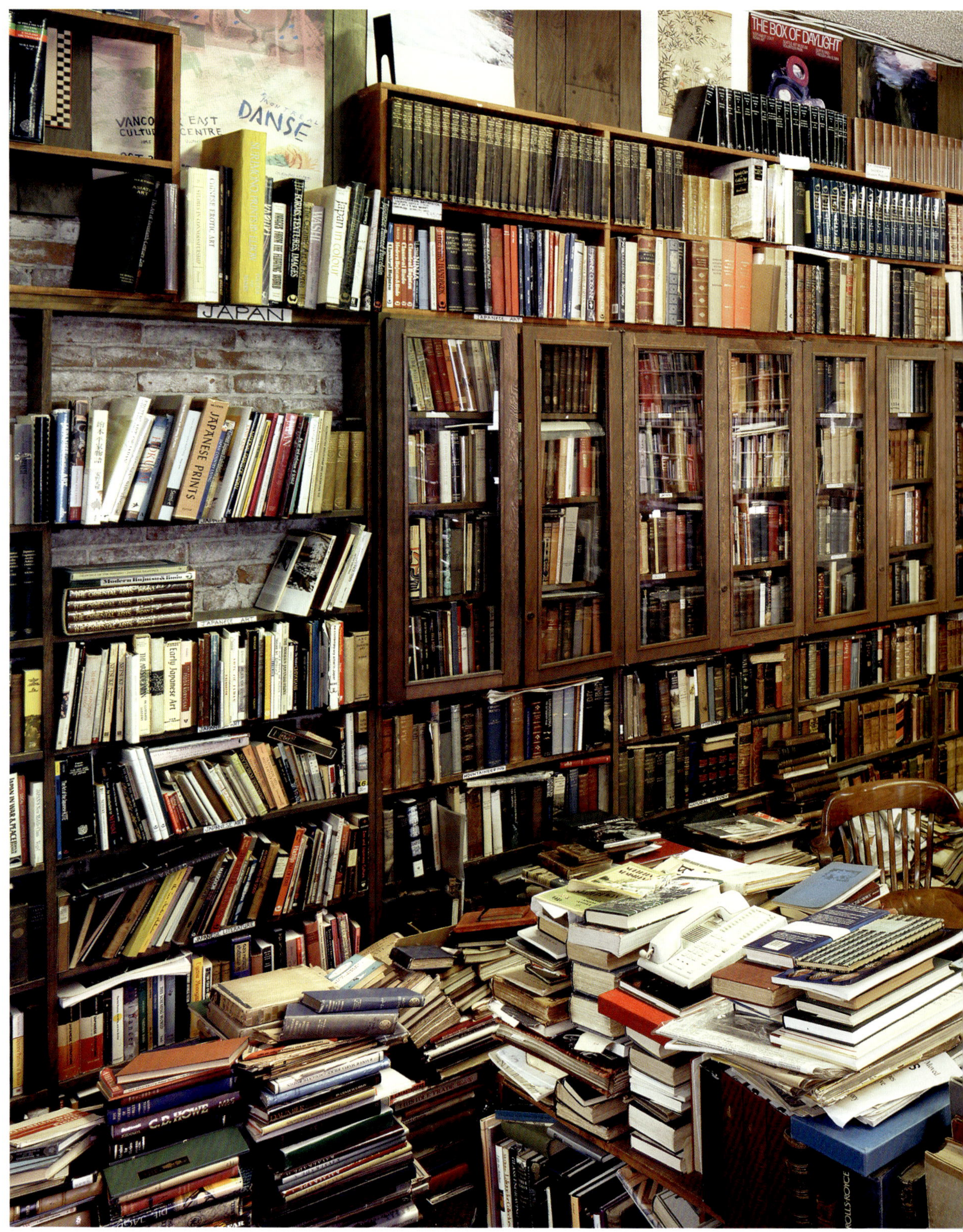

Stan Douglas (b. 1960)
MacLeod's Books, Vancouver, 2006
chromogenic print
178.0 × 305.0 cm
Gift of Michael Audain and Yoshiko Karasawa; Audain Art Museum Collection, 2015.020

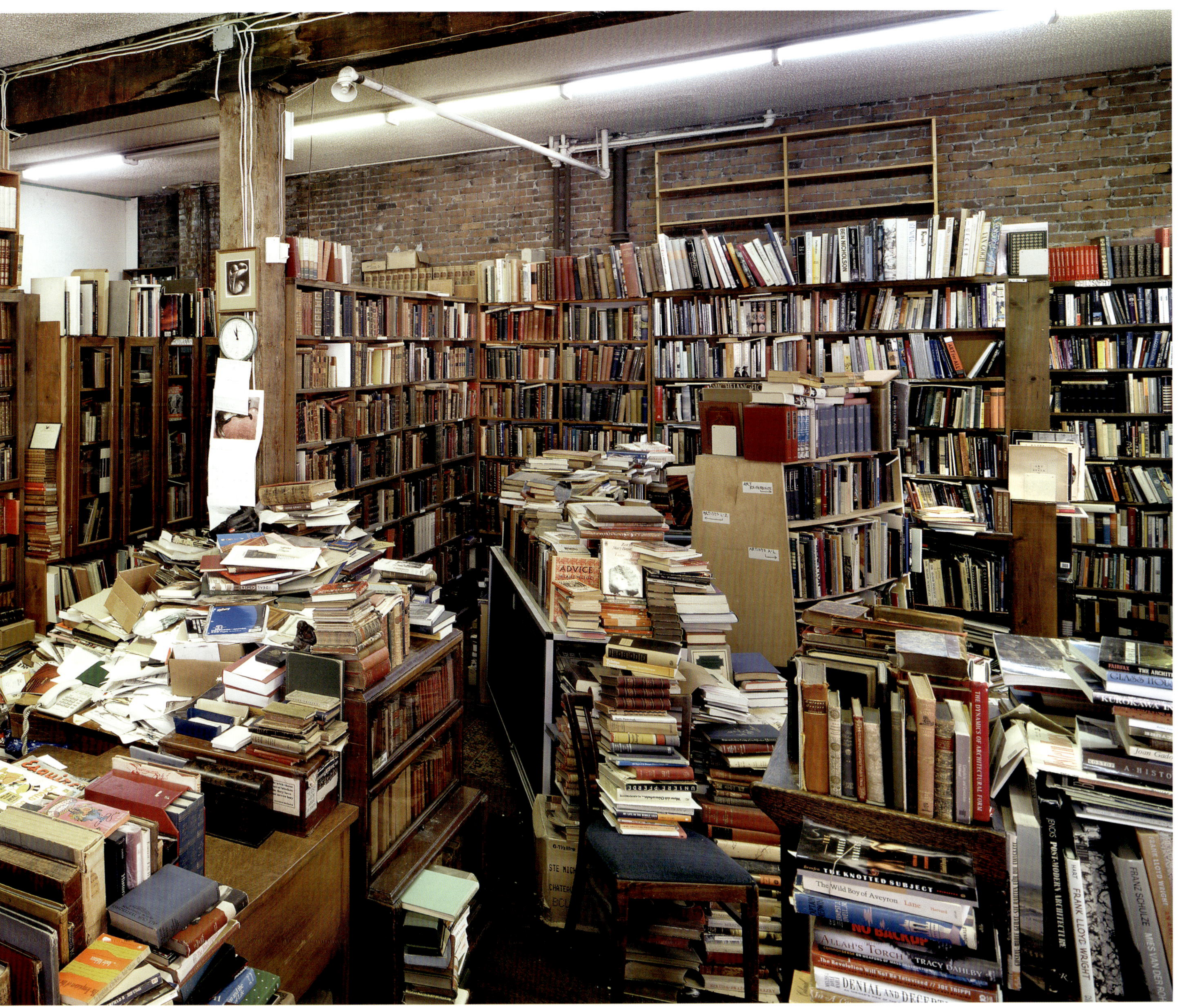
BEN NICHOLSON
VAN GOGH
ADVICE
THE DYNAMICS OF ARCHITECTURAL FORM
FAIRFAX
THE KNOTTED SUBJECT
The Wild Boy of Aveyron
Lane
NO BACKUP
ALLAH'S TORCH
TRACY DAHLBY
The Revolution Will Not Be Televised // JOE TRIPPI
POST-MODERN ARCHITECTURE
FRANK LLOYD WRIGHT
FRANZ SCHULZE

Rodney Graham
The Drywaller
2012

Rodney Graham began making work that included himself as a protagonist in 1994, with the video *Halcion Sleep* (Vancouver Art Gallery). Since that time he has made a number of works, both video and photographs, in which he positions himself in meticulously constructed or reconstructed situations. He has appeared as everything from a French country bumpkin to a shipwrecked sailor, a sous-chef and a classical musician, to name just a few of his identities. In each case, Graham has created a setting and worn a costume that allows him to inhabit both the character and the space in which that character acts. As the artist Jeff Wall (b. 1946) wrote, "Rodney Graham's work implicates itself in a complex of philosophical, aesthetic, historical and social issues and does so in novel and unexpected ways."[1]

Born in Abbotsford, British Columbia, in 1949, Graham attended the University of British Columbia, where he studied art and art history. He has worked in a variety of media, including sculpture, photography and painting, and, since his first solo exhibition in 1979, has gone on to exhibit widely internationally. He represented Canada at the Venice Biennale in 1997.

The Drywaller is a life-sized diptych with a one-to-one equivalence between the image and the lived experience. In the left panel, Graham, in the character of the drywaller, is standing on a pair of stilts, which would allow him to reach the upper portions of the walls and ceiling. He thus towers over us, just as he would if we were actually in the pictorial space. The goggles and face mask hanging around his neck give him a casual appearance as he takes a cigarette break, but there is a remarkable elegance to the positioning of his left arm, which suggests a deliberateness to the pose. Critic Michael Vass has described the work as follows:

> The black and red of his plaid shirt in the left panel rhymes with the black space heater bearing glowing orange filaments in the right panel, while an off-white wall marked with a grid pattern and dots stretches across both panels. This faux–Abstract Expressionist backdrop, along with the listless expression worn by Graham's worker and the incidental vaudeville of his stilts, emphasizes in a darkly humorous manner that this is, decidedly, a portrait of a non-artist as an aging man.[2]

This is not a glamorous image. Graham appears as a working man but, as Vass has suggested, the image is highly considered visually. In addition to the red and black in each panel, Graham has repeated the pattern of the drywaller's labour and details such as the light switch and the electrical outlets that help to visually animate the space. Graham's meticulous attention to detail is evident: the crooked antenna on the boom box echoes the electrical cord of the heater, and everything in the photo is in focus. This outcome would not be possible in a single photograph. The image we see is a digital knitting together of images of the background and of the artist himself, each of which is shot separately and then combined

PROVENANCE: *Artist; 303 Gallery, New York; Audain Art Museum Collection, 2013.003*

▸ **Rodney Graham** (b. 1949)
The Drywaller, 2012
aluminum lightboxes with transmounted chromogenic transparencies
diptych, each 303.8 × 181.9 cm
Audain Art Museum Collection, 2013.003

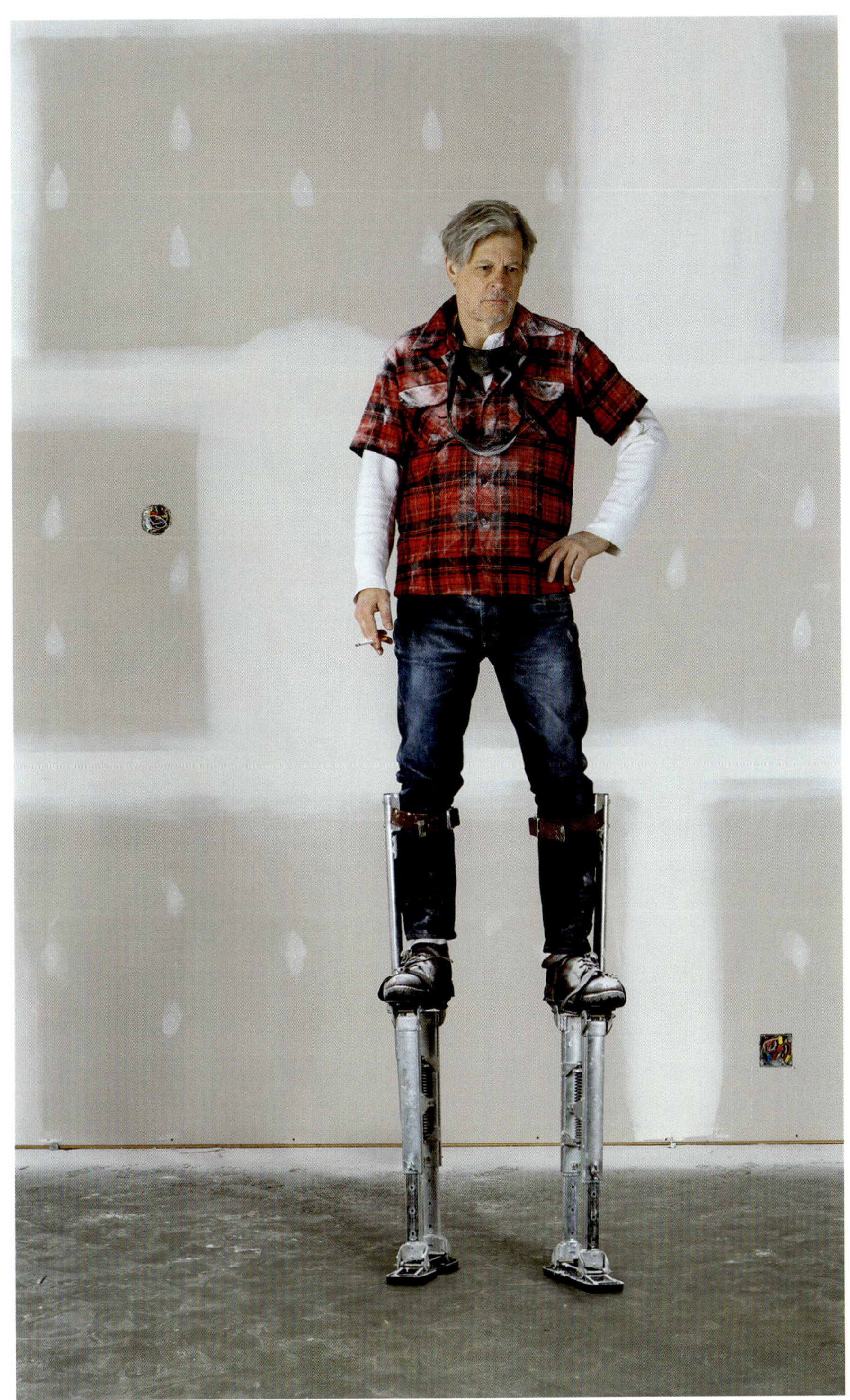
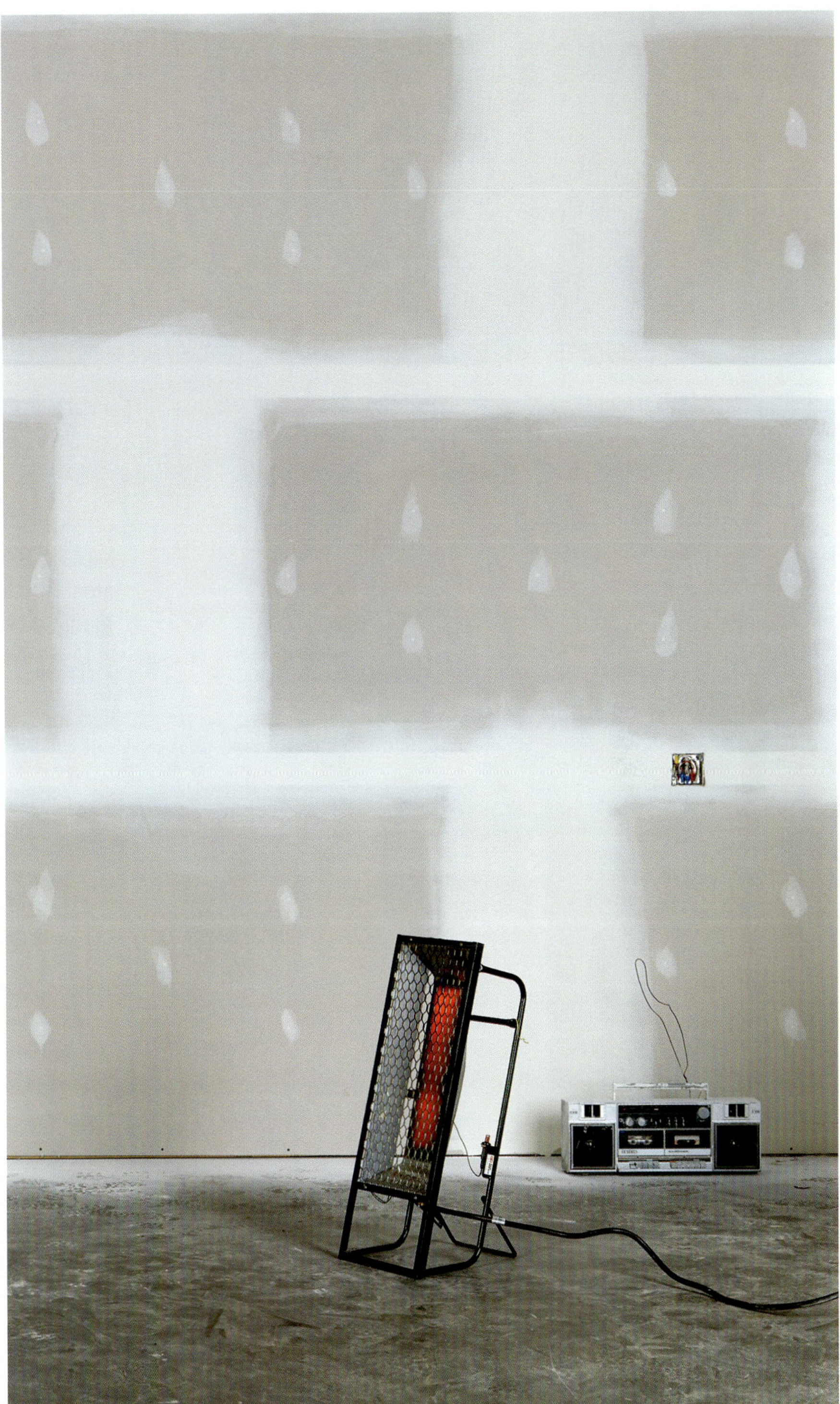

to create the finished image. This enhanced perception, which is not immediately evident, is critical to the success of the image.

Works such as *The Drywaller* are the result of a crew of people working to create them. Rodney Graham is the artist and subject, but the work has a deliberate and theatrical aspect to it. This is theatre that elevates the quotidian and commonplace to the level of spectacle. Both the scale and the backlighting of the image provide the spectacle, but it is, paradoxically, a spectacle that is absolutely deadpan—and this deadpan presentation only heightens the humour. ■

Attila Richard Lukacs
Love in Loss c: Painting the Lovers' Portrait
1991

Attila Richard Lukacs has largely devoted himself to depictions of the male figure, a reflection of his own sexuality and of his interest in the long traditions of Western figurative art. The grand scale of many of his images recalls the enormous history paintings of artists such as Théodore Géricault (1791–1824) and Eugène Delacroix (1798–1863), and like his predecessors, Lukacs is generally concerned with contemporary or near contemporary history. He takes his inspiration from a wide variety of art-historical models, such as Jacques-Louis David (1748–1825) and Michelangelo Merisi da Caravaggio (1571–1610), Indian miniature paintings and Hungarian folk painting, as well as from his studies of the model. His choice of subject matter initially made his work somewhat controversial. However, the open expression of his own homosexuality, combined with increasing acceptance of lesbian and gay people within society as a whole, have made his work more appreciated by a wider public.

Born in Calgary, Alberta, in 1962, Lukacs attended Emily Carr Institute of Art and Design (now Emily Carr University of Art + Design) and graduated in 1985. That same year his work was included in the exhibition *Young Romantics,* which was held at the Vancouver Art Gallery. This marked the launch of Lukacs's professional career, and since that time he has exhibited widely in both Canada and abroad. Lukacs left British Columbia in 1986 for a period of residence in Berlin and then spent several years in New York after 1996, moving to Hawaii in 2001 and returning to British Columbia in 2005. He continues to live and work here.

Love in Loss c: Painting the Lover's Portrait is the final image in a cycle of fourteen monumental paintings completed in Berlin in 1991–92. First exhibited in Vancouver at the Diane Farris Gallery in the exhibition *Varieties of Love,* the image, in the context of the larger series, might be read as the conclusion of a complex and tumultuous romantic relationship. This, however, would be an erroneous reading because Lukacs never conceived of the paintings within the exhibition as a continuous narrative.[1] Rather, the painting should be seen as an individual composition and is, in Lukacs's view, a work that is about painting itself. The work is inevitably reflective of his own circumstances in Berlin in the early 1990s as

PROVENANCE: *Diane Farris Gallery, Vancouver; Audain Collection, purchased 1999; Gift of Michael Audain and Yoshiko Karasawa; Audain Art Museum Collection, 2015.021*

▶ Attila Richard Lukacs (b. 1962)
Love in Loss c: Painting the Lovers' Portrait, 1991
oil, bitumen, enamel, tar, gold leaf on canvas
284.0 × 152.4 cm
Gift of Michael Audain and Yoshiko Karasawa; Audain Art Museum Collection, 2015.021

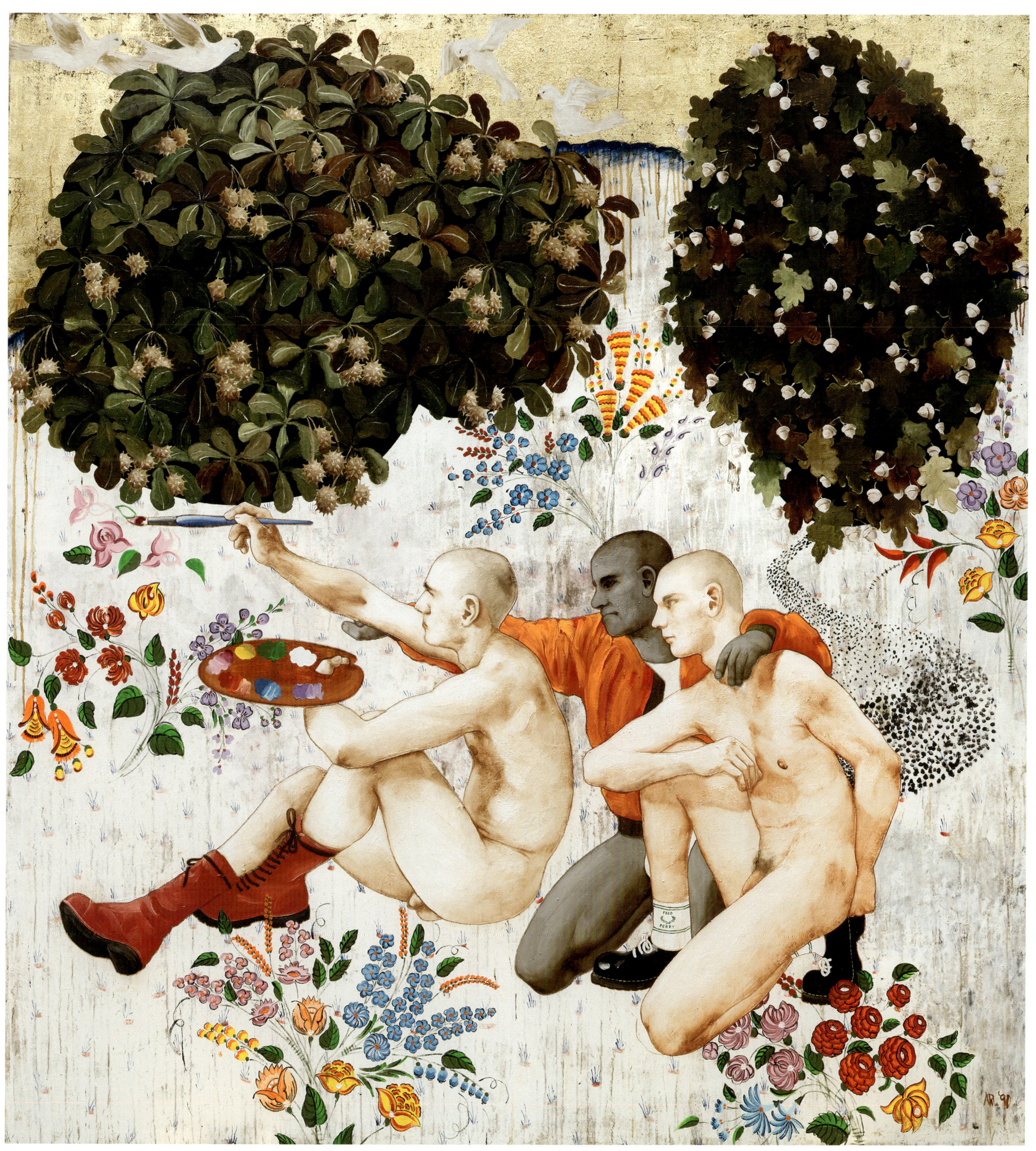
FRED
PERRY
AR. '90

well: there he found himself able to live more freely as a gay man but also, and more importantly for his work, was exposed to a wealth of painting within the museums of the city. Lukacs saw the work of Karl Friedrich Schinkel (1741–1841), Caravaggio and others and realized that it was possible to depict the world from a gay perspective. Deeply influenced by the examples from the past, Lukacs was also invigorated by the men of Berlin and by his ability to obtain models to pose for his work.

This work was inspired by a drawing by Schinkel that was used as a decorative panel in one of the architect's many buildings in Berlin. Lukacs used the drawing as the basis for positioning or posing his model. His process was to then extensively document the model or models in a series of Polaroid images. During this period in Berlin, many young men were sporting Doc Martens footwear; Lukacs found this appealing and posed the principal model for this work, a young man named Stephan, in them. Indeed, Stephan appears twice in this work: he is both the solo figure and one of the pair (with another model, Marek).[2] These Polaroids, some of which have been published, reveal that Lukacs has been remarkably faithful to the photographic images in his painting.[3] This is particularly noticeable in his use of light and shadow on the figures; however, when the composition requires it, Lukacs is not afraid to change things dramatically. For example, the skin colour of one of the figures is darkened in the painting. This simple device means that the grouping of two figures reads more coherently as three-dimensional.

Although Lukacs has spent a lot of time considering the history of Western art, this series of paintings has been importantly informed by his study of Mughal miniature paintings, Chinese art and other non-Western sources. One of the attractions of these non-Western visual sources for Lukacs is the lack of conventional approaches to space. Here Lukacs has been more interested in the idea of pattern and design than in creating a unified pictorial space. Indeed, it might be said that he has deliberately avoided creating such a space. For example, the three figures, one of whom is engaged in the act of painting (although we do not see what he paints on or his subject), seem to be suspended before the distressed white ground. Lukacs has paid a great deal of attention to the variety of surface pattern and texture, ranging from the flat gold leaf of the sky (recalling medieval panel paintings) and the scraped surface below it to the richly detailed foliage of the chestnut and oak trees. Not only do these plants evoke the flora of Berlin, they can also be read symbolically. This was Lukacs's intention. The seed pods of the chestnut tree recall human testes, and the German word for "acorn" *(Eichel)* is slang for the head of the penis. So when this and other works from the period are seen within the German context in which they were painted, they are highly sexualized. Within the North American context, where they were first shown, they lie more within the realm of a fantastic world.[4]

Indeed, part of the power of *Love in Loss c: Painting the Lovers' Portrait* is the series of paradoxes within it. Although the work relates to the compositional strategies of the Indian miniature, it explodes that paradigm by using life-sized figures. The realism of the foliage of the trees is in direct contrast to the extreme artificiality of the doves and the golden sky. The naturalism of the figures is contradicted by the fact that they float, casting no shadows on the ground. The illusion of three dimensions is in opposition to the flat patterning of the floral forms that Lukacs has derived from Hungarian folk art found in his childhood home.[5]

And what about the title? Lukacs thought that it came from an Indian miniature, but when he reflected further, he commented that the work was about painting and therefore the title was appropriate because "painting is my lover."[6] ■

Tim Lee

Upside Down Water Torture Chamber, Harry Houdini 1914

2004

Tim Lee's work draws on both popular culture and the traditions of the avant-garde. Born in Seoul, South Korea, in 1975, he grew up in Edmonton, Alberta, and graduated from the University of Alberta with a degree in design in 1999. He worked as a commercial designer for a couple of years, but after hearing a lecture by artist Stan Douglas (b. 1960), Lee decided to abandon design and pursue further art studies at the University of British Columbia, where he earned his master's in 2002.

Initially interested in the idea of pursuing a practice that was based on text, in 2001 Lee made a breakthrough that has determined the direction of his subsequent work. His initial artwork, *The Move, The Beastie Boys, 1998,* was a video installation of Lee performing the song "The Move" by the well-known hip-hop group Beastie Boys. While the camera was used in a direct and uninflected way, Lee complicated the message by dividing the image between three monitors, thus amplifying his performance and requiring viewers to reunify the images in their own minds. Lee's interest is in indexical moments (moments that may be defined by many different points of view)—here the song that defined Beastie Boys, who were, improbably, a group of young Jewish men trying to make a name for themselves in hip hop, a genre of music usually associated with African Americans and Latino Americans. By using himself as the protagonist in the video, Lee references the work of earlier video performers such as American Bruce Nauman (b. 1941) but also further complicates our understanding of hip hop by introducing yet another unexpected disjuncture of race. If Beastie Boys were seeking to deracinate themselves through hip hop, Lee is calling our attention to both the seminal nature of this moment in popular or mass culture and to their strategy by inserting himself into a new, restaged scenario. The specificity of the moment is clearly implied in the title, which he describes as being "bibliographic, like you would see in an old card catalogue."[1] We have the title of the song, the year of the song, the authors of the song and the year in which Lee has recreated this "seminal moment."[2]

Lee chose Vancouver to do his graduate studies and continues to live there because he feels that this community has a distinct relationship to the larger world of conceptual art, or art based on ideas. It has nevertheless been important for Lee to distinguish himself from the photo-conceptual practices of more senior artists such as Jeff Wall (b. 1946), Stan Douglas and Rodney Graham (b. 1949), and one of the ways he has done so is by re-examining some of the issues of the past, both artistically and culturally. He is deeply interested in the work of Robert Smithson

PROVENANCE: *Artist; Vancouver Art Gallery auction (lot 12, October 2, 2006); Audain Collection; Gift of Michael Audain and Yoshiko Karasawa; Audain Art Museum Collection, 2015.022*

▸ Tim Lee (b. 1975)
Upside Down Water Torture Chamber, Harry Houdini 1914, 2004
chromogenic print
135.5 × 110.0 cm
Gift of Michael Audain and Yoshiko Karasawa; Audain Art Museum Collection 2015.022

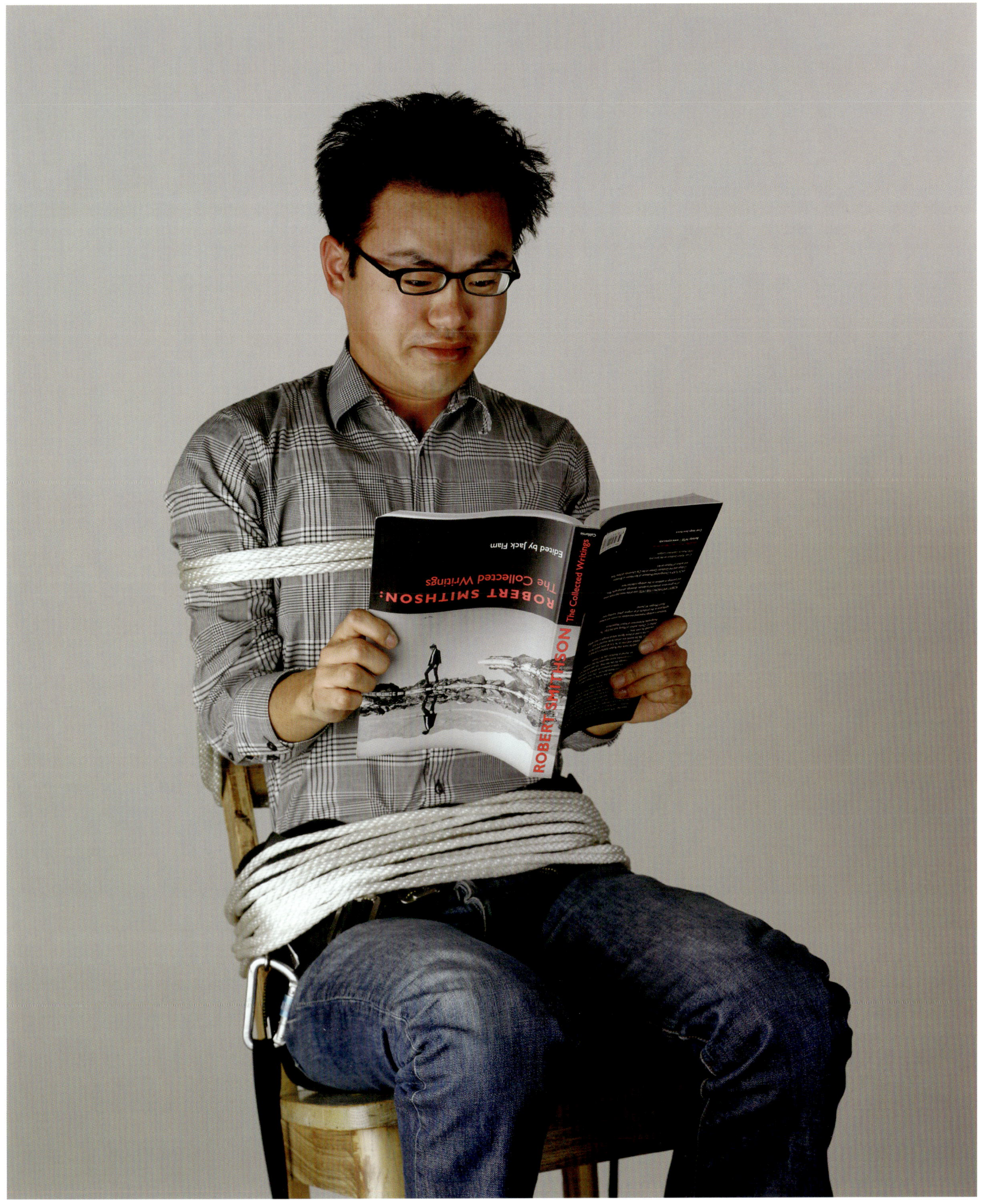
ROBERT SMITHSON:
The Collected Writings
Edited by Jack Flam
ROBERT SMITHSON
The Collected Writings
California

(1938–1973), Dan Graham (b. 1942) and other important pioneers of conceptual practice in the 1960s, but he is also interested in broader aspects of popular culture—music, hockey, stand-up comedy, magic—and has produced a body of work that brings together a broad range of references.

Upside Down Water Torture Chamber, Harry Houdini 1914 operates on a striking number of levels. In it we see Lee, life-sized, tied to a chair at both the waist and chest, holding a book, *Robert Smithson: The Collected Writings,* upside down. Closer examination reveals a large buckle at Lee's waist on his right side and a belt that extends beyond the picture frame below it. Another belt or cord is visible between his legs. Lee's facial expression seems somewhat strained. What is not immediately apparent is that Lee was actually upside down when this photograph was taken. He has presented us with a series of inversions, or reversals: he is upside down, but he is presented as right side up and the book as upside down. However, for Lee to be able to read the Smithson book in his inverted state, it is actually the right way up.

Lee's work is an allusion to the Upside Down Water Torture Chamber, or Chinese Water Torture Cell, which Harry Houdini (born Erik Weisz, 1874–1926) staged in 1912 and which was one of the defining moments of magic in the early twentieth century. This illusion—in which Houdini's feet were locked in stocks and then he was hung upside down, immersed in a tank full of water and locked in that position before making his escape—made Houdini's name and cemented his celebrity. In Lee's words, this moment marked when Houdini's "name became proper."[3] Ironically, with his hair pulled away from his scalp by gravity, Lee bears an uncanny resemblance to Houdini, which he did not initially intend.[4] How is Houdini related to the American artist Smithson? Smithson, who is seen on the cover of the book Lee is holding, is walking along his celebrated land artwork, *Spiral Jetty,* and is reflected in the waters of Great Salt Lake in Utah. Although this was not Smithson's first earthwork, it is the work that made Smithson's name proper.

Lee has taken two important moments in history and restaged them in his own, contemporary moment. He does not historicize the image. He wears his own clothes, and he employed two riggers from Cirque du Soleil to secure him to the chair and a photographer (Robert Keziere) to take the image. *Upside Down Water Torture Chamber, Harry Houdini 1914* was inspired by an exhibition of Smithson's work at the Vancouver Art Gallery during which Lee reflected that Smithson and Houdini were both anti-mystical individuals even as they were illusionists. Houdini created his persona and put himself at risk to entertain. Smithson took great intellectual and artistic risk by creating works of art at considerable cost in remote locations that few will ever see. Therefore, Lee, who is interested in "counterintuitive thinking," brings these two figures together in a provocative and thought-provoking way. As he explains of his objective in creating this work, "I guess just this idea that maybe conventional thought is the worst thought of all. That viewing something straight and as direct as possible is the most boring way to view something. I think that is something that was essential to me—the essential thing I learned from Smithson. He reminds us of the questions we should be asking of ourselves and they can be performed with a simple twist of viewing something from the weirdest angles."[5]

Upside Down Water Torture Chamber, Harry Houdini 1914 is open ended. Each viewer must bring his or her own perspective to the work, and there is no right way to view it. However, Lee has clearly met his goal to have us think in unconventional ways. Few artworks are both immensely funny and deeply thought provoking, but this is a rare example of a work that succeeds in making us both laugh and think. ■

Ken Lum
Nancy Nishi, Joe Ping Chau, Real Estate
1990

Ken Lum has an interest in exploring our relationship to the contemporary world—the realities of our complex perceptions of who we are and the boundaries of art or our perception of what art is. Lum's work has been informed by the history of modernism, photography, advertising and typography as well as, due to his Chinese ancestry, by his own experience of being thought of as "other."

A Vancouver native, Ken Lum was born in 1956. Initially, he had little intention of becoming an artist and attended university to study biology. However, while at Simon Fraser University, he took classes from artist Jeff Wall (b. 1946), who was teaching there, and this changed the course of Lum's life. He later studied art education at New York University and, in 1985, graduated with a master of fine arts from the University of British Columbia. He began exhibiting while still a student, and his work has been exhibited extensively in both solo and group exhibitions around the world.

Lum has employed a number of strategies in his work, and has made sculpture, photographs and paintings. *Nancy Nishi, Joe Ping Chau, Real Estate* is one of a series of photographic portrait works in which Lum has placed actors into roles and then paired these highly contrived images with what might be described as visually activated text. This image is very specifically placed in Vancouver; indeed, it was shot on the balcony of a West End apartment that Lum lived in at the time. In this image, the protagonists Nancy Nishi and Joe Ping Chau[1] are placed before the vista of the city's urban life. In the distance, almost lost in the fog or mist, is the Vancouver neighbourhood of Kitsilano, and in front of it, a glimpse of English Bay as it narrows to become False Creek. Clearly, the implied narrative is that these two real estate agents are selling us on the apartment because of the view and the location within the city. They are presented in business attire, with Ms. Nishi in a demure blazer and striped skirt. Colour is kept to a minimum, and there is an interesting contrast between the encouraging hint of a smile on Ms. Nishi's face and the broad grin that turns the face of Mr. Chau into a cipher. Each of the agents employs a different strategy and body language to sell us, the client.

This image, in common with all the "attribute" portraits in this series, devotes equal attention to the text portion of the composition. Although he uses only seven words in total, Lum, by varying the scale of the words, the boldness of the type and the style of the font, has given what might have been a flat, dull area of the image considerable visual energy. He has also toyed with our perceptions of depth and space. The rusticated letters of the words "Real Estate" are given implied dimension through the use of shadow and texture. They appear to be made of stone, which implies solidity and permanence despite being subtly pockmarked, and gives the viewer or buyer a sense that the investment that Ms. Nishi and Mr. Chau are proposing is a good one.

PROVENANCE: *Artist; Andrea Rosen Gallery, New York; Audain Collection, purchased 1998; Gift of Michael Audain and Yoshiko Karasawa; Audain Art Museum Collection, 2015.023*

► Ken Lum (b. 1956)
Nancy Nishi, Joe Ping Chau, Real Estate, 1990
chromogenic print
242.8 × 152.4 cm
Gift of Michael Audain and Yoshiko Karasawa; Audain Art Museum Collection, 2015.023

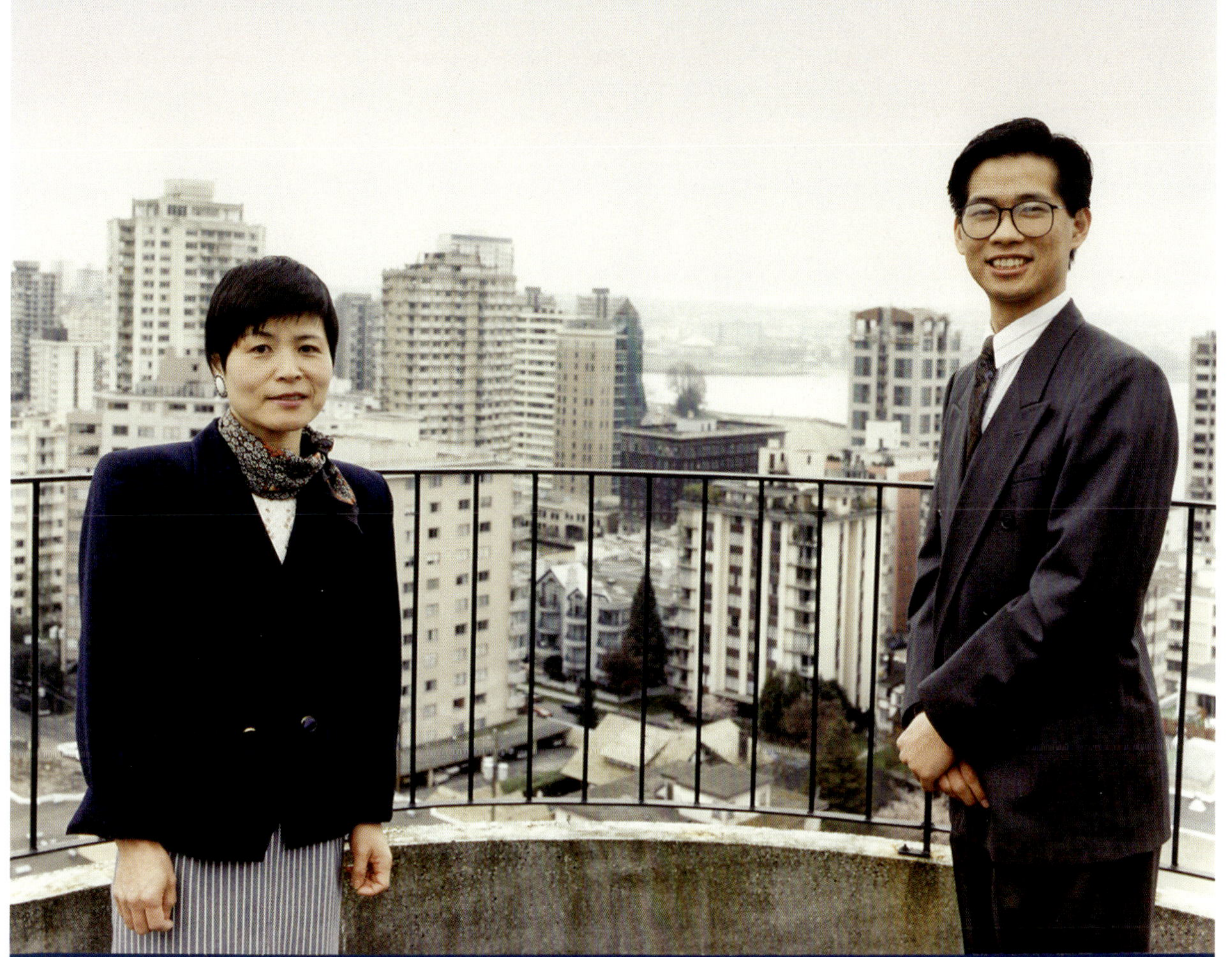

Nancy NISHI

Joe Ping CHAU

REAL ESTATE

Like many attribute portraits, this work also raises significant social questions. Vancouver has a large and important population of Canadians and immigrants of Chinese ancestry. Knowing this, and looking at this image, how do we perceive people of Chinese ancestry within the broader population of Vancouver, British Columbia and Canada? What of their relationship to real estate and the implications of ownership of a portion of the sky? Do the postures and expressions of the figures in this image change the way we view them? All these questions and many others flow from the image, and one of the strengths of this work is that there is no single answer. Each of us must come to our own conclusion. Lum's skill has been to express a profoundly complex nexus of aesthetic, social, cultural and political issues in what is, at first glance, an apparently simple and straightforward work of art composed of a single photographic image and a seven-word text. If we take the time to consider it, however, we quickly realize that the image is far from simple.

When recently asked about this work, Lum wrote:

> It was clear to me by the start of the 1990s that a new and sustained wave of Asian migration (particularly from China) would transform Vancouver, rendering it anew in ways that would radically upset the Vancouver as it has been defined since 1886. The redefinition of Vancouver is most visually evident in the changing countenances of its citizens and in the city's intensively monetized geography. Like all change, it comes also at a cost. *Nancy Nishi, Joe Ping Chau, Real Estate* was my way of asking the question of what will be the cost.[2]

Now, more than twenty years after Lum created this work, the prescience of this image is evident. ■

Steven Shearer
Guitar #5
2002–3

PROVENANCE: *Artist; State Gallery, Vancouver; Audain Collection, purchased 2004; Gift of Michael Audain and Yoshiko Karasawa; Audain Art Museum Collection, 2015.024*

Born in 1968, Steven Shearer grew up in Port Coquitlam, British Columbia, and, like many young men of his generation, was fascinated by the culture of rock 'n' roll—both its glamorous television stars, such as Leif Garrett and David Cassidy, and its darker side, heavy metal. He is also fascinated by the life of images, and has compiled a massive archive of images of people and objects, which he uses in some of his art. Although he works in a variety of media and formats, he has become very well known for a series of works that draw on his archive images and reflect his own interests and those of the larger culture.

Guitar #5 is a collection of images of a single male figure with one or more guitars, drawn from Shearer's larger collection. Gleaning individual images from the Internet, Shearer classifies them by type and then knits them together in a kind of mosaic. Here Shearer has taken what are, for the most part, singularly banal snapshots of unidentified men and boys in both relaxed and mock heroic poses and reassembled hundreds of them into a vast, scintillating field of images. None are remarkable in and of themselves (though, tellingly, the pictures were important enough to the individuals depicted in them to post them online), but the whole takes on a much greater meaning than the individual parts, causing us to reflect on the importance of the guitar to popular culture, the ubiquity of imagery and the tsunami of that imagery that is now available to us on the Internet and through social media. As Shearer has noted, "What is powerful or poetic is when people relate to the experiences of others."[1]

Like Shearer's other archive works, *Guitar #5* has an almost incantory aspect to it: the repetition of similar but not identical images adds up to a visual experience that is both powerful and poetic. These works share something of the interest in typologies seen in the more formal work of the German artists Bernd and Hilla Becher (1931–2007; b. 1934), but at the same time they reflect both the ambitions and dreams of amateur guitar players all over the world and the organized chaos of the online world. Although this work predates Facebook and other popular photo-sharing sites, amassing such image archives has now become dramatically more possible. Shearer has characterized his interest in images thus: "My image archive stems from a serious, almost forensic interest in how images are made, how they're formed both physically and theoretically. I'm interested in making things that explore how we all remember and idealise each other. Today's images are echoes of how people have always been depicted, throughout history."[2]

Clearly, we are meant to identify with these men and boys whose interests and activities may reflect our own lives or the life of the artist himself. While a discrete border of white surrounds each image, the whole field of images seems like a complex pattern in constant motion, the eye never resting in any one place for longer than a moment or two. The experience of *Guitar #5*, rather like the

Internet itself, is deliberately immersive. This Shearer has accomplished through the large scale of the work. It rewards the casual viewer with its rich overall pattern and visual activity, and the close observer with the humour, bravado, modesty and delight of the individual images that make up the whole.

Shearer adds, "Collecting all of these pictures can also have an anthropological or sociological feel to it."[3] Fortunately, for his viewers, his arrangement of these pictures transcends the dry realms of anthropological or sociological categorization to become an arresting work of art. ■

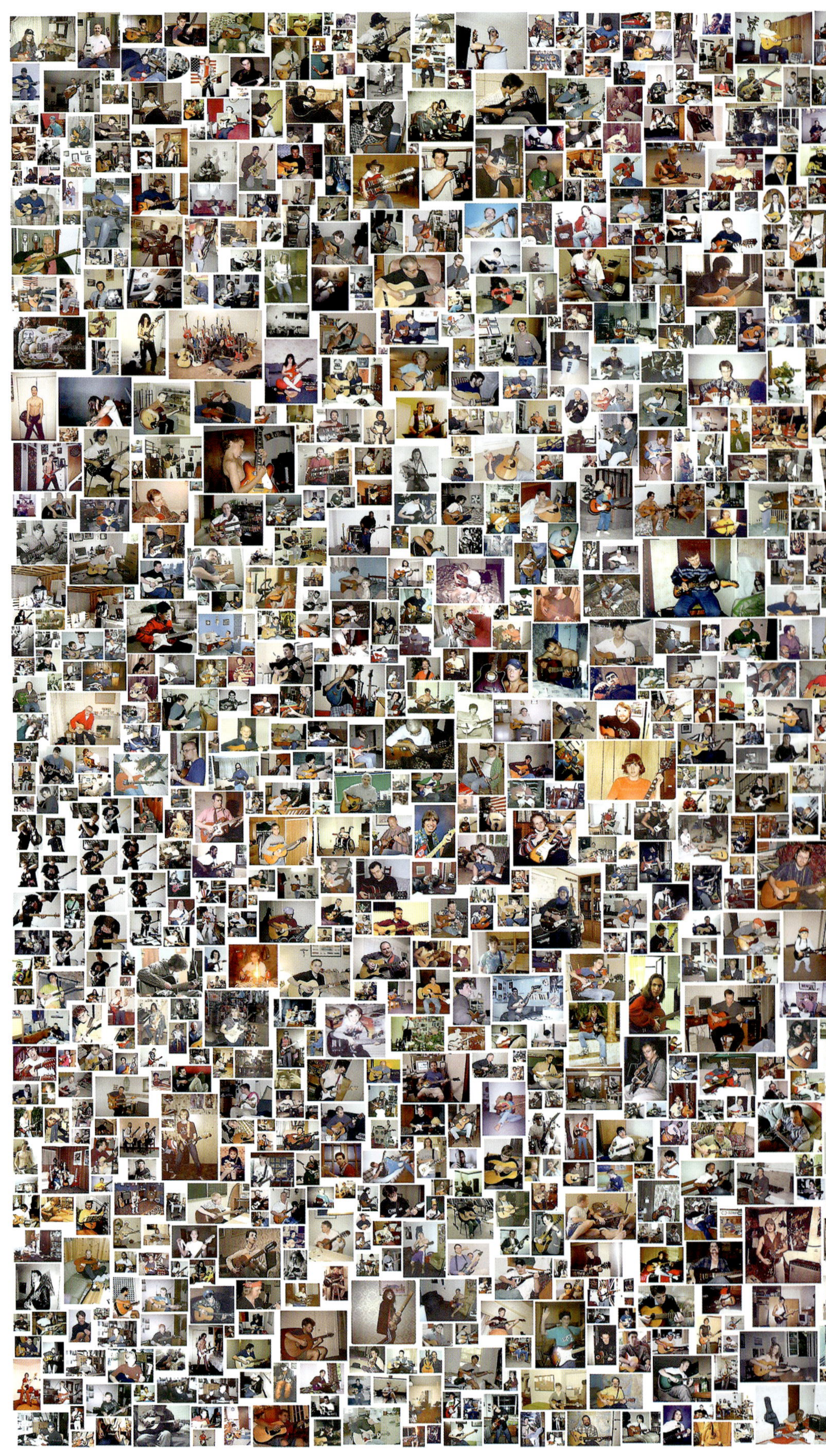

▸ **Steven Shearer** (b. 1968)
Guitar #5, 2002–3
inkjet print on archival paper
185.0 × 292.0 cm
Gift of Michael Audain and Yoshiko Karasawa; Audain Art Museum Collection, 2015.024

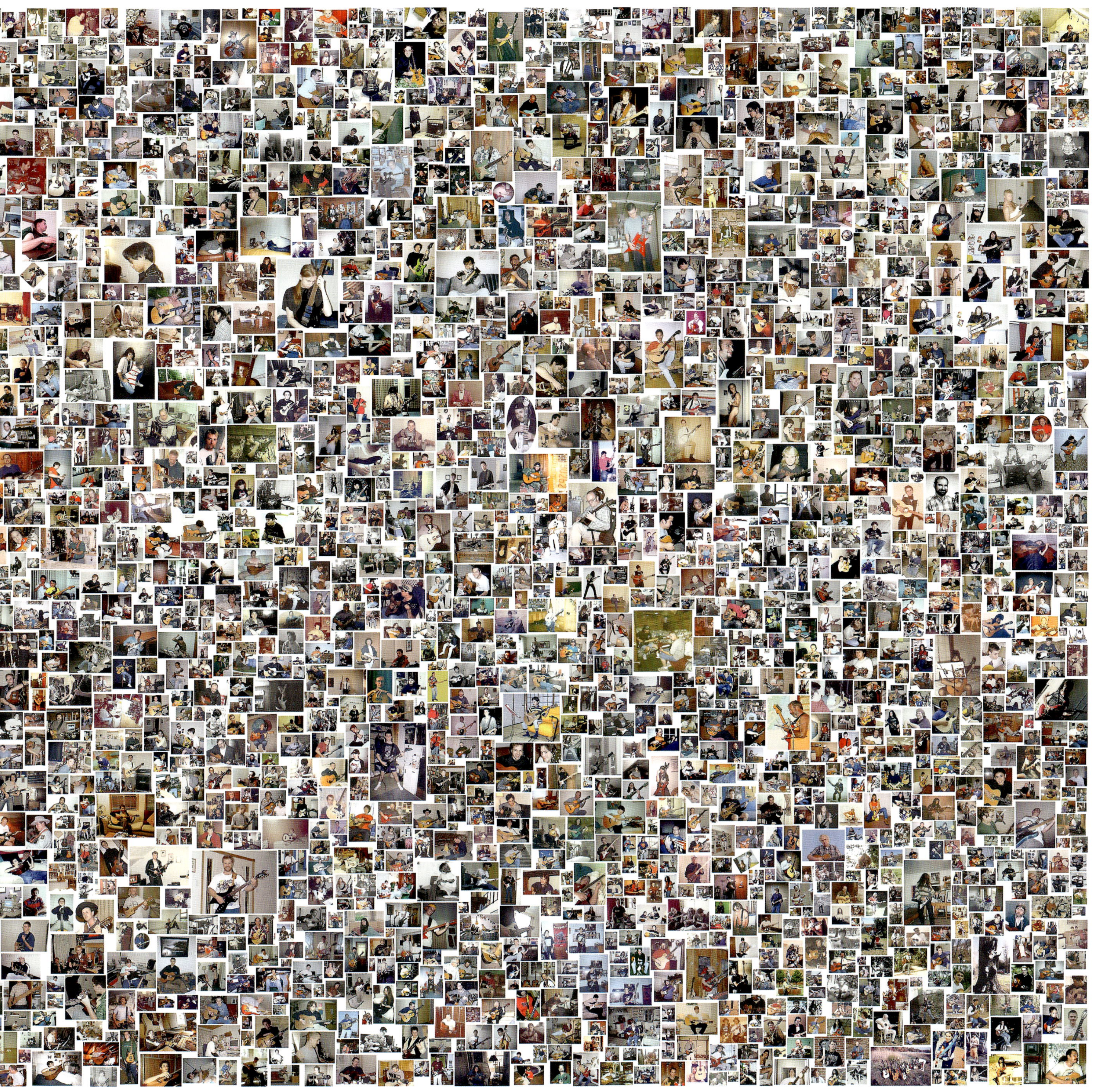

Jeff Wall
The Crooked Path
1991

Born in Vancouver in 1946, Jeff Wall initially studied art history and received a master's degree from the University of British Columbia in 1970. He then went to London to study at the Courtauld Institute of Art, where he worked for several years on a doctorate and spent considerable time looking at historical paintings. This immersion in art history continues to influence his work today, though ultimately he decided that it was not the best expression for his ideas.

While exploring photography and the idea that photography could convey something of the monumentality of painting of the past, Wall realized that commercial advertising is in part so compelling because it is often illuminated from behind. Wall chose to explore this idea in his art, and in 1978 he exhibited his first large-scale colour transparency, *Destroyed Room,* in Vancouver's Nova Gallery. Soon he realized that using an aluminum lightbox equipped with powerful interior illumination would allow him to control light, the essential ingredient in all photography. It was a revolutionary move in photography. As curator Gary Dufour has recently written, "This new medium—a colour transparency in a lightbox—afforded Wall an opportunity to link three areas of personal interest: the scale and affection for nature he found appealing in painting; the expanded capacity for storytelling and the imaginative licence cinema offered to documentary reportage; and the medium of photography itself."[1]

The images that Wall has created, though all based on everyday experiences, are of two types: those that involve the construction or recreation of a setting in which to tell the narrative and those that are documentary. *The Crooked Path* is among the second of these. We see a slightly dispirited landscape, neither fully urban nor completely natural. The image, which was probably shot in December,[2] has a foreground of green grass but the trees and bushes are still bare. Across the image, leading into it from our vantage point, is the pathway of the title, a path that has been made by people walking across the space, perhaps to tend to the hives that are visible on the left side of the composition, or perhaps to move towards the industrial buildings that form the backdrop of the scene. There are flashes of red throughout the composition—some of the hive boxes, and the building and signage in the background—and these provide an element of formal interest to the composition. They were naturally present in the scene, as was the relatively blank, white sky, which offers an important foil to the visual detail of the lower portions of the image.

Wall writes of such spaces, which often appear in his work,

> They are urban areas, left over from an earlier moment of development and captured by something else, at least for a time. They remind me of when Vancouver wasn't so completely filled in as it is now, when there were empty lots and fragmented, undeveloped zones all over town. At one time downtown Vancouver was really pitted with parking lots, just empty lots gravelled

PROVENANCE: *Artist; Mai 36 Galerie, Zurich; private collection, Switzerland; Christie's, London (lot 47, October 18, 2013); Audain Art Museum Collection, 2013.013*

► **Jeff Wall** (b. 1946)
The Crooked Path, 1991
lightbox with chromogenic transparency
165.1 × 134.9 × 21.9 cm
Audain Art Museum Collection, 2013.013

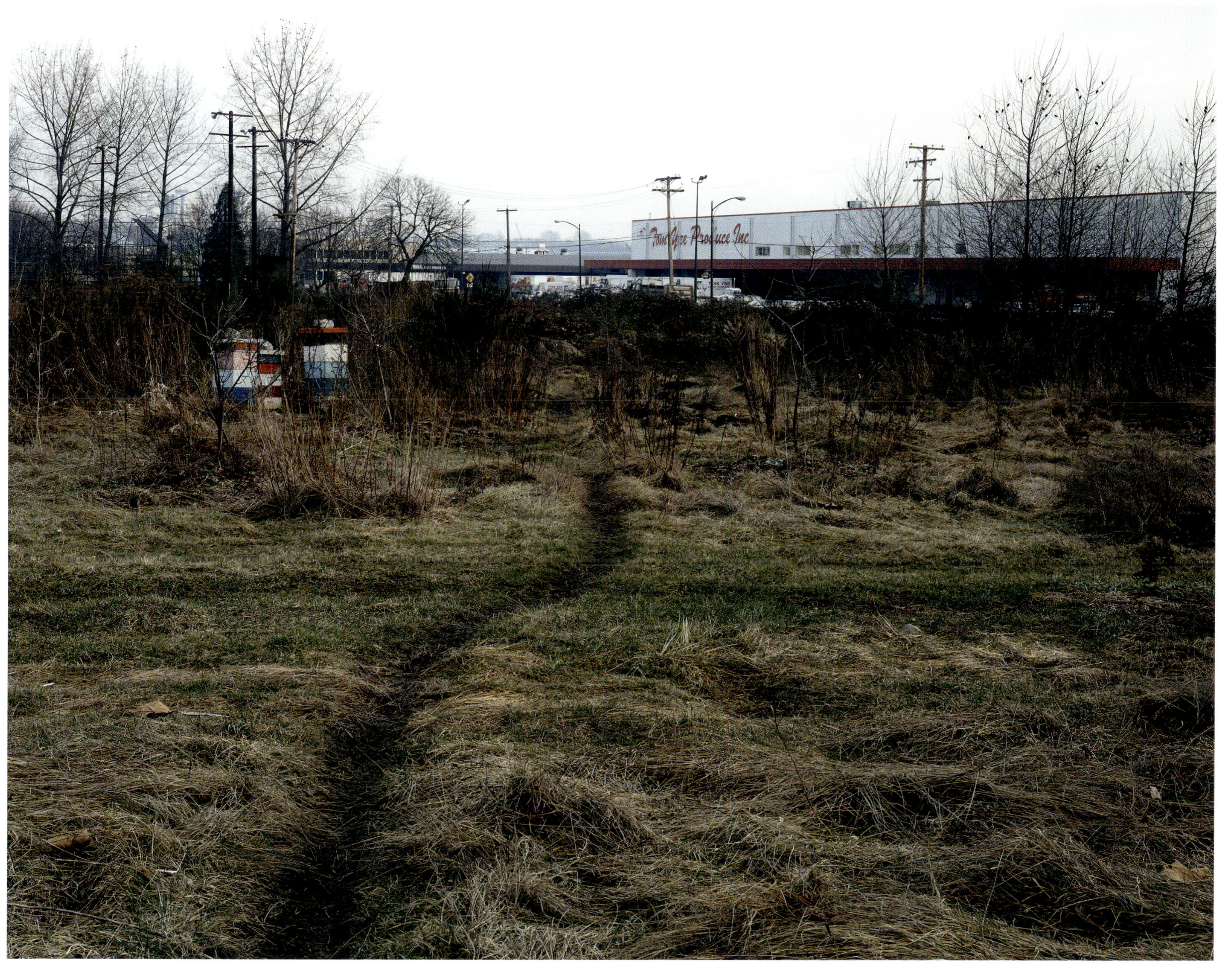
Tom Yee Produce Inc

> over, no structure, just a "parking" sign. These spaces seem full of potential and introversion since they've been neglected—or spared having to take part in the development process.[3]

The "potential" of these spaces that Wall speaks of is realized in the narratives that we, as viewers, create for ourselves when we view the image. This is the mark of Wall's genius: he has been able to spot a scene that is rich in possibility and, when most of us would simply pass it by, capture it on film and make an image. He explains, "It seemed right when I saw it and it couldn't have been different now, looking back. That's the documentary mode—either the thing and the moment make it instantly, or they don't."[4]

How, then, are we to read this image? The affinities between this image and the landscapes "shaped by humanity" of painters James M.W. Turner (1775–1851) and John Constable (1776–1837) have been noted by writers Ulrich Bischoff and Alexander Vasudevan,[5] and others have observed that this image manages, in what is essentially a snapshot, to imply a sense of time. This crooked path has been created over time, implying that it has a history but it also has a contingency that reinforces the contingency of this urban space. There is, as Wall has noted, enormous potential, but how that potential is realized remains to be seen. At present there are some hives and bees, which are dormant in December. The grass, though still green, is not growing. The path leads somewhere, but we are not sure where. We know that when spring arrives this scene will be transformed, and that this space may be here for twenty years or may be gone tomorrow. *The Crooked Path* is a powerful and memorable image, and part of its power is this sense of ambiguity. It suggests both a history and a future, but it is up to each of us to define those narratives. ■

Ian Wallace
Times Square NYC (July 11, 2003) I
2003

PROVENANCE: *Artist; Catriona Jeffries Gallery, Vancouver; Audain Collection, purchased 2006; Gift of Michael Audain and Yoshiko Karasawa; Audain Art Museum Collection, 2015.025*

Artist, musician and art historian Ian Wallace was born in Shoreham, England, in 1943. His Canadian parents returned to Canada the following year, and after a period living in British Columbia's Okanagan, the family settled in North Vancouver in 1952. Wallace began his studies at the University of British Columbia (UBC) in 1962 and graduated with a master's degree in art history in 1968. During that time, in 1965, Wallace began to exhibit his paintings, and his work has been extensively exhibited internationally since 1973. He has also had a distinguished teaching career beginning in 1967 at UBC and then the Vancouver School of Art (now Emily Carr University of Art + Design) from which he retired in 1998. In 1969, Wallace began to work with photography, and in the 1970s he produced a number of large-scale photographic works that reflected his interest in art history and cinema. Beginning in 1982, in a pivotal series entitled *Poverty*, Wallace began to combine photographic images with paint.

Times Square NYC (July 11, 2003) I continues a long-term investigation of urban life that Wallace began in 1969 when he turned his attention to the theme of the street. This investigation has encompassed paintings of intersections in Vancouver and several other cities in North America (New York, Chicago, Los Angeles, Toronto), and Wallace has written eloquently about these works. He notes, "In all of these series the urban intersection with pedestrians in the crosswalk form the core motif of the imagery… The image of the urban intersection and crosswalk remains a key subject in my work."[1] Intersections, as Wallace observes, provide an important nexus for people to locate themselves within a city. They are at once fairly universal within the Western world and individual within specific cities by virtue of the surrounding architecture, signage and landscape. In this image, we are securely placed within the heart of the major North American metropolis and the intersection requires a heightened sense of awareness among all who pass through it if they are to negotiate it successfully.

The title of this work is very specific because Wallace intends these paintings to be "a form of contemporary 'history painting' which often uses a date to note the occasion of an 'event,' however quotidian, and are a testimony to a specific moment in the flow of contemporary life that in the future will take on another meaning."[2] For Wallace, "Deep investigation of the phenomena of the 'everyday'… tells us as much or more about our culture than any rhetorical analysis."[3]

This work is part of a series of New York images. In them, Wallace has employed two types of proportion: earlier images such as *Jazz Street I* and *Jazz Street II* (2001) are substantially more vertical in format, half again as tall as they are wide, whereas *Times Square NYC* is square—two monochrome bands, one green and one white, frame the photolaminate image of the intersection. There is a striking contrast between the reality of the photographic image and the abstraction of the two painted areas, and also congruence between the rectangle of the image of the intersection and the rectangles of the two monochrome elements in the painting, although they differ proportionally.

Wallace's long interest in the history of modernist art and his desire to make work that reflects his own time led him to explore photography. As he says, photography "opened up new areas of thinking about contemporary life while still maintaining a connection to the formal and critical strategies of modernist art."[4] Wallace admired the strategies of N.E. Thing Co.—the duo of Iain Baxter (b. 1936, now Baxter&) and Ingrid Baxter (b. 1938) who, with artist Marcel Duchamp (1887–1968) in mind, photographed ordinary objects in the environment and presented them as art. In Wallace's words, "Photographic appropriation converted the city and its suburbs into an endlessly open-ended source of readymades."[5]

Wallace wrote his master's thesis on the work of the great Dutch abstractionist Piet Mondrian (1872–1944), and his street works, including *Times Square* NYC, make reference to some important innovations in modernist art, as does much of Wallace's artistic practice. He explains, "The urban environment provided me with visual references to three fundamental technical innovations of twentieth-century avant-garde art: abstraction, the readymade, and collage."[6] Within the city, Wallace found a particular focus: "The street became an icon or cipher for the space of modernist reality."[7] All of these elements are part of this image. The monochrome elements evoke the history of abstraction and the experiments of Mondrian and others. The photographic image of this intersection is the readymade, complete with anonymous actors. Finally, Wallace has used collage to place the photographic image on the pictorial surface. He has produced an image that is absolutely of its time yet draws tellingly from the lessons of art history. In Wallace's own words, "The referential power of photography preserved the connection between monochrome painting as a trope of modernity and the space of the everyday as a site of political and existential presence."[8]

Equally important for Wallace is his ongoing exploration of his relationship with the history of painting and abstraction. In these works he has, like Mondrian, deliberately imposed some limits on the compositions. He writes:

> Since the late 1980s I have worked out a strict structure for the relation of the photographic image to the canvas ground that not only involves colour but also the placement of the image on the ground or support. This compositional structure is as follows: the image is positioned to the left-hand side of the pictorial field so that there is revealed a bar of (coloured) canvas that

▸ **Ian Wallace** (b. 1943)
***Times Square* NYC *(July 11, 2003) 1*, 2003**
acrylic, photolaminate on canvas
183.5 × 183.5 cm
Gift of Michael Audain and Yoshiko Karasawa; Audain Art Museum Collection, 2015.025

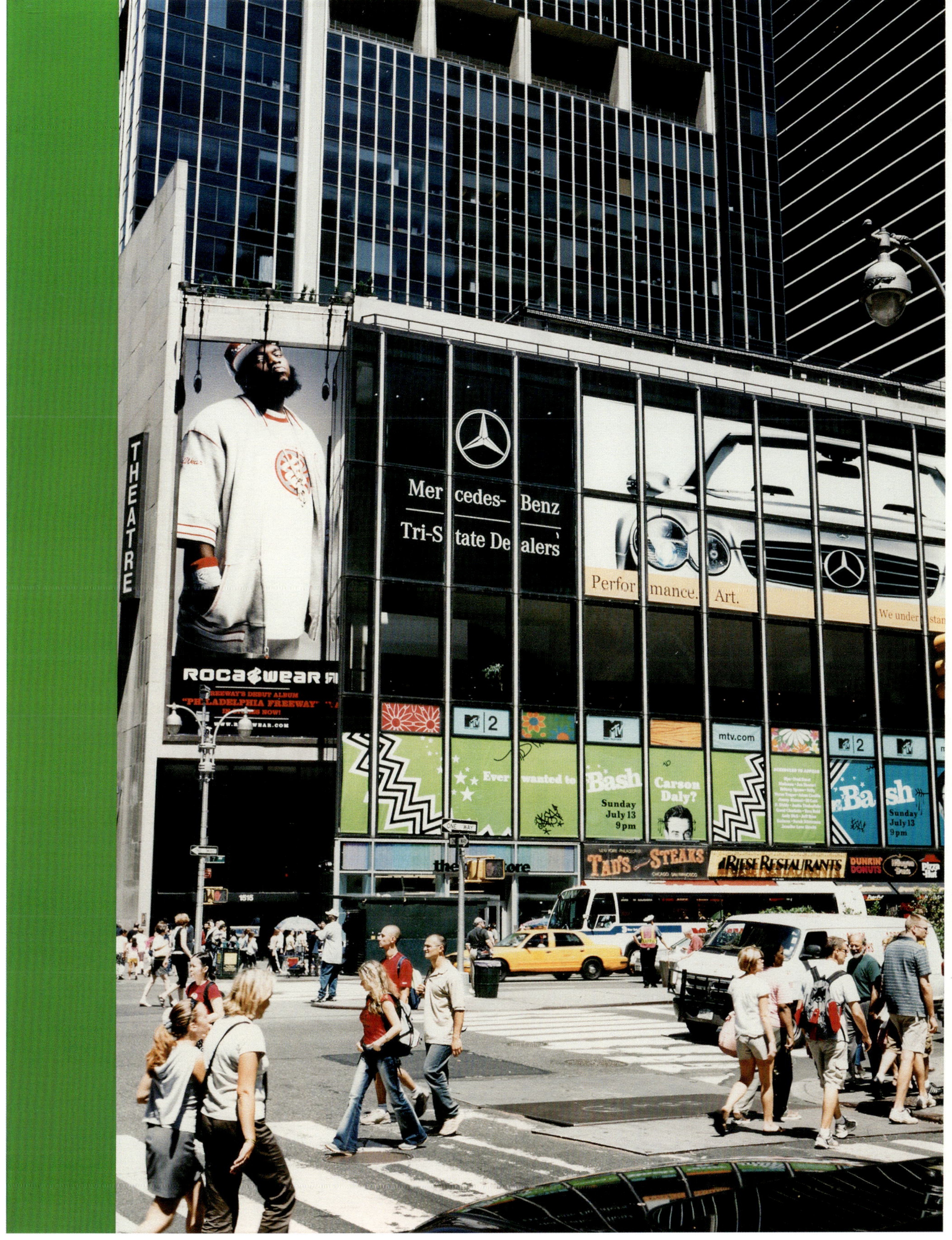
THEATRE
Mercedes-Benz
Tri-State Dealers
Performance. Art.
mtv.com
Bash
Sunday
July 13
9pm
Carson Daly?
TAD'S STEAKS
RIESE RESTAURANTS
DUNKIN' DONUTS

is approximately half the width of the bar (always painted white) on the right-hand side. The photographic image (which runs from top to bottom of the pictorial field) is cropped to allow for the proportions of this composition that reveals the canvas support as well as the significant pictorial features of the photograph. As noted, the bar to the left is always coloured, and the bar to the right is always white.[9]

Within these formal restrictions Wallace has been able to make a remarkable series of images of the urban world that are at once closely connected to each other and distinctly different as works of art. *Times Square NYC (July 11, 2003) I* works because of the subtle tension between the "reality" of the photographic image and the flat expanses of monochromatic colour on either side. Bringing these apparently disparate elements together so successfully marks Wallace as an image maker of great imagination and skill. ■

Xwalacktun (Rick Harry)
He-yay-meymuy (Big Flood)
2014–15

PROVENANCE: *Commissioned for the Audain Art Museum Collection, 2014.024*

Born in 1958, in the town of Squamish, British Columbia, Xwalacktun (Rick Harry) is of Squamish (Coast Salish) and Kwakwa̲ka̲'wakw ancestry. He was given the ancestral name Xwalacktun in a ceremony, but the exact meaning of that name has been lost to history. What is clear is that Xwalacktun is "a very old, ancestral name to be passed on" and that he has the responsibility "to carry that name in the best way I can and do not mud that name, do not dirty that name because many ancestors before you carried that name in a good way and I have to carry myself in a good way."[1]

He became interested in art as a child, or, as he explains, "I have been doing artwork since I was five. My brother was in Grade 7 at the time and I loved his drawings and I thought I want to be able to do that, so I started to draw and I have never stopped since."[2] He received his artistic training at Emily Carr College of Art and Design (now Emily Carr University of Art + Design) and Capilano College (now Capilano University) and worked with sculptors Bill Koochin (b. 1927) and Gerhard Class (1924–1997). While Xwalacktun was in art school, there was no First Nations training, and when he began to make work upon graduation, it was in a Northern rather than a Coast Salish style.[3] It was exposure to the work of Coast Salish artist Charles Elliott (b. 1943) that led him to think about and explore Coast Salish design for himself, a process he describes as "finding [his] own way and looking at designs, and looking at similarities, not just in Squamish or Coast Salish but in other art, to kind of piece things together."[4]

▸ Xwalacktun (Rick Harry) (b. 1958)
He-yay-meymuy (Big Flood), 2014–15
aluminum
487.7 × 167.6 cm (diameter)
Audain Art Museum Collection, 2014.024

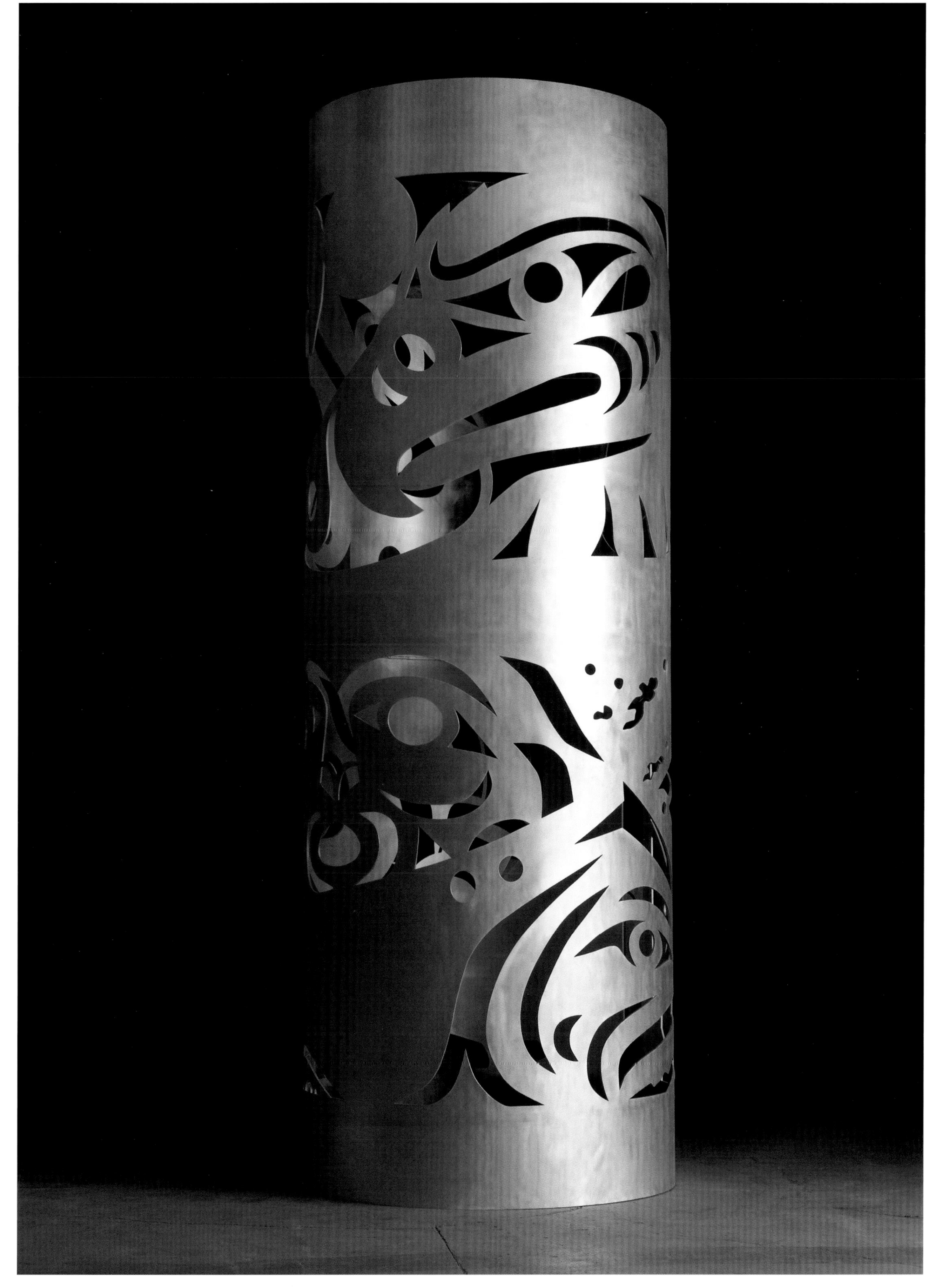

This piecing together of his own understanding of Coast Salish design has led to a major career as both a carver and a traditional healer within the Squamish First Nation. Xwalacktun has completed a number of major public art projects in Canada and overseas, including several carved poles in Scotland, a country he has visited several times, beginning in 2002. He has completed more than eighty public art works in British Columbia's Lower Mainland and has worked extensively with schools and with students at Emily Carr University of Art + Design. In 2007, he completed his major Cor-ten steel sculpture *Spirit of the Mountain,* in West Vancouver's Ambleside neighbourhood.[5] He was awarded the Order of British Columbia in 2012, in recognition of his artistic practice and his work with young people.

The Audain Art Museum commission is of particular significance to Xwalacktun because the museum lies on part of the traditional territories of his Coast Salish people. In accepting the commission, he considered the museum's location on the flood plain of Fitzsimmons Creek and chose a story from Salish legend that refers to a great flood in the area. As he explains,

> Well, looking at it and knowing that they were building the building on the flood plain, I thought that maybe we should tell the story of a flood story. We have an old story of the great flood that happened here. What we did is, we tied our canoes up to what we now call Mount Garibaldi; we call [it] Nch'kay. When we were tied there, we ran out of food and the Creator, the thunderbird, sent the eagle to get, to gather some salmon and dropped it into our canoes when we ran out of food, and that is how we survived the great flood. So the eagle is important to us.[6]

The building site and the proximity of the Audain Art Museum to Nch'kay made this the appropriate story for the sculpture, which Xwalacktun considers a contemporary Coast Salish house post. He describes the work:

> There is the eagle. We have the eagle here; we have the human lifting his hands up to give thanks to something greater than ourselves. The thunderbird, to show respect the paddles are up; we have the salmon here but also the front of the canoe here and we have a salmon just underneath the canoe here. We have ideas of the rope here to symbolize tying, water coming up higher. So I think of things, like these [two circles] represent balance on the canoe. You need balance. Mind, body, spirit, going by threes here.[7]

Xwalacktun chose aluminum as the principal material because of its colour and light weight. The piece is lit from below and above, creating a rich variety of shadows.

He-yay-meymuy (Big Flood) is the first piece of art that visitors to the Audain Art Museum will see. For Xwalacktun it is an important expression of Squamish and Coast Salish identity and an affirmation of Coast Salish culture. He expresses his hopes for the sculpture: "I would like people to learn just a little bit more about Salish design and also stories. That there are still stories, stories being told of the area. Just to learn that the people are still here and still working."[8] Equally, however, it is a work about his own evolution as an artist and the evolution of Salish art: "I sort of just like to focus on who I am as an artist and that is what I reflect on. If we just stuck to tradition, we would still be rock painters or cave painters, so we are always evolving as people. We now have all the intermarriages so the artwork is changing."[9] ■

Interview with Michael Audain

Ian Thom: What motivated you to build the Audain Art Museum?

Michael Audain: Well, it wasn't a snap decision. My wife, Yoshi [Karasawa], and I had been mulling over building a home for our art for years. We held off for a long time because we were hopeful that the Vancouver Art Gallery would relocate to new quarters. Our thinking was that if they had a new and larger building, there would be more chance of our art being exhibited than simply tucked away in the vault. But as prospects for the Vancouver Art Gallery's early relocation dimmed, we became concerned that it wouldn't happen in our lifetime.

IT: Did you follow any particular model in creating your museum?

MA: Not really. It's true that we were very influenced by a visit in the early 1990s to the Maeght Foundation in Saint-Paul de Vence, which is a lovely small museum set on a sunny Provençal hillside. I generally prefer small museums. But Yoshi and I determined our own set of criteria.

IT: What were they?

MA: First and foremost, we were interested in a naturally landscaped site of at least two to three acres. In other words, not just a lot on a city street. In fact, we hoped for the natural landscape to dominate the building. Then we wanted the site to have convenient pedestrian or public transit access. Finally, we thought it would be nice if someone would donate the land for us to build on.

IT: What about the building itself. Did you have a particular style in mind?

MA: Yes, we initially leaned towards something fairly residential, preferably built out of wood and British Columbia granite. But obviously the building we ended up with looks quite different.

IT: How do you account for this difference between your vision and the final design?

MA: Well, while in the call for architectural proposals we did specify "the liberal use of wood," we decided it would be best if we just let the architect marry the site characteristics and the functional objectives for the museum.

IT: Are you happy with the building in its completed form?

MA: Yes. I am no architectural critic, but I believe that architects John and Patricia Patkau have done quite a remarkable job in creating an environment that will allow visitors to enjoy our art collection while also experiencing the natural beauty of this mountain valley.

IT: What led you to build in Whistler?

MA: We received proposals from some other places, but our friend Jim Moodie suggested that Whistler would be ideal from the point of

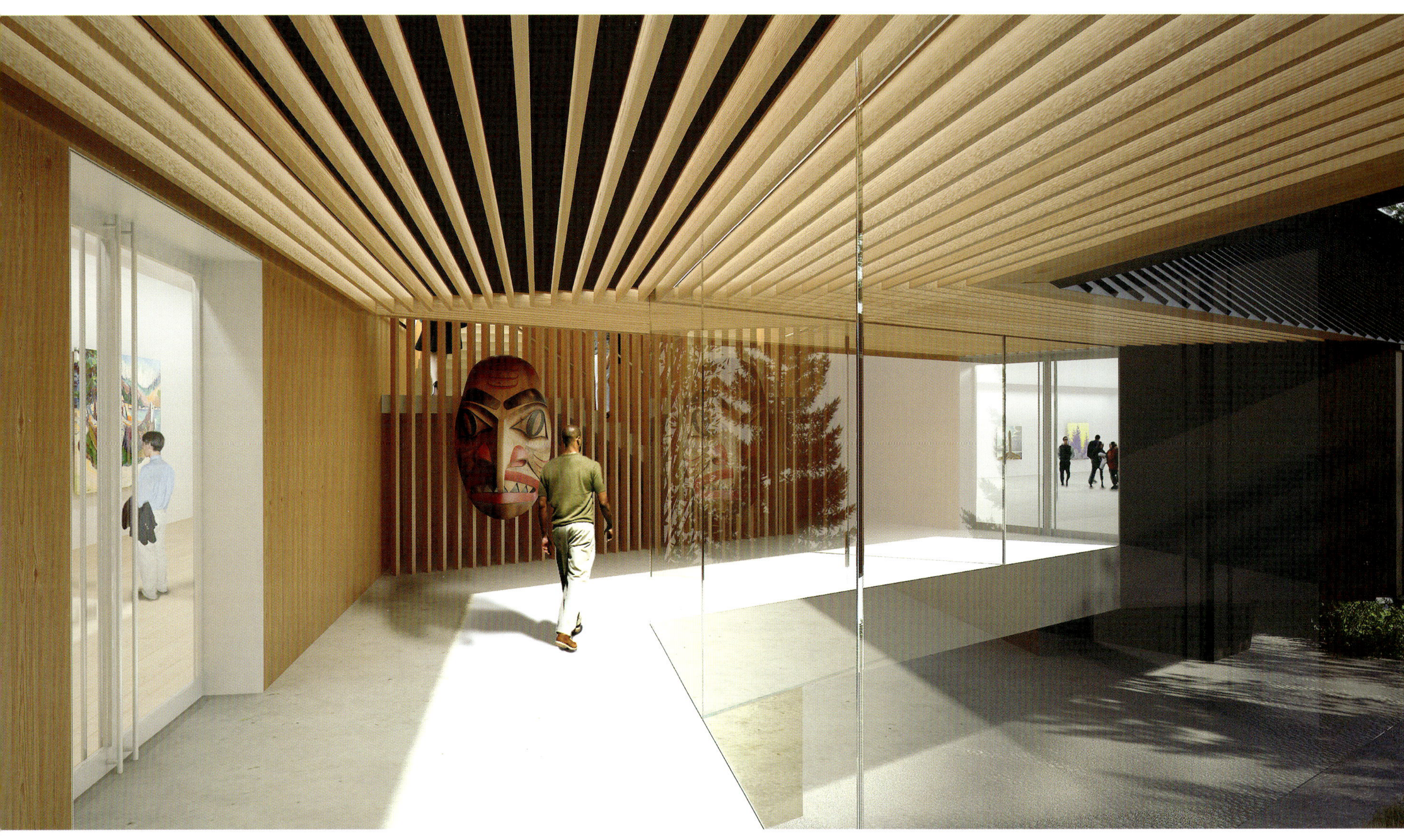

view of being a four-season resort which also had the virtue of being close to Vancouver. Certainly, the mayor and council of the day were very keen to have the museum in Whistler and went all out to convince us to locate here by providing our land on a long-term leasehold.

IT: Did you have a long relationship with Whistler before you decided to build the museum here? For example, are you and your wife avid skiers?

MA: Oh, I must confess that neither of us are skiers, although we both tried it when we were young. I have always preferred to live on the waterfront, perhaps because I am a keen sailor. On the other hand, Yoshi comes from a village in the foothills of the Japanese Alps and absolutely loves mountain vistas. So it wasn't difficult to convince her that Whistler would be a good home for our art, especially since it's just over an hour's drive from our home.

IT: What led you to select Patkau Architects?

MA: We actually interviewed eight architectural firms, all of whom appeared very capable, but John and Patricia Patkau, besides having a stellar reputation, seemed to understand the understated, quiet ethos that we wanted for the museum. They have certainly been wonderful to work with.

IT: Why the focus on British Columbia art?

MA: I have always thought it is interesting to learn about the development of a country's art over time, and, by the way, British Columbia, with over ninety-five million hectares, is larger than France and Germany combined. I have taken an interest in British Columbia art because this is my home. This is where I grew up, my family having lived in these parts for over 160 years. It's also that the art of this region ranks among the world's most important, whether one is referring to our early nineteenth-century First Nations works or Vancouver's celebrated photo-conceptual school, which has achieved such an international following over the last couple of decades.

IT: Can I take it that you have always only acquired work by British Columbia artists?

MA: Yes, principally by British Columbia artists. But, of course, Yoshi and I have some other collecting interests—for example, Mexican eighteenth-century works, as well as Mexican modernism. We also have a passion for Quebec's Automatiste school. But, it became apparent that space limitations would have to limit the scope of the museum's permanent collection.

IT: How long have you been collecting art?

MA: Well, since I was a teenager I have been putting prints and photographs up on the walls of the scores of rooms and apartments that I inhabited, well before we tentatively started paying money for pictures in the early 1960s, back then usually twenty-five or fifty dollars.

IT: Is it fair to ask, what are your favourite items from the museum's permanent collection?

MA: Actually, I have a deep attachment for all the art that we have endowed the museum with. It's true that perhaps thirty or forty years ago I used to speculate about if I was sentenced to a desert island, which painting would I select to accompany me? Today I am convinced that all the artworks in this museum share attributes of excellence.

IT: And by "excellence," what exactly do you mean?

MA: I suppose that one first thinks about the originality of the work. In other words, does it add something to the story of art from the beginning of time? A tall order! And then I think about technical competence, as well as whether the work was relevant to the time in which it was created. Finally, I am interested in whether the work is, to my mind, amongst the best that the artist has executed. Now, having said this, there is no doubt that whether or not I'm emotionally drawn to the artwork when I first see it plays a very important role.

IT: Some people might feel that it's a bit of an ego trip to put your family name on a museum. How would you respond to that?

MA: Yes, I guess that it is "a bit of an ego trip," as you call it. I had originally thought of naming the museum after Princess Diana, whom I greatly admired for her bravery in teaching the world about AIDS and the importance of clearing land mines. But I was persuaded that because the permanent collection has such a personal bent, it would make sense to put our name on the building that has been created to accommodate it. Also, I suppose that in bearing a family name, the museum doesn't purport to have just a Whistler scope. But, who knows, one day a future board might decide to rename the building.

IT: In your opinion, is the museum likely to attract people to make the drive up from Vancouver?

MA: Hopefully! For architecture buffs, the building could be considered interesting. In terms of its respect for the natural landscape and its appearance, the museum is obviously very different from what has been built before in Whistler. But then, after all, Patkau Architects have received fifteen Governor General's Awards—more than any other firm in this country!

There are also several unique aspects to the permanent collection. There is a strong presentation of work by the original peoples of the Northwest Coast, whom Jonathan King of the British Museum has called the most sophisticated art makers of any of the world's hunter-gatherer groups. This includes what I am told is one of the most important collections of old Northwest Coast masks, which have been repatriated from all over Europe and the United States. Besides being interesting artworks, they also have served important ceremonial roles in the interaction between the First Nations and their nearby relatives: the creatures of the sea, land and sky. I personally feel a great affinity for these objects and was so sad to see them depart from our home on the ocean shore. I gave them all a pledge that they will never leave the coast, nor be resold again. And it is going to be the job of the museum to ensure that pledge is fulfilled for all time.

There is also some wonderful work by today's leading First Nations carvers, foremost amongst them being James Hart's dance screen, which is a tour de force that museums throughout the world would love to own.

Then there are the Emily Carr works, which capture life on the Northwest Coast and the mystery of the coastal forest in a manner that has never been equalled. Emily Carr, who was so often ignored by art connoisseurs in her lifetime, is now receiving exposure in London and Paris exhibitions and finally gaining the recognition she deserves as one of the twentieth-century's great artists. Thus, if you are an Emily Carr fan, you will need to come here to see one of the strongest collections of her work. E.J. Hughes's picturesque paintings of the British Columbia coast also have many admirers. Fortunately, the museum offers the most important collection of his work.

Finally, there are many contemporary artists in the collection who made their homes in British Columbia, perhaps the most famous being Jeff Wall, who to this date is still the only Canadian to have been offered a full-scale retrospective at New York's Museum of Modern Art. You will see his work here, as well as that of other important Vancouver photographic artists to whom I have been attracted, such as Rodney Graham and Stan Douglas.

One thing I would like to point out, though, is that the collection is by no means comprehensive. There are many distinguished artists in British Columbia that I simply didn't get around to collecting. And because I never had an opportunity to study art history, a very untutored eye selected what you see in the Audain Art Museum collection.

IT: So it sounds like there are many styles of art for visitors to enjoy. How did you end up with such an eclectic collection?

MA: I have never taken time nor had the inclination to analyze why I acquire an artwork. If it speaks to me, and it meets my standard of excellence, I just have to have it, whether or not we have space to exhibit it—and frequently to the detriment of my bank account. But isn't that common to most art collectors?

IT: What do you hope people will take away after seeing the museum's collection?

MA: First of all, I would hope that they will discover those parts of the collection that they particularly enjoy. It would be too much to expect someone to like everything. On top of that, I hope that connoisseurs with specialized interests—say, First Nations or Emily Carr—will be able to learn something from the depth of the museum's collection in these areas.

Most importantly, for schoolchildren, I hope that exposing them to the variety of art that we have in this museum will stretch their minds and perhaps make them more receptive to visual art when they grow older. I grew up in a town without a public art gallery, so missed that opportunity.

Finally, it's my hope that our international visitors—and Whistler gets a lot of these—will be impressed with the wonderful art making that has happened in our corner of the world. Who knows? It may add enough to the Whistler experience that they will return or at least tell their friends that there is an interesting cultural dimension in this beautiful mountain resort.

IT: And what about the future—what do you see evolving in the years ahead?

MA: That will be up to the museum's board and staff. But I hope that the museum will attract sufficient interest and visitors, plus the crucial financial support that the museum will need not only to keep solvent but to enable it to grow in stature in the years to come. All my wife, Yoshi, and I have done is give the museum a head start. It will be up those who come after us to determine what lies ahead.

IT: I am told that you moved remarkably swiftly to get this museum underway.

MA: Yes, at my age I cannot afford to waste much time! Mayor Nancy Wilhelm-Morden and her senior staff showed me the site at 10 a.m. on September 21, 2012, and over a sandwich lunch that day I told her that if the municipality made the site available, I would build here. We actually started construction work less than a year later, and it will have taken just slightly more than three years to complete the building. That's thanks to a lot of hard work by a great many folk.

IT: Finally, they say that you are among Canada's most important visual arts philanthropists. Why do you do it?

MA: Well, I don't keep score. I am not much of a psychiatrist, so I won't venture to explain it except to say that some years ago I realized that the visual arts are certainly the most important art form out here on the Pacific Coast. There's a tremendous indigenous heritage, and Vancouver undoubtedly has Canada's best art school. To my surprise, I was recruited to join the board of the Vancouver Art Gallery in the late 1980s, and that coincided with growing our own collection. Thus, when we started our family foundation in 1997, we decided that the strengthening of the visual arts in British Columbia would be a good focus. It's a great privilege to give, but, frankly, writing cheques is a lot easier than the challenges that face artists and others who work one way or another in the field. The good thing is many more people in our part of the country are finally waking up to the realization that if arts and culture are going to flourish, those among us with the resources need to open their wallets rather than just relying on government.

IT: Anything else you would care to add?

MA: Well, things like art museums obviously don't just happen. There are an awful lot of people Yoshi and I are indebted to, most especially our friend Jim Moodie, who convinced us that Whistler was the right place for this museum.

It's been a stimulating learning experience to relate to such remarkable architects as John and Patricia Patkau. Then there's been the great leadership from Executive Director Suzanne Greening and a host of museum and family foundation board members, as well as the many Polygon Homes Ltd. people who went above and beyond their usual remit to ensure everything came together.

Naturally, Yoshi and I owe our greatest debt of gratitude to all those artists represented in the museum. Through their carving, painting, photography and sculpture, the artists will be communicating tirelessly in the centuries to come to all who care to visit.

About the Contributors

Michael Audain OC OBC, Chairman of Polygon Homes Ltd., is one of British Columbia's leading home builders. A fifth-generation British Columbian and an alumnus of the University of British Columbia, Audain is also one of Canada's leading cultural philanthropists, supporting the artistic life of this province and country for many years through the Audain Foundation. He is honorary chairman of the Vancouver Art Gallery and a past chair of the National Gallery of Canada, the Vancouver Art Gallery and the Vancouver Art Gallery Foundation. He has received honorary degrees from four universities, as well as the Queen's Diamond and Golden Jubilee Medals. Married to Yoshiko Karasawa, Mr. Audain has two children and four grandchildren, all of whom reside in British Columbia.

Suzanne E. Greening, Executive Director of the Audain Art Museum, has embraced her passion for the arts through a lifelong career in the arts community in Canada and the United States. She has had extensive experience starting up new museum facilities, previously acting as the director of the Canadian Clay & Glass Gallery in Waterloo, Ontario; the Museum of Glass and Chihuly Bridge of Glass in Tacoma, Washington; and The Reach Gallery Museum in Abbotsford, British Columbia. She has also been actively involved on cultural and community-based boards, such as the Chamber of Commerce, the Glass Art Society, KCTS 9 and Rotary International.

John and Patricia Patkau CM are founders and principals of the Vancouver-based Patkau Architects. Their contributions to architecture and Canadian culture have been recognized by numerous Governor General's Awards, as well as the Royal Architectural Institute of Canada Gold Medal. Patricia is professor emerita at the University of British Columbia, and her significant commitment to architectural education was recognized with the Tau Sigma Delta Gold Medal. John and Patricia are also honorary fellows of the American Institute of Architects and the Royal Institute of British Architects. They represented Canada at the Venice Biennale in 1996.

Ian M. Thom CM is Senior Curator–Historical at the Vancouver Art Gallery, where he has been involved since 1988 in more than fifty exhibitions, including retrospectives of Emily Carr, E.J. Hughes, Takao Tanabe and Gordon Smith. Collaborating with Grant Arnold, Audain Curator of British Columbia Art at the Vancouver Art Gallery, Thom organized, in 2011, the first major showing of the Audain Collection: *Shore, Forest and Beyond: Art from the Audain Collection.* He previously served in senior posts at the McMichael Canadian Art Collection and the Art Gallery of Greater Victoria. A graduate of the University of British Columbia, Thom has published extensively on Canadian art.

Acknowledgements

My first thanks must be to Michael Audain, who has long been supportive of my work and who kindly invited me to write this book. He, and his wife, Yoshiko Karasawa, have been enormously generous at every turn in this process.

Two of Michael Audain's employees, Barbara Binns and Georges Dordor, have been instrumental in this project. My sincere thanks to them both for all that they have done to assist me. I would also like to thank Chantal Shah, Executive Director of the Audain Foundation, for her assistance.

I am extremely grateful to all the artists who have agreed to speak to me about their work. Their words have been crucial.

Scholar, curator and writer on Northwest Coast art Bill McLennan has been an enormous support in guiding me through the intricacies of historical First Nations masks and the literature on the subject. His highly informative interviews with contemporary artists about some of the historical masks have been most helpful. I am extremely grateful for both his expertise and his grace under persistent questioning.

Audain Art Museum Executive Director Suzanne Greening has been encouraging of my efforts, and I appreciate her confidence and her help in obtaining the copyright permissions for the works of art.

The architects of the Audain Art Museum, John and Patricia Patkau of Patkau Architects, have also been very generous with their time and ideas. I am grateful for their contribution to this book.

Many photographers, especially Trevor Mills, have made a significant contribution to this project. This book would be nothing without good images of the works of art, and I want to thank all those whose images are used here.

Colleagues at the Vancouver Art Gallery have graciously advised me from time to time, and I would like to thank them, particularly Grant Arnold and Bruce Grenville. I am also grateful that Vancouver Art Gallery Director Kathleen Bartels was agreeable to my taking on this project.

The publisher, Figure 1; designer, Jessica Sullivan; and editors, Lucy Kenward and Stephanie Fysh, have all made this book much better. To you all, many thanks.

Finally, my husband, Darrin Martens, has been a constant strength and my sounding board for this project. To him, my deepest thanks and love.

Ian M. Thom

Notes / Photo Credits

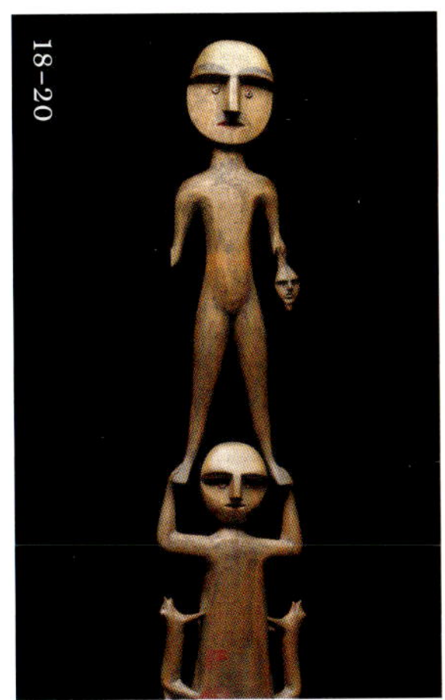

Salish Artist
Figure

NOTES

1 My discussion of this object has benefited greatly from conversations with Northwest Coast art curator, scholar and writer Bill McLennan.

PHOTO Courtesy of Vancouver Art Gallery (Trevor Mills)

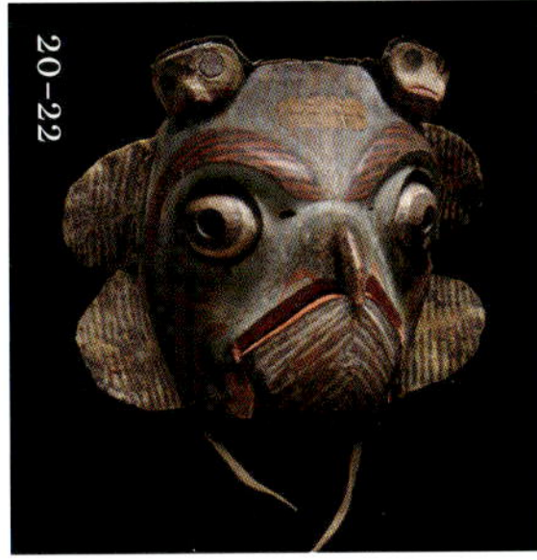

Heiltsuk Artist
Articulated Mask (Owl)

NOTES

1 Steven C. Brown, *Transfigurations: North Pacific Coast Art: George Terasaki, Collector* (Seattle: Marquand Books, 2006), entry 33 (unpaginated).
2 Ibid.
3 Ibid.
4 Bill McLennan, in conversation with the author, August 5, 2014.
5 Norman Tait, in an interview with Bill McLennan, July 20, 2014.
6 Ibid.

PHOTO Courtesy of Vancouver Art Gallery (Trevor Mills)

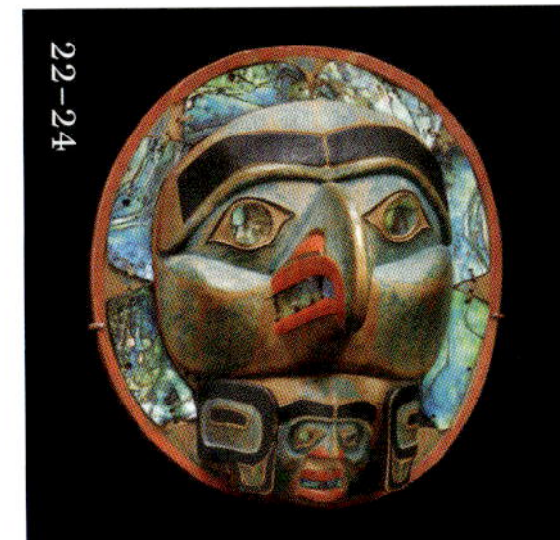

Heiltsuk Artist
Frontlet

NOTES

1 Bill McLennan, in conversation with the author, August 5, 2014.
2 Beau Dick, in an interview with Bill McLennan, March 11, 2014.

PHOTO Courtesy of Vancouver Art Gallery (Rachel Topham)

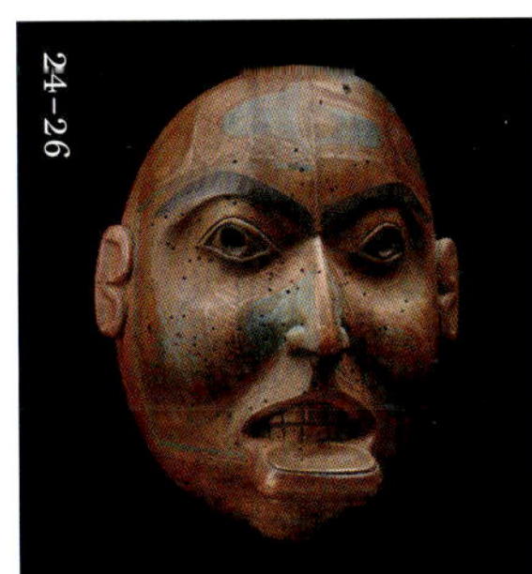

Haida Artist
Female Portrait Mask

NOTES

1 Bill Reid and Bill Holm, *Form and Freedom: A Dialogue on Northwest Coast Art* (Houston, TX: Institute for the Arts, Rice University, 1975), pp. 218–20.
2 See Bill McLennan and Karen Duffek, *The Transforming Image: Painted Arts of the Northwest Coast First Nations* (Vancouver: Douglas & McIntyre, 2007), pp. 92–98.
3 Robert Davidson, in an interview with the author, July 8, 2014.
4 See SMNH 89049 and UPMAA 45-15-2. The example at the Smithsonian was collected in Skidegate in 1883. Bill McLennan, in an email to the author, August 10, 2014.

PHOTO Courtesy of Haida Gwaii Museum (Trevor Mills)

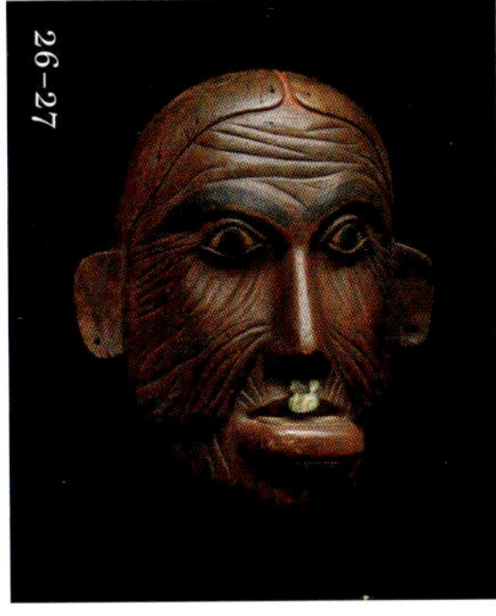

Haida Artist
Old Woman with Labret Mask

NOTES

1 Steven C. Brown, *Transfigurations: North Pacific Coast Art: George Terasaki, Collector* (Seattle: Marquand Books, 2006), entry 42, unpaginated.
2 Robert Davidson feels that the carving of this mask is not fine enough to be the work of Sdiihaldaa; in an interview with the author, July 8, 2014.
3 Brown, *Transfigurations*, entry 42.

PHOTO Courtesy of Vancouver Art Gallery (Trevor Mills)

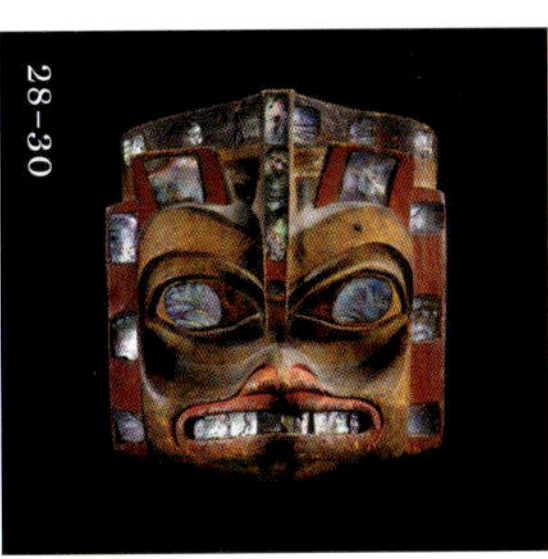

Haida Artist (Kaigani)
Frontlet

NOTES

1 Bill McLennan identified the abalone as being of "typical California colour" in a conversation with the author, August 5, 2014.
2 Bill Reid, in Bill Holm and Bill Reid, *Indian Art of the Northwest Coast: A Dialogue on Craftsmanship and Aesthetics* (Houston, TX: Institute for the Arts, Rice University, 1975), p. 184.
3 Dempsey Bob, in an interview with Bill McLennan, March 14, 2014.
4 Norman Tait, in an interview with Bill McLennan, July 20, 2014.

PHOTO Courtesy of Sotheby's, New York

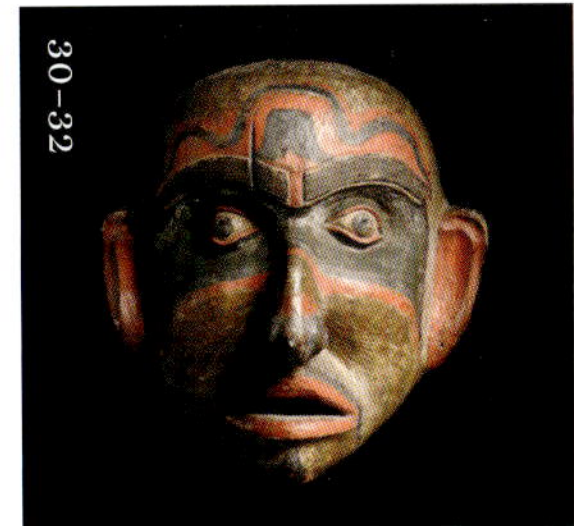

Kwakwaka'wakw Artist
Ancestor Mask

NOTES

1 This was part of the *1895 Report of the National Museum* (Washington: The Smithsonian Institution, 1897), pp. 468–99.
2 Ibid., p. 468.
3 Ibid.
4 Ibid., p. 469.
5 Beau Dick, in an interview with Bill McLennan, May 11, 2014.

PHOTO Courtesy of Sotheby's, New York

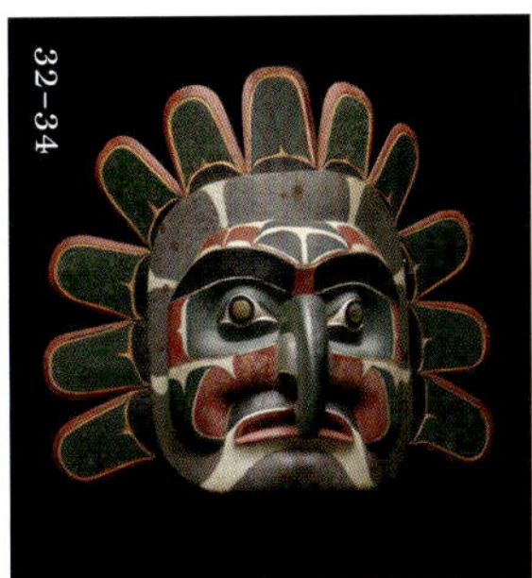

Kwakwaka'wakw Artist
Sun Mask

NOTES

1 Beau Dick, in an interview with Bill McLennan, March 14, 2014.

PHOTO Courtesy of Vancouver Art Gallery (Trevor Mills)

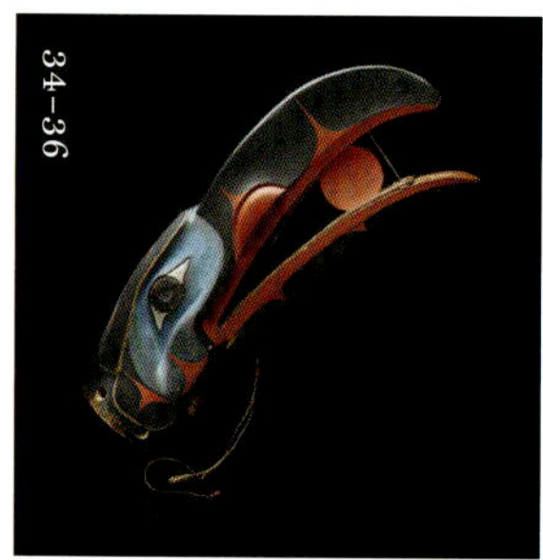

Nuxalk Artist
Raven Mask (Bella Coola)

NOTES

1 T.F. McIlwraith, *The Bella Coola Indians* (Toronto: University of Toronto Press, 1948), vol. 1, pp. 82–83.
2 Ibid., p. 298.
3 Latham Mack, in an interview with Bill McLennan, March 19, 2014.
4 Ibid.
5 Ibid.
6 Ibid.

PHOTO Courtesy of Vancouver Art Gallery (Trevor Mills)

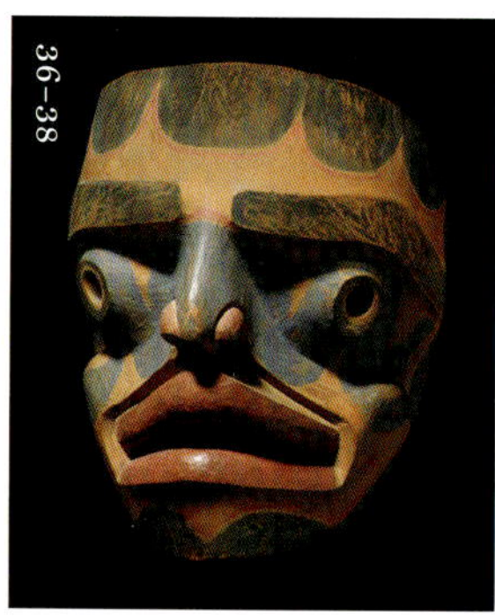

Nuxalk Artist
Earthquake Mask

NOTES

1 T.F. McIlwraith, *The Bella Coola Indians* (Toronto: University of Toronto Press, 1948), vol. 2, p. 42.
2 Franz Boas, "The Mythology of the Bella Coola Indians," in *The Jesup North Pacific Expedition, Memoir of the American Museum of Natural History* (New York: American Museum of Natural History, 1898), vol. 1, p. 37.
3 McIlwraith, *The Bella Coola Indians*, vol. 2, p. 237.
4 Latham Mack, in an interview with Bill McLennan, March 19, 2014.

PHOTO Courtesy of Vancouver Art Gallery (Trevor Mills)

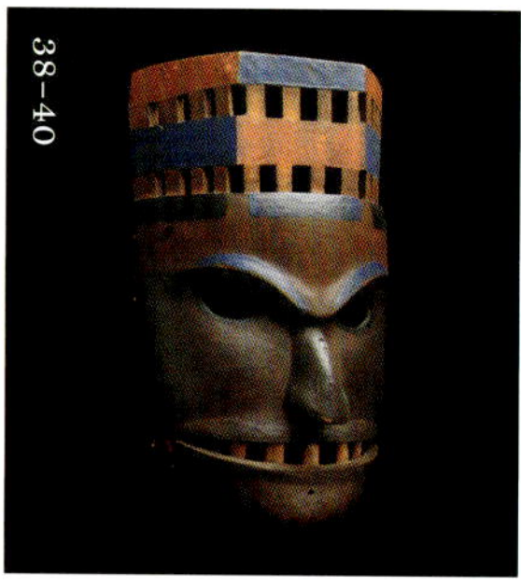

Nuu-chah-nulth Artist
Articulated Mask

1 This characteristic is shared by two Nuu-chah-nulth masks in the Royal British Columbia Museum (catalogue numbers 1338 and 14114). This mask, however, is much more finely carved.
2 Bill McLennan, in conversation with the author, August 5, 2014. McLennan believes that the Glenbow Museum mask is by the same carver as the present mask.
3 The American Museum of Natural History has a striking example of this type of rattle (AMNH 16/1966).

PHOTO Courtesy of Vancouver Art Gallery (Trevor Mills)

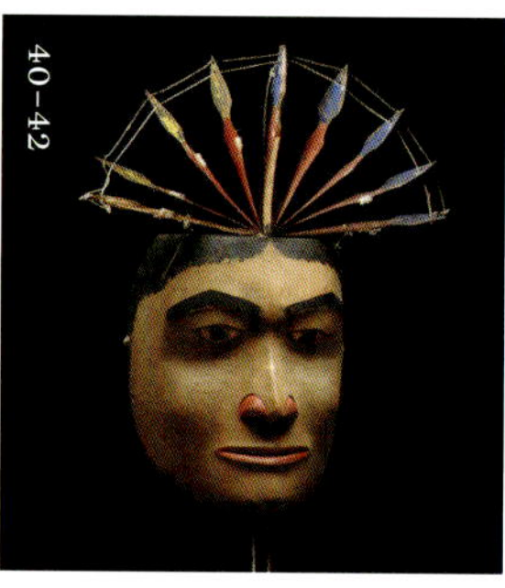

Gitxsan Artist
Portrait Mask

NOTES

1 Distinguished Northwest Coast art scholar Bill McLennan has been a consultant to the Audain Collection, and examined and researched the historical First Nations objects for the Audain Art Museum. McLennan confirmed his belief that the two masks were by the same carver in a conversation on August 5, 2014.
2 Rocque Berthiaume, in an interview with Freda Diesing School of Northwest Coast Art staff and students, conducted by Bill McLennan in Terrace, BC, on March 19, 2014.

PHOTO Courtesy of Vancouver Art Gallery (Trevor Mills)

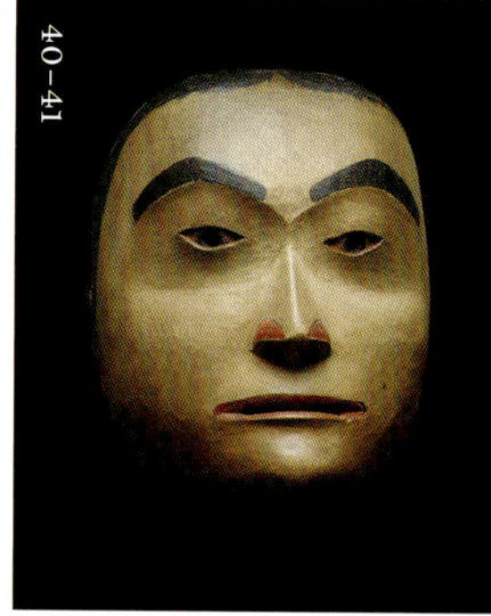

Gitxsan Artist
Portrait Mask

PHOTO Courtesy of Vancouver Art Gallery (Trevor Mills)

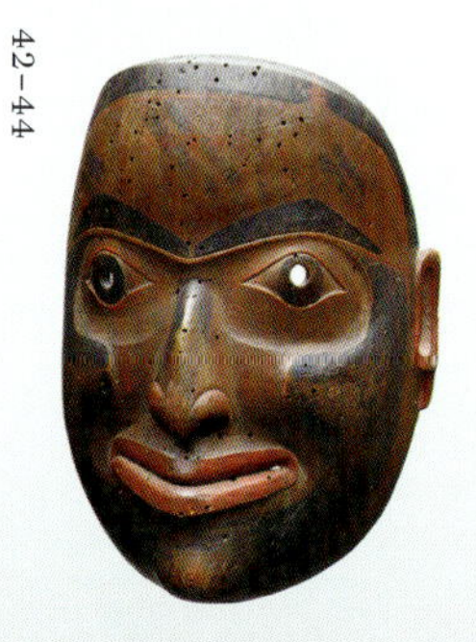

Tsimshian Artist
Portrait Mask

NOTES

1 Daniel Francis, ed., *The Encyclopedia of British Columbia* (Madeira Park, BC: Harbour Publishing, 2000), p. 158.
2 Stan Bevan, in an interview with Bill McLennan, March 19, 2014.
3 Bill Holm, in Bill Holm and Bill Reid, *Indian Art of the Northwest Coast: A Dialogue on Craftsmanship and Aesthetics* (Houston, TX: Institute for the Arts, Rice University, 1975), p. 241.
4 Bill Reid, cited in ibid.

PHOTO Courtesy of Donald Ellis Gallery, New York and Vancouver (John Bigelow Taylor)

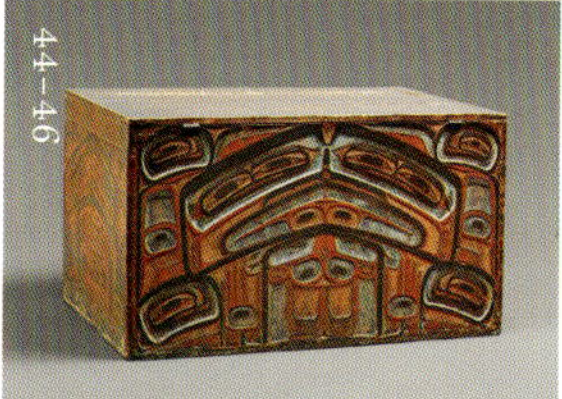

Tsimshian Artist
Chest

NOTES

1 See Alan L. Hoover, "The History of the Dundas Collection," in *Tsimshian Treasures: The Remarkable Journey of the Dundas Collection*, edited by Donald Ellis (New York and Toronto: Donald Ellis Gallery Ltd.; Vancouver: Douglas & McIntyre; Seattle: University of Washington Press, 2007), p. 41.
2 The exhibition opened on March 1, 2007, at the Museum of Northern British Columbia, Prince Rupert, and then travelled to the Royal British Columbia Museum, Victoria; the Art Gallery of Ontario, Toronto; the Canadian Museum of Civilization, Gatineau; and the Museum of Anthropology at the University of British Columbia, Vancouver, where it closed on June 7, 2008.
3 Hoover, "History," p. 68.
4 Bill McLennan, in a conversation with the author, August 5, 2014.
5 Dempsey Bob, in an interview with Bill McLennan, March 11, 2014.
6 Bill McLennan and Karen Duffek, *The Transforming Image: Painted Arts of the Northwest Coast First Nations* (Vancouver: Douglas & McIntyre, 2007), pp. 126, 129.
7 Ibid., p. 129.
8 Hoover, "History," p. 68.

PHOTO Courtesy of Trevor Mills

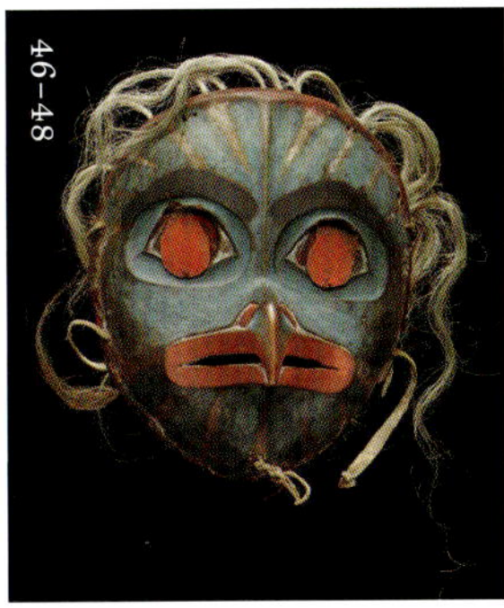

Tlingit Artist
Owl Mask

NOTES

1 The lower edges of these eyelids have a small deformation that indicates that rigging would have been connected to allow the lids to open. George T. Emmons reports that it is not clear if the Tlingit made this type of articulated mask, even though masks of this type have been collected from them (*The Tlingit Indians* [New York: American Museum of Natural History, 1991], p. 379). Articulated masks, even though they have long been associated with the Tlingit, may have been made by either Haida or Tsimshian carvers.
2 Bill McLennan, in conversation with the author, August 5, 2014.
3 See, for example, at the American Museum of Natural History, AMNH 19/852, 19/853 and 19/855, all of which have similar painted eyebrows.
4 Rocque Berthiaume, in an interview with Bill McLennan, March 19, 2014.
5 Ibid.
6 Stan Bevan, in an interview with Bill McLennan, March 19, 2014.
7 Frederica de Laguna, *Under Mount Saint Elias: The History and Culture of the Yakutat Tlingit* (Washington: Smithsonian Institution, 1972), vol. 2, pp. 829–30.

PHOTO Courtesy of Vancouver Art Gallery (Trevor Mills)

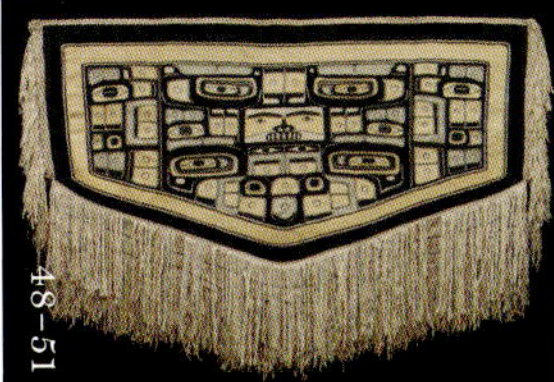

Tlingit Artist
Chilkat Blanket (Robe)
[Diving Whale Design]

NOTES

1 George T. Emmons, *The Tlingit Indians* (New York: American Museum of Natural History, 1991), p. 224.
2 A Tlingit pattern board for a Chilkat robe of similar design is in the Museum of Anthropology at the University of British Columbia, Vancouver (A8326).
3 Entry for Chilkat Blanket E/627 collected by G.T. Emmons in 1894, Manuscript Catalog, section 1, pp. 92 and 93, Collection of the American Museum of Natural History, New York.
4 See Ian M. Thom, *Challenging Traditions: Contemporary First Nations Art of the Northwest Coast* (Vancouver: Douglas & McIntyre, 2009), p. 156.

PHOTO Courtesy of Vancouver Art Gallery (Trevor Mills)

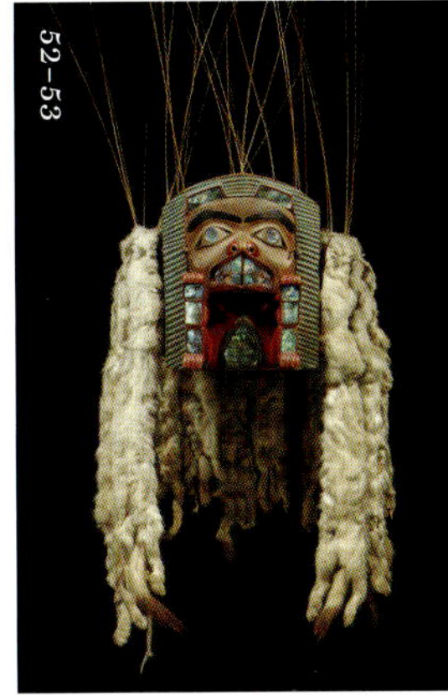

Tlingit Artist
Headdress Frontlet

NOTES

1 There are three Tlingit headdresses in the American Museum of Natural History (16.1/303, 16.1/304 and E/1062). Each of these has a more elaborate ermine train; however, they all seem to date from slightly later in the century.
2 An ermine is a stoat (a kind of weasel), the fur of which, in winter, turns white, with the exception of the tip of the tail, which remains black. This means that the fur could be harvested only in winter, when hunting is more difficult. Ermine has thus always been a fur reserved for the most illustrious members of any society.
3 Steven C. Brown, "Note on Headdress," WC8808021, Warnock Collection, www.splendidheritage.com/nindex.html.
4 Ibid.
5 Ibid.
6 Dempsey Bob, in an interview with Bill McLennan, March 19, 2014.
7 This robe would likely have been a Chilkat blanket such as the one in this collection (page 48).

PHOTO Courtesy of Donald Ellis Gallery, New York and Vancouver (John Bigelow Taylor)

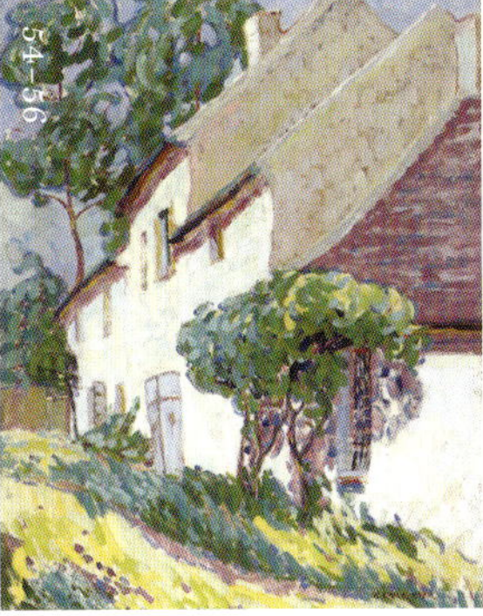

Emily Carr
House with Slanted Roof ~ Brittany

PHOTO Courtesy of Heffel Fine Art Auction House

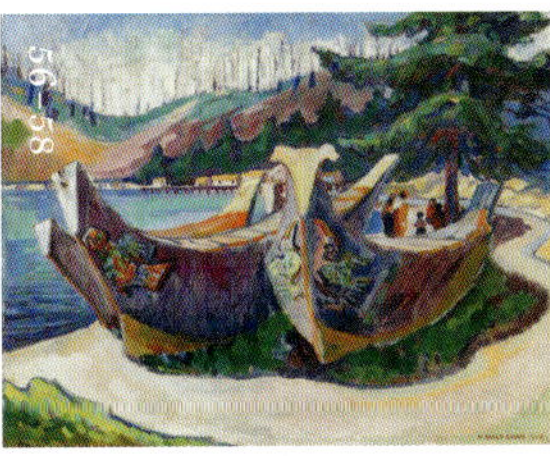

Emily Carr
War Canoes, Alert Bay

PHOTO Courtesy of Vancouver Art Gallery (Rachel Topham)

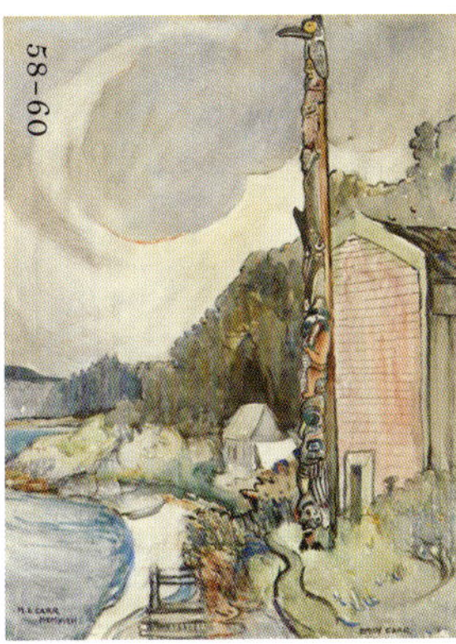

Emily Carr
Memkish

NOTES

1 Emily Carr, "Lecture on Totems," in *Opposite Contraries: The Unknown Journals of Emily Carr and Other Writings*, edited by Susan Crean (Vancouver: Douglas & McIntyre, 2003), p. 177.
2 Ibid., p. 203.

PHOTO Courtesy of Vancouver Art Gallery (Rachel Topham)

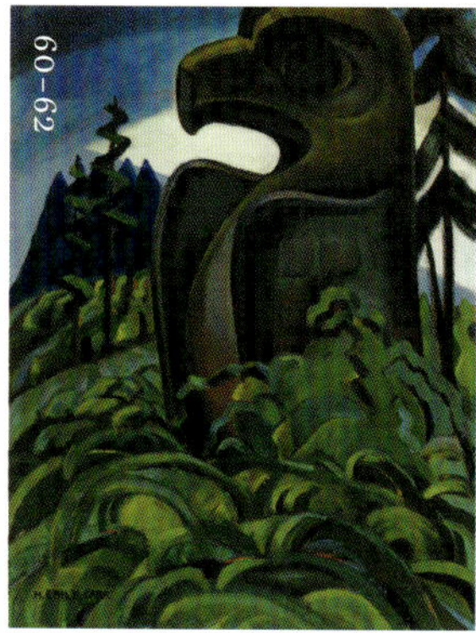

Emily Carr
Eagle Totem

PHOTO Courtesy of Heffel Fine Art Auction House

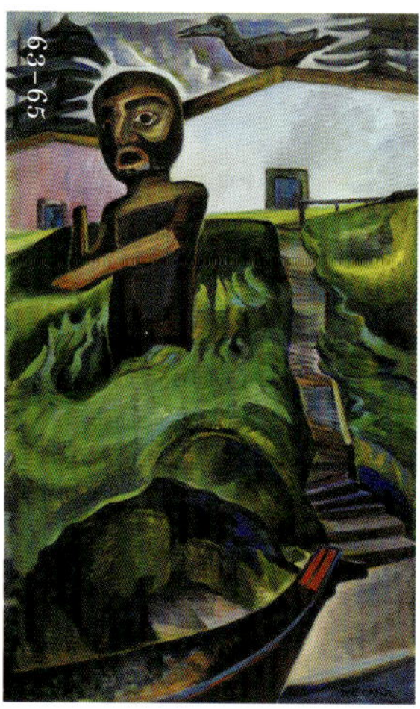

Emily Carr
The Crazy Stair (The Crooked Staircase)

NOTES

1 The work was known as *The Crooked Staircase* and exhibited and published with that title. During conservation of the painting in 2013, the back of the canvas was uncovered for the first time in many years and revealed a title inscription, almost certainly by Carr: *The Crazy Stair.*

PHOTO Courtesy of Heffel Fine Art Auction House

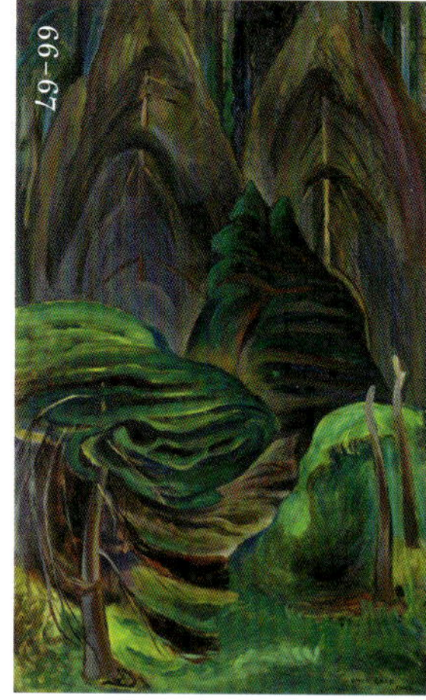

Emily Carr
Quiet

NOTES

1 Doris Shadbolt, *Emily Carr* (Vancouver: Douglas & McIntyre, 1990), p. 211.
2 Doris Shadbolt, *The Art of Emily Carr* (Toronto and Vancouver: Clarke, Irwin/Douglas & McIntyre, 1979), p. 182.

PHOTO Courtesy of Heffel Fine Art Auction House

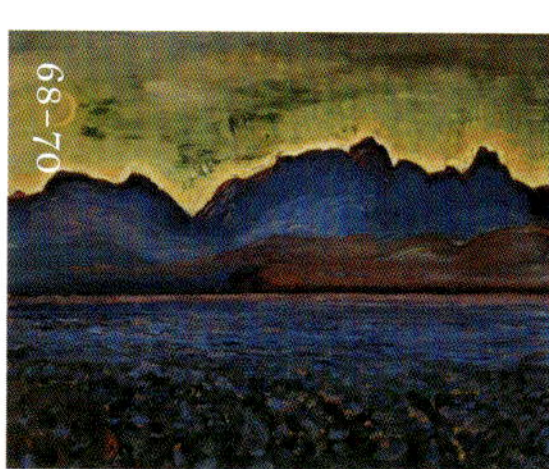

Frederick (Fred) Horsman Varley
Dusk—Tantalus Range

NOTES

1 Fred Varley to Elizabeth Nutt, January 1, 1932, National Gallery of Canada Archives.
2 Jock Macdonald, "Vancouver," in *F.H. Varley, Paintings 1915–1954* (Toronto: Art Gallery of Toronto, 1954), p. 7.

PHOTO Courtesy of Heffel Fine Art Auction House

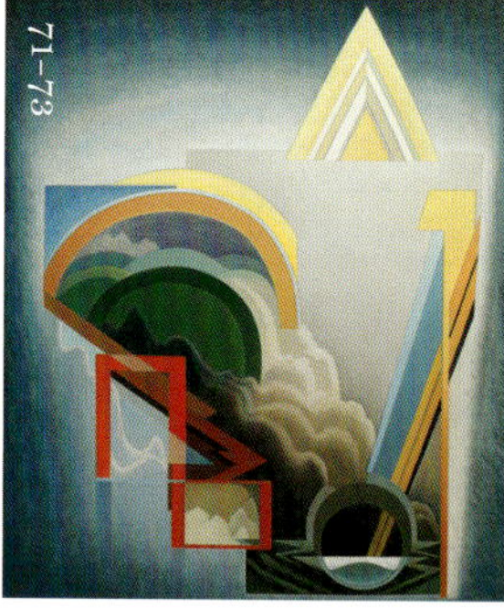

Lawren Stewart Harris
Abstraction 119

NOTES

1 Peter Larisey, *Light for a Cold Land: Lawren Harris's Work and Life—An Interpretation* (Toronto: Dundurn Press, 1993), p. 163.
2 Ibid.
3 Lawren Harris, *A Disquisition on Abstract Painting* (Toronto: Rous & Mann, 1954), p. 16.

PHOTO Courtesy of Vancouver Art Gallery (Rachel Topham)

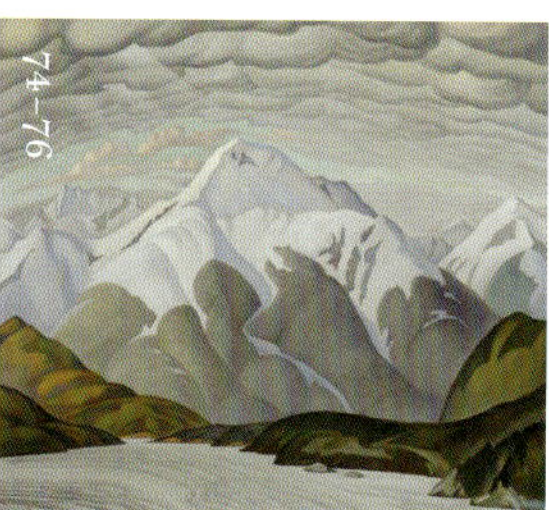

William Percival (W.P.) Weston
Jötunheim

NOTES

1 William Weston, in an interview with Marjorie Dallas, Spring 1962, Collection of the Glenbow Museum Archives.
2 Undated note, formerly in the possession of the Weston Family, quoted in Ian Thom, *W.P. Weston* (Victoria: Art Gallery of Greater Victoria, 1980), p. 12.
3 Weston, in an interview with Marjorie Dallas, Spring 1962.
4 Joan Lowndes, "Weston—imposes his will even on clouds," *Vancouver Province*, September 16, 1966.

PHOTO Courtesy of Vancouver Art Gallery (Rachel Topham)

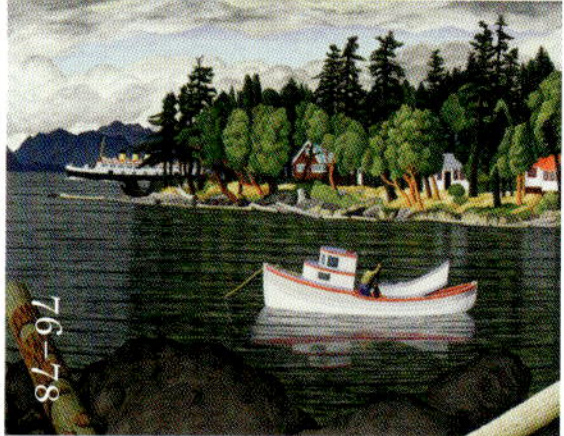

Edward John (E.J.) Hughes
Taylor Bay, Gabriola Island, BC

PHOTO Courtesy of The Barbeau Owen Foundation Collection

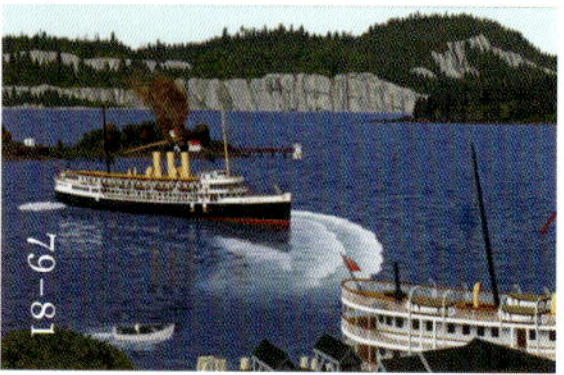

Edward John (E.J.) Hughes
Departure from Nanaimo

PHOTO Courtesy of Granville Fine Art

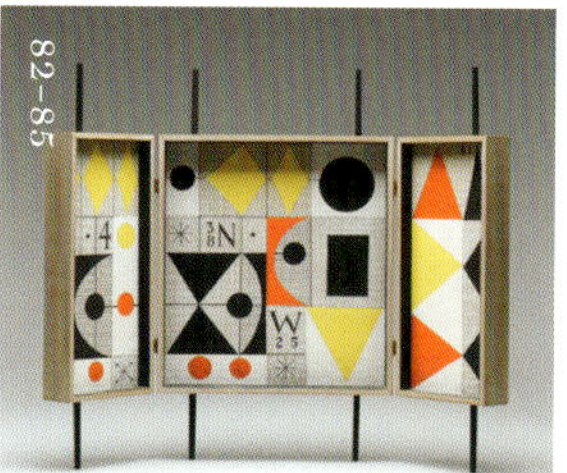

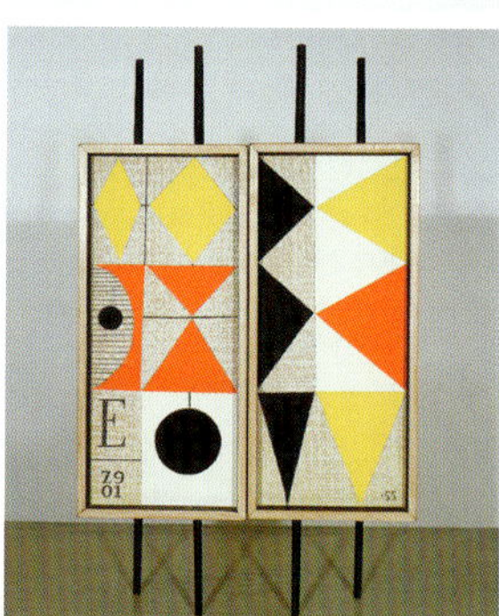

Bertram Charles (B.C.) Binning
Triptych of Nautical Symbols

PHOTOS Courtesy of Heffel Fine Art Auction House

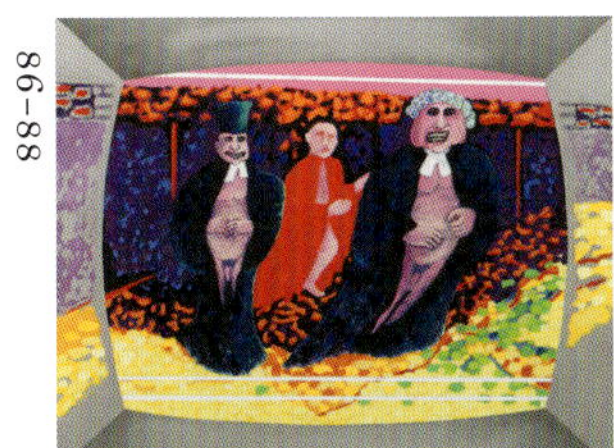

88–89

Claude Herbert Breeze
Transmission Difficulties: The Dignitaries

NOTES

1 Claude Breeze, in an email to the author, August 8, 2014. The exhibition that Breeze refers to is *Persian and Indian Miniatures from the Collection of Edwin Binney III*, organized and circulated by the Portland Art Museum and shown at the Vancouver Art Gallery in February and March 1964.
2 Claude Breeze, in an email to the author, August 4, 2014.
3 Ibid.
4 Unidentified newspaper clipping reproduced in *Claude Breeze: 10 Years* (Vancouver: Vancouver Art Gallery, 1971), unpaginated.
5 Claude Breeze, quoted in Richard Simmins, "Down with social depravity," *Vancouver Province*, October 8, 1971, p. 6.

PHOTO Courtesy of Vancouver Art Gallery (Rachel Topham)

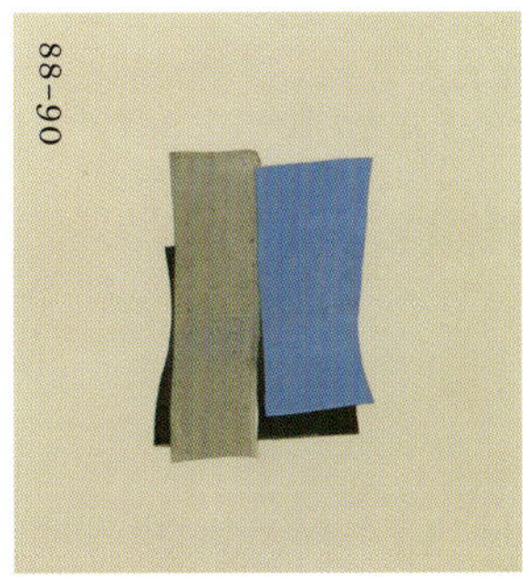

88–90

Norman Antony (Toni) Onley
Juno

PHOTO Courtesy of Vancouver Art Gallery (Rachel Topham)

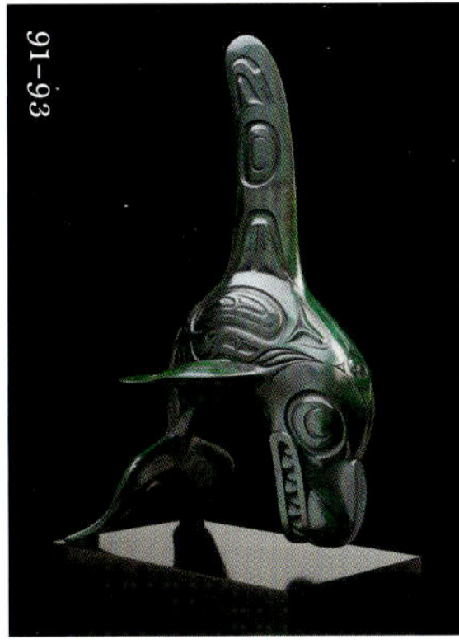

91–93

William Ronald (Bill) Reid
Killer Whale

NOTES

1 Doris Shadbolt, *Bill Reid* (Vancouver: Douglas & McIntyre, 1986/9), pp. 13–61.
2 The commission came through University of British Columbia anthropologist Dr. Harry Hawthorn, who knew Reid and his work.
3 It is not, however, the first ever work created in bronze by a British Columbia First Nations artist. That distinction belongs to a totem pole that James Hart (b. 1954) made in 1982.

PHOTO Courtesy of Vancouver Art Gallery (Trevor Mills)

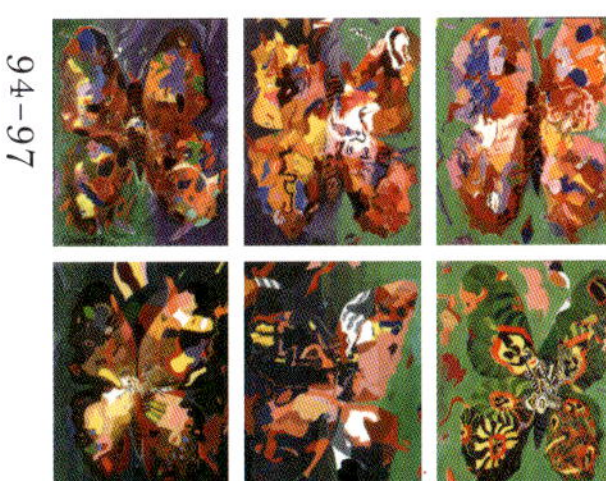

94–97

Jack Leonard Shadbolt
Butterfly Transformation Theme 1981

NOTES

1 Scott Watson, *Jack Shadbolt* (Vancouver: Douglas & McIntyre, 1990), p. 196.
2 Jack Shadbolt, "Artist's Statement," in *Jack Shadbolt: Butterfly Transformation Theme* (Victoria: Art Gallery of Greater Victoria, 1988), unpaginated.
3 Jack Shadbolt, "Journal, March 30, 1981," quoted in Watson, *Jack Shadbolt*, p. 198.

PHOTOS Courtesy of Rare Books & Special Collections, University of British Columbia Library Jack Shadbolt Fonds, Box 45, BC 1935/227

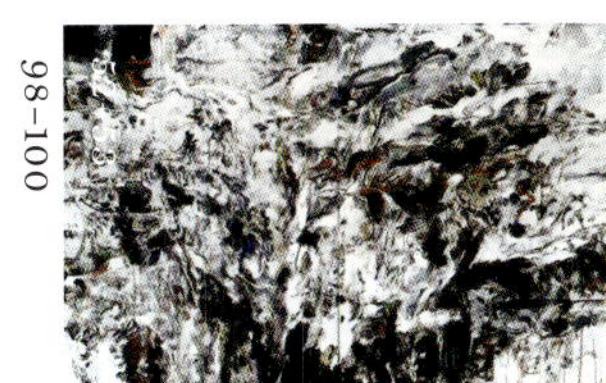

98–100

Gordon Appelbe Smith
Winterscape

NOTES

1 Gordon Smith has been awarded several honorary doctorates, the Order of British Columbia, the Order of Canada, the Governor General's Award in Visual and Media Arts, and the Audain Prize for Lifetime Achievement in the Visual Arts, to mention only a few.

PHOTO Courtesy of Vancouver Art Gallery (Trevor Mills)

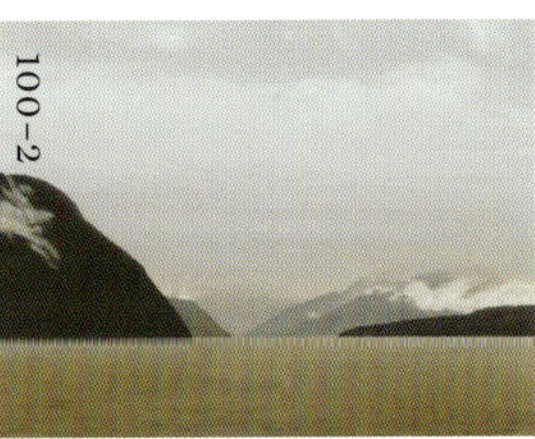

100–2

Takao Tanabe
Straight of Georgia 1/90: Raza Pass

PHOTO Courtesy of Vancouver Art Gallery (Rachel Topham)

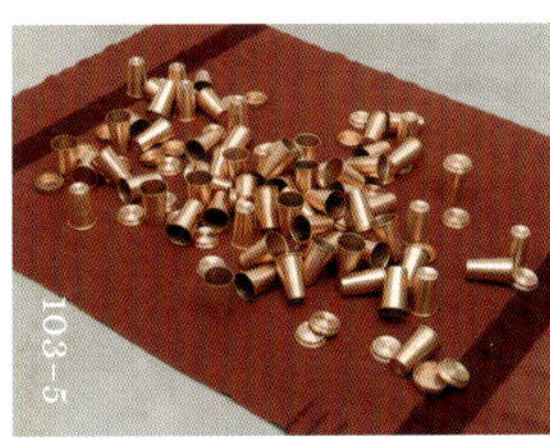

103–5

Sonny Assu
1884–1951

NOTES

1 Sonny Assu, quoted in Ian M. Thom, *Challenging Traditions: Contemporary First Nations Art of the Northwest Coast* (Vancouver: Douglas & McIntyre, 2009), p. 13.
2 Assu, in an interview with the author, June 27, 2008.
3 Ibid.
4 Assu, in an email to the author, March 5, 2015.
5 Assu, in an email to the author, July 2, 2014.
6 Ibid.

PHOTO Courtesy of Vancouver Art Gallery (Rachel Topham)

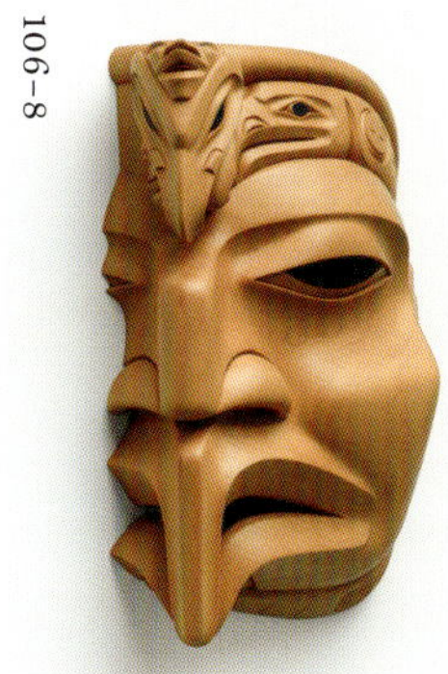

106–8

Dempsey Bob
Northern Eagles Transformation Mask

NOTES

1 All Dempsey Bob quotations are from two interviews, a first with the author on July 26, 2008, and a second with First Nations art consultant Bill McLennan on March 20, 2014.
2 The Tlingit have two large phratries, or clan groupings—Eagles and Ravens—each of which has subgroups that identify with helper animal spirits. In the case of the Eagles, these creatures are the grizzly bear, wolf and shark.

PHOTO Courtesy of Trevor Mills

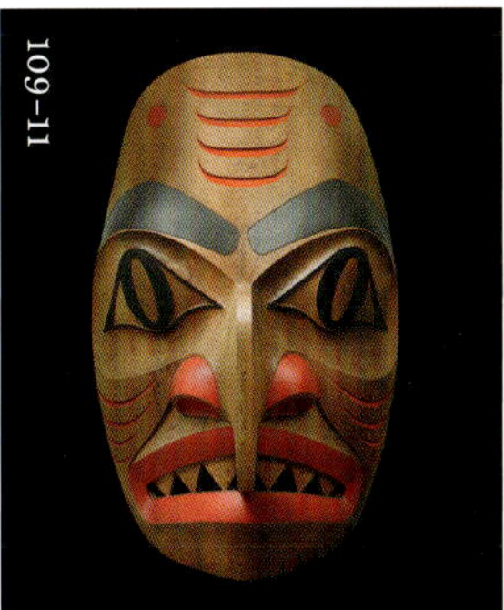

109–11

Robert Charles Davidson
Dogfish

NOTES

1 Robert Davidson, in an interview with the author, July 8, 2014.
2 Ibid.
3 Ibid.
4 This idea first appeared in *Dogfish Mask* (1974), which is now in the collection of the Royal British Columbia Museum and Archives.

PHOTO Courtesy of Trevor Mills

112–14

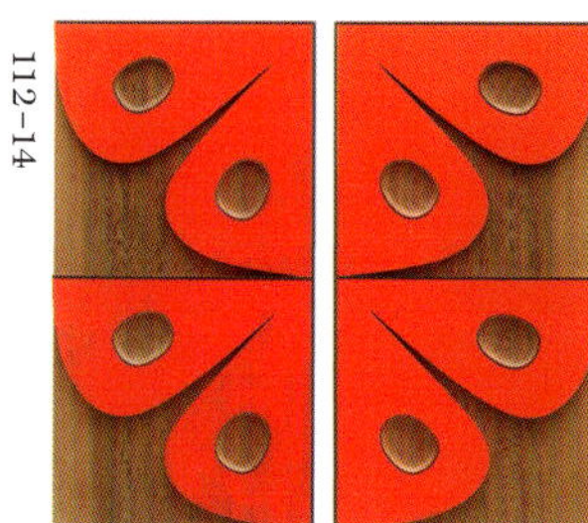

Robert Charles Davidson
Relaxed Symmetry

NOTES

1 See Charles S. Rhyne, *Expanding the Circle: The Art of guud sans glans, Robert Davidson* (Portland, OR: Douglas F. Cooley Memorial Art Gallery, Reed College, 1998).
2 Robert Davidson, in an interview with the author, July 8, 2014.
3 Ibid.
4 Ibid.
5 Davidson, in a message to the author, July 23, 2014.
6 Davidson, in an interview with the author, July 8, 2014.
7 Ibid.
8 Ibid.

PHOTO Courtesy of Vancouver Art Gallery (Trevor Mills)

115–20

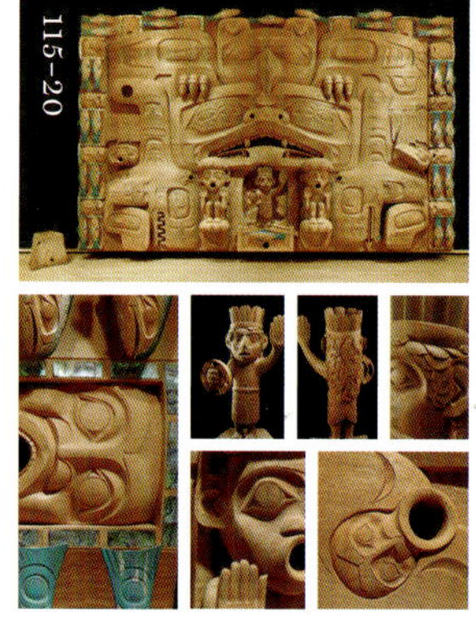

James Hart
The Dance Screen (The Scream Too)

NOTES

1 The James Hart quotation is from an interview with the author on February 22, 2008, and the information about this work from an interview on February 13, 2013.

PHOTOS Courtesy of Vancouver Art Gallery (Trevor Mills)

121–23

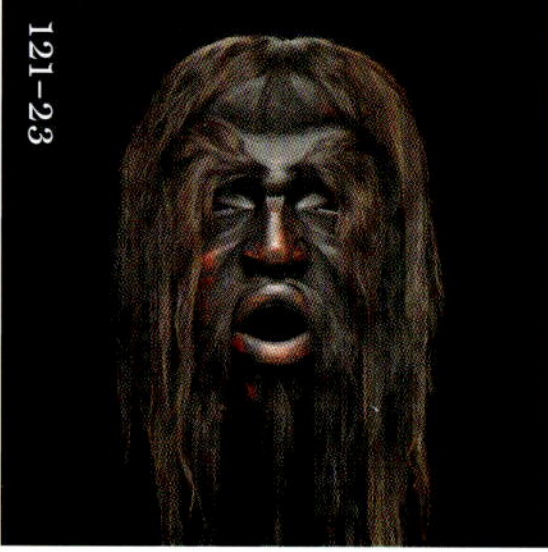

Beau Dick
Dzunukwa Mask

NOTES

1 All Beau Dick quotations are from an interview with the author on May 16, 2008.

PHOTO Courtesy of Vancouver Art Gallery (Trevor Mills)

124–26

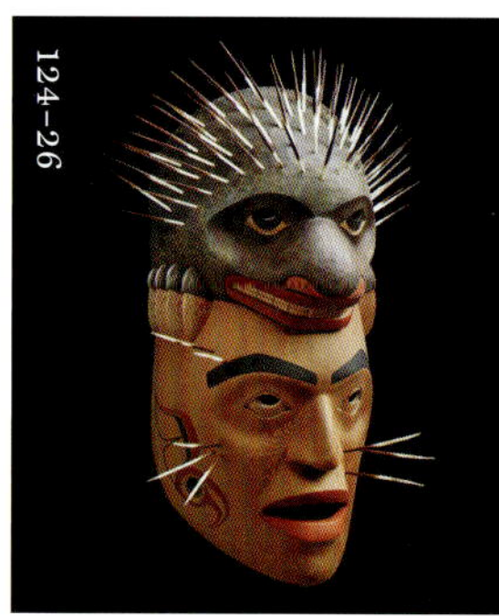

Philip Gray
Porcupine Hunter Mask

NOTES

1 Philip Gray, in an interview with the author, February 4, 2008.
2 Ibid.
3 Gray, in an email to the author, June 14, 2014.

PHOTO Courtesy of Vancouver Art Gallery (Trevor Mills)

126–28

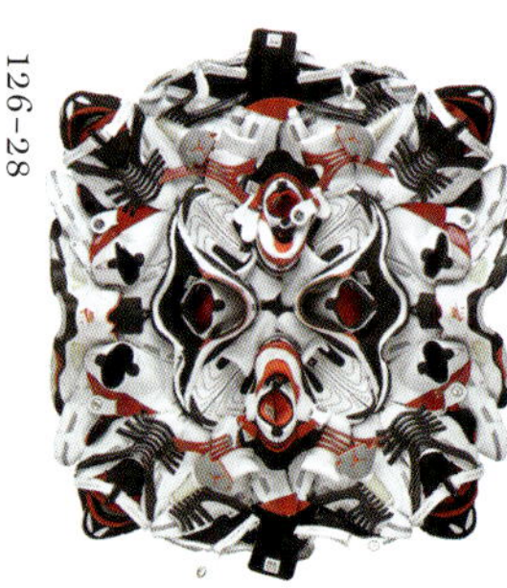

Brian Jungen
Variant I

NOTES

1 Brian Jungen, "Brian Jungen in conversation with Matthew Higgs," in *Brian Jungen* (Vienna: Secession, 2003), p. 25.
2 Perhaps significantly, *Variant II* is owned by Michael Jordan himself.

PHOTO Courtesy of Vancouver Art Gallery (Trevor Mills)

128–31

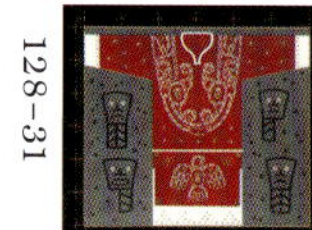
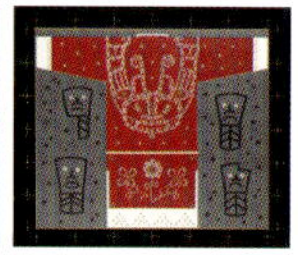

Marianne Nicolson
Tunic for a Noblewoman: In Memory of 'Wadzidalaga

NOTES

1 Marianne Nicolson, in an interview with the author, February 18, 2008.
2 Ibid.
3 Petra Watson, "Introduction," in *Continuum: Vision and Creativity on the Northwest Coast* (Vancouver: Bill Reid Gallery of Northwest Coast Art, 2009), p. 7.
4 Marianne Nicolson "Artist's Statement," in *Continuum*, p. 19.
5 Ibid.

PHOTOS Courtesy of the artist

132–34

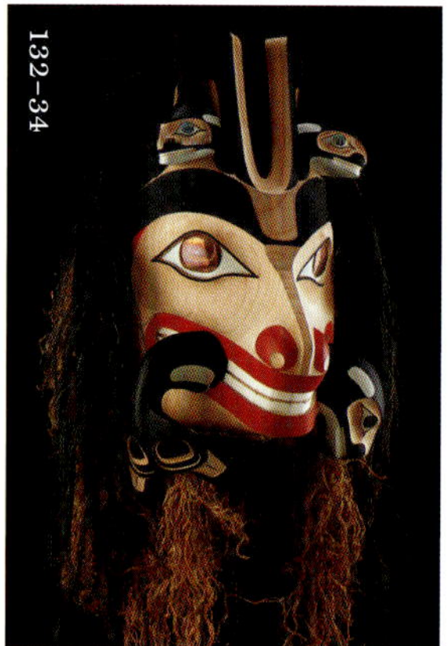

Jay Simeon
Sea Wolf and Killer Whale Mask

NOTES

1 All Jay Simeon quotations are from an interview with the author on February 5, 2008.

PHOTO Courtesy of Spirit Wrestler Gallery (Kenji Nagai)

134–36

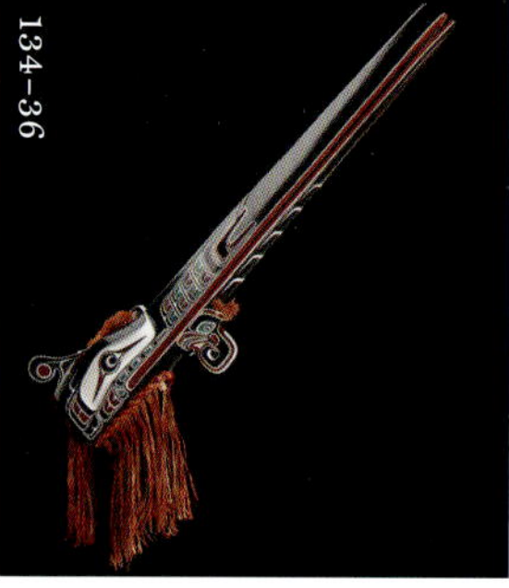

Henry Speck Jr.
Hok Hok Headdress

NOTES

1 All Henry Speck Jr. quotations are from an interview with the author on September 30, 2008.

PHOTO Courtesy of Vancouver Art Gallery (Trevor Mills)

137–39

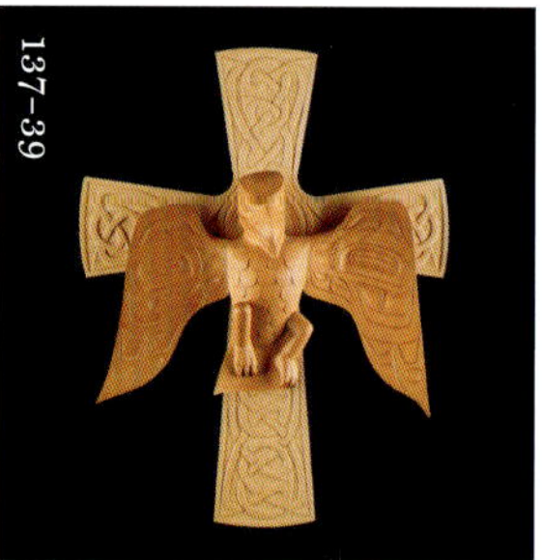

Don Yeomans *Creator*

NOTES

1 All Don Yeomans quotations are from an interview with the author on July 18, 2008.

PHOTO Courtesy of Douglas Reynolds Gallery

140–43

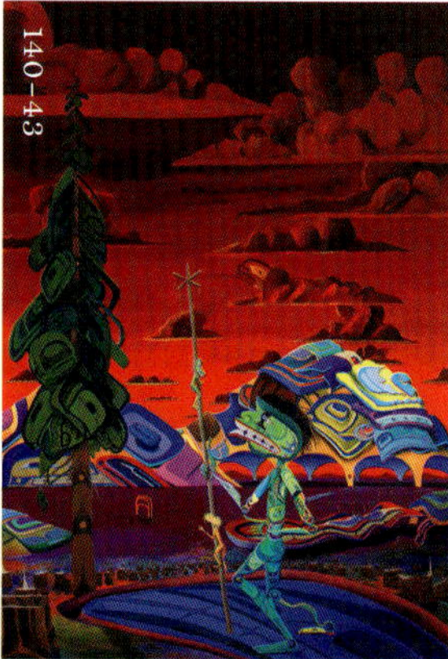

Lawrence Paul Yuxweluptun
Clearcut to the Last Old Growth Tree

NOTES

1 All Lawrence Paul Yuxweluptun quotations are from an interview with the author on June 10, 2008.

PHOTO Courtesy of Trevor Mills

144–47

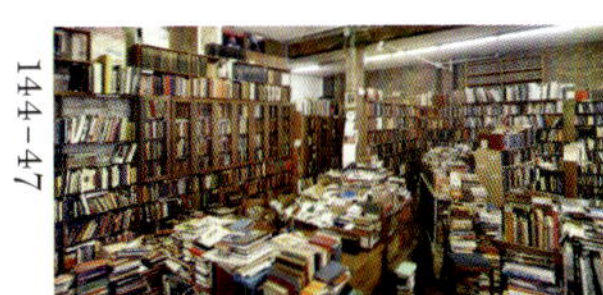

Stan Douglas
MacLeod's Books, Vancouver

NOTES
1 All Stan Douglas quotations are from an interview with the author on August 18, 2014.
2 Officially, this building is known as the Maritime Labour Centre.

PHOTO Courtesy of the artist

148–50

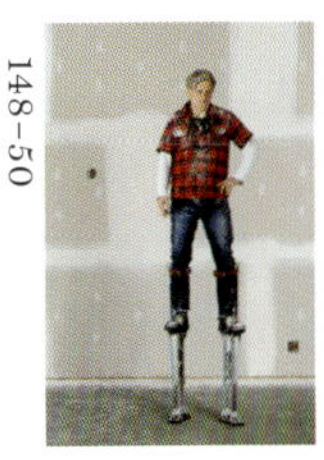

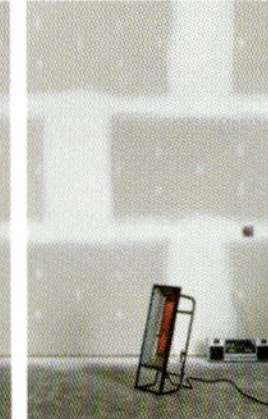

Rodney Graham *The Drywaller*

NOTES
1 Jeff Wall, "Into the Forest: Two Sketches for Studies of Rodney Graham's Work," in *Rodney Graham* (Vancouver: Vancouver Art Gallery, 1988), p. 9.
2 Michael Vass, "Rodney Graham reflected anew in NYC," *Canadian Art*, June 26, 2013, at www.canadianart.ca/reviews/2013/06/26/rodney-graham-2/#sthash.YIWIKYYB.dpuf.

PHOTO Courtesy of the artist

150–53

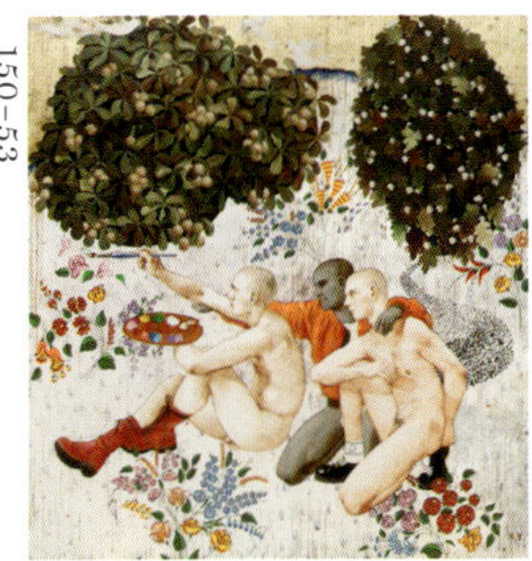

Attila Richard Lukacs
Love in Loss c: Painting the Lovers' Portrait

NOTES
1 Attila Richard Lukacs, in an interview with the author, July 11, 2014.
2 Ibid.
3 Source Polaroids for this work are published in Michael Morris, ed., *Attila Richard Lukacs/Polaroids* (Vancouver: Arsenal Pulp Press, 2010), pp. 35, 37.
4 Lukacs, in an interview with the author, July 11, 2014.
5 Ibid.
6 Ibid.

PHOTO Courtesy of Vancouver Art Gallery (Trevor Mills)

154–57

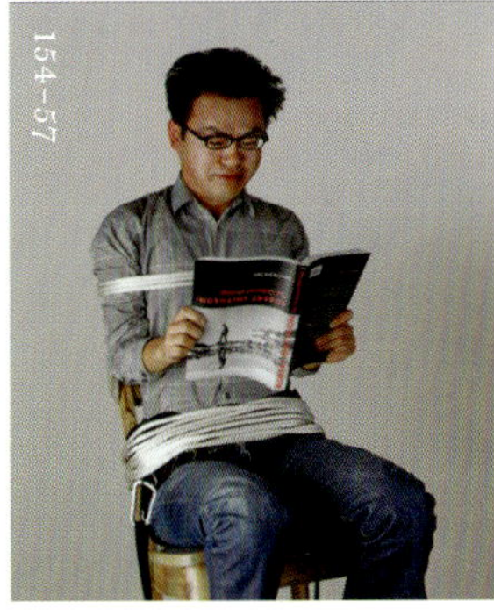

Tim Lee
Upside Down Water Torture Chamber, Harry Houdini 1914

NOTES
1 Tim Lee, in an interview with the author, July 21, 2014.
2 Ibid.
3 Ibid.
4 Ibid.
5 Ibid.

PHOTO Courtesy of the artist

158–60

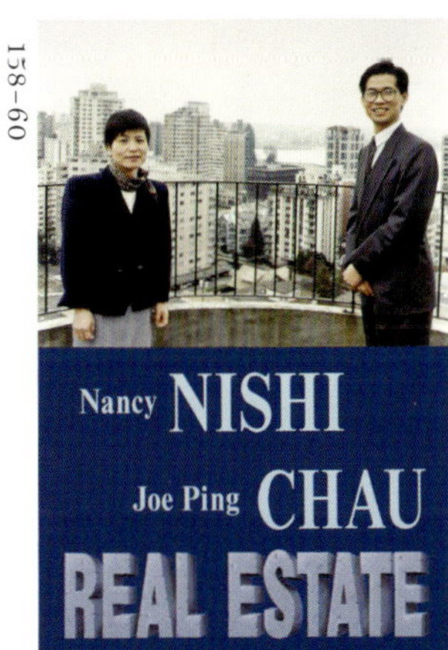

Ken Lum
Nancy Nishi, Joe Ping Chau, Real Estate

NOTES
1 Ken Lum made up the names (Lum, in an email to the author, June 21, 2014).
2 Ibid.

PHOTO Courtesy of the artist

161–63

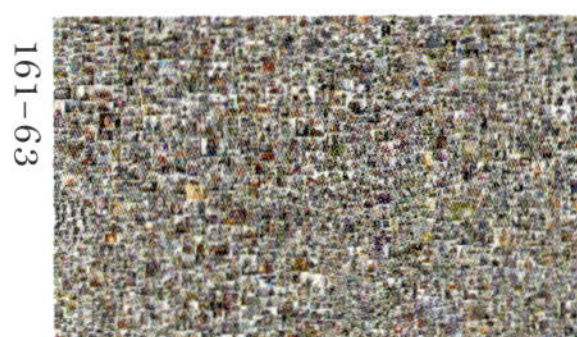

Steven Shearer
Guitar #5

NOTES
1 Steven Shearer, in an interview with Vanessa Nicholas for *The White Review*, July 2011, at www.thewhitereview.org/art/interview-with-steven-shearer.
2 Ibid.
3 Shearer, quoted in Shannon Heth Vergette, "Steven Shearer," *Montecristo Magazine*, March 21, 2011, at montecristomagazine.com/magazine/spring-2011/artist-steven-shearer.

PHOTO Courtesy of the artist

164–66

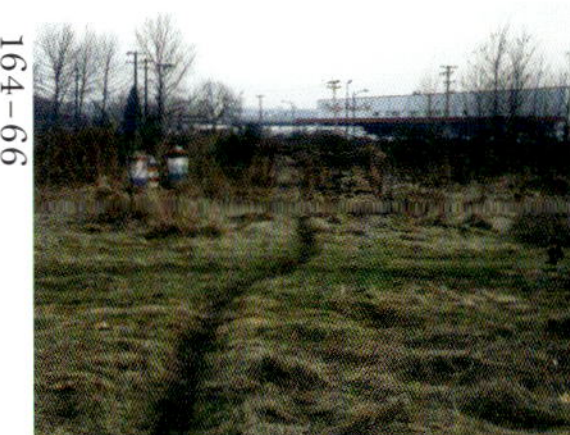

Jeff Wall
The Crooked Path

NOTES
1 Gary Dufour, "Look, and Look Again," in *Jeff Wall Photographs* (Melbourne: National Gallery of Victoria, 2013), pp. 1–2.
2 Jeff Wall, in an email to the author, August 3, 2014.
3 Ibid.
4 Ibid.
5 Ulrich Bischoff, "The Crooked Path," in *Jeff Wall: Transit* (Dresden: Schirmer/Mosel, 2010), p. 101; Alexander Vasudevan, "'The photographer of modern life': Jeff Wall's photographic materialism," *Cultural Geographies* 14, no. 4 (2007), p. 577.

PHOTO Courtesy of the artist

167–70

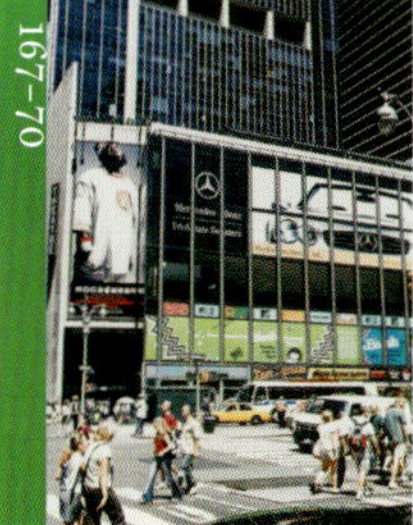

Ian Wallace
Times Square NYC (July 11, 2003) I

NOTES
1 Ian Wallace, "Street Photos 1970," republished in Daina Augaitis et al., *Ian Wallace: At the Intersection of Painting and Photography* (London: Black Dog Publishing/Vancouver Art Gallery, 2012), p. 177.
2 Wallace, in an email to the author, June 13, 2014.
3 Ibid.
4 Wallace, "Street Photos 1970," p. 178.
5 Ibid.
6 Ibid., p. 182.
7 Ibid., p. 181.
8 Ibid.
9 Wallace, in an email to the author, June 13, 2014.

PHOTO Courtesy of Vancouver Art Gallery (Rachel Topham)

170–73

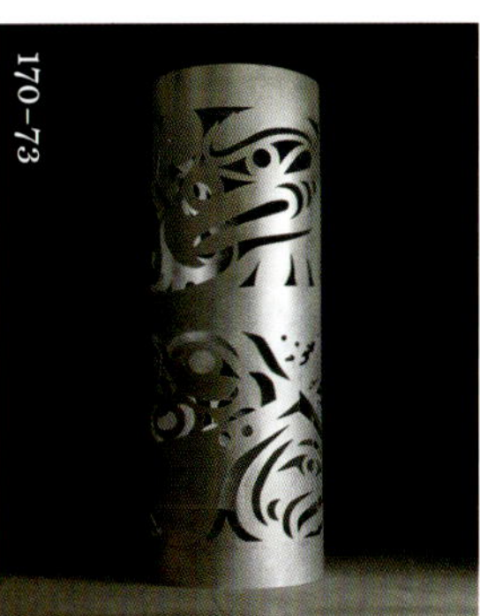

Xwalacktun (Rick Harry)
He-yay-meymuy (Big Flood)

NOTES
1 Xwalacktun, in an interview with the author, August 19, 2014.
2 Ibid.
3 Ibid.
4 Ibid.
5 This was Xwalacktun's first large-scale metal sculpture.
6 Xwalacktun, in an interview with the author, August 19, 2014.
7 Ibid.
8 Ibid.
9 Ibid.

PHOTO Courtesy of Trevor Mills

15 16 17 18 19 5 4 3 2 1

Cataloguing data available from Library and Archives Canada
ISBN 978-1-927958-49-0 (hbk.)

Design by Jessica Sullivan
Copy editing by Stephanie Fysh

Cover images: *Front:* Emily Carr, *The Crazy Stair (The Crooked Staircase)* (detail), c. 1928. Photo: Courtesy of Heffel Fine Art Auction House. *Back:* Takao Tanabe, *Straight of Georgia 1/90: Raza Pass*. Photo: Courtesy of Vancouver Art Gallery (Rachel Topham).

page ii: Emily Carr, *War Canoes, Alert Bay*, 1912. Photo: Courtesy of Vancouver Art Gallery

Photo credits are separately noted
Artist renderings on pages 4, 9 and 176 courtesy of Patkau Architects

The dimensions of all artworks are given in centimetres, in the order height × width × depth.

All works of art purchased by the Audain Art Museum and illustrated in this book have been purchased with funds from the Audain Foundation.

Printed and bound in Canada by Friesens
Distributed in the U.S. by Publishers Group West

Figure 1 Publishing Inc.
Vancouver BC Canada
www.figure1pub.com

Audain Art Museum
Whistler BC Canada
www.audainartmuseum.com

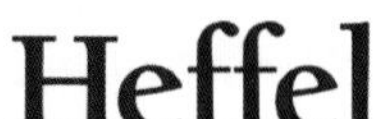

This book is generously supported by
Heffel Fine Art Auction House. www.heffel.com

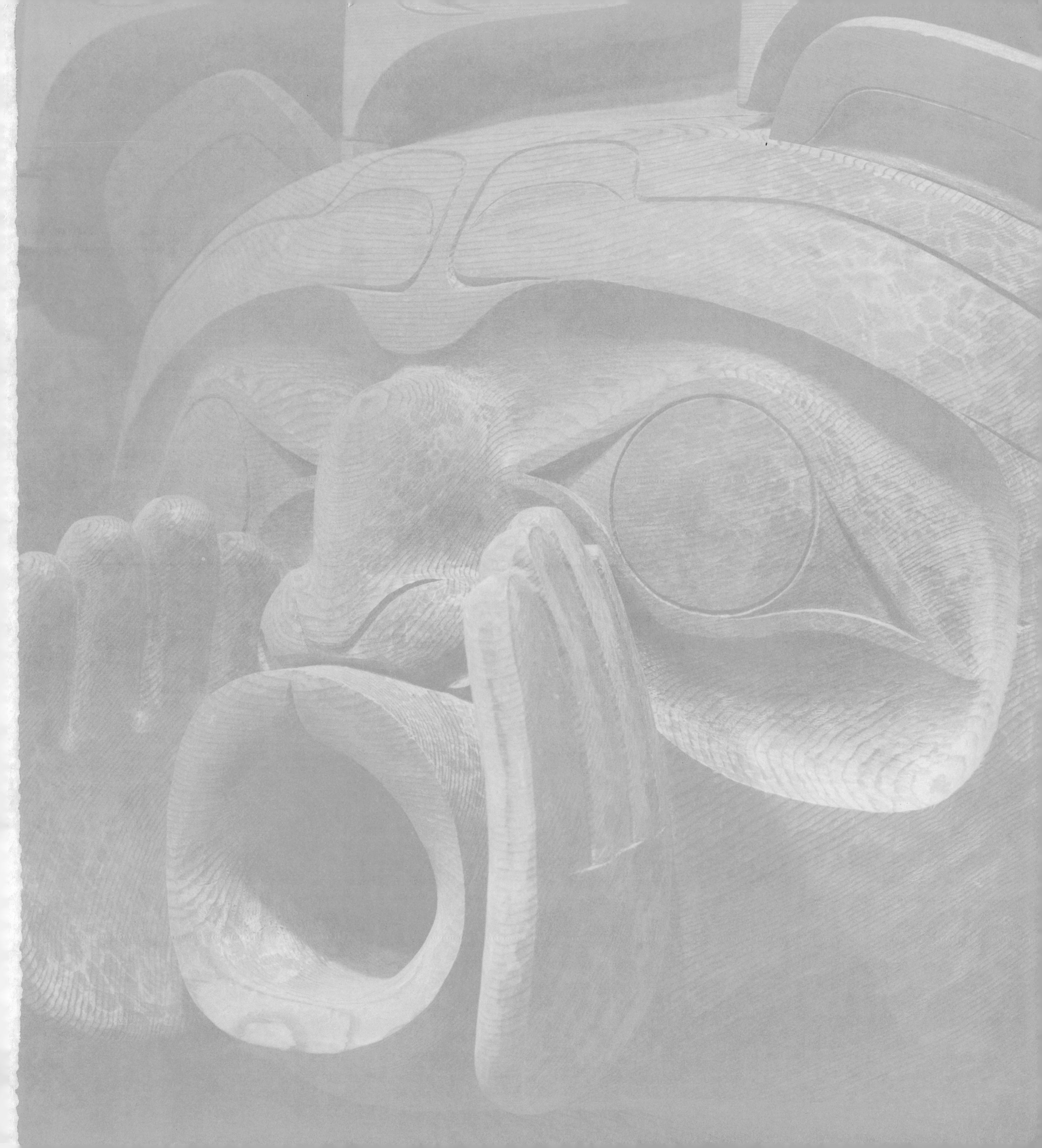

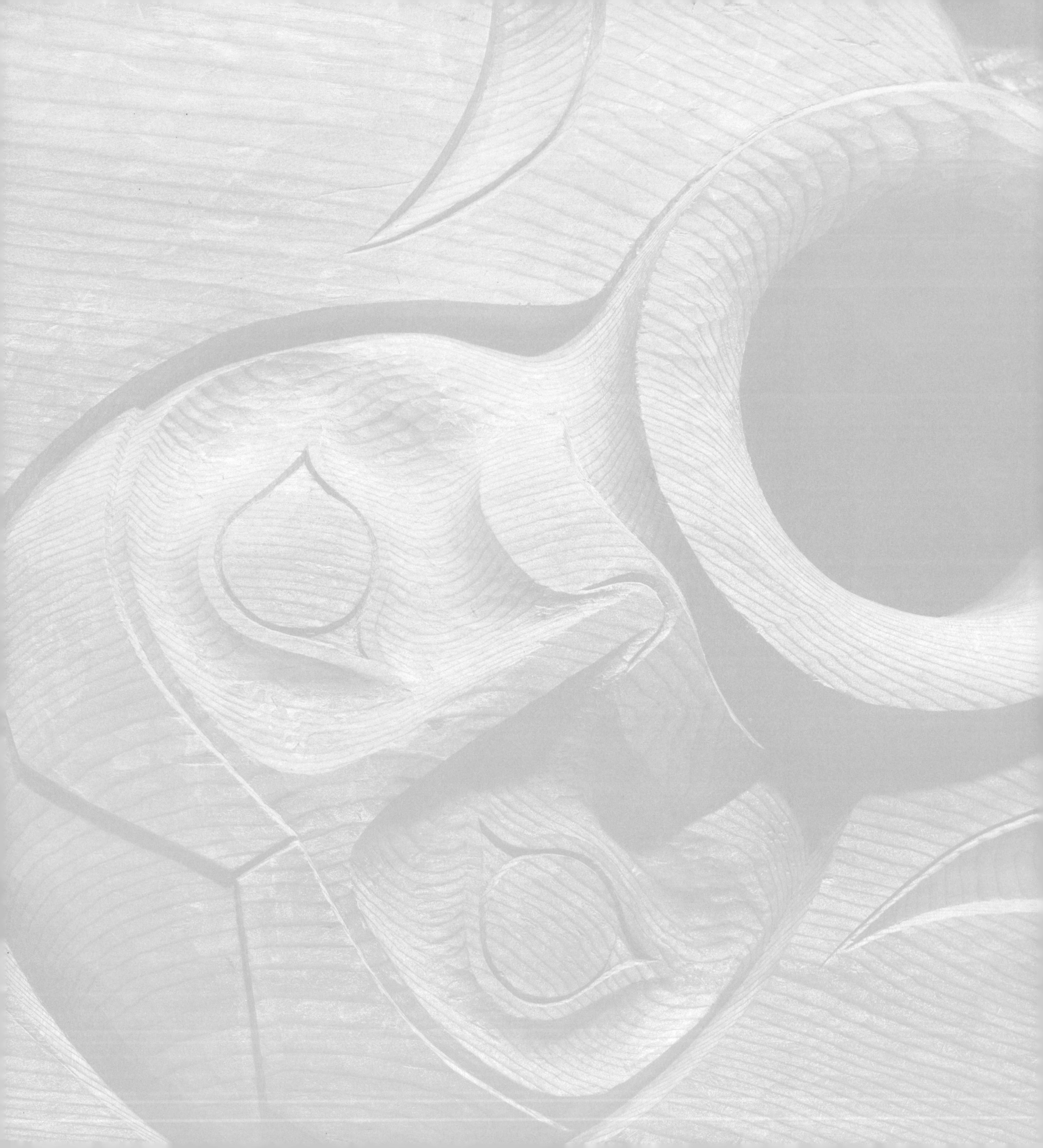